PRAISE FOR *CLOSER READING*

"Garrett Stewart is arguably the finest close reader of English texts on the planet. This new book of essays offers a cornucopia of delights on a wide range of literary and cultural topics. Its release is an occasion for celebration—and for devouring its contents as soon as possible."
—N. KATHERINE HAYLES, Distinguished Research Professor of English, University of California, Los Angeles, USA

"It is never enough for Garrett Stewart merely to write, down or out, the results of his reading, whether of literature, film, or art. His impulse is rather to strain ever closer to the objects of his close readings, to attain a propinquity intimate enough to enter into composition with them. The results, in what Stewart calls the 'textual prismatics' arrayed here, are uniquely collusive alloys of reading and writing, which magically protract, dilate, and reinflame the works that they treat."
—STEVEN CONNOR, Grace 2 Professor of English Emeritus, University of Cambridge, UK

"To read Garrett Stewart's expansive readings is to enter an expanding world: texts, images, and forms come more alive than they were before we read his account of them. His attention to novels, films, art objects, and criticism enlarges our very senses and makes us see how active reading can be."
—FRANCES FERGUSON, Mabel Greene Myers Distinguished Service Professor of English, University of Chicago, USA

"This book offers a welcome opportunity to retrace and to connect some of Garrett Stewart's brilliantly eccentric footsteps. These essays—on Dickens, Hopkins, and Conrad, on Le Carré, Cavell, and conceptual art—are *technically* eccentric because, as they maintain an elliptic or parabolic orbit around criticism's shifting centers of gravity (New Historicism, postcolonial theory, surface reading, etc.), they use the official history of literary scholarship as a spur to Stewart's *unofficial*, beautifully errant, and always exciting thought."
—KENT PUCKETT, Professor and Ida May and William J. Eggers Jr. Chair in English, University of California, Berkeley, USA

Past Praise for the Ever Closer Reading of Garrett Stewart's Critical Writing

"A characteristically dazzling, intellectually inventive, almost preternaturally informed tour d'horizon and analysis of the interplay between spaces of exhibition and recent (and not so recent) developments in video, film, medial manifestations of all sorts."

—Michael Fried, on *Cinesthesia* (2021)

"Garrett Stewart's unique sensibility—which combines textual perception with a vigilant receptivity for changes in technology—here affords us rich insights [...]. This is wonderful reading and thinking."

—Fredric Jameson, on *Framed Time* (2007)

"[… A] consummate study by (that rare thing) a scholar of genius. It gives us new ears and eyes for what we read and a new conceptual armature for thinking about how."

—Herbert F. Tucker, on *The Deed of Reading* (2015)

"[… A] continuously responsive, marvelously informed mind inspired by as surprising a range of films and as ample a range of serious writing about film as you will find in one place."

—Stanley Cavell, on *Between Film and Screen* (1999)

"With his most unusual gift for subtle stylistic interpretation, Garrett Stewart is more or less *sui generis*, belonging to no particular school of criticism."

—J. Hillis Miller, on *Death Sentences* (1984)

"In this remarkable book, [...] Stewart's innovative and imaginative concept of 'narratography' draws attention to those points at which both narrative and technological uncertainty erupt symptomatically into both image and idea on the screen."

—Laura Mulvey, on *Framed Time* (2007)

"At last, a scrupulous and sustained—'earsighted'—study of that shadowy yet vital intersection of sound and sense [...]."

—Geoffrey H. Hartman, on *Reading Voices* (1990)

"[… A] dazzling, transformative book. Garrett Stewart's supple, lambent, witty prose is itself a laboratory of the effects to which he pays attention."

—Susan J. Wolfson, on *The Deed of Reading* (2015)

"Stunningly articulate. [...] Stewart offers new and dazzling interpretations of the 'poetics of prose. [...] The book is a *tour de force*, no doubt about it. [... It] will have not only a wide but a lasting reception.'"

—Hayden White, on *Reading Voices* (1990)

"That peerless verbal acrobat/analyst Garrett Stewart has given us a new feast of words and images."

—Ross Posnock, on *The Metanarrative Hall of Mirrors* (2022)

"Stewart's style has a quality that most critical styles utterly lack: it's thoroughly vocalizable. To appreciate its rhythms and sonorities, you practically have to speak it aloud."

—D. A. Miller, on *Streisand: The Mirror of Difference* (2023)

"Garrett Stewart is a multi-media close reader extraordinaire whose answerable style rewards close reading in turn."

—Paul H. Fry, on *Attention Spans: Garrett Stewart, a Reader* (2024)

"In staging a critical rereading of his own work, Stewart offers us an exhilarating history of aesthetic theory since New Criticism, which is also a virtuosic display of fine readerly attention. Continually unsettled, continually restless, it is written in what Stewart himself calls a 'language not quite gelled into the print that transmits it.' To read it is to feel, again and again, the lifted joy of shared thinking."

—Peter Boxall, on *Attention Spans: Garrett Stewart, a Reader* (2024)

"… [E]ngages the major developments of recent criticism. A *tour de force*."

—Jonathan Culler, on *Attention Spans: Garrett Stewart, a Reader* (2024)

"Here is a volume of writing about voices, faces, sentences, songs, paintings, spelling, mirrors, reading, technology, time, and other objects of considerable interest. How could one evoke and study such diverse matters without getting lost? We may not know the answer, but this book does. […] An amazing work of critical theory and practice."

—Michael Wood, on *Bandwidths: Reading Across Media with Garrett Stewart* (2025)

"Garrett Stewart's longtime readers will be familiar with a feeling of pleasant incredulity: how can anyone read this widely and always this well? In gathering an A-team of equally intense critics around him, *Bandwidths* offers something else almost beyond belief: a dazzling group intellectual experience that is also intensely moving—a snapshot of literary and cultural criticism at its collective best."

—David Kurnick, on *Bandwidths: Reading Across Media with Garrett Stewart* (2025)

"With the vast philosophical erudition and rigorous analytical skills that are his trademark, David LaRocca here brilliantly introduces Garrett Stewart's unique body of readings and writings, 'across media,' while bringing together an original and reasoned set of critical interventions by distinctive commentators […]. What results is a groundbreaking and wide-ranging work, an intellectual adventure of dazzling intensity, that is bound to become a standard reference for any future engagement with—and further elaboration of—Stewart's 'inter-medial' approach."

—Hent de Vries, on *Bandwidths: Reading Across Media with Garrett Stewart* (2025)

Also by Garrett Stewart

Dickens and the Trials of Imagination
Death Sentences: Styles of Dying in British Fiction
Reading Voices: Literature and the Phonotext
Dear Reader: The Conscripted Audience in Nineteenth-Century British Fiction
Between Film and Screen: Modernism's Photo Synthesis
The Look of Reading: Book, Painting, Text
Framed Time: Toward a Postfilmic Cinema
Novel Violence: A Narratography of Victorian Fiction
Bookwork: Medium to Object to Concept to Art
Closed Circuits: Screening Narrative Surveillance
*The Deed of Reading: Literature * Writing * Language * Philosophy*
Transmedium: Conceptualism 2.0 and the New Object Art
The Value of Style in Fiction
The One, Other, and Only Dickens
Book, Text, Medium: Cross-Sectional Reading for a Digital Age
Cinemachines: An Essay on Media and Method
Cinesthesia: Museum Cinema and the Curated Screen
The Ways of the Word: Episodes in Verbal Attention
The Metanarrative Hall of Mirrors: Reflex Action in Fiction and Film
Streisand: The Mirror of Difference

Authored, Edited, or Coedited Books by David LaRocca

On Emerson
Emerson's Transcendental Etudes by Stanley Cavell
The Philosophy of Charlie Kaufman
Estimating Emerson: An Anthology of Criticism from Carlyle to Cavell
Emerson's English Traits and the Natural History of Metaphor
The Philosophy of War Films
A Power to Translate the World: New Essays on Emerson and International Culture
*The Bloomsbury Anthology of Transcendental Thought: From Antiquity to the
    Anthropocene*
The Philosophy of Documentary Film: Image, Sound, Fiction, Truth
*The Thought of Stanley Cavell and Cinema: Turning Anew to the Ontology of Film
    a Half-Century after* The World Viewed
Inheriting Stanley Cavell: Memories, Dreams, Reflections
Movies with Stanley Cavell in Mind
Metacinema: The Form and Content of Filmic Reference and Reflexivity
*The Geschlecht Complex: Addressing Untranslatable Aspects of Gender, Genre,
    and Ontology*
Television with Stanley Cavell in Mind
Attention Spans: Garrett Stewart, a Reader
Music with Stanley Cavell in Mind
Werner Herzog / Rogue Filmmaker
Bandwidths: Reading Across Media with Garrett Stewart

Guest Edited

Conversations: The Journal of Cavellian Studies No. 7: Acknowledging Stanley Cavell

CLOSER READING

Garrett Stewart's Essays in Refraction

Edited by
David LaRocca

BLOOMSBURY ACADEMIC
NEW YORK · LONDON · OXFORD · NEW DELHI · SYDNEY

BLOOMSBURY ACADEMIC
Bloomsbury Publishing Inc, 1359 Broadway, New York, NY 10018, USA
Bloomsbury Publishing Plc, 50 Bedford Square, London, WC1B 3DP, UK
Bloomsbury Publishing Ireland, 29 Earlsfort Terrace, Dublin 2, D02 AY28, Ireland

BLOOMSBURY, BLOOMSBURY ACADEMIC and the Diana logo are
trademarks of Bloomsbury Publishing Plc

First published in the United States of America 2026

Copyright © David LaRocca and Garrett Stewart, 2026

Cover design by Eleanor Rose
Cover images: Object (attributed to Gerard C. A. Fonte) © John Opera, 2007;
Beam of light © Flavio Coelho / Moment / Getty Images

Bloomsbury Publishing Inc does not have any control over, or responsibility for, any
third-party websites referred to or in this book. All internet addresses given in this
book were correct at the time of going to press. The author and publisher regret any
inconvenience caused if addresses have changed or sites have ceased to exist, but can
accept no responsibility for any such changes.

Library of Congress Cataloging-in-Publication Data

Names: Stewart, Garrett, author. | LaRocca, David, 1975- editor.
Title: Closer reading : Garrett Stewart's essays in refraction / edited by David LaRocca.
Description: London ; New York : Bloomsbury Academic, 2025. |
Includes bibliographical references and index.
Identifiers: LCCN 2025006676 | ISBN 9798765140277 (hardback) |
ISBN 9798765140260 (paperback) | ISBN 9798765140307 (eBook) |
ISBN 9798765140291 (ePDF)
Subjects: LCSH: Literature, Modern–20th century–History and criticism. |
Motion pictures and literature. | Close reading (Literary analysis)
Classification: LCC PN771 .S75 2025 | DDC 814/.54–dc23/eng/20250527
LC record available at https://lccn.loc.gov/2025006676

ISBN: HB: 979-8-7651-4027-7
          PB: 979-8-7651-4026-0
          ePDF: 979-8-7651-4029-1
          eBook: 979-8-7651-4030-7

Typeset by Integra Software Services Pvt. Ltd.
Printed and bound in the United States of America

For product safety related questions contact productsafety@bloomsbury.com.

To find out more about our authors and books visit www.bloomsbury.com
and sign up for our newsletters.

For Readers Dear—and Enduring

CONTENTS

INTRODUCTION

READING PRISMATICALLY /
A SPECTRUM ANALYSIS

David LaRocca

So as to be read in itself prismatically, from all of its invited angles, *Closer Reading* stands to benefit from exactly the introduction its author doesn't need. Which isn't to say it is too late to encounter Garrett Stewart's work for the first time—the representative breadth and depth of his writing—and in fact, under compression, right here in this volume. If you're such a reader, you'll be brought excitedly up to the mark and the moment among the equally curious return visitors. Stewart is the author of twenty books that range with imponderable competency across Victorian narrative, contemporary American fiction, written auralities, poetics and prose stylistics, cinematic evolution from silver oxide to screen pixel, book art, scenes of reading in painting, and most recently, the vocal drama of Barbra Streisand. The distances between his disciplinary terrains are as vast as his close readings of them are coordinated and trenchant. Given the stamina and span of his publications, such a summary of his achievement speeds by in inverse ratio to the professional decades clocked in by the potential audiences for his writing. And, as I say, you don't "have to have been there" when. If you were, you are still likely to have missed some part of this tireless multi-media trajectory. If not, *Closer Reading* opens onto the range and energy of its typifying variety—with close(r)-grained analysis and bursts of semiotic invention from 1981 to 2025—by single-essay exemplifications. And singular they are.

Stewart's ongoing experiments in interpretation could have been collected under a subtitle's straightforward descriptive rubric: Test Essays, New and Selected. But the emphasis on "refraction" better demonstrates the three-dimensional valence—and material reorientations—inherent to Stewart's multidirectional, cross-medial method. With the term's reminder that light *bends* as it passes from one medium to another (air to glass), we marvel at the energies and effects of Stewart's angles of vision, especially at those volatile transfer points—of medial crossover/overcrossing—where his exacting practice roves from novel to film to song to Conceptual art. At those proliferating cruxes of canted illumination, we behold how the *more* closely read a text is (in his company), the more surprising its subsequent dimensions of inference, the more ample its ranging gamut of chromatic forms. Along this route of interpretive surplus we approach the very practice—and effects—of prismatic reading.

At the same time, in this collection's familiar but newly inflected stress on "close/r" reading, the incremental *r* captures a complementary method of closing-in still further than "close," which entails—by linguistic (in this case elided phonetic) paradigm, and as if by definition—the ever-close*r* results. Close/r/eading collapses into a unified operation, becoming over time a transtemporal program inherent to the decades of Stewart's labors therein: from *Reading Voices* (1990) and *Dear Reader* (1996) to *The Look of Reading* (2006), *The Deed of Reading* (2015), *Attention Spans: Garrett Stewart, a Reader* (2024), and *Bandwidths: Reading Across Media with Garrett Stewart* (2025). Students of whom a daunting "closeness" is feared expected may still approach such reading with an unstudied dread. In contrast, where professional literary protocols have grown all too inured to the once-vaunted "close" of analysis, perhaps to the point of deeming it moribund, a vestige of lost eras and antiquated semiotic regimes, *closer* reading catches us up to—and with—the special potencies of Stewart's "cross-sectional" art of interpretation.

When reading down the right edge of the contents page, what you will see tabled there (Part II) across the first of four new chapters is not just a linked affiliation but a reliable overview all its own. Proposed at a glance is how the phonetics of a poet's *script*, being its own mode of subvocal *punctuation*, finds its prose equivalent in the actual marking out of syntax as the lower limit of *plot* and its rhythms as well as an often emphatic feature of *style*, the latter transferred—and transvalued—from linguistic to visual craft in the marked "anti-style" of negative imaging in Conceptual *art*. Four separate chapters serve in this way to square one circuit of an adventurous career in transmedial reading on the way to a more speculative meditation (Part III) on interpretive energies found "ghosting" prose *style* and its often phonetic *art* even beyond the *punctuated script* of *finis*, this through the half-phrased reverbs of closure—like specters partly raised from the dead-end of plot, revenants ready for (re)interpretation. Ever so cleverly, the deferral of closure results from (yet) *closer* reading.

What *occasions* these essays bears little weight in comparison to the occasion they constitute, but the moment does invite mention in regard to the rationale of their arrangement. A question perhaps hangs in the air. What makes possible this present embarrassment of riches: five new essays, previously unpublished, by Garrett Stewart? They result from the opposite of embarrassed expectations in a previous volume I edited; rather, from a certain modest caution on my part there. In scheming out how to achieve what the subtitle of *Bandwidths* had in mind, namely *Reading Across Media with Garrett Stewart*, I cast the net broadly, if strategically, hoping to attract a dozen or so distinguished scholars whose engagement with Stewart's work, not just over the years but in new conversation, might help to pinpoint its own unique role across several decades of trend-(up)setting innovation. In approaching such scholars without of course knowing what statistical return I might garner by way of committed contributions, I found Garrett willing in the meantime to stockpile some of his recent writings (he sardonically admitted that "the world could wait") so that they might round out a full volume if too many of the approached critics demurred or came in short. It was hardly to be considered a makeshift or default option, since the contributors would then in a heightened sense, true to our subtitle, be writing "with" Stewart—and he with them, at full analytic throttle and, even then, full prismatic tilt, rather than just in his ad hoc response to the arriving pieces.

Ah, but the best laid fallback plans found no laid back prospective contributors! In an incoming flood of fortuitous good will, almost everyone in the invited "band" of essayists affirmed their enthusiasm and eagerness to write, so that the anthology's contractual page limit was quickly reached. Hence this "spin-off" volume: propelled, in effect, by exactly the welcome and specific centrifugal force of those gathered voices—of varied critical persuasion and styles of articulation—on issues Stewart habitually takes up. That "habit" is manifestly prolonged—and in a representative subdivision of topics— in the three originally tabled essays to follow (on John le Carré [chapter 6], Conceptual art [chapter 7], and narrative closure [chapter 8]) and, sprung from invitations since, in two fuller essays developed out of a conference paper and an anthology assignment (in order, on Gerard Manley Hopkins [chapter 4] and Charles Dickens [chapter 5]). Again via microreadings in Stewart's inimitable hands, these two latest essays, along with the trio previously held in abeyance, focus, respectively, on phonetic nuance in poetry and the subliminal metrics of punctuation in prose, as well as (there in waiting) so consequentially "focusing" on cinematographic style in popular fiction, the ironic inversions, reversals, and material negativities of Conceptual art, and—quite literally last, but in just that respect not least—touching on the interpretive impulse to put extra words in the mouth of novelistic closure, writing "beyond the end" under the pressure of accumulated narrative tension. Touching on, as idiom would have it—but more to the point in all these new pieces: hitting hard after landing on, bearing down, digging in, and coming up with remarkable new insights. And while there was no space for even the latter three of these pieces after the omnibus interchanges in *Bandwidths*, here there is room, not just for all five, but for some predecessor articles never before collected (chapters 1, 2, and 3), nor otherwise incorporated into the twenty monographs excerpted for the predecessor to *Bandwidths*, titled with the same appeal to scope, *Attention Spans: Garrett Stewart, a Reader*. In the spirit of that subtitle as well, the present collection could only benefit from some tapping of the author's critical backlog in order to bring out salient emphases in his return to certain verbal, visual, and conceptual demands made on "reading" at large. And, maybe just as interesting, to watch him feeling and finding his way through the interdisciplinary crossfire of earlier decades to which he was instinctively drawn, including screen semiotics, literary theory, and repeated returns (however ambivalently because skeptical of its methods) to philosophy—from Bergson to Deleuze, Wittgenstein to Cavell, Heidegger to Derrida, Kristeva to Agamben. So not just explaining the contingent origins of this volume, I am glad to enhance it with a look back into the origins of Stewart's own critical practice.

Ample introductory oversight can be gleaned for this collection's new essays, literary and otherwise, from a single reloaded delivery system in Stewart's multiple arsenal of critical attack across media: the wedge driven by his neologisms. One arc of the unconventional "reader" called *Attention Spans* straddled this career of Stewart's analytic coinages from *nom de plumage* (Fanny Cleaver renaming herself Jenny Wren in his first book—and first book on Charles Dickens, 1974) to an appendix—amounting to a full glossary— of his typically portmanteau compressions down through (and beyond) the 2018 book titled *Cinemachines*, concerned as he was there with the evolution of screen apparatuses from celluloid cell to pixel. Little surprise how his new essays collected here—oriented by samples from his backlist that help widen a magnifying lens on the prismatic spread of interpretive chromatics under scrutiny in diverse textual objects over the decades, along with the "schools" and "turns" that have inevitably shaped (and altered the outlets of) such discussions—continue to generate similarly fascinating and felicitous coinages. But, this time out, there is reason to summarize their *effects* rather than just flag site-specific contexts (since the full essays that embed these new appearances are all at hand below); worth reviewing and accumulating, in other words (somewhat other), the logic that so often elicits these widely foraged and then newly forged wordings from the kind of cross-medial and multisensory analysis being performed in Stewart's wide-ranging critical enterprises. Spotlighting the latest avatars of his long-standing vocabular habit—such is its earned centrality—affords a clearer (over)view of the work these intertwined terms, in fact and in effect, accomplish.

Admittedly, and for good reason, some of his portmanteau packings come so naturally as to seem almost etymological, as if tracing origins bi- and trilingually: like *gestalterity* in the Gerard Manley Hopkins essay (chapter 4), where such Germangling of the English lexicon feels drawn forth from the thematically dominant imbrication between pattern-spotting eye and phonemic ear in the rhythms of this transcendental poet and prolific coiner himself. The full force of this emergent terminological process, in respect to Hopkins and in the field of Stewart's innovative attentions more generally, comes out in the newly prompted dialogue following these essays—and does so, surprisingly enough, by cybernetic analogy. For the coinages are often minted in the same foundry as Stewart's own stylistic findings—which is to say, as conversation at the end brings to light, by reference to the stratum of "concatenated" digital textuality at the "subword" level of the bigram or trigram. Well before critical uptake, such are the code-like phonetic clusters that are slipped over—under enunciative pressure—from one lexeme to the next in writing of anything like Hopkins' density.[1]

Garrett has mentioned to me his pleasure that the new writing in this volume sets out, in Part II, with an essay in which Hopkins' locutionary play has pressed him to revisit two linked foundational debts in his critical career: namely, to the supple analyses of syntax, word, and syllable in Christopher Ricks and Geoffrey Hartman (see endnotes 17 and 23, respectively). The chapter thus does more than return to and extend Stewart's previous analytic encounter with Hopkins' poetry—including the "rhymed treason" of the poet's run-ons as well as his internally soldered wording ("in-jammed"). Stewart's labor also serves to rehearse the whole tenor of such phrasal tension in his more extensive work on prose fiction—and thus gets apt pride of place in this further sampling of his textual "prismatics." As is characteristic of Stewart's interpretive instincts, always fueled by an enriching indebtedness, he ultimately outdistances all precedent, critical included, except that set in motion by the cadenced faceting (call it audiovisual) of the writing—or screen framing or cinematographic editing—to which his interpretation is directed.

Nowhere is his cultivated gift for the (purposive) play offered by language clearer than in the field of nomenclature on display in the Hopkins chapter. Stewart's longtime penchant for invented portmanteau terms—devised to catch the action of convergent textual forces under pressure and discussion (whether on page or screen, in medial artifact or textual remnant)—goes into overdrive in encounter with a poetry, and its poet's own metacommentary, very much engaged with such compressions, resulting as they do from a syllabic "over-roving" more widely disposed than just at line's end. The incremental syllabics of a linguistically identified "gradience" lead Stewart—in the audition of such modularity, and beyond wording's internal anagrammatic combines—to the *transgram*. A newly minted word identifying the hinges by which letter sounds pivot and slip (phonemes beneath graphemes) between the unpoliced borders of abutting lexemes. We can almost, *almost*, track Stewart's whole argument along these paths of neologism in the Hopkins essay, making it unmistakable how these compressed phrasings—not (mere) tics of the critical stylist—bear evidence of the poet's own virtuosity with the substrate of grammars, English and otherwise, as they are taken up by the analyst's labors. To wit: the strain exerted by the poet in the tension between script and the rhythm of its "sprung" intonations, in the gestalt *auralterity* of their own *oculaurality*, induces a *kaleidophonic* shimmer of signifiers in sound play's *acoustic prism* (pertinently mixed metaphor rather than portmanteau). Admixture and interpenetration, inner/otherness, results—across the intertwisted warp of the poet's phrasal "infrascape"—from what Stewart builds on a rare Hopkins adverb for things intermingled ("throughther"), its own portmanteau at that, to term a syllabic *throughtherness*. Variously "refracted" in such prismatic cases, in the oscillation between script and enunciation, is the license that translates "inscape" into "instress," by way of what Hopkins asks one to imagine as the declaiming "paper" itself of the poetic page. In the aural pleating of any such sheaf, the contouring of script—transferred to mental impress/ion by acoustic stress—invokes not the print manifestation of an only posthumously published poet, but the subjective *inpress* of an intoned devotional *wor(d)ship*—all rendered in sacred service to an art of *logopoetics*.

Locally revisited in this way, Hopkins might have seemed an inevitably fertile turf for any such "rescaped" wording—in which the terrains of texts are perpetually alive beneath our critical gaze and metered feet. Newly apparent in this collection, however, what tends to organize Stewart's coinages in the all but "title essay" is the overarching metaphor of reading prismatically: its lenses precision-ground to the specifications of Hopkins' verse nuance, for instance, but applicable more broadly to the shifting surfaces of Stewart's own attention across periods, genres, media, and the sentences that under-/overwrite the transmissive/gressive reports. Surfaces—and their refractive depths, entailing many a beveled edge (his trope, again, from *The Metanarrative Hall of Mirrors*)—sheering off at some subtle angle of perception with a recombinatory glint. That glancing spark(le) is proof positive of the lucid exegesis ever underway (as when we peer into the microscope to study the surprising cliffs, glyphs, and angles of otherwise—i.e., to the "naked" eye—pedestrian salt crystals or grains of sand). This prismatic tack—or say its acoustic form, in that just-invoked coinage from the Hopkins analysis, as *kaleidophonic* shimmer—comes through even in Stewart's writing for a philological volume on punctuation in Dickens (chapter 5). From amid such specialized linguistic denotations as "commash" (for comma-plus-em-dash)—some of them obviously portmanteaus in their own right—Stewart borrows the primal unit of the "punct," the onetime floating period between every word in Latin manuscripts. He applies this term for his own stress on contrapuntal effects. Make that detonations of marked narrative inflection in Dickens. These effects include a micromanaged syntactic melodrama—visible to the unaided eye/I—in the first-person grammatical cliff-hangers (glyph-hangers) of *Great Expectations'* narrative consciousness.

Elsewhere in the present volume, coinage is again raised to titular status in the essay on medial reversibility in Conceptual art (chapter 7), where negation—elicited in detail as *negactivity*—is performatively engaged across the startling invertability of a pictographic logic. Instress now by impress—and occasionally obliteration. By such determinations, the radical Not A (~) is revisualized as a productive third term. The compression-cum-elision may place the poetically minded (and trained) in proximity to John Keats' "negative capability" or David Miller's "'negative' epiphany."[2] But in his penultimate essay here, Stewart finds unsuspected and sometimes bizarre materialities and technical executions bent to such abstract notions, all but re-conceptualizing them. Backed by one of Stewart's trustiest portmanteau conflations (in which media are sensed to foreground, as if with one breath, their own *medi/a/rchaeology*), an early subhead in this "negaction" essay renames Conceptual art—for its closely knotted relation of medium to mentation—as "Ideart." And then proceeds to illustrate such an operation, in one of its most complex materialist ideations, in the negative paintings of American artist Matt Saunders (b. 1975) when projected into the photogram/mar of inversion as all but dialectical *oppositives*. Expanding the borders of what the chapter's last paragraph terms "photontology," work of this transmedial sort is taken up in Stewart's reconceptualizing notice (and by another portmanteau) for the lexically self-illustrated permeability of its "permediations" in the tantalizing play between pigment treatment and light-seared imprint. Beyond Saunders' photo-painting and its occasional mobilization as animated image sequence—and Stewart's reflections on a kindred artistic practice by photographer, John Opera (b. 1975), a physics-focused painter of incandescent impressions[3]—this essay, alone among the new works comprising *Closer Reading*, takes Stewart back at key points to his interest in international cinematic experiments, narratographically tracked across directors as far afield as Iran, Taiwan, and Great Britain. Other dovetailed coinages invited by the conceptualist exhibits thus entertained include the pivotal elisions, each lexically reflexive, of *mirrorotation* and the explicitly linguistic *doublentendre*, with certain questions of intent, anything but negligible, reconfigured by the end under the near-anagrammatic rubric of the *neglegible*. Stewart is so unsparing in the subpoena to such terminological ferment that it can seem a continuous—and still continuing—spur to his interpretive urgencies.[4]

Finally, hived off into its own deliberate aftermath slot (chapter 8 featuring the virtual postmortem specter of such spectral reading practices), there is Stewart's eccentric, but still demonstrably essential, venture in scriptive intervention—in this case, in writing's wake, after the novelistic sentence has ended. In the classroom preamble to this final essay on prose closure (and beyond—to the immediate afterlife of criticism), Stewart can't resist—given mention of a verbal artist boasting, according to T. S. Eliot, the greatest ear of any English poet—a sense of Tenny*sonics* as prompt to a different scale of prose audibility and analysis. Or resist (Who would wish him to?)—closer to the nub of his own argument—a bivalve sound bite logged to allegorize a generalized (rather than pointedly phonetic) sense of prose fiction's latent *extratext*. By this he means a surplus, a supplement, as inertial and self-imbricated as the coinage makes it sound, at times potentially swallowing its own tale ouroboros-style, the coinage taking a bite of sound from its own syllabic coil. What Stewart is, in every sense "after" here, is story's subliminal narrative addendum, an *aftertext* generated in the reading, not just of final paragraphs, but of closure as such—with its potential discursive sediment(ation) figured again, in phonetic play and in broader portmanteau terms, as a *textension*. Here we find Stewart attending to the taut and sprung features of a text—all the while positioned to assess what might have exceeded, in felt phrasal inference, the writing's last (but tacitly outlasted) sentence remnant. With an ending sufficiently suggestive to be no ending after all, reading tracks the leftovers of a narrative leave-taking as plot's own "afterwording." In effect, Stewart's reading of the last paragraph of John le Carré's *Absolute Friends* (2003), among the works he discusses in another new essay (chapter 6) as the *film gris* of the novelist's inner stylistic cinema-on-the-page, has already applied this technique of extratextual extrapolation to that contemporary novel's muted symbolic truncation. Even before returning, in that same book, to gloss the penultimate irony of the vanished *decedent* in a grammatical slip of memorial *antecedence*, Stewart has thus anticipated, with some lingering figural fallout, the more fully exfoliated experiment of the "closing" essay's "Ghost Reading." And he has done so, indeed, with a passage of incompletely lifted mist at the end of *Absolute Friends* that seems almost directly to echo the ruminated last sentence from *Great Expectations* returned to in this final ghost-sighting report (after discussion of the latter as well in "Charles Dickens and the Plotting of Punctuation" [chapter 5]).

Such analysis approaches closure as a *ghostext* re-mediated in an almost ventriloquial literary de-briefing of residual thematic tension. Even in that latest ectoplasmic coinage, there might seem a fleeting spectral fleck of imitative disappearance, but in general more is at stake in these portmanteau nodes than the kind of syllabic mimesis Stewart often detects in literary writing—or in the visual puns of both cinematic editing and transmedial installation art. In his own coinages, that is, more method is underway than with, say, a detection of strategic wordplay in le Carré's *A Perfect Spy* (1986)—where, as flagged in Stewart's ekphrastic decoding, the mother's "empty" figure in a lone photo is anagrammed via the four-syllabled "permanently" into a voiding psychic imprint upon the surviving and narrating son. Given such attention to the ludic dimensions of literary invention, and the retention of its energy in coinages of Stewart's own casting, it isn't just that the word is cousin to the interpretive deed, but that it conjures new connections in response to the materiality (maternality) under analysis, plastic or linguistic, video or phrasal. In the special case of "afterwording"—tending-to-read-beyond-the-end—the orphan sentence or dissolving frame or whispered acoustic succession operates as its own kind of textual blood/line, self-inheriting narrative's own generativity. In all such neologisms as *ghostext*, then, there is a dialectical logic: or call it helical, bifocal, dialogic, stereoscopic, prismatic. (Those readers wishing to follow out the thrust of previous coinages along the beveled edges of Stewart's innovative lexical engineering may wish to consult the supplementary "Terms of Use: Coinages Cashed Out," that selective glossary featured in *Attention Spans* [340–47].)

Among the characteristic valences of Stewart's stylistic chemistry, we find here as well—in the pieces both retrieved and newly featured, and thus illustratively fused to a more complete cross-sectional archive—this critic's evolving way with the play of analytic titles and their programmatic terms.

In the earliest of the reprints, from 1981, Francis Ford Coppola's reworking of Joseph Conrad replays the depredations of colonial history in both forgotten political lessons and metanarrative recycling (chapter 1, "Coppola's Conrad: The Repetitions of Complicity"), a study that follows Stewart's most anthologized essay, "Lying as Dying in Conrad's *Heart of Darkness*," published the previous year in *PMLA*. Stewart has mentioned to me, by contrast, how "The Foreign Offices of British Fiction" (chapter 2), when first a lecture delivered at Stanford University's Center for the Novel in the late nineties, even as it was already on its way to print (in 2000), had required a brief give-and-take in the subsequent discussion period to bring out what his title meant to compass, not just geopolitically but methodologically, given the essay's comparison between the colonial fictions of Dickens' *Dombey and Son* and Forster's *Howards End*. Each plot entails the proverbial "home office" of mercantile enterprise over against its international outposts, of course, but the latter plural of "offices" was also meant to make space—and stoke recall—for novelistic "functions" or "services" (here ideological) as well as locales, which at Stanford the author realized could more helpfully have been pointed up early on in the paper. As readers of *Attention Spans* are well aware, Stewart is typically quick to note, looking back on any of his work, the missed chances (he rightly calls them "opportunities") for clarifications that might have been inserted without blunting the subtlety of his distinctions. Backfiled there, as if by uncharacteristic restraint in the foregrounding of wordplay, was the critic's intended sly sense of instant recognition for a trending postcolonial thematic under immediate reconsideration as an explicitly formal negotiation of subtexts. With the third of these revisited pieces—another methodological position paper called "The Avoidance of Stanley Cavell" (chapter 3), published in 2005—the title didn't fall short in this way, since the essay's lament for resistance to Cavell after the Foucauldian turn in literary studies was made clear as a working allusion to the philosopher's famous crossover essay on *King Lear*, called, as if in anticipation of Cavell's own subsequent fate, "The Avoidance of Love," situated as the concluding—far from conclusive—entry in his own "book of essays," *Must We Mean What We Say?* (1969).

The variety in Stewart's topics, not just of genre but of gender, and recently of race as well in contemporary practice—from extensive work on Jane Austen, George Eliot, and Virginia Woolf to engagements made and met in contemporary art and letters with Black artists from Glenn Ligon through Toni Morrison to Colson Whitehead—are part of what makes the commodious scope of his work, without loss of probing analytic focus, as hard to summarize as to represent by piecemeal sampling. At this valedictory moment in the long sweep of Stewart's career, it would be presumptuous to believe his achievements needed hyping, since they speak impressively, inimitably, for themselves. No superfluous effort here at giving him his (over)due. And yet, appreciating how Stewart's critical life overlapped with the major trends of aesthetics as well as literary, cinematic, and media theory over the last fifty-plus years—delivering an unintended shadow history of more than one field—readers may yet crave a modest announcement of acclaim and a modicum of advocacy to get their bearings with this book: not just what it is but when it is. Which is to say, who can presume to know which readers arrive here—and what they need to hear (if anything) before reading. If they are Stewart veterans, then, a few fresh dollops of orientating analysis, mostly rendered as reminders of past pleasures and benefits, may suffice. For novitiates (and you are very deliberately invited with this tempting spread of ex/samples), expounding on features and their merits could be called for in nominating Stewart as a candidate worthy of your over-subscribed attention within a crowded marketplace of contenders. In the twilight of an era (or more than one of them), a few lumens cast upon a deserving emissary of method would, in fact, be welcome. And having read this far, you have already found no few.

But there is one further phase of emphasis worth placing at the outset. Beyond the invigorating rigors of an attention so "close" that it often needs new names for what it finds are the electrifying and cauterizing connections it founds. What readers new to Stewart's methods ought most to know going in: how often, in bearing down, he tends also to stand back, to lift off, theorizing the intimacy of his sightings and auditions. There is his landmark theoretical account of the "phonotext" from Shakespeare forward in English letters, prosecuted from *Reading Voices* (1990) to *The Deed of Reading* (2015). Beyond this inflection, and equally in evidence in the pages to follow, he has initiated a discipline—in both senses: as a regimen of attention and as an intermedial practice—called "narratography" that was fashioned in the interplay between *Framed Time* (2007), on the shift from celluloid to digital cinema, and *Novel Violence* (2009), on the conflicted vectors of prose in Victorian fiction. Operating across narrative media, and modeled on the "detailed" mapping of cartography rather than the writing of calligraphy, this scale of analysis traces out issues dear to theoretical narratology (the "science" of narrative) at the more tightly-gauged (and engaged) level of a given narrative's stylistic "microplot."

Reading the entries in the *Closer Reading* ledger, one falls under a spell of vertiginous agitation, yet it is a *pleasing* symptom, neither a disorienting nor deranging one (such as might be felt in the imbricated backroads of highfalutin deconstruction). Here by contrast, Stewart brings the page alive with kinesthetic pleasure verging on proprioceptive awareness. We ask: Are such effects solicited (and by what strategic means?) for studies (and students) of grammar and diction, punctuation and ellipsis, film frame and narrative construction? Why, yes, in Stewart's stimulating company one can almost hear the sound of the classroom's evocative magic (more on this in a moment).

Chapters, ledger entries, lesson plans—or think: tracks on a long-playing methodological demo. (Still other trains of thought find rails laid to capitalize on the positive inertia of Stewart's onward experiments.) Taking stock of accumulated findings, there is something about the eclecticism of this collection of essays that surprises by its (uncanny) consanguinity; the cobbled together doesn't customarily cohere so emphatically, so persuasively. The exception is explained in this case by recalling that Stewart's ruminations are addressed to realms and regions he's already written whole books on (in all cases, improbably, more than one). Reading along with him at the scale of chapter-length rather than book-length, one can better hear the track change—a silent in-between, a pausal *punct*, that signals he is headed for yet further texts and methods. This isn't a greatest hits album (the predecessor volume, *Attention Spans*, delivered with capacious liner notes, holds that position), but instead a fresh session of virtuosic performances from a seasoned artist-critic at work in the studio (call it home office). Feeling the freedom—as befits his elevated stature (as well as his characteristic down-to-earth *bonhomie*)—to switch up his objects of interest and his approaches to them.

Once the needle is down, the disc spinning swiftly, sounds amplified beyond the silent page, our ears are surrounded and delightfully impinged upon by the pedagogical force of Stewart's critical practice. We readers come as close (as we can come) to inhabiting the classroom with him—listening to him articulate his reading of texts (films, novels, poems, songs, Conceptual art—in close-up and in cross-dissolve). Even as we privately hear him subvocally enunciated in our own heads, these pages call out—all too ideally—for the transition to audiobook (the dialogue voiced to incarnate a podcast episode). Other trade practices come indirectly to mind as well. To underwrite and overhear, that is, to make more readily available these specific jolts, the chapters could be individually glossed as variations on the (practical) strategies familiar to mass-marketed ventures—not *Garrett Stewart for Dummies* (that's a self-defeating jest) but something more like *How to Read with Garrett Stewart*. So think again: tracks as cuts—incisive cross-sectionings of his method as well as track-listed results, the needle picking up every vibration of his own original stylus—

1 / at the intersection between cinema (frame, editing, dialogue, song) and literature's lines of prose, ligatures of syntax, loops of metaphor;
2 / where both Victorian and Edwardian fiction find, and ideologically fine-tune, their pitch at once domestically, nationally, and at the farthest reaches of Empire;
3 / regarding the uneven inheritance of another scholar transgressing disciplinary property lines—a philosopher at work in literary regions, writing literature disguised (and distinguished) as philosophy;
4 / when the demands of experimental Victorian poetry are nourished and reactivated a century after the fact by vigorous and invigorating attention to lexicon, syllable, rhyme, and exotic mark;
5 / as Dickens' fiction is pressed into scrutiny to reveal the microplots of punctuation as a stylistic register all their own;

6 / when a master novelist's spy fiction seems itself monitored from within by the viewfinders of cinematic technique;

7 / where negative reversal in art practice is pursued as its own mode of material disclosure rendered inside-out;

8 / in residual discursive response to novelistic closure when found ghosted by afterthoughts that seem internal to the text's own thematic haunts;

—all in such a way that lets Stewart make audible the microplot at macro level, narratography expanded to the scale of the essay-as-form.

Chapters, entries, tracks, reworked studio takes. Or cuts again, this time having in mind (anticipating two explicitly "Negative" sculptures by Cornelia Parker encountered in chapter 8) laser shavings at the lapidary studio of the diamond cutter or silver engraver as well as the laid-down grooves of the audio engineer. Such precision work works not (just) as a metaphor for the faceted sheen of the essays themselves, eight polished cuts yielding a rainbow-tinged octahedron of a volume—but rather as figuring the various textual(ized) objects coming under Stewart's scrutiny, whose glancing illuminations the essayist seeks to catch and hold, light-beams as waves at once distinct *and* overlapping, "mixing" in their visual and audiophonic dimensions. Prismatic. While we are framing the ambitions of Stewart's first "essay collection"— aggregated after a career of book-length monographs—a brief clarification of the intended potencies of the subtitle's preposition. Stewart's essays don't conspire to refract one another at whatever angle or diagonal. Rather, as with the spectrum analysis attempted in this introduction, the intended emphasis— including subtly promoted affiliations to his forebears—should underscore how these are *essays in the mode of refraction*: Stewart responds to, and filters, various medial prisms as perceived in varied art forms and specific art works. The essays operate on the grammatical model too, in this respect, inheriting the mantle of Matthew Arnold's *Essays in Criticism* (1865) or Christopher Ricks' *Essays in Appreciation* (1996). At last, Stewart's *Essays in Refraction*.

One result is a book-length monograph as a workshop for experimentation (Montaigne's French sense of the *essai* as assay, attempt) in the fashioning of new words and the insights they yearn to compass. In the end-cap dialogue, Stewart addresses the service his books have offered him—a way to preprocess thoughts for the classroom (in the spirit of a syllabus, if in the style of a critical manifesto) and later to further process classroom conversations, and reflections occasioned by teaching, to make the analytic books of even more acute pedagogical use down the line. A book *of* essays at this late stage yields a culminating prismatic lesson: that his admirably diverse objects of critical study (proving an insatiable curiosity) are linked by certain methodological talents and tendencies—taking up narratographic mapping, micro-reading, and the sonic texture of text—to sound the depths of otherwise silent prose, to make visible that which so often rests before our eyes, stands in need of a coaxed and artful articulation. The impressive display of Stewart's books (of essays, as essays), their chromatic/thematic range, should nevertheless—looking back from this volume's multivalent angles of refraction—allow light to break on their endogenously practiced pedagogical motive. However much Stewart's writing makes a claim to artful achievement—analysis at once probing and persuasive, enterprising and enticing—the prose makes contact with terra firma in the training of new generations.

Let *Closer Reading*, then, stand as a bid for Stewart's engagement with a third major genre in what amounts to a trilogy: After (1) a "reader," entitled *Attention Spans*, we undertook the labors of (2) a group portrait in critical retrospect under the auspices of the *Bandschrift*, a dossier presented beneath the heading *Bandwidths*; and now (3) "essays in refraction" that coalesce under the title—and implied interpretive action of a zoomed-in—*Closer Reading*. Repeating this tripartite structure but at a different angle of approach—to facilitate the glimmer of yet other features—my editor's purview, though locally focused on each initial then successive/successor volume, has *also* been applied cumulatively across these three books con/sequentially concerned with Stewart's reading (writing) practice, given their shifting agenda and agencies: one book *about* him in self-chosen examples accompanied by self-correcting, context-enlarging, post-facto commentary; one *with* him in exchanges with other leading critics; one *by* him in predominantly new essays (the recovered suite of three previously published feeling new enough in this shared context, the essays neighboring one another in complementary ways). Suited to the master trope of the entire verbal and verb-driven venture, we encounter here a multifaceted effect, which in its coruscating way is exemplary rather than merely posted as career addendum. The virtuosity of Stewart's prose exemplifies its own virtues by providing a dynamic spread of intensity. His verve remains an abiding and appealing feature of every analysis, such that we fans find it hard to time-stamp his experiments: his contemporaneous review of *A Star is Born* (1976) would reside comfortably in Stewart's *Streisand: The Mirror of Difference* (2023); like his subject there, Stewart time and again proves his timelessness—and, as a compelling dividend, his timeliness. With over four decades between his two books on the Victorian novelist (*Dickens and the Trials of Imagination* [1974], *The One, Other, and Only Dickens* [2018]), it is the same unstinting and instantly recognizable enthusiasm that carries him through to different revelations.

However one may privately "spotify" the five new-release tracks as a personal playlist (and with no reason to begin at the beginning just because it is the most explicit of this book's new experiment in textual prismatics), one question, along with the pleasure, may emerge more obviously than before from the nonsequential variety of Stewart's concerns and discernments here (liberated as they are from any sense of methodological *non sequitur* even across ordinarily segregated media). Is there really a method in all this gladness? Or just an attitude made possible by such altitude: leaning in to the object for detections (and delectations) that are then lent out to more "readers" than one? Is the quite open secret, then, merely Stewart's habitual stance of close inspection tu(r)ned with strenuous exercise to a multi-platform aptitude: for listening harder, seeing more keenly, caring more carefully? But, "How?," one may still want more specifically to know. Whether imagined as prismatics or narratography, what kind of toolkit dependably equips such "micro" analysis when the desired results are always so elusively site (and sound) specific? Whatever comes to hand on aesthetic demand, it would seem, in all the code switching of the variable "texts" to which he responds. Sometimes a syllabic stethoscope, sometimes bifocal lenses, sometimes 3-D glasses, now sonogram tracing, now X-ray—and always the mind's own manifold aperture held open to the makings and markings of culture as signifying and therefore legible acts. And this is, after all, eminently teachable in the root sense: by example and practice together, *educible* from students and their chosen texts at once.

Though seldom teaching his own work, as explained in *Attention Spans*, when Garrett emailed a document to me for inclusion, he accidentally attached a note he had once appended to "The Foreign Offices of British Fiction" (chapter 2), in his rare sharing of published work with his students. He has now authorized the reproduction of the proviso so we can all benefit from the window it opens onto the extemporaneous build of his classroom practice, depicting, as the essay does, a deeper glimpse into the complexity of his wide-ranging pedagogical competencies (more of which we learn about in this book's concluding—and freshly constituted—entry, "A Dialogue in Diffraction"). Even as we are grateful for the author's own gloss on the chapter (a handout to his students that generously extends a hand out), the special attribute that catches my ear is (as Stanley Cavell would say) the "sound of the classroom."

To economize on the anti-Surface Reading, anti-anti-Critique you folks have requested from me, I attach my most Jamesonian/Lukácsian essay—on the merchant marine (parallel to the Imperial Rubber Company, as in Forster) frame around Dickens' most colonial novel, *Dombey and Son*, and its aura of mortal "totality." The titular "Offices" was a play on colonial outposts as well as imperial aegis or functions. This was done for an anthology in the first phase of a resuscitated formalist critique—before it was thought best (in some quarters) to divorce such reading from ideological "suspicion." We all read then for what's on the page surface, of course, but only in the sense that the explicitly *verbal* surface—if one has taken onboard anything from the readings we've explored in this course—is itself layered and braided, often laced with ideological blind spots and contradictions, impinging "deep structures," political as well as grammatical. These I draw out here by an approach to Riffaterre's odd borrowing of Derrida's odd use of syllepsis just to mean double meaning—or adapted by Riffaterre to split the difference between text and intertext. With such matrix payoffs as "sea changes" and the economic dead metaphor "ships have come in," I also do versions in the attached of the semiotic square (based on Jameson's Activity/Value antinomy in Conrad's *Lord Jim*) but without graphs, in purely discursive form (always one option), in order to show how Dickens anticipates the geopolitical occlusions of the "unseen" in Forster. A Surface Reading—who knows?—might thrill to the melodrama and comedy of *Dombey* without sensing its anticipation of Forster regarding the residual Victorian work ethic in precisely its exclusion of the female. But we don't really know, since there are no extended examples that I've seen. And I'm the first to admit that it's too easy to trivialize such results when there are no strong counter-examples in print, just sensible polemics *against*. Confronted with calls for, without instances of, this rallying around surface resembles claiming that we should read for plot, not theme, without having (unlike in Peter Brooks) real narratological results to show for such apparent back-pedaling reductionism. More Thursday.

That semester Thursday came and went, but the essay had already been long "on the books," with its exemplary microstylistic negotiation between the euphemized Victorian/Edwardian abstractions of geopolitics and macroeconomics. Stewart's account is "punctuated" by his favored rhetorical device of syllepsis, returning with a vengeance, brio, and unique political edge in the essay—when submitted, in quite different ways, to the tactical watering down of that grammatical term (a twinning itself standing as the terminological twin of "zeugma" in Anglo-American rhetoric) by the overdeterminations of structural semiotics and deconstruction alike. More recent writing by Stewart finds that trope of syllepsis less thickly embedded in the prose or poetry under analysis than in his comparison of Dickens and Forster, but always, in its departure from syntactic norms, of note and use. Before you know it in this essay (again, chapter 2), though Stewart revels in their slow transitions and escalations, such issues flower from philology into narratology. And, by extrapolation, into aesthetic philosophy.

Anticipating the conversational envoi that concludes this volume in the spirit of another new beginning, I had the opportunity for a similar conversation with Garrett in the pages of the journal *Philosophical Investigations*, in a special issue devoted to the variable, sometimes vexed, relations between literature and philosophy. The précis commenced with a question, the probing spirit of that conversation very much shared with the present volume's: "What does a famed literary theorist have to say about the interaction between literature and philosophy?—Well, if he's Garrett Stewart, the celebrated agent of pyrotechnic style in the service of durable insights between disparate disciplines and media," then, I stressed, we have much reason to listen up. In the interview there and in these pages, Stewart fields questions from me, who "asks how he, if he, thinks about the program of literature and philosophy." He does, and "from there the interview tracks the urgency of our moment," as I say:

in which literature and philosophy are independently besieged and yet may concede little rapprochement. Where does philosophy happen in literature (a philosopher's question) is turned around by Stewart such that we see literature conjuring philosophy at the level of the sentence. We are not peering "in" so much as looking "at" the art of literature teaching philosophy through refined reading and the analytical inquest of the syllable and the sayable. Anyone who works at the fraught fissure of these realms will benefit from the ways Stewart makes literature and philosophy sensible to one another—even as he productively unsettles the terms and conditions of their affiliation.[5]

While affirming the virtues of *Closer Reading* in that light and others, the previous endorsement of distinguished and philosophically minded critic Paul Fry, among others, in his enthusiasm for the first of these Stewart volumes, *Attention Spans*, intuits the promise of its next installments: "An astonishing volume concluding with yet newer directions." Adding in his fuller commendation: "Even bolder moves and still wider horizons may yet lie ahead." Awaiting you now, along with three durable forays (until now unattached to any prior project), are five emboldened new essays that confirm and ramify this heartening sense of remaining promise. Rounded out here is a true trilogy, then: a score of excerpts in retrospect, *Attention Spans* calibrated in review; a dozen-and-one paired commentaries and responses engaging the scope of those twenty books, their variable *Bandwidths* dialed in by interchange and debate; and now a clutch of new essays extending their analytic grasp in fresh directions, a further *Closer Reading* under spectrum analysis for the light shed by the unique wavelengths of its diffractions. Do consult those two predecessor collections in collecting your thoughts about the challenging and rewarding work by Garrett Stewart that follows. Across the terrain of the three-volume set, readers will come to appreciate anew the fervor with which Stewart monitors crest and trough of untold undulating passages. Unique among readers, Stewart rides the wave of pulse and interval—noting the sounds as well as silences, tones and pitches along with the rhythms of textual syncopation and amplifications of conceptual resonance. The refined grain of his particular attention to the particles of prose—from articles to participles—appears here under the scope of an anomalous microstylistics of reading. With his trained vision and sensitized sonic sense, Stewart makes the seemingly continuous admit its partic/ularity—thereby granting readers the rare chance to perceive the workings of the word up close, articulated at the sliding scale of every letter's singularity, syllabic coalescence, phrasal bravura, and sentential potency. That he can bring the same scale of analysis to the serial photograms or pixel splay of screen narrative, to the ligatures and elisions of shot change, lap dissolve, and acoustic bridges, and most recently, the at-times off-putting output of artificial intelligence, makes this narratographic downscaling all the more obviously a transmedial method rather than just a temperamental habit of response.

At the end of the present volume, a special addendum to close-out the endeavor, one that delivers on promises made: the continuation of a conversation underway across all three volumes, this installment is named

"A Dialogue in Diffraction" to keep pace with the marshalled metaphors—a conversation conducted with candor and interpretive flare, tracing critically the felt spread of radiating pathways, particles *and* waves alike—found in *Closer Reading.* There is one undergirding scene near the midpoint of this final interchange (see pp. 251–52) that proposes its special relevance (also) at the outset, summarizing as it does the *kind* of reading experience upon which we're about to embark. Allow me, then, to co-opt the episode and install it here by way of introductory emphasis—while also designating it as an invitation to revisit its crystalizing moment in the dialogue's fuller context:

DL: [...] One of your avowed narratological heroes, Roland Barthes, famously distinguished in literary history between the classical "readerly" novel and a postmodern "writerly" fiction, but I always think of your close "readings" as inherently writerly in themselves. Acknowledging you as among the most intricate and accomplished living stylists in the critical academy—and certainly as unflagging as any in the urge to *phrase your way* to insights, rather than just deposit them—I wonder if this isn't, after all, the open secret of your transmedial offerings, including your productivity? You write as a prose stylist about the style of prose, but you discourse in a comparable manner (as if you were actually "translating" image into words) in your extensive and vividly written work on painting, sculpture, assemblage and installation art, and of course, film. Is this writerliness, verging so often on a texture of imitative form, some kind of baseline common denominator?

GS: How can I agree, let alone thank you for noticing, without congratulating myself on some anomalous artistic bent? But I guess such tendencies of mine were after all why I thought, overconfidently, that I could teach creative writing, as if it were continuous with film criticism under the rubric of the "cinematographic sentence." Why should screen analysis be limited to the straightforward terms (vocabulary and determining limits) of journalistic movie reviews? Reactions are one thing, analytic enactions another. Why shouldn't an interpretive paragraph be as carefully shaped and edited as the montage sequence it seeks to evoke as well as report on? Or the solution to a narratographic puzzle be as tightly grooved and interlinked as the increments it has troubled to decode and reassemble? So yes, the urge to think through a formal pleasure or conundrum, on screen or wall or page, is always for me an intuitive (aesthetic) wish to find not just words for it, but the keenly right (just) ones, as multifaceted in syntax as the work's own structure. There is no dream of interpretive poetry here, but the means are not "merely" prose. I once wasn't so alone—and certainly had inspiring precedents in this line (including, beyond my own literary discipline, philosopher Stanley Cavell, of course, and art historian T. J. Clark)—but it seems to me a vanishing wish in criticism. When I can inculcate its thrills in a student here and there, now if mostly then, I know I'm still teaching.

After the coming chapters of such "writerly" analysis, unrestricted to written media, join us for an afterclass supplement of multiple portent. Once the full measure of Stewart's eight deep cuts in *Closer Reading* is taken, Garrett sits down with me for an extempore jam session as a last recorded bonus track, reflecting back—or rather, refracting outward—on the proceedings (and their radiating relevance to his previous twenty books—including their offshoots, *Attention Spans* and *Bandwidths*). At work in those pages at the broadest disciplinary scope, far from any play-by-play recap, is a contemplative rendering of where we have been, what has been and gone, and, more auspiciously, what might still be done: a modest nod toward where things may be heading in light of Paul Fry's "yet new directions . . . even bolder moves . . . still wider horizons" potentially in wait for work at this level of intensity. Sidling up to Garrett Stewart at the height of his considerable critical powers, we settle in for a series of sonorous valedictory riffs, not just on the writing he gave us but also on the classroom priorities to which it has responded over the years—the very decades, as it happens, which align coextensively with the major trends of literary study since the mid-twentieth century.

Notes

1 Of similar note: the pitch-b(l)ending and legato slide between cadenced microtones in vocal performance. Consider the pressing, not just peripheral, interest coming into genuine tangency with new writing in this volume, when the author of the opening essay in its predecessor, *Bandwidths* (so titled "Voiceover," by Herbert F. Tucker), compares the effects Stewart intuits and attunes to in his audition of Barbra Streisand's vocals with the tiered, recursive sound play one might expect to find under a phonetic analysis of Hopkins' poetry. See Herbert F. Tucker, "Voiceover" and Garrett Stewart's reply, "Writing the Voice," in *Bandwidths: Reading Across Media with Garrett Stewart* (New York: Bloomsbury, 2025), 15–25.

2 See David Miller, "'Negative' Epiphany," in *W. H. Hudson and the Elusive Paradise* (London: Palgrave Macmillan, 1990), 52–56.

3 See remarks on John Opera's works of art in *Attention Spans: Garrett Stewart, a Reader*, ed. David LaRocca (New York: Bloomsbury, 2024), 290–92, 325.

4 In both of the new essays Stewart has written—composed after the holdover pieces from *Bandwidths* that round out this volume—he is once again up to his familiar upping-of-the stakes with resonant terminological in(ter)ventions. In "Transmit by Intermit: Between Metatextual and Metamedial" forthcoming in the *Routledge Companion to Metafiction*, ed. Josh Toth and Lissi Athanasiou-Krikelis, we encounter—in Stewart's characteristic link between literary and film reading—the notion of *intramittence* in the matter (and motion) of frame advance or syllabic overlap, as well as the screen-specific *techno(ideo)logy* that filmic or digital effects can sometimes symptomatize. These fresh castings lead to Stewart's latest quintessential portmanteau phrasings for the articulation of theme by medial technique: *techxt* and its *metatechxtual* overlay. Comparably, when

pursuing the question of inverted optical process across the spectrum of visual representation first developed in chapter 8 of the present volume—while also returning on invitation to his earlier concept of "demediation" in the logic of the *bibliobjet*—Stewart contributes the lead essay (under the title "Medium Neg(activ) ated") to a forthcoming special issue of *Textual Practice* named for his own reinvested coinage, "Demediation," ed. Juri Joensuu and Mikko Keskinen. Here is an essay that again shows the structural and often transmedial leverage exerted by portmanteau conflations as being so central to Stewart's concerns that the argument organizes itself across such subheads as "Xphrasis" and "Textirpation" on the way to the borrowed syllabic contraction of "Negentropy." Either Stewart finds—or, if not, finds himself fashioning—the categorical pressure points he needs.

5 See David LaRocca, "'It's All There in the Language'—A Conversation with Garrett Stewart," special issue, "Literature and Philosophy," ed. K. L. Evans and David Rozema, *Philosophical Investigations*, vol. 47, no. 3 (2024): 278–97.

I

REVISITATIONS

1 / Weighing in for the second time with his newly combined media interests, fiction and film, in the leading interdisciplinary journal of its day, *Critical Inquiry*, Stewart follows his sense of Dickensian industrial satire (*Hard Times*) in Chaplin's *Modern Times* ("Modern Hard Times," 1976) with a sustained response to Frances Ford Coppola's adaptation of Joseph Conrad's *Heart of Darkness* in the Vietnam update of *Apocalypse Now* ("Coppola's Conrad: The Repetitions of Complicity," 1981). Building on what has become his most often anthologized essay, "Lying as Dying in Conrad's *Heart of Darkness*" (*PMLA*, 1980), and on contemporaneous structuralist thought about repetition and ritual violence, Stewart's turn to the screen version of this imperialist plot is less an adaptation study than a tryout for the critic's later textually-focused work in "narratography" across literature and cinema, and, in the latter medium, across the transition from celluloid to digital thematizations.

1 / *Coppola's Conrad: The Repetitions of Complicity*

It was like a weary pilgrimage amongst hints for nightmares.

—Marlow in *Heart of Darkness*

It smelled like death in there, malaria, nightmares [...]. This was the end of the river all right.

—Willard in *Apocalypse Now*

FRANCIS FORD COPPOLA'S FILM *Apocalypse Now* (1979) takes up Joseph Conrad's *Heart of Darkness* (1899) as an aesthetic repetition within a human history of repetition, a returning nightmare of plunder, blunder, and malignity as old as the motives of empire. *Heart of Darkness* does not come easily to *Apocalypse Now*, yet the film's real power derives from its sustained attempt to transpose the story's incremental repetitions of style, plot, and psychology into a new cinematic register and a new century. Film stands to tale as the brutal duplications within each stand to one another: signaling a replication beyond either or any text, an irreversible cyclic violence that threatens to turn history itself into one long sacrificial ritual. Conrad's politics thus predict rather than merely provide the heart of Coppola's darkness, *Apocalypse Now* emerging as both historical deduction and aesthetic debt. Film not only overhauls or reinhabits but extrapolates from a piece of classic fiction. The result, for all its extravagant lapses, is an American movie of risk, scope, extraordinary impact, and rare challenge.

The aesthetic and commercial coup of Coppola's first *Godfather* picture (1972) gave rise to the speculation that mediocre books make the best movies. Would the trouble most everyone notices toward the end of *Apocalypse Now* therefore have to do with the fact that Conrad is too good for Coppola's own good? (Certainly in estimates to date the book is seldom set against the film without being used against it.) Or is there a problem in Conrad's own ending for *Heart of Darkness* which Coppola tries to face up to and work through, not routinely borrowing his source so much as recapitulating it in yet a bleaker key? Coppola is trying to address by spectacle the dilemmas of moral complicity that Conrad manipulates by tone and metaphor, trying to find in visual chiaroscuro and collage the equivalent of the writer's brooding, rhetorical cadences and driven iterations. The film he builds in this way, spellbound (or thunderstruck) at times by its own reverberations, still burrows as Conrad does down to the shadowed underside of event, even in its troubled and cumbersome finish. This final phase of the story, with Kurtz at last confronted, offers perhaps the best place to measure the angle of Coppola's deflection from Conrad and so to assess the dimensions of his film as a whole. Departing from Conrad, Coppola gains access to their common theme at a deep level. The revisionary impulse becomes a second look, harder and darker.

To see what befalls and refashions Kurtz on his way from book to film, where Marlon Brando's version of him can too easily seem redundant, is to see something of the internal workings of narrative, its genius for repetition, multiplication, and mirroring, and its itch for the rounding out of a narrative line, the spatialization of temporal form. Conrad's Marlow recounts a narrative of infectious evil which there is every reason to suppose he has told before and will tell again, a story inexhaustible, never exorcized, the oldest story of all: the truth about human nature that links in one unbroken narrative the corrupting power of Roman colonization and the imperialistic pride of Victorian England. Coppola extends this historical line forward into American militarism. As atrocities in his film repeat and compound themselves and psyches duplicate and fuse, Coppola presses his symbolism a step beyond Conrad, turning the screw of cyclic history and spiral plotting one more notch into violent confrontation—not only between national armies but between separate entities innately bonded, between antihero and villain, executioner and Antichrist.

Two influential recent critics, J. Hillis Miller and René Girard, coming at the question of repetition so separately as never to repeat each other, see repetition on the one hand as the central habit of story, not only as retold but as internally disposed, and on the other as the basis of violent ritual, not only as replayed on schedule at sacred intervals but within the very structure of violence as determined by sacrificial duplications and displacements. A few years back in these pages, Miller argued that it was the nature of every major narrative line to trace itself by some return or repetition, looping over its own length, crisscrossing, knotting up.[1] Which zigzags, folds, and intersections are definitive for *Apocalypse Now*? What Girard says about the structure of sacrifice should also bear on a movie that ends in a bloody scapegoat ritual where the tense thread of plot is split into parallel symbolic strands by a crosscutting of the cinematic line. Incision yields doubling, psychological exchange, violent equivalence. In the rudimentary forms of tragedy, Girard explains, "violence invariably effaces the difference between the antagonists," for it is "the act of reprisal, the repetition of imitative acts of violence, that characterizes tragic plotting."[2] Coppola further suggests that when the violent reprisal is of self against alter ego, in a repetition of previous violence committed in the first person, the logic of repetition is complicated by the power of two. The "line" Willard must get on Kurtz is the plot line of his own examined story drawn to the breaking point.

In both Conrad and Coppola, a river journey offers from the first a linear figure (doubled in Conrad, where the story of the Congo passage is told on the Thames) for the steering of their plots along what Marlow calls "streams of death in life." The briefest summary should sketch a map. Conrad sends his narrator Marlow, agent of an international trading company, up the Congo River in search of another European agent in the ivory trade named Kurtz, a once humanistic mastermind of inordinate personal energy and intelligence, whose burning idealism, but not his hubris, has been lost to festering empathy with the jungle where he has been installed, it seems, as a kind of ruthless godhead among cannibals. Rumors of Kurtz's genius and eloquence begin to preoccupy Marlow as he nears his destination, but by the time Marlow reaches him, Kurtz is feverish, skeletal, and doomed. Kurtz dies shortly afterward with Marlow in nearby attendance, Kurtz's eloquence dwindled to that famous death gasp, "The horror! The horror!" Allegorically charted, the story's true voyage of discovery, together with its true point of no return, is the gradual convergence of Marlow's imagination with the dark churnings of Kurtz's heart. To borrow from another Conrad title, Marlow must come to admit himself as a "secret sharer" in Kurtz's vile will to power, must come face to face with his gruesome double across the very brink of the grave.

In the film script by Coppola and John Milius, Brando plays Kurtz, now a brilliant Green Beret colonel, as swollen rather than emaciated by evil, a man gradually maddened by the Indochina conflict who has retreated into the Cambodian jungle to play out in the guise of a demonic Buddha his vision of terrorizing and remorseless warfare. There he has divested himself of his uniform and been lifted to rule over a tribe of whitewashed, spectral natives who seem to travesty the pale Anglo villain who has come among them. Martin Sheen plays Captain Willard (Coppola's version of Marlow), the steely willed classified agent sent upriver by the Intelligence Corps to slay Kurtz before it is too late. The symbolic stream that runs straight from Conrad's African river through the turbulent flood of Coppola's apocalyptic imagery is implied early on by Willard's reference to a main circuit. His metaphor, a technological conceit that modernizes a linear metaphor in Conrad, suggests the plot circling around to self-confrontation. Marlow repeatedly describes the inauspicious river as a twisted snake, suggesting an Edenic promise corrupted by serpentine and sinister trade routes. In the gritty vernacular of the *Apocalypse* narration, written after the original script by Michael Herr (author of the Vietnam journal *Dispatches*), Willard says of the fatal river, as if it were the visual delineation of the movie's whole plot, that it "snaked through the war like a main-circuit cable plugged directly into Kurtz." The two men are thus stationed at different points along the same systematic malfunction, a chain of command overloaded by stupid brutalities and constantly in danger of an explosive short circuit.

By the standards of screen borrowings, a surprisingly high percentage of Conrad is there in Coppola, imported but transmuted. Marlow's Black helmsman reappears as Chef (Albert Hall), the pilot of Willard's craft who tells him of his immediate predecessor on the river, an officer who has mysteriously committed suicide in a fatal omen of self-confrontation. Willard, like Marlow, fixates on Kurtz's voice long before he is encountered, a voice that "put a hook" in Willard ever since he heard a tape recording of the colonel's psychotic fantasies and genocidal ravings. Conrad's Russian in motley, stupefied by admiration for Kurtz, is a role inherited by Dennis Hopper as a loony (and unnamed) photojournalist, devoted fool to Kurtz's mad lord. Such proliferating details from Conrad pace and focus Coppola's wartime narrative down to its finale in private violence, where the line "Exterminate all the brutes!" scribbled on Kurtz's supposed humanistic report on methods for civilizing the natives is transposed into a nuclear key as "Drop the bomb! Exterminate them all!" And through both plots runs, seductive and bedeviling, that almost hallucinatory magnetism Kurtz exercises over the protagonist's imagination, a dark linkage that gives the true psychic axis to the gloom and gore of story. In one of the head-on ironies of Conrad's narration, Marlow disclaims his own integral part in the tale as another European soul struggling with guilt at least by association: "I don't want to bother you much with what happened to me personally," he would have us believe, yet he admits as an afterthought that the eventual meeting with Kurtz did seem "somehow to throw a kind of light on everything about me—and into my thoughts," invoking there an apt play on "about" as "around" but also "concerning." Atmosphere *is* spiritual comment in the story, but Coppola's Willard is more to the point. "There's no way to tell Kurtz's story without telling my own," he announces toward the start of the film, "and if his story is really a confession, then so is mine." The plot's deepest logic is a rhythm before it is an argument. Paired, split, and parallel syntax, antithetical or double-tracked cadences, all give the seal of deadlock or the pull of contradiction to the pace of voiceover narrative even before it has accumulated to theme. "They call me an assassin," says Kurtz's voice on the tape Willard first hears. "What do you call it when the assassins accuse the assassin?" It is a rhetorical question meant only to instill its ironic and repetitive rhythm until such circular hypocrisy can be explored by actual drama.

Apart from the clear parallels between Conrad's story and Coppola's script, two salient divergences, one in framing structure and the other in climactic plot, go far toward gauging the thematic differences between these two versions of the tale. Coppola has dropped the coda in which Willard returns to Kurtz's once humanizing and domestic connections (fiancée in the story, wife and son in the film) to deliver a sugar-coated fabrication of Kurtz's terrible end, a lie that (however speciously well-intentioned) binds Marlow, in the tale, to the worst delusions of hubris, blind idealism, and intellectual superiority. Coppola's dismantling such a structure of receding irony provides a cinematically more forceful, if at one level ethically simplified, narrative: Willard's collusion in the brutal heart of Kurtz's darkness speaks for itself—or whispers pitilessly on the closing soundtrack with "The horror! The horror!" Willard's moral complicity does not need a white lie shading to black to confirm it because his deepest guilt and identification with Kurtz inform Coppola's most obvious departure of all from Conrad: the fact that Willard does not, as Marlow before him, simply watch Kurtz die but becomes his bloody executioner.

The circular trap by which savagery must be performed in order to purge itself entangles Willard in a tragic repetition of Kurtz's own tactics of fiendish expediency that implicates in the prevailing bloodshed the very agent come to exorcize it. Conrad's turn-of-the-century critique of amoral imperialism and the sins of pride to which it falls prey is not lazily appropriated, compromised, or updated by Coppola. Rather, he rigorously projects it into its own augured future, exposing idealistic colonialism's inevitable violent issue in capitalist military aggression. By being at times so infernally faithful in drawing on the prehistoric jungle imagery of his source, Coppola may seem to have surrendered his chances to mount a definitively contemporary war epic. Yet the lurid primeval atmosphere of the movie's climax, if dramatically miscalculated, appears far less anachronistic, exotic, and derivative when proper weight is given to the episode Coppola invents which has no parallel in Conrad at all and which doubles his plotline's power to move toward a conclusion. The swaggering, sociopathic Colonel Kilgore (Robert Duvall), in the thick of his mad command, serves as a preliminary exposure to evil, anticipating his more profound counterpart in Kurtz.

Kilgore (the compound pun of his name a double indictment straight out of the satiric techniques of *Catch-22*) strafes, bombs, and napalms an entire enemy village mainly to clear a beachhead for surfing. Kilgore and his men descend out of the skies like winged supernatural furies, piping Wagner's "Ride of the Valkyries" through loudspeakers mounted on their helicopters (the colonel's inscribed with the apocalyptic motto "Death from Above") [...] But it is Kurtz's own unfolding history which finally clarifies the imagery of satanic descent in the helicopter mission. His demonic proficiency has also, we learn from his dossier, taken the form of death from above: we discover with Willard that Kurtz rose to national prominence and a *Newsweek* cover story by spearheading an unauthorized air strike with the code name "Archangel." As Willard says about the whole matter, "The bullshit piled up so fast in Vietnam you needed wings to stay above it." When the wings turn malign, the Archangel is confessed as Lucifer, who must be struck down by a central command whose code name in the last scenes, broadcast repeatedly over the ship's intercom, is "Almighty." This religious imagery is not idly strewn about but built up from episode to episode. When we first encounter Kilgore in a cleanup operation, there are shots of a priest shouting mass to genuflecting soldiers in the middle of the still chaotic battleground, while above the offered Eucharist the netted body of an ironically sacred cow is being helicoptered out of the fray—an image that anticipates the slaughter of the sacrificial water buffalo at the film's conclusion. Just before the encounter with Kurtz, Willard's crew must pass through the deserted scene of a satanic sabbath, altars heaped with severed heads and flanked by votive torches guttering amid a forest of charred, ashen crucifixes. Such cumulative repetitions of religious iconography are not incremental so much as regressive, moving back beyond the Christian myth, defunct and desecrated, to more primitive communions and sacrifices.

Apocalypse Now certainly keeps its title before us with its imagery of fallen archangels, antichrists, satanic auras and emanations, and fiendish halos. The Intelligence Corps general who assigns Willard to his top-secret mission says that Kurtz is one of those men whose dark sides have usurped the "better angels of our nature," and Kilgore is introduced into Coppola's plot to illustrate an aggravated but not yet final stage in this corruption, a willful and foolish cruelty still held in check by the trappings of command. He is, says Willard, a soldier "with a weird kind of light around him"—a braggart's hellfire made literal in Kilgore's case—which signals the fact that he would never get so much as a scratch in battle. In the last dossier photograph of Kurtz Willard studies (taken in Cambodia by the Hopper character?), Kurtz too, backlit, seems to radiate such a glow but is himself all in shade, a black silhouette rimmed with fire. This photograph, like a spiritual X-ray, anticipates with its hellish aureole the man's actual appearance at the end, Kurtz no more than a brooding and tortured bulk emerging from darkness, catching the light only dimly, as if he barely remains in the phenomenal world at all—a ghostly presence that outlines the abstract form of his doom as the embodied core of darkness.

The absurd homicidal spectacle of Kilgore's methods suggests to Willard that it could not be "just insanity and murder" that headquarters holds against Kurtz, for "there was enough of that to go around." Instinct tells Willard that as he moves from this colonel to the other (the viewer moving with him), the sequential encounter with brutality will not be redundant but will plumb corruption to a new depth. What singles out Kurtz for extermination is not the scale of his slaughter but the excoriating self-knowledge (up to a point, beyond which Willard is necessary) and fevered independence that fuel his brutality and carry it beyond the reach of containment or subordination by his military superiors. To discover this about Kurtz, however, Willard must confront himself even more deeply, must respond in kind, as we will see, to Kurtz's self-awareness—answer to it and indeed complete it as he turns the other's suicidal instinct into murder, turns Kurtz's craving for a way out into an exit by execution. It is a sentence Willard carries out against himself as well, for in killing Kurtz he will not only answer the colonel's introductory question— "Are you an assassin?"—but own up to it for the second time. One of the finer ironies of Coppola's story is that the official reason for terminating Kurtz includes his having summarily executed a number of double agents without permission from central command, yet such assassination is precisely Willard's credential for his mission against Kurtz in the first place. As the film opens, we discover our narrator raving drunk in Saigon, in a grueling lull between assignments, wondering how many men he has killed by this point and waiting for yet another mission to be allotted to him "for my sins"—a penance, an expiation in more blood. It is a perfect irony that he first assumes he is being arrested rather than assigned a new duty and asks, "What are the charges?" Willard is interviewed in the next scene by the Intelligence staff, and we find that his last assignment was in fact the assassination of a tax collector. When Willard's voice later breaks onto the soundtrack reading a letter from Kurtz to his son about being accused of murder by the army, Willard's own "I" seems to take upon himself the burden of defense. Whereas in Conrad, Marlow *does* nothing wrong, Willard meets Kurtz on equal terms, mutual even when they turn punitive. His new "charge" is indeed an accusation after all.

Though Willard's previous acts of murder are only alluded to, two subsequently staged events spell out the violence in which his psyche is mired. When his trigger-happy crew massacres a sampan full of innocent Vietnamese only to discover one woman still alive, they want to rush her to medical attention. Knowing that this would endanger his mission, Willard cold-bloodedly kills the woman with a single bullet. In the immediately preceding scene, Willard has read a letter from Kurtz about ruthlessness in combat as a kind of clarity in which one does "what there is to be done, awake, looking at it," without being rendered impotent by the "timid lying morality" of official codes of conduct. As if taking dictation from Kurtz's words, Willard acts directly in line with their fearful insight. After a long-held shot of him isolated on the prow of the ship, bulking to a silhouette edged by the wasted light of the setting sun (much like Kurtz's photograph in the preceding scene), the screen goes dark, blank, for a disconcerting (and in this film unprecedented) stretch—no slow and decisive cut but more like a wound in narrative. We have here, for a full half-minute, the visual equivalent of the heart of darkness, the instinct toward cool, callous, efficient action bluntly confronting itself within a gulf of voided narrative, voided nature. When images begin to emerge, resolving back into light and focus, Willard's resumed voiceover (in what would ordinarily be part of the same continuous scene) acknowledges that, although the crew will never look at him the same again, he has in a single act of violence learned "one or two things about Kurtz that weren't in the dossier"—by learning, of course, more about himself as one of the two men. This brief hole in linear narrative is a small masterstroke of editing and editorializing at once. The pitch-black hiatus at this turning point opens our eyes with Willard's to the plot's own abyss, a fracture at one level of the story that drops its hero through to a closer bond than ever with Kurtz as an alter ego in calculated ferocity.

Such a lacuna in narrative is a breach in telling that reaches out, for it opens us to our own space of contemplation as well as to Willard's. I am obviously verging here on a cinematic correlative to that reader-response criticism so much in vogue of late for literary studies. An even more direct example of this in *Apocalypse Now* comes early with the film's one explicit allusion to the metaphor in Conrad's title. When Willard is getting his orders over lunch with the general, he looks straight into our eyes (the eye of the camera) as the general mentions the phrase "dark side of our natures." Willard's gaze snares all of us, too, in the complicity he must so relentlessly share with Kurtz. A later violation of the cinematic frame also challenges our supposedly safe distance from the confines of plot. After a machine-gun assault from the invisible enemy on shore, the ship's Black navigator, staring straight into the camera, reaches below and past the frame, as if into our own laps, and brings back his fist bloodied with the gore of the other Black seaman on the boat, just gunned down. These two men thus become blood brothers in the most sickeningly literal sense. At the same time, by a camera angle that can only be described as a corpse's-eye view, we are drawn into a drama of mortal soul mating in a cinematically unorthodox way. Our point of view demonstrates, visually and viscerally at once, how in such nationally sanctioned carnage the soldier always dies for us, in our very place and space—we *are* our dead—and how, too, in all art death can be turned (as it will be again in the case of Kurtz at the end) into an act of sacrificial surrogacy, the participant as scapegoat for the spectator.

The tragic bonding of these two black men at the point of death is reversed for Chief's own fatality shortly afterward, the second scene of violence that helps mark the change from Marlow to Willard. [...] In Conrad the helmsman seems to stand for physical instrumentality abstracted from any reflective capacity, brawn to Marlow's brain, and so to form with him a composite and complete human agent, each half of which recognizes his deep link to the other only at the "supreme moment" of death. Coppola stays as close to the original dichotomy of this conception as he can. Of course his "chief" speaks English, being an American soldier, but when asked his opinion for the first time by Willard, Chief replies flatly, bitterly, "I don't think," leaving the decisions entirely to the clear-sighted but compunctionless Willard. When Chief is stabbed in the back by a spear, he tries to embrace Willard not as he did his slain black brother but in an unexpected attempt to yank his superior officer down upon the spear's point as it protrudes from above his heart. Conrad's deployment of mortality as the supreme test of human brotherhood is converted in the film to the reprisal of an enraged death grip, white and Black man face-to-face across the narrowed breathing space of their interdependence and their enmity. When Willard has to administer, in effect, the death blow to Chief in order to preserve his own life, we see again that heightening of violence over the Conrad original that leads to the even more fatal doubling of Willard and Kurtz at the river's end. Willard has informed us early in his narrative that, while he has killed many enemy soldiers at close enough range to feel their dying breaths, the attack on Kurtz, his military superior, would be different. On his way to this fateful confrontation, Willard feels the death breath of a soldier under his command (speared by what Willard claimed were only toy arrows), as if he were struggling with an enemy in mortal combat and must look into the face of his own murderousness as a symbolic negative image of his responsibility as an officer.

"A part of myself," notes Willard, is afraid of what that "I" will do upon meeting Kurtz, and it is that part of himself (though he doesn't yet guess this) which *is* Kurtz, or which dwells with him in the dark recesses of the will. Orson Welles had just the right idea: on first coming to Hollywood, before conceiving the *Citizen Kane* project, he had intended to film *Heart of Darkness* with himself playing both Marlow and Kurtz. Trying to explain why Kurtz transferred to a Green Beret airborne unit, Willard says, "He could have gone for general; he went for himself instead." That second phrase can be taken in the idiomatic sense of an assault on the self, worded differently later when Willard suspects that Kurtz not only broke with his family (as Willard has agreed to a divorce from his wife) but "broke with *himself*." Violence for the reflective soul is always in the long run reflexive, self-divisive, a rending of identity. Kurtz has split, that is, into both Willard and himself together, cold-blooded clarity of purpose and the more bestial promptings into which it can degenerate, and so he knows, says Willard, "more about what I am going to do than I do myself." Again the cadences of parallelism and antithesis accompany the reflexive syntax of splintered identity. When Willard first describes Kurtz in his temple, he says he has never seen a man so "ripped in half," and this helps explain the alternating dialogue of their first dramatic encounter, verging as it does on the echoing stichomythia of ritual tragedy:

> "Are you an assassin?"
> "I'm a soldier."
> "You're neither. You're an errand boy."

Disjunctions, wavering rapidly enough, fuse into equivalence.

At the same time, certain imagistic repetitions momentarily double back past their own debasement to an unfallen purity. "This was the end of the river all right," remarks Willard when he first enters Kurtz's compound. Unfortunately, the only arresting speech he encounters there, the only one truly suited to Brando's gift for bizarre yet delicate eccentricity, is Kurtz's halting, pained nostalgia for the undespoiled land of home. In a Huck Finn–ish evocation, he searches for words to recall a gardenia plantation along the Ohio River he knew as a boy, where it seemed several miles of heaven had fallen on the earth. Now all the skies have fallen, and hell has erupted onto the face of a defiled earth. "Did you live near the river?" Kurtz begins by asking his fellow middle American from Ohio. No matter, he responds, all rivers lead here. The pastoral has gone purgatorial.

"In the destructive element immerse [yourself]," commands Conrad in *Lord Jim* (1900), and some such idea, a baptism in the primal, must underlie one of the most peculiar scenes in *Apocalypse Now*. For his fated last audience with Kurtz, Willard chooses, for some undermotivated and thus presumably symbolic reason, and although far readier access is available, to enter the virtual throne room of Kurtz's Cambodian temple by way of a complete submergence in the river's backwash that abuts on the portals of the fortress. This scene also recalls Willard's first trespass onto Kurtz's terrain, where moral disorientation and debasement are oddly symbolized by the natives' turning him upside down and rolling him in the mud, an initiation doubtlessly ordered by Kurtz. Wilard's later and last approach to the temple becomes an amphibious ambush, as he surfaces from the muddied waters of precivilized life. And when he emerges, he too is painted like a savage in that brand of pagan war paint which is modern military camouflage, the same livid disguise that Kurtz wore on his very last military mission when he de-capitated one of his own nation's soldiers aboard Willard's boat. Such camouflage is a would-be subterfuge turned ironically to spiritual unmasking, the lethal truth spelled out in the perverse colors of its own primitive reversion. Rising smeared with paint and mud, as if for the ritualized murder of some crazed Caesar, Willard hacks Kurtz to pieces with a machete. The grotesque spectacle is a Black Mass of sacrificial vengeance, staged in operatic counterpoint to the natives' ceremonial butchering of an animal outside, recalling the dire ironies of conjunction between cathedral baptism or religious street procession, respectively, and the various vendetta murders in Coppola's *Godfather* films. This twofold blood sacrifice as purging retribution also recalls Kurtz's recorded voice earlier, announcing his intention to exterminate the enemy "pig by pig, cow by cow." As he would slay, so he is laid low. Added to this, and complicating the whole pageant of atrocity and contrition, is the deadly reflexive logic of Willard's sacerdotal slaughter, performed in the painted mantle of primitive rites doubling as the guise of modern warfare. By an inescapable irony, this mission for his sins becomes Willard's ultimate collusion in brutality as well as his ceremonial cleansing.

Like a dying and rising god, his private hell harrowed and fled, Willard, after a few moments alone with Kurtz in the reciprocal precincts of damnation, steps beyond the entombing death chamber into the native throng. He is suddenly bowed down to as the new lord, his lower impulses forced now to contend with the lure of their own deification. This is just where one rough cut initially screened for preview audiences ambiguously ended, with the unsettling sense that Willard might, depraved by power, take up where Kurtz left off. Such a closure seemed to complete the prognosis of the scene in which the general initially orders Kurtz's death, musing that "out there with those natives it must be a temptation to play God." Instead, in the finished version, Willard's purging murder accomplished and his soul's greater doom—dark incarnation as a god-head—avoided, he throws down his bloodstained weapon and returns homeward with his own kind. The drugged and deranged young soldier Lance, the sole member of the crew to make it alive, having preserved his life, it would seem, only by being detached from his sanity, is retrieved by Willard from the barbarity in which he has so passively taken part, first at war and now in pagan ritual. He is led out of hell by the hand of the man who has always kept his head, if only by annihilating that lost mind which Kurtz represents. The movie is ready to close—close round—upon its opening image, Willard's head superimposed, in a subjective or hallucinatory framing, alongside an equally scaled close-up of the stone idol recently beside him at the temple door, an image eyeless, impassive, dead, but seeming to whisper now from its own cold lips the repeated "horror" of Kurtz's last words. Coppola has resisted most ordinary temptations to blend the human images of Willard and Kurtz in any melodramatic visual equation, whether by intercutting craftily between them or superimposing one upon the other. Instead he has referred them both back to the blasphemous stone image, idolatrous and blind. The prophetic icon of their blurred fates, it fades out in the movie's last evaporating shot.

But to what resolution does this dissolve? Through what variation on the themes of its source does this ending do its work? One of the major surprises of *Apocalypse Now* is that the movie does not address Vietnam in overt political terms. Conrad's largest political irony embraced and satirized the whole of Western colonial idealism. As he had Marlow blandly declare, even after the terrible revelations both embodied and voiced by Kurtz:

> The conquest of the earth, which mostly means the taking it away from those who have a different complexion or slightly flatter noses than ourselves, is not a pretty thing when you look into it too much. What redeems it is the idea only. An idea at the back of it; not a sentimental pretence but an idea; and an unselfish belief in the idea—something you can set up, and bow down before, and offer a sacrifice to [...].

With ideas like that, what need of delusions? Yet it is dangerously easy to take this as Conrad's own redemptive point, mouthed by his narrative stand-in, just as there is no little risk in *Apocalypse Now* of taking Kurtz's amoral futilism about the darkness in all men as a complacently acknowledged inevitability. Yet Willard is there to rebuke and cure, even as he corroborates, this levelling vision. Where Marlow half-admires the original Kurtz straight to the end, Willard must murder him. Coppola's protagonist is more jaded than Marlow even before he has heard Kurtz's name, more embroiled in a carnage that may have begun as foreign but has grown only too familiar. The psychological trajectory of the film thus takes the curve, the moral downswerve, of the source story and continues it further into incriminating recognition. Conrad's epoch of colonization—with the idealism, hypocrisy, and greed that spawned it and the delusions of European moral grandeur that ennobled its rhetoric— has atrophied in Coppola's film beyond mere political expediency to urges so violent and atavistic that they have left articulation itself behind. No one in the film thinks even to allude to reasons for being involved in the Vietnam War and this is not Coppola's fault but the fault of the military action itself, the barbarism of which is after a point self-generating as well as, so his ending would suggest, self-revenging. Kurtz may once, before volunteering for the Green Berets, have had the intellectual compulsion to rationalize his nation's political role in Indochina, but rapidly obsessed by the means of brutality, he has long since lost interest in any end but his own.

By the time we meet him, Kurtz wants to die. He knows right away that Willard is the man for the job, but he must train him to his Black task by torture and disclosure at once. Where Conrad's Marlow was a minor satellite of Kurtz's tragedy, Willard and the new Kurtz are bound up in a deadly symbiosis. Coppola's Kurtz knows his own evil to some degree and waits for the man who will know himself well enough *in Kurtz* to will the eradication of that self, someone in no position to "judge" him, who will permit him to die a "soldier's death" even at the hands of one of his own, just as he has killed the last GI on Willard's boat. It takes an assassin to slay one, as Kurtz intuited when first asking his visitor if he fit the description. By answering in deed rather than word, Willard seems once again, as in the sampan scene, to be acting under indirect orders from Kurtz, who recognizes with colder clarity than ever "what there is to be done." Private and public renunciation merge again in another of Willard's parallel constructions: "Everyone wanted him dead, himself most of all." Looking up knowingly as the blade descends, Kurtz has finally found an antagonist whose reciprocation of wicked instinct enacts on a private scale the internecine nature of the whole war. The martial epic has shrunk to a revenger's tragedy with a cast of one.

Complex moral narratives like *Heart of Darkness* and *Apocalypse Now* are likely to twist back over themselves in order to find an exit from the ethical labyrinth of their own intricacy, to fit their length to a finish. We need Coppola's Kurtz precisely because we have seen him in other shapes before. Ariadne's thread (Miller's term) can only strengthen itself by doubling up. Kurtz is Kilgore understood from within; Kurtz is Willard in the act of understanding. And these understandings complement the archetypal structure of the conclusion. Ritual is psychologized; public bloodbath is the opening of an inner vein of meaning. It is no accident that Girard's remarks about the brutal duplications of ritual sacrifice and surrogacy turn out repeatedly to be statements about repetition. "In a tragedy the reciprocal relationship between the characters is real, but it is the sum of nonreciprocal moments. The antagonists never occupy the same positions at the same time, to be sure; but they occupy these positions in succession."[3] This is just what we recognize in Coppola's tragic narrative when we discover his antagonists as successive stages of the same protagonistic urge. Kurtz is not a redundancy but an uncovered double; and doubly, for there are, in those ritual sacrifices in which tragedy is rooted, two phases of displacement simultaneously illustrated by Coppola's violence. As Girard says, "All sacrificial rites are based on two substitutions. The first is provided by generative violence, which substitutes a single victim for all the members of the community."[4] But here we have two communities, the American military establishment and the Cambodian natives. Kurtz, defector from one, lord and protector of the other, is explicitly chosen by the first as a substitute for more than one Kilgore still within the fold and implicitly chosen by the second as a mad deity overstaying his secular reign. There follows "the only strictly ritualistic substitution, [...]that of a victim for the surrogate victim. As we know, it is essential that the victim be drawn from outside the community."[5] The victim can be an animal, as for the natives, or a white interloper, as for Kurtz, or a self-exiled pariah, as on the American side of this equation Kurtz has become. It is only after Willard realizes how far beyond the pale Kurtz has slipped in his programmatic depravity that he can murder Kurtz not as his officer's duty but as a ritualistic performance. Hacked beast outside, hewn ruler within: a simultaneous repetition that offers us a complex instance of ritual duplication, cruel but illuminating.

Finally, there is a further substitution: Kurtz's will to be exterminated taken up by Willard as a will to return. The demonic impresario of his own slaughter, Kurtz has staged both a private and a communal end to his quasi-divine rule. "From the purely religious point of view," writes Girard, "the surrogate victim— or, more simply, the final victim—inevitably appears as a being who submits to violence without provoking a reprisal; a supernatural being who sows violence to reap peace; a mysterious savior who visits affliction on mankind in order subsequently to restore it to good health."[6] Willard is Kurtz's delegate in this unspoken urge toward restitution, declining one last repetition of assumed godhead, breaking the pattern by retracing his steps along the line that, until severed, bound him inextricably to Kurtz. "The surrogate victim, as founder of the rite, appears as the ideal educator of humanity, in the etymological sense of *e-ducatio*, a leading out. The rite gradually leads men away from the sacred; it permits them to escape their own violence"—only temporarily, of course, for the rite as ritual is by nature recurrent, like history and like film.[7] But it is this role of leading out that is specifically bequeathed by Kurtz to Willard when Lance is guided out from the sacred temple to whatever community is left, led away and back. That Kurtz can be taken in any sense to have intended this, that such matters are meant self-consciously to preoccupy him as well as Coppola, is lamely indicated when the camera spots James Frazer's *The Golden Bough* (1890) and Jessie Weston's *From Ritual to Romance* (1920) lying allusively about, a pretentious sampling of Kurtz's acquaintance with cultural anthropology. But this movie, begun as a soured romance, undergoes its own generic erosion back to ritual tragedy, reversing the history of art in the formal equivalent of its own ethical reversions.

The plot is still, however, to suffer one more reverse, the ritual again internalized at the last minute, engorged by psychology. Willard, leading out, is led back into his own mind where the reciprocal violence must once more be replayed. Psychic reprise becomes its own worst reprisal, self-knowledge its own demythologizing scourge. Kurtz was the agent of ravage; Willard had to become the will of outrage, the mind and arm of a deed both lethal and cathartic. To extirpate, even to curtail a darkness, one must know and loathe it at close range. In the interchanged psychologies of the film, Willard must come to know it both in himself and *for* Kurtz, who seems in some measure inured to his own depravity and defensive about his vision of "moral terror" and its satanic tactics. This is the true territorial imperative of the allegorical journey in both story and film: we must explore and colonize our own dark natures certainly not in order to glorify them, even to acquiesce in them, but only the more guardedly to stand watch, at times to wage war, against their aberration and excess. Only full recognition can expunge an evil. The movie's Kurtz talks about logic and clarity but is still committing horrible and arbitrary murder right up to the time of his death. Someone must know better, but it can only be the self—or second self—if that knowledge is to be made potent, as mighty as the sword that would do it in and so drive it out. This is the ultimate parable of Coppola's bloodbath, the higher logic of its ferocity. We may all harbor the savage in our souls, wish at times to send it abroad, while a part of us must remain on hand to suppress or punish that desire. But if, on one framing of their duality, Kurtz stands for what is reprehensible in the human spirit as against Willard's power of comprehension and so of containment, the price paid for this further clarity is that such knowledge can never be shaken off, cannot help but follow Willard back down the river, echoing on the soundtrack over and above the film's last images.

In *Heart of Darkness*, just before Marlow enters the house of Kurtz's Intended to tell a lie by which (certainly through which) he cannot escape pollution, he "seemed to hear the whispered cry, 'The horror! The horror!'" Yet this echo, this insistent epiphany from the past, is denied to the world in the person of Kurtz's fiancée, euphemized away. The moral vacillation in Coppola's narrative takes a different double turn. Instead of accepting the natives' adulation in brutality, the hero who slew the true scapegoat while the natives were offering up the animal surrogate suddenly discards his weapon.

Mindlessly following suit, so do they, their guns layered across his path like palms in the footsteps of the new savior. Nemesis has become Messiah. Lest Willard believe in this finer deification, invest faith in this precipitous pacifism too good to be true—Coppola treading here a fine line between political satire and Hollywood melodrama, between irony and facile uplift—lest he submit to this external image of himself, as dangerous in its healing apotheosis as is the previous temptation to lord his murderous power over the natives, he must be reminded in his own mind's ear that the darkness is with him still, a whispering and perpetual admonition.

The ending of neither story nor film is confusing, but rather in each case bifocal. In Coppola we find writ large, for Willard as well as for us, what Conrad seems to keep from Marlow by ironic distance: that the return to civilization from primitive haunts can never lay the ghostly image of that bestial horror lurking within us, the horror that finds such kinship, regressed beyond any ethical restraint, in the jungle's heart of darkness. It is a horror that the tropical rain droning on the soundtrack as the film's last trace can scarcely wash clean. For just before, staring straight at the camera and through it at us for one final time, confirming earlier suggestions of the universal complicity in evil, Willard's disembodied face—the reflective mind as if unmoored from its whole self, decapitated—slides out of view to the right behind the dead but deathless carved image. With the film's narrator absorbed into the immemorial icon of that anthropomorphic vanity and villainy which has comprised his tale, Kurtz's "horror" comes onto the soundtrack as a primal echo in the soul, an echo drenched from without by the sounds of a world that outlasts but cannot quench it.

Yet we are made to sense this destination in the premature fusion of imagery, including the stone idol, in the film's opening scene. Here may be a framework of repetition that encompasses and composes all the rest and that does so in an indirect reworking of Conrad's own ironic temporality. Shortly after a startling and awesome shot of napalm invading the silence of the jungle in the prologue, we see Willard practicing karate to keep in shape for whatever penitential mission will be assigned him, bloodying his hand against a mirror in his squalid hotel room. The right hand he injures here is the one he stares at and repeatedly flexes just before killing Kurtz, just before directing his earlier violence outward from the self toward an embodied reflection of it rather than a mirror image. But even before this mirror scene, our first glimpse of Coppola's narrator has been upside down and queasily disoriented: we discover him staring up at the rotation of an overhead fan. Blade becomes propeller in his mind's eye and ours: insignias of circularity in a prediction of the jungle encounter that will itself spin back in the end to that hovering image of the stone idol which now flanks Willard right-side up at the other side of the screen. As yet we have no way to sound the import of this fugitive, dreamlike image or of the other split-second subliminal premonitions that erupt on screen. Unassimilated glimpses forward into the Cambodian sequence, they suggest as well visual traces, psychic scars, left over from Willard's earlier forays into the jungle. Though Coppola's rhetoric at this point is entirely visual, this notion of circularity and proleptic repetition is one he could have taken indirectly from Conrad. [...]

Circular imagery, itself symbolized by wheeling blades like the mechanism of a spinning brain, can be made to serve the purposes not only of retelling, as with the tradition of twice-told, obsessively repeated tales of an Ancient Mariner or a Charlie Marlow but also of unconscious recurrence, compulsion, and inbred penance. There is a curious circular link in Conrad's story that anticipates in this way the underspecified, dreamlike prologue of *Apocalypse Now* and its fulfillment later by plot. Conrad's tale opens upon an aura of foreboding that we have no means to interpret. Marlow's auditors are gathered round him on board ship near the mouth of the Thames, but the clouded horizon suggests, by a pathetic fallacy we are unequipped so far to explain, "a mournful gloom, brooding motionless" over the entire earth. Only when the story's narrative course has aligned the sinuous Congo with the Thames estuary in an unbroken indictment do we understand that the British river, too, in the last clause of the tale, "seemed to lead into the heart of an immense darkness." Apropos of nothing so far but of everything to come, Marlow's first words amount to a disconcerting non sequitur that suggests a profound and fearsome continuity: "'And this also,' said Marlow suddenly, 'has been one of the dark places of the earth.'" Answering nothing, knotted to nothing, the conjunction seems linked only to the story in his mind, as told and retold again, though never before to us or to his immediate listeners on the scene. Only after traversing the length of *Heart of Darkness*, as it threads together its two waterways and dovetails its historical epochs, is the brooding, elliptical conjunction justified, bridging the gap between now and then, us and them, empire and tribe, civilized codes and vile rites, progress and savagery—and between this instance of such a story and all those which precede it, as if every important "once upon a time" is premised on a "so too here and now." Coppola wants this sense at the beginning of his film and devises the disjoint visual "and" he needs to convey it. Willard has been there before too, far down into the nether reaches of his soul, perhaps in earlier missions, certainly in unshakable visions.

When the stone idol absorbs and displaces, or repeats and thus deletes, Willard's own face at the end, we are ready to probe the deeper logic by which Coppola has chosen to have his film swallow its own tail in a snakelike vicious circle. Classic symmetry has turned (inward) to psychology. *Apocalypse Now* is thereby detached from the immediate temporal designation of its title to suggest the human mind's recurrent nightmare of its own abyss, time out of mind. When Kurtz's "horror" haunts the soundtrack for the last time as a moral echo knowing no end to its repetitions, the idea articulates what was only latent visually in the film's inchoate first images. We realize in final retrospect that the stench of "nightmare" Willard encounters in the sanctum sanctorum of Kurtz's retreat is his own opening nightmare of blood, fire, and idolatry come true.

Though the disoriented and disorienting first images of *Apocalypse Now* may suggest Willard's previous jungle missions, they are flashbacks, repetitions, half in the more disturbing sense that they tap race-old dreams or memories of terror, secrets from the collective unconscious of our savage origins. They are what ritual would defeat by repeating, the inescapable scourged by symbolic recurrence only to come again. Neither just retroactive nor, by poetic license, entirely clairvoyant, neither guilty dreams nor prefigurations pure and simple, they are prophetic in the original sense of a soothsaying. For Willard's disorder of soul, long before he faces his alter ego in Kurtz, is a nightmare of demonic complicity of the most tormenting sort, a fever in the will that is complicity both before and after the fact. It is a torture of self-knowing that must be embodied and made assailable in the person of Kurtz. The "confrontation" Willard lives and is willing to die for is disclosed as a long appalling stare at the true form, the human form, in that broken, bloody, distorting, but still functional mirror with which the film so loadedly opens. Apocalypse, now or to come, means in its own original sense, after all, not only Doomsday but Revelation.

Notes

1   J. Hillis Miller, "Ariadne's Thread: Repetition and the Narrative Line," *Critical Inquiry*, vol. 3 (Autumn 1976): 57–77. The deliberately embedded image of a thread as analog for any story as yarn is apparent in Conrad not only with the map Marlow studies before his setting out, of the sinuous Congo River as linear synecdoche for the trek and track of coming narration, but with that "uncanny and fateful" old woman in the company's office whose act of "knitting black wool as for a warm pall" marks the point of departure for Marlow in his journey from civilization to the jungle. Symbol of plot as fate, her work draws and fastens into pattern—into a premonition and a destiny—the originating thread of a symbolic quest narrative that recognizes itself as a complex reticulation of advances and returns, a webwork of inevitable doubling.

2   René Girard, *Violence and the Sacred*, trans. Patrick Gregory (Baltimore: Johns Hopkins University Press, 1977), 47.

3   Girard, *Violence and the Sacred*, 158.

4   Ibid., 269.

5   Ibid.

6   Ibid., 86.

7   Ibid., 306.

2 / With Francis Ford Coppola's updating of Joseph Conrad no doubt in mind, Stewart's more direct later engagement (in a 2000 issue of *MLQ: Modern Language Quarterly*) with the analytic parameters of postcolonial studies turns his attention to two other narrative structures he finds "officiating" over the ironies of imperial outreach on either side of the Victorian perspective, Charles Dickens' *Dombey and Son* (1846–48) and, from the ensuing Edwardian moment, E. M. Forster's *Howards End* (1910). His metacritical argument enters upon the waning hegemony of New Historicism and the then-current trend of a supposedly corrective "neoformalism." He does so in order to entertain an amalgam between the most rigorous of previous semiotic methods—the seemingly antithetical reading practices of Michael Riffaterre (1924–2006) and Fredric Jameson (1934–2024)—that reveals a cognate power of both "subtext" and "intertext" in each critic half a decade before Stewart pursues such issues, now reoriented by his microstylistics, under the sign of "narratography." And under a title which, as he explicates it now in retrospect, "was meant in its double sense to negotiate the colonial novel's off-shore interest(s)."

2 / *The Foreign Offices of British Fiction*

THIS ESSAY SETS ITSELF TWO INTERLOCKED TASKS, at cross-purposes, only if we settle for business as usual. It attempts, first, to resuscitate the formalist mandate in the study of prose fiction; and, second, to test it out on one of those burgeoning subfields of cultural criticism, colonial and postcolonial literary studies, where such formalism, to judge from current practice, seems far from urgent when not downright suspect. This second effort is less perverse than corrective. The formalist imperative is to read, to read what is written as a form (and formation) of meaning, both authorially designed and culturally inferred.[1] The nationalist and imperialist bias of classic narrative is now widely presumed, but what shape might be assumed in turn by the local linguistic forms of this bias? How might a recommitted formalism demonstrate not only literary structure's configuring access to the cultural terms of narrative production but form's now strategic, now unconscious reprocessing of such *idées reçues*?

Seen in this way, formalism is an account of what makes things work, or what makes out of language a work. For those interested in the cultural labor performed by literature, what could be more useful even now? Toward this redirected task of interpretation, a bridge needs to be built—and more two-way transit needs to be encouraged—between an intertextual semiotics of absent causes and a structuralist Marxism of underlying historical determinants. To name names, as they never do each other's: between Michael Riffaterre and Fredric Jameson, our most unrepentant formalist of literary production and our most intrepidly literary of social critics, respectively. What would bring them together is the surface-depth model in both of their systems: the role of the unconscious in the generative formation of literary meaning. In Riffaterre, certain unsettling textual features ("ungrammatical," in his sense) are like the neurotic symptoms of a structuring unsaid.[2] In Jameson, surface disturbances (contradictions) are the return of a repressed ideological instability in the text's structuring historical absences. The divergent "formalisms" (formativisms) of these two critics thus meet, or might, on the common (hidden) ground of the buried assumption.

Novelistic formalism could well sharpen tools—and combine forces—for the unearthing of such assumptions, but only by remembering that the best clues remain in plain view: the permutations by which a novel's textual surface lets its political unconscious come up for narrative air. Jameson takes us to the edge of such recognition in his powerful 1990 essay on E. M. Forster and James Joyce.[3] In a continuing effort to "get beyond the windless closures of formalism" (beyond, if you will, the prison-house of language), he isolates modernist "style" as a cognitive process in its own right, semiautonomous and pervasively reified.[4] Such verbal practice is a symptom not only of bourgeois capitalism, as Jameson has long argued, but of imperialist myopia, as he now proposes. His argument, briefly, is that Forster's style stages a perceptual dissociation between the quotidian here and now and the othered and elsewhere, between self and a ruse of infinitude, ultimately between the consolidated values of the metropole and the shaping absence of the colonies, with all the obscure interdependency their conjured removal half-summons to mind. Such is for Jameson the true cognitive mapping, always and already geopolitically projected, of early high modernism—a foundational interplay between center and periphery, the seen and the hazily unseen. Granting this intuition should not exempt us, however, from the need to ask what subformations of diction and syntax tend to absorb the shock of macroeconomic anxieties.

The question leads us to—and beyond—the most unabashedly text-bound of procedures in Riffaterre's *Fictional Truth* (1990). He retrieves from the dustbin of tradition, as the linchpin of his method, the dated trope of syllepsis, emphasized as a lexical conundrum rather than a syntactic fulcrum, punning doubleness rather than swing grammar.[5] Syllepsis becomes for Riffaterre, however, no mere stylistic device but the very structure of intertextuality as a duplex but unified function. Syllepsis names the stumbling block in mimesis at large (rather than in local wording) that alerts us to the operation of the "subtext."[6] But what if sylleptic splitting in the conduct of actual sentences, of little concern to Riffaterre, also reported a more encompassing doubleness? What if, in fiction itself, such a device were extrapolated to a formal principle, even as that formal principle of divided cognition were reinjected into the ideological content of the narrative? Style might well emerge as the thinnest (and hence sharpest) wedge of a text's cultural exertion. If one were to detect something like a sylleptic paradigm, a consistent stylistic register, for the obfuscations of colonial ideology not only in Forster but in Charles Dickens, then Jameson might well be on to something that in fact antedates the arena of his investigation.

Since the political stakes become clear only in view of Riffaterre's elevation of the sylleptic figure to a master trope of intertextuality, we need a fuller blueprint of his semiotics, best dispatched by example. With an irony I have never seen discussed, the full title of Dickens' 1848 study of mercantile power and collapse reads as follows: *Dealings with the Firm of Dombey and Son Wholesale, Retail and for Exportation.*[7] The subject is not character but trade. Familiar with the fictional subcode of titling (especially of chapters), we might have expected *Dealing with the Firm* in the sense of taking it as a topic: treatment rather than transaction. The first "ungrammatical" (hence "sylleptically" reorienting) signal of this brief text is, therefore, the pluralized first word, now commercial rather than self-referential—or, more to the point, the latter via the former. *Dealings*, that is, becomes the semiotic "model" (Riffaterre) for the Dickensian transfer from commodity text to commodity market at large—in an interplay that goes both ways at once, since *Wholesale* and *Retail* (especially when initially unpunctuated and thus seeming to modify *Dealings* rather than *Firm*) have, in their dictionary senses, textual as much as mercantile associations. A novel can be narrated with "wholesale" irony and "retailed" in gripping melodramatic precision at the same time. Further, as Dickens would have been keenly aware (fresh from his battles over international copyright), here is another text by Boz destined for, as well as an imperialist shipping firm specializing in, a certain lively (even if "pirated") export trade. Once arrived at the firm's own name, of course, the reader encounters another "model": the first sign of that conversionary irony by which the "sociolect" of family businesses (where sons are unnamed placeholders of inherited partnership) will be commandeered, in the authorial "idiolect," for a satire of unfeeling paternity.

The relay between these two discursive levels is an exemplary mode of what Riffaterre calls intertextual "double-take."[8] This is only the beginning. In *Dombey and Son* the structure of intertextuality not only runs deep but intersects directly with the novel's explicit imperial thematic of divided vision, now terrestrial (territorial), now transcendental. The amorphous expanse of colonial dominion is in this way further delimited by a more metaphorical (hence metaphysical, and politically equivocated) frontier. Together, these receding horizons offer the twin vanishing points of oceanic trade and the intertext of death's "immortal sea." In their service, style schools us in the doublethink necessary to hold both perspectives in mind—because never in view—at once.

Double Dealings

Before Derrida one would have scarcely been inclined to see a sylleptic structure in the slippage of *Dealing/s,* reserving that rhetorical term for more obviously split syntactic collocations. In Anglo-American tradition, from George Puttenham through H. W. Fowler to Richard A. Lanham, "syllepsis" and its sibling "zeugma" are phrasal rather than lexical. Instead of dividing against itself as a pun may be thought to do, the sylleptic or zeugmatic gesture reorients in progress. Its forced junctural coupling bifurcates rather than collapses meaning, with the phrasal counterpart an indicated rather than alternate designation. Borrowing the textbook example from Alexander Pope, it is not that "stain" *might* be figurative as well as literal when it is collocated at one and the same time with "honour" and "brocade." It must be. The incompatibles are copresent at the same level of grammatical immanence.

In Riffaterre's lexical rather than syntactic version of this trope, syllepsis is meant to topple New Critical ambiguity, as well as to elude Derridean undecidability, by erecting in its place a functional semiotics of "overdetermination." I give the italicized summary from Riffaterre's seed essay "Syllepsis," a decade before *Fictional Truth:* "*Syllepsis is a word understood in two different ways at once, as meaning and as significance.* And therefore, because it sums up the duality of the text's message—its semantic and semiotic faces—syllepsis is the literary sign par excellence."[9] In syllepsis, the apparent discrepancy between two meanings leads to a dialectical synthesis called intertextual comprehension. Meaning may be confounded just where significance is consolidated: through the resolution of incompatibles. Mimesis yields to semiosis as the truth of the text.

What happens, then, when one encounters a classic narrative blatantly arranged to foreground the tension (rather than the wedding) between text and intertext, in particular between a bourgeois melodrama with imperial trappings and an extraterrestrial chastening of mortal ambitions? Would not a splintered but still forcibly bonded phrasal parallelism, repeatedly pivoted around material versus spiritual reference, be one way to capture this tension as a strained synthesis in the very grain of description? If this reading of *Dombey and Son* starts small, this is (1) just as it should be and (2) formalism for you. Only then does it deserve its name and your time. For literary things are built up, not just set or taken down, constructed from within rather than dictated by overarching design. Syllepsis can be one of the internal hinges of such construction.

As Dickens would have practiced it, with or without recognizing its name, syllepsis is a device borrowed from his favorite comic predecessors. Like zeugma, and whether strictly grammatical or not, syllepsis predicates in two different senses of its main verb.[10] Amid the panoply of grammatical forkings in *Dombey* there is one thrilling transgression of the grammatically illicit sort, attributed to Cockney ingenuity in the dialogue of the irrepressible

Susan Nipper. She is about to tell Dombey off at last: "What I mean, Sir, is to speak respectful and without offence, but out," with *out* retrofitted as part of a suddenly compound verb.[11]

This is the ungrammatical exception that proves the rule of Dickens' typical bifold phrasing, so frequent in *Dombey and Son* as to become its metatrope.

Repeatedly, this device, in which a predication splays out in two different but syntactically absorbable senses, is a manner of yoking unlike things together by a logic somewhere in the middle zone between metonymy and metaphor. Once diagnosed in an alliterative skewed parallelism, like "the beadle of our business and our bosoms" to describe Mr. Dombey, the spiritual collapse of outer on inner can be read in the least insignia of costume or demeanor, as in "stiff with starch and arrogance."[12] In his first separation from his son after the mother's inconvenient death in childbirth, the boy is given out to wet-nursing "born by Fate and Richards," where a laboring woman's embrace is ominously linked to the failed self-sufficiency of Dombey's bourgeois world.[13] As with the forking between *starch* and *arrogance*, the corporeal (bodily removal) again emblematizes the spiritual (human destiny) across a single grammatical frame. This toggling between literal and figurative is the deepest common denominator of the sylleptic trope, in both *Dombey and Son* and elsewhere. In another sartorial metonymy just barely avoiding the repressed Riffaterrean "matrix" (or suppressed truism) of "stout-hearted," Captain Cuttle is put before us as "one of those timber-looking men, suits of oak as well as hearts."[14] [...]

Enough minuscule syntactic wrinkles of this sort accrue to a pleated pattern. Once the sylleptic paradigm—call it divided consciousness grammatically instantiated—has been established in the early chapters, across the "high" and "low" strands of the plot, it can be proliferated at will. There is the exit of Major Bagstock, who "took his lobster-eyes and his apoplexy to the club," as if such eyes were a synecdoche as well as a medical symptom of his bulging and convulsive self-importance.[15] Or note the play, once more, between spiritual and material cause (verging on a radical confusion of the intrinsic and the contingent) when Mr. Dombey confronts his wife-to-be "with a lofty gallantry adapted to his dignity and the occasion."[16] Later, when Mr. Toots laments Florence's announced marriage, he bemoans the "banns that consign her to Lieutenant Walters, and me to—to Gloom, you know."[17] Revealed here again, in a comic key, is the cleaving between novelistic fate and its embodied nemesis in character.

Clearly, the term *syllepsis* appeals to Derrida and Riffaterre for the way its lexical sense retains certain vestiges of its syntactic version, where its twofold character is dynamized by grammar.[18] They wish to stress the *unfolding* shift of levels, verging at times on incompatibility. This fine-grained slide between literal and figurative, physical and immaterial, perfectly suits a novelistic structure whose chief ideological work is to render implicitly mutual, without exploring too closely, the dimly twinned realms of matter and spirit, the worldly and the eternal, the palpable and the unglimpsably distant. For the poles of the tangible and the intangible are ultimately redistributed in *Dombey and Son* around the narrative pivot of heroic imperial enterprise and the obliterating intertext of eternity. By this point, in its prose form (and formalism), the pronged grammar of syllepsis has become a tuning fork of the novel's finessed conceptual dissonance.

Toward a Global Poetics

JAMESON FINDS IN FORSTER a "closet modernist" whose verbal tendencies manifest the way "the structure of imperialism also makes its mark on the inner forms and structures of that new mutation in literary and artistic language to which the term 'modernism' is loosely applied."[19] The hypostatized category of "style" per se—style divorced from content, or put at a recuperative distance from fixed or localizable content—is the pressure point in this new aesthetic. Conceived in this way, style is a figurative register that can only evoke rather than capture the alienating distances on which metropolitan dominance must ground itself. Style vibrates with an unmanageable sense of "a global space" that, "like the fourth dimension" of time, "somehow constitutively escapes" the regime of representation, evading the metropolitan consciousness it helps shape from the margins.[20] Taking his point of departure from a description early in *Howards End* (1910), in which the great North Road out of London is found "suggestive of Infinity,"[21] Jameson wants to show that this positive valuation, *in all* its admittedly vague and undecidable nature, is later compromised by the degradation of the infinite—at least the indefinitely distant and inconceivable—to the sheer mercantile reach of a new colonial economy whose peopled places are "structurally occluded" from the First World vantage of the metropole. Style transvalues the vast and shapeless—colonialism's unglimpsed horizons—into sheer perceptual intensity, diffuse and perfumed. To borrow the title of a more recent book by Jameson, modernism becomes a massively suppressed "geopolitical aesthetic," instituting through style the very form of the formless. Whereas geographic "'infinity' (and 'imperialism') is bad or negative" in Forster, "its perception, as a bodily and poetic process," becomes "a positive achievement and an enlargement of our sensorium."[22] This is a gripping insight. What seems aggressive, domineering, and hegemonic in political fact, as well as socially dispersive and intellectually unmanageable, is found redeemed by figuration as imaginatively expansive.

The effect is more pervasive in the very texture of Forster's writing than Jameson's cursory glance indicates. Just before the passage he quotes, the second chapter has developed a full-blown set piece concerned with the British railway system, which also "suggested infinity."[23] The earlier passage unfolds altogether like a Riffaterrean laboratory specimen. No sooner is Margaret Schlegel numbered with the Londoners who attach emotional value to "railway termini" than we read how these stations "are our gates *to* the glorious and the unknown."[24] The sense of "terminus" as something more like "ingress" than end point, a usage recruited from the sociolect, abets the idiolect of this lyric passage. Once a "sylleptic" model has been set in place at this switch point between a national railway and its intertext in spiritual *transport* (the passage's unsaid matrix), stylistic latitude can sustain the double paradigm across two instances of quietly forking grammar. First, transit's destination in "the glorious and the unknown" suggests not glory and all that might or might not be glory but rather all that is glorious simply because it is unknown, instinct with mystery. So, too, with the more obvious syntactic glissade of the next sentence: "Through them we pass out into adventure. And sunshine."[25] Again there is the forced "twinning" associated with rhetorical hendiadys, as if the prose should more accurately read "sunny adventure," like "the glorious unknown" just before it. Bonding immaterial energies to corporeal warmth, this new phrasing evokes romantic excursions in the countryside (the purlieus of the estate at Howards End, say) rather than colonial expeditions (to which, of course, no railroads can directly connect the British national imagination). The sudden shift of gears between the immaterial and the meteorological— between mentality and climate—is precisely *not* suborned to the colonialist dyad of economic venture and tropical heat associated with Mr. Wilcox's West African rubber company.

The perspectives availed by technological outreach are further trans-valued over the next several sentences through the epithetical chain of "remoter" through "illimitable" to "eternal" (the last two adjectives favored by Dickens as well for the metaphysical aura of his own overseas subtext). Whatever the "eternal adventure" may be for the metropolitan imagination, thinks Margaret, it is one whose "issue might be prosperous, but would certainly not be expressed in the ordinary language of prosperity."[26] The sylleptic double tracking installed here and inaugurating its own subtext—as if she were to say "it may swell one's accounts in heaven rather than the bank"—begins to elaborate an anti-imperialist vocabulary with a biblical intertext in the miscalculated "profit" of gaining the world and losing one's soul.[27] Against such worldliness, the "unseen" gradually takes precedence over the "infinite" in regard to the motto "Only connect," since such connection must be achieved in a manner wholly antithetical to a spreading commonwealth of co-opted colonial interests. As Jameson leads us to see, the cognitive rarefaction of transcendental experience in bourgeois capitalism, manufactured in part by the stylistic engineering of its prose masterworks, converts its geopolitics to an escapist poetics.

In discussing Forster, Jameson twice mentions "cognitive mapping" as his continued purpose, but never works it out schematically in his favored way, via the Greimasian foursquare grid of semiotics by which a signifier is put in play by contrast with its contrary and by diametrical opposition to its contradictory.[28] Yet *Howards End* offers a dialogue that could in its own right be an *explicit* rethinking of the quintessentially protomodernist cultural contraries of "activity" versus "value" in *Lord Jim* of the previous decade, as diagrammed by Jameson in *The Political Unconscious.*[29] The binary banter in question occurs between the insistently idealist Margaret and her spiritless brother, Tibby, fresh from the languors of the University of Oxford. Margaret admits that "an Empire bores me, so far, but I can appreciate the heroism that builds it up."[30] The cultural contradiction tightens into a chiasmus: "I want activity without civilization. How paradoxical! Yet I expect that is what we shall find in heaven." The return volley from Tibby: "And I . . . want civilization without activity, which, I expect, is what we shall find in the other place."[31] Against Tibby's desire for elite leisure, Margaret dreams of finding meaning in a means without an end, sheer labor without product, energy without power. This is Forster's vestigial faith in the Victorian work ethic, somehow disentangled from the ideology of progress to become something more like a work ethos.

While Greimasian mapping points to an attempted resolution at the primary level (between activity and civilization *in* the mythology of empire), it also generates, in the bottom sector of the usual grid, the neutral term of double negation (neither activity nor civilization). Such is the cognitive zone of the impalpable and "unseen" by which Margaret is drawn away from politics (the Schlegels failing to "follow our Forward Policy in Tibet with the keen attention that it merits"[32]). But, forced into this same conceptual sector, other things unseen by the middle class are also situated by the negation at once of civilized value and of activity. "We are not concerned with the very poor," says the narrator in a famous digression, since this is a novel of "gentlefolk." The destitute "are unthinkable, and only to be approached by the statistician or the poet." They do not have stories or operate within plot. The "abyss" is where people "dropped in and counted no more."[33] The desperately poor may work, may labor, but that necessitated expenditure cannot be dignified by the purist term activity. Here, too, a Greimasian schema unsettles the dichotomies that organize it. The unsayable of the sublime risks being lumped with the unspeakable of the lumpenproletariat. The abyss of squalor and the high road of visionary intuition slip together past the attention of the workaday and clear-eyed. Insight, a perception of the unseen, must therefore be redeemed by plot as an *activity* in its own right that rescues civilization from the nightmare of progress for the dream of bourgeois perfectibility.

As semiotic mapping demonstrates, then, Margaret's equivocations are telltale for the novel as a whole. She attempts to bridge contradictions rather than follow out consequences. Forster generalizes this tendency on her behalf in a later passage that recalls Dickens' sylleptic rewiring of syntax itself. Once again grammar takes the strained form of its own disjunct content. "It is impossible," writes Forster, "to see modern life steadily and see it whole, and [Margaret] had chosen to see it whole. Mr. Wilcox saw steadily."[34] Keen sight versus the broader ken of insight: these are the now divisive terms of the passage, descended as they are, by allusion, from an explicit Arnoldian touchstone in his verse celebration of Sophocles, who, as stressed by the comma in the shift of scale, "saw life steadily, and saw it whole."[35] Under exactly the burden of colonialist enterprise and its inherent blindnesses, the allusion takes on an extra twist—and not least because Arnold's accolade is bestowed on one whom, unlike Mr. Wilcox, "Business could not make dull." As in the Arnoldian intertext, Margaret's skewed parallelism shifts the expected adverb "whole" some uncertain distance toward the adjectival status of "see it complete" (totalized in itself) rather than "completely." At the same time, in the eddying ironies of the passage, to "see modern life" at all is to court reduction (and moral diminishment) to something like the intertextual "know the world" or "take life on its own terms"—namely, the contrary idiom of a Wilcox, plugged self-servingly into the complacent sociolect.

In Dickens, too, broken parallelism can expose a spiritual disparity. If, by some deep rhetorical logic, the colonial armatures of the British economy are to be found inscribed into such a figural pattern in *Dombey and Son*, then new literary-historical bets are on. Beyond confirming that the stylistic fallout from colonialism in British fiction is less exclusively modernist than Jameson claims, this would also be to say, before showing how, that the imperial dimensions of British fiction are prominently intertextual, developed by allusion and skewed truism. "Dombey was about eight-and-forty years of age. Son about eight-and-forty minutes," opens the second paragraph of a novel bound in 1848. Dombey is in every way *the man of the century*. Bourgeois to his fingertips, he is the picture of a nineteenth-century capitalist, Mr. Wilcox *avant la lettre*. The title of chapter 3, "In which Mr. Dombey, as a Man and a Father, is seen at the Head of the Home-Department," invades domestic nurture with the patriarchal hierarchies (man and father both) of the capitalist bureaucracy and further suggests a tacit imperialist network, as managed only indirectly from the insular seat of power, via the inferential supplement of the Foreign Office. Compared to the novel's prolonged analysis of the railroad's urban upheaval, to be sure, explicit mentions of the empire do seem peripheral. But that is just the point. Within mid-Victorian society, as in Forster's Edwardian era, everyone confronted the railroad, few the colonies. The impact of the latter in *Dombey and Son* would necessarily be oblique and pervasive, a structuring of consciousness rather than a conscious object. That is why the least allusion now and then does the trick. Captain Cuttle's home in Brig Place is on the brink of the "India docks."[36] Paul goes to school with the repatriated "Master Blitherstone (whose temper had been made revengeful by the solar heats of India acting on his blood)"—a kind of mutinous contagion from the colony.[37] Reverend Howler is shipped back from the West Indies for stealing rum.[38] Dombey, whose fame extends to "the British possessions abroad," is the cynosure of certain "minnows among the Tritons of the East," the shipper gods of foreign trade.[39] The sliest irony in this line has a colonial subaltern, once brought into the boudoir of the English military man Bagstock as valet and slave, referred to as "'the native,' without connecting him with any geographical idea whatever"—thus disguising a blanket racism with the false etymology of the indigenous.[40]

Among such disparate contextualizing gestures, however, there is one recurrent strain of allusion that prepares for the novel's conversion of the imperial into the unseen and eternal, an extrasecular version of Forster's "glorious and unknown." For at several points the empire strikes back in the form of death. There is the mention of Bagstock's older brother, who "died of Yellow Jack in the West Indies";[41] of Mrs. Pipchin's husband, who died of "pumping water in the Peruvian mines";[42] of that "junior dead in the agency at Barbados" whom Walter goes out to replace.[43] More central to the plot, young Paul's figurative death by water—borne on that hallucinated "dark, dark river" that "rolled toward the sea," toward exactly the "unknown sea" that, in a different turn of the verb, "rolls round all the world" at his mother's death—must be transformed into the nautical success story of Walter Gay.[44] A massive and sustained figural relay is needed to purge shipping of its negative bonds to colonial mastery and economic oppression and associate it instead with impulses immemorial and redemptive: the immortal obverse of the railroad as a "type of the triumphant monster, Death."[45]

Where British railways are positively associated early on in Forster's novel with a limitless expanse of possibility, in *Dombey and Son* the mercantile aspect of locomotion is more immediately stressed. Together, the industrial convulsions of railway transit and the flurry of international shipping are paired implements of capitalism and colonialism, local change and global transformation.[46] They represent exactly that myth of empire that makes common cause between industrial "activity" and aggressive "civilization" in the typically Victorian form of so-called progress. Again cognitive mapping tells a fuller story.[47] And again Margaret Schlegel offers clarifying terms, in her ambivalent Edwardian battle against such progressivism, when her antinationalist streak leads her to intuit that "any human being lies nearer to the unseen than any organization."[48]

Opposed to empire and its literalized engines of progress in the uppermost quadrant of false ideological resolution in *Dombey and Son* would fall (in the bottom slot of double negation) all that remains unseen of the "immortal sea," all that draws a limit to terrestrial motion and ambition. Stationed between, to embody a progress that overrides mere transient activity, would lie the Dombey business as firm at one lateral extreme. As patrilinear bastion, the House of Dombey remains a conservative enclave more important as an invulnerable temple to capitalist accumulation than as a place of ongoing work. It has the stasis of the status quo. Not decadent in the usual sense (like Tibby's place in a comparable slot of civil inaction in the earlier schema), still the firm's unyielding stature has no truck with temporal ripening. "Dombey and Son know neither time, nor place, nor season, but bear them all down."[49] A site of spiritless emotional inertia, representing a paradoxical progress without change in the commercial sphere, the rigid perpetuity of the House is thereby contrasted with the vivid nostalgic datedness of the Wooden Midshipman's in the opposite lateral quadrant (defined by activity and nonprogress). Here is an "establishment" holding on by energetically (rather than complacently) holding out against change. In polar contrast to the firm, where all progress is fiscal accumulation, the busyness of the Midshipman's is the zone of what we might well call nonprofit enterprise. With its unsalable stockpile of superannuated nautical gadgetry, it is the store(house) become a museum, a shrine to all that is "old-fashioned."

This is also the zone (activity without progress) that first situates and then releases Walter, the lone character who can functionally negotiate between the world of the Midshipman's, in which he was raised, and the House whose fortunes he seems to revive by proxy after Dombey's bankruptcy. Walter's valuable—and only incidentally lucrative—activity is thus to transcend both the stagnation of the Midshipman's and the strangulation of the firm, renovating vigor from within the precincts of its decline by passing from one sector to the other. But not before Dombey himself, from the pinnacle of imperial command in Dickens' novel, like Wilcox brought low in Forster's, is made to face the humiliating collapse of all he knows as civilization, progress, acquisition. Only then can that abasement be understood not as the bottomless pit of degradation (poverty, death: again the double negation of the "abyss") but as the resuscitating fund of the greater "unseen."

The Rescue Action of Dickensian Metaphor

IN THE ACTUAL GRAIN AND FORMS of semiotic signaling, tainted metaphors may return purified in a recognizable variant, even if still repressed as part of a subtext rather than foregrounded as obvious rhetoric. This happens across those two opposed sectors of the plot, Dombey's shipping House and the surrogate home of the Midshipman's. Look closely at Dombey's spiritual cum financial restitution. Of his "saving" attachment to his granddaughter, Little Florence, the novel says simply, half a dozen paragraphs from the end, in one of its shortest sentences, "He hoards her in his heart."[50] Inveterate covetousness is one thing, but what is far more surprising is that, after almost a thousand pages of satire undermining the foundations of the firm as mercantile concern, we are asked to root for it as well as its figurehead in the end. This, as Raymond Williams was quick to see, is "almost a terrible irony."[51] Almost. Instead we are coached in our enthusiasm by the reported prognosis of none other than Dombey's once bravest critic, Susan Nipper, now Mrs. Toots, who sees in Walter's successful business venture—a colonial entrepreneurship untarnished by old, dead money—the probability that "another Dombey and Son will ascend—no 'rise'; that was Mrs. Toots' word—triumphant!"[52] Susan's taste for assonance is Dickens' own. Note the "sylleptic" echo as well, splitting along the seams of the novel's abiding tropology. The Victorian innovation of train travel as an emblem of death's "triumphant monster" has been purged in an exact chime ("rise triumphant") of its oppressive and leveling overtones.

We are, in brief, still "dealing" with the firm of Dombey and Son—trafficking with its ideology of commercial validation—long after it has been in every sense discredited.

In the contrary zone of nonacquisitive domesticity at the Midshipman's, economic upswings also require figurative validation. At the close of *Dombey and Son*, we are a far cry from Margaret Schlegel's faith in imaginative prospects, whose success is "not . . . expressed in the ordinary language of prosperity." In Dickens it is—but with a softening overlay of oceanic metaphors that develop out of an unsaid matrix whose earliest deflected manifestation is a crucial and explicit Wordsworthian intertext. In her trumped-up pastoral nostalgia, Mrs. Skewton has driveling recourse to "undeveloped recollections of a previous state of existence—and all that," garbling the title of Wordsworth's "Ode: Intimations of Immortality from Recollections of Early Childhood."[53] Numerous other allusions, including the "waves" of Paul's fatality, collect around "that immortal sea / Which brought us hither," with its "mighty waters rolling evermore."[54] All such romantic vistas of unnavigable origin have, of course, been desecrated throughout *Dombey and Son* by the coerced grandeur of the tides, a sublimity tamed by the implacable forays of the merchant marine. By the book's second page we have heard how, in the megalomania of Dombey and Son, "rivers and seas were formed to float their ships."[55] Even when all this self-aggrandizing plunder in the overseas subtext leads only to the torture of Dombey's "rolling sea of [...] pride"—an inward roiling antithetical to the "unknown sea" that "rolls round all the world" at the death of his wife, making the very world roll round in the process—even then, the metaphorical sense of humanity's tides and times still clings to narrative life.[56] For the novel's deepest figural evasion, localized in closure by the twin financial successes of Walter and his uncle Sol, still tries to hover somewhere between the nautical and the metaphysical, to keep the figure of tidal vastness itself in productive flux.[57] Intertextual syllepsis may be the best account we have of such operations, and it comes closer than ever at this turn to the political unconscious of Jameson's alternate approach.

Without saying so, this novel is first and foremost about *sea changes*, but it must bring the economic (as in the stock exchange known as 'Change) together with the mortal associations that attach to the time-honored cliché of this embedded matrix. Empire receives its comeuppance in death, global waterways in the continuity between the river of time and the sea of eternity. To this extent, structuring dichotomies are firmly in place. Any "invisible" far harbor can be imagined only from a vantage "upon the margin of the unknown sea"—or, in the novel's penultimate sentence, from the near shore of the more explicitly Wordsworthian "mighty" sea.[58] Just before, the waves murmur "of the love, eternal and illimitable [those two epithets that recur in Forster], extending still, beyond the sea, beyond the sky, to the invisible country far away." If this last is a circumlocution for heaven, it is also a transvaluation of the colonial annex by way of a Shakespearean intertext cannily dodged and conjured at once. Chastening the cultural truism of England as an empire on which the sun never sets, Dickens would rebuke the ends-of-the-earth trope for colonial dominions by dashing its illusions on a daunting "immortal shore." But how to arrange this when the novel aspires as well to the secular apotheosis of this globalizing vision, without irony, in its concluding symbolism? For it is from the remote shores of the same imperial world system, productive and fructifying, that the daughter of Dombey comes home with a child from her venture on the waves, the now repatriated reward for her colonialist solidarity with Walter. As the marine becomes maritime, and on the way to its own Shakespearean intertext, the novel is indeed to double business bound.

Just in time to bankroll Walter's further shipping enterprise, his uncle Sol, discovering that some long-fallow stock investments have made good, has only one rhetorical groove in which to configure his delight. He thereby expands a vernacular cliché to a modest conceit by announcing that "some of our lost ships, freighted with gold, have come home [...]. Small craft [...] but serviceable to my boy."[59] All capital gains, all financial successes, are humanized by Sol's rhetoric in terms of nautical transit.[60] Not incidentally, this phrasing highlights the same subtext that generates out of Dombey's side of the story, as an image for the annuity provided him by Harriet Carker, the one salvaged buoy ("annual sum") that "drifted to him from the wreck of his fortunes":[61] a reiterated seafaring metaphor that, in Riffaterre's metaformal terminology, would be the structural equivalent of a rhetorical "antanaclasis."[62] In other words, always other words, what goes unspoken so that it can help the novel say all that remains to be told—not only about Dombey's reclamation but also about its facilitation by the once shipwrecked hero returned to build his fortune—is a complementary form of the buried matrix (sea changes) drawn straight from the discourse of venture capitalism while being domesticated characteristically in Sol's plural variant ("some [...] have come home"): namely, his *ship has come in.*[63]

From where, exactly? From shipping's semiotic contrary, a boundless eternal sea? In this highly Shakespearean novel, where Dombey plays Lear to Florence's Cordelia and a cuckolded Othello to his envious lieutenant Carker, the other great tragic topos that is alluded to without being named is, beyond the parodistic debts of Bagstock and Skewton to *Antony and Cleopatra*, the famous lines in *Hamlet* about death as "the undiscover'd country, from whose bourn / No traveller returns."[64] Under Dickens' transforming control, this matricial intertext passes through such antanaclastic variants over the course of the novel as appear reconvened, in fact, back to back in the last two paragraphs: moving from the "invisible country" to the attenuating assonance of "unseen region." Reasons for this muting of the Shakespearean echo are, on any cognitive map of the novel's ideological horizons, not far to seek. The intertext must of structural necessity be suppressed—along with the no doubt geopolitical irony of Shakespeare's own original formulation—to avoid the undue negation of precisely those *discovered* countries of the imperial enterprise that, from the Renaissance forward, provided England with much of its offshore riches and that lend their exotic glamour now, in tacit remembrance of Paul's purifying waves, to the grand reversals of the hero and his uncle alike.

Here we can appreciate the full grip of a transformational semiotics when historically contextualized: its ability to grasp the definitive cultural tensions that generate in fiction the inferences that it must, for ideological as well as aesthetic reasons, avoid spelling out. Always intertextual to begin with, the cultural nugget of the given, the semiotic as well as ideological matrix, must be held in suspension in order to permeate. Take *sea changes*—as it ripples the text with both the Shakespearean near miss and the not-quite-idiomatic "ships come home." Ideology's ongoing effort to naturalize the constructs of the social could scarcely be clearer than in this dispersed cliché of vicissitude as it saturates everything in *Dombey and Son*, from market cycles to the broader flux of socioeconomic ascendancy across classes, nations, and races to the rhythms of human mortality itself. Keeping such a cultural truism at the level of dead metaphor is essential, whatever freshness animates its variants at the surface of dialogue or description. In the dialectics of interactive reading, prevailing cultural forms must remain sufficiently distanced so that they can return as an intuitively *achieved* rather than received truth. Like all ideology, so with the clichés of an age. Their naturalization of the made works best by being left unsaid. In the literary register, the very necessity for hermeneutics is the proof of subtle associative webworks, rather than blatantly advertised norms. The better readers a novel seems to demand, the more cogent its inculcations, imaginatively discovered rather than imposed. And so with that Shakespearean touchstone, voucher of both national and international literary resonance. In the transactional economy of our dealings with *Dombey and Son*, it is the circulation value of literary-historical capital that is drawn on to reinvest colonial horizons with metaphysical glow. In league with the diverted truism of sea changes, no example could make more evident how the "intertextual unconscious" reveals itself as an exacerbated symptom of the political unconscious. What we come upon here, once and for all, is the styleme as ideologeme.

Truth or Historical Consequences

IN THE INTERESTS OF RENEWING FORMALIST CONVERSATION in the critique of novelistic ideology, I have drawn on two indisputably major—and teasingly congruent—position papers of the early nineties and on the career-long methodologies that underlie them. The evidence is before us, but not yet the findings. The two methodologies, I need finally to show, are not so much at cross-purposes as at right angles to each other and hence are wholly coordinate in their diverging thrusts. If we cannot learn from bringing one method alongside its counterpart, then we have missed the force of their separate agendas.

Marshaling some of the same vocabulary, though as if from different lexicons, Riffaterre and Jameson sound strangely interchangeable up to a point, at least when their leading propositions are herded into terminological line. As derived from the intertext and dependent on it, the concatenated "subtext" in Riffaterre is "not a subplot and must not be confused with a theme, for it has no existence outside the text in which it appears."[65] As a "unit of reading," the subtext is a "hermeneutic model" that helps the reader "decode the significance of long narratives."[66] So too in Jameson, but in a pointedly different way. For him, a literary text can operate only as "the rewriting or reconstruction of a prior historical or ideological subtext."[67] This historical substrate is something "fundamentally non-narrative and nonrepresentational" (Jameson is very close to Riffaterre here), appearing only within and through the formal constraints of representation.[68] For Riffaterre, the subtext is the fragmented but aggregate Truth (not a transcendental signified but the internal poetics of signification) that overrides the narrative text in its forced deference to the intertextual system. This Truth has to do with aesthetic veracity rather than external verification, of course, but that makes it all the less like documentation or chronicle and all the more like an undergirding abstraction such as History. At least one thing seems abundantly clear. Historical Necessity in Jameson, like Truth in Riffaterre, is the prime mover without priority, immanent only in its effects, radically atemporal in its truth to time.

Such is Jameson's deepest Lukácsian legacy (if not explicitly acknowledged in the essay on Forster and Joyce): to see the novel form inserted into a cultural declension from the epic through the Romantic-realist-naturalist era in prose fiction to the modernist reification of the epiphanic fragment. This is a transformation that mirrors the withdrawal of a cosmological totality from human life. In the negation of theological transcendence, only history exists as absent if not first cause, a history traceable only in the epiphenomena of textual notation. As the irreversible law behind the linearity of narrative time, Historical Necessity is therefore figurable only, not plottable, and figurable by the very form of novelistic totality. So, in Riffaterre, with fictional truth, which "obtains when the mode of the diegesis shifts from the narrative to the poetic."[69] His argument comes to rest on just this closing note: "Subtexts, therefore, and the intertextuality that sets them in motion, do not unfold along an axis of duration. Like the unconscious described by Freud, the unconscious of fiction, and, therefore, its truth, stands outside the realm of time and is impervious to its ravages."[70] So does Historical Necessity in Jameson, and before him in Lukács, for whom it is impervious in a special sense: indifferent to the very ravages it brings about. In the absence of all divine assurance, the novel participates directly, according to Lukács, in modern life's "invention" of the self-contained "productivity of the spirit," where art must now generate rather than mirror the formal order for which it yearns.[71] Modernism's late and signal stage in the evolution of novelistic style poses a kind of epistemological quandary: how to test for reality—rather than its travesty, cosmopolitan worldliness—in an interface with the "invisible," what Lukács would call the former immanence of the divine in the epic life-world.[72] What is needed by the formal dialectic of conservative modernism, one might then claim, is nothing less than a rarefied synthesis between the conflicting pulls of psychological realism and the coterminous supernatural strain in Victorian gothicism, synthesized in a new aesthetic (and ethic) of the unseen: spectral, epiphanic, and potentially escapist. As is apparent by now, my only demurral from Jameson's account of *Howards End*, in its historical rather than literary-historical terms, is that one can locate the first stirrings of this culturally impacted synthesis exactly half a century earlier, in Dickens' muted supernaturalism well before Forster's.

For *Dombey and Son* is the novel that most of all, at least first of all, in the geopolitical context of the Victorian canon, in contriving to secure its formal symmetries, lays bare their structured rather than organic nature, their conceptual desperation. Here without flinch or deflection is the "fundamentally abstract nature" of the novel's systematizing project, a formal recompense for totality's absence from every other life sphere.[73] Never more openly than in *Dombey and Son* does the domestic melodrama of Dickensian fiction reach out to embrace an entire global vision. Its formal compass is put in the national service of representing an imperialist (and therefore anything but organic) world system, but only so that its spiritual authentications can proceed "by recognizing, consciously and consistently, everything that points outside and beyond the confines of the world"—just over the edge of its geopolitical horizons, formally manifest only by intertextual summons.[74]

When narrative verisimilitude gives way to poetics, to mythopoetics, the intertextual unconscious of imperial representation works, that is, to mystify (and narrow) the unseen into the one psychic space that cannot be territorialized: all that unknowably outstrips the "bourn" of death, falling forever beyond the colonial pale. History as Necessity is reduced (in an eminently ideological reduction) to the intractable limits of the single life, no longer global, no longer even communal. "Death destroys a man, but the idea of death saves him," writes Forster in one of his most cryptic antimetaphysical epigrams: novelistic through and through.[75] This antimaterialist ethic might have served as the epigraph to *Dombey and Son*, as of course to any number of Forster's novels. In terms of the novelistic chronotope, death as a form of closure—necessity writ small—redeems the very characters who, undergoing it or not, are willing to contemplate it. Such is Forster's quintessential attempt, but Dickens' equally before his, to humanize necessity as an *escape* from history. Death remains the one thing we wish always to intuit only, rather than to know. If only empire's "unseen" could be made to satisfy the spirit in the way the ideation of death does, then totality could be reined in as a purely abstract value, hazy and bracing. Literature intercedes for us just here, not only in its vicarious content (characters who die for us, heroes whose ships come in) but in its form:

with its whole panoply of equilibrated structural contradictions. At the stratum of intertextually generated truth alone, we are to think, can the novel help us confront with impunity, through stylistic mediation, the aestheticized return of the historical repressed. In *Dombey and Son*, then, every bit as much as in *Howards End*, the tenuous ligatures of colonial interdependency come to us refigured as immaterial, distanced, disembodied, impersonal, abstracted to all that remains unseen to be believed, believed in as British fortitude rather than exploitation. If, stretched to the breaking point, this figuration can be further redirected—away from the territorializing entrenchments of power and into a manifest destiny common to all (death rather than domination)—then the novel has performed its true ideological foreclosure. It has done so, yet again, by pointing to a realm of latent value stripped of all action, an unknown shore that cannot be properly confronted in the collective (and hence politically) but only in the individual reconciliations of the spirit.

We have traveled a long way from the tensed phrasal duality of our opening examples, but only around again to the reverberations of their verbal byplay. The broadest "sylleptic" (or intertextual) tendency in *Dombey and Son*, generated by the oceanic matrix and maintained by the nautical subtext, plays ultimately, as it does in *Howards End* afterward, between the global circuit of colonial exchange and a psychic economy of human mortality. Whether as generalized nickname for intertextuality or as specific internal deviance, syllepsis emerges as the figure of (and for) a strategic—and forced—unification. In its grammatical form, such unabashed shiftiness is the lower limit of an at least potential mystification, equivocation degree zero, naturalizing the incompatible by the aggregate force of grammar itself. We are now ready to see in sum, that grammatical forking emerges as one of style's rudimentary formal models of an otherwise uninstantiable desire: the desire for a specifically *willed* inclusiveness. It is the figure not of paradox or antithesis, deeply ideological in their own right, but of that more culturally sanctioned thing: the attempted resolution of incommensurables. Syllepsis, by any other name, is the division from within that overtly sustains two simultaneous strata of apprehension. It is therefore, to vary Riffaterre, not only the literary but the *ideological* trope par excellence, subsuming the divisive in a totality never wholly present to consciousness. In Forster, topographic vanishing points (roads or railways) and receding spiritual vistas, sunshine and adventure, seeing whole and seeing steadily; in Dickens, shirt fronts and false fronts, suits and hearts, servants and an always insubordinate Fate, colonial dockings and eternal harbors: each dyad abdicates under stylistic pressure to an absent—and somehow unifying—common denominator. Such stylistic insistence, shearing between fields of reference, often holding the coarsely literal and the diaphanously metaphorical in the same syntactic vector, operates for Dickens and Forster, in short, as the historically specific training ground of a *double vision* that is both the essence of fictional poetics and the stuff of political self-deception.

In the formalist amalgam ventured by this essay, then, its reciprocal corrective amounts to this. Not only would the nuances of verbal intertextuality help carry a Marxist semiotics, as a principle of form rather than of content, beyond the structuring framework of narrative ideology into the very crevices of literary formation itself—and back again—but, conversely, a truly exploratory rather than merely resolute formalism would discover from text to text, rather than presume, the inevitably political structure of the intertextual unconscious. In transactional dealings with *Dombey and Son* or *Howards End*, symptomatically "modern" texts each, the act of reading, like the (always interpretive) spiritual life in Forster, is meant to "pay." But in the semiotic economies of decipherment, such reading may institute an intermediate credit check—through a double-edged, double-ledger attention. Trafficking as it does with the fluctuations of metaphor, renegotiating its transfers and exchanges, only a *formative* encounter with the literary page can bear witness to that silent partnership between mimesis and poesis by which the invested (the simultaneously lured and constituted) reader is invited to abide.

Notes

1 In this sense of a formalist obligation, I allude to Susan J. Wolfson, *Formal Charges: The Shaping of Poetry in British Romanticism* (Stanford: Stanford University Press, 1997).

2 See Michael Riffaterre, *Semiotics of Poetry* (Bloomington: Indiana University Press, 1978), 19. "The text functions something like a neurosis: as the matrix is repressed, the displacement produces variants all through the text, just as suppressed symptoms break out somewhere else in the body."

3 Fredric Jameson, "Modernism and Imperialism," in *Nationalism, Colonialism, and Literature*, ed. Seamus Deane (Minneapolis: University of Minnesota Press, 1990), 43–66; his discussion of protomodernist figural "style" in E. M. Forster is followed by a reading of James Joyce as antistylistic and already postmodern.

4 Fredric Jameson, *The Political Unconscious: Narrative as a Socially Symbolic Act* (Ithaca, NY: Cornell University Press, 1981), 42. I allude as well to Fredric Jameson, *The Prison-House of Language: A Critical Account of Structuralism and Russian Formalism* (Princeton: Princeton University Press, 1972).

5 Riffaterre in fact defers to Jacques Derrida's preference for the lexical rather than syntactic usage, following French and German rhetorical traditions, in Michael Riffaterre, "Syllepsis," *Critical Inquiry*, vol. 6 (1980): 629 n. 10.

6 This last is a somewhat slippery (because broad) term in Michael Riffaterre, *Fictional Truth* (Baltimore: Johns Hopkins University Press, 1990), where perhaps the most instructive example is the "fragile porcelain" subtext from George Meredith's *Egoist* (2.1–2.8), somewhere between a motif and a symbolic pattern.

7 This title has gone through various mutations in punctuation, including none at all, in editions over the years; I touch again on the phrasing in just those terms, via the original title page, in the essay below on Dickensian punctuation, "Point/Counterpunct."

8 "Double-take is the perception of syllepsis." Riffaterre, *Fictional Truth*, 86.

9 Riffaterre, "Syllepsis," *Critical Inquiry*, 638.

10   H. W. Fowler, in the terminological minority here, cites syllepsis ("taking
     together") as the grammatical "doubling" of Augustan wit, zeugma ("yoking")
     as its ungrammatical cousin (*The New Fowler's Modern English Usage*, 3rd ed.,
     ed. R. W. Burchfield [Oxford: Clarendon, 1996], 758, 863). Richard A. Lanham,
     following George Puttenham, reverses the priority, so that zeugma ("single supply")
     covers Alexander Pope's "stains her honour or her new brocade," whereas syllepsis
     applies to such "double supply" problems of incongruent verb number as "the
     Nobles and the King was taken" (A *Handlist of Rhetorical Terms*, 2nd ed. [Berkeley:
     University of California Press, 1991], 160, 145); so, too, *The Oxford Companion to
     the English Language*, ed. Tom McArthur (Oxford: Oxford University Press, 1992),
     1146. Terminology aside, it's no accident that a web encyclopedia should look to
     Dickens for an illustration of syllepsis, citing from *Pickwick Papers* the penultimate
     sentence of chapter 35, where the agitated Miss Bolo "went straight home in a flood
     of tears and a sedan chair." Bringing the two complements of the predicate into a
     more complementary relationship, rather than simply a jarring discrepancy, is the
     more usual, and subtler, work of a later novel like *Dombey and Son*.
11   Charles Dickens, *Dealings with the Firm of Dombey and Son Wholesale, Retail and
     for Exportation* (Harmondsworth: Penguin, 1970), 703.
12   Dickens, *Dombey and Son*, 113, 151–52.
13   Ibid., 122.
14   Ibid., 179.
15   Ibid., 661.
16   Ibid., 513.
17   Ibid., 887.
18   This point is dearer in the original Derrida passage than when Riffaterre calls
     the figure "simply a pun" ("Syllepsis," 629). Derrida stresses an "internal" syntax
     in Stéphane Mallarmé's grammatical as well as lexical play on the "hymen" (as
     both marriage and blockage) "entre" ("between" in both senses) desire and
     fulfillment in Jacques Derrida, *Dissemination*, trans. Barbara Johnson (Chicago:
     University of Chicago Press, 1981), 221. Derrida is out to deconstruct the very
     difference between diction and syntax, with every word entailed by system, every
     relationality inscribing the content of its own form.
19   Jameson, "Modernism and Imperialism," *Nationalism, Colonialism, and Literature*,
     44–45.
20   Ibid., 51.
21   E. M. Forster, *Howards End* (Harmondsworth: Penguin, 1992), 29.
22   Forster, *Howards End*, 58.
23   Ibid., 27.
24   Ibid.; italics added.
25   Ibid.
26   Ibid.
27   The subtext ("the nonordinary language of prosperity") is capped near the end of
     the novel in a single resonant sentence, when Margaret's unquestioning love has
     rescued Helen from Henry's abusive dismissal: "The inner life had paid" (ibid.,
     292). If one is faced with the strangling effect of international materialism, the
     instinct to bank on invisible values may, in other words, still be cost-effective.
28   Jameson, "Modernism and Imperialism," *Nationalism, Colonialism, and Literature*,
     52, 58. For an image of the semiotic square by A. J. Greimas, see *Attention Spans:*

Garrett Stewart, a Reader, ed. David LaRocca (New York: Bloomsbury, 2024), fig. 1, 82.

29　Jameson, *The Political Unconscious*, 254.

30　Forster, *Howards End*, 119.

31　Ibid., 112.

32　Ibid., 41–42.

33　Ibid., 58.

34　Ibid., 165.

35　See the sonnet "To a Friend," *The Poems of Matthew Arnold*, ed. Kenneth Allott (New York: Barnes & Noble, 1965), 105.

36　Dickens, *Dombey and Son*, 178.

37　Ibid., 201.

38　Ibid., 278.

39　Ibid., 188, 778.

40　Ibid., 144.

41　Ibid., 187.

42　Ibid., 158.

43　Ibid., 241.

44　Ibid., 295, 60.

45　Ibid., 354.

46　Because of the railroad's limited symbolic utility, Terry Eagleton exempts *Dombey and Son* from his claim about later Dickens novels: that the centralized social structures under satiric attack, in their labyrinthine and oppressive symbolic inclusiveness, tend to grow homologous with the complex organization of the text itself (*Criticism and Ideology: A Study in Marxist Literary Theory* [London: Verso, 1978], 130). My own view is closer to Ian Duncan's in *Modern Romance and Transformations of the Novel: The Gothic, Scott, and Dickens* (Cambridge: Cambridge University Press, 1992), where *Dombey and Son*'s narrative sprawl is related to organizational circuits of imperial trade. In this sense, the famous passage from chapter 34 about "this round world with many circles within circles"—in which the "world" is usually taken metonymically for something like "this vale of laughter and tears"—carries instead the hint of global circumnavigation (579). Duncan aptly finds this virtual dead metaphor related to imagery of "mysterious systems, patterns and connections" in *Bleak House* and *Little Dorrit*, concluding that the role of such systemic webbing is performed in the earlier novel by "a global energy system" within a "universal economy" (241).

47　Steven Connor, in drawing less directly on Jameson, has attempted Greimasian schemata for *Dombey and Son* that are very different from those to follow here (*Charles Dickens* [Oxford: Blackwell, 1985], 36–43).

48　Forster, *Howards End*, 44.

49　Dickens, *Dombey and Son*, 611.

50　Ibid., 975.

51　Raymond Williams, introduction to *Dombey and Son*, 30.

52　Dickens, *Dombey and Son*, 974.

53　Ibid., 371.

54　Ibid., 164–65, 168.

55　Ibid., 50.

56　Ibid., 649.

57　Forster's imperialist mystification commits a similar slipperiness with oceanic figures, so that Mrs. Wilcox dies like "the seafarer who can greet with an equal eye the deep that he is entering, and the shore that he must leave" (ibid., 111). Even the compound secretes the false parallelism of an ungrammatical zeugma or syllepsis (you do not greet the shore you leave behind, only the one you may dream of reaching). Forster's nautical conceit is then extrapolated to nationalism's secular destiny in Margaret's later reflections at Poole harbor both about England "sailing as a ship of souls"—narrowly deflecting the heroic cliché from the imperial sociolect, "ship of state"—and also about the turbulent effect, nonetheless, that private gestures of love make on "the world's waters" (ibid., 178).

58　Ibid., 676, 976.

59　Ibid., 974.

60　A historicist account of the socioeconomic cycles of market fluctuation in the period of *Dombey and Son*'s setting and composition confirms quite precisely, even without quoting, the force of this idiom and the larger repressed matrix of capitalist "sea changes." See Mary G. McBride, "Contemporary Economic Metaphors in Dombey and Son," *Dickensian*, vol. 90 (1994): 19–24, an article that ties the "wavelike cycles of the Victorian concept of economic change" into the novel's guiding motif (rather than local metaphors) of the waves (23).

61　Dickens, *Dombey and Son*, 971.

62　Instancing the actual trope of "antanaclasis" from Dickens, we find this in *Great Expectations* (Harmondsworth: Penguin, 1965), 225: "Bentley Drummle, who was so sulky a fellow that even he *took up* a book as if its writer had done him an injury, did not *take up* an acquaintance in a more agreeable spirit" (italics added). For Riffaterre, such a figure of marked variation is paradigmatic of fictional structure as it unfolds over textual duration: "This trope is therefore a corollary of *syllepsis*. Text production by narrative derivation from a syllepsis may be achieved by transforming the syllepsis into an antanaclasis" (*Fictional Truth*, 125), as with the widely dispersed "*passe/passer/passé* subtext" in Proust (103).

63　*Hamlet*, 3.1.78–79. To measure the imperial girth of the figurative net cast by this tacit phrasing, compare it with the yet deader metaphor associated with Mr. Wilcox's colonial rubber venture, when Margaret says, "I gather he is launching out, rather" (Forster, *Howards End*, 114).

64　*The Riverside Shakespeare*, ed. G. Blakemore Evans (Boston, MA: Houghton Mifflin, 1974), 1160. On a similar Shakespearean intertextuality in *Little Dorrit*, where the patriarchal watch containing the letters "D.N.F." ("Do Not Forget") repeats the ghost's words to Hamlet, see Jonathan Arac, "*Hamlet, Little Dorrit*, and the History of Character," *South Atlantic Quarterly*, vol. 87 (1988): 316–18.

65　Riffaterre, *Fictional Truth*, 131.

66　Ibid.

67　Jameson, *Political Unconscious*, 81.

68　Ibid., 82.

69　Riffaterre, *Fictional Truth*, 111.

70　Ibid.

71　Georg Lukács, *The Theory of the Novel: A Historico-philosophical Essay on the Forms of Great Epic Literature*, trans. Anna Bostock (Cambridge, MA: MIT Press, 1971), 33–34.

72 According to Lukács, in the novel of abstract idealism, the ambient space of selfhood—"the ability to experience distances as realities"—has been lost (97). The "metaformal grace" of fictional shape alone is counted on to redeem the spirit in the representation of a world where "distance, losing its objective reality, is turned into a darkly beautiful ornament"—perfected, we may say, in the recuperative ornamentality of modernist style when faced with the unfelt distances of empire (102). In the clearest anticipation of Jameson's sense of a "bad" infinity in Forster ("Modernism and Imperialism," 58), Lukács notes the risks involved in idealism's "metaformal" displacement as those of "'bad' abstraction, 'bad' infinity" (101).

73 Lukács, *The Theory of the Novel*, 71.

74 Ibid., 71. To be sure, Lukács everywhere relegates Dickensian fiction to "mere entertainment literature," incapable of grappling with the foundational problematic of the novel form as an epic in the absence of a totalized organic culture underwritten and overseen by transcendental sureties. It may well be, however, that the figurative subtext of *Dombey and Son* comes closest to exposing Dickensian anxieties—and recuperative powers (deceits)—in just this regard, and hence to exposing the hastiness of Lukacs' dismissal.

75 Forster, *Howards End*, 315.

3 / With a focus on philosophy and its discontents not typical of Stewart's writing, "The Avoidance of Stanley Cavell" has turned out to be widely cited in the American philosophical community—and not just for its spirited defense of Cavell's own work on literature, theater, and film but for its unstinting regret over what the reigning paradigms of literary study tended to blind themselves to in their response to Cavell (New Historicist Shakespeare studies in particular). What emerges is an appreciation not just of Cavell on literature but of the philosophic writer's own distinct literary qualities.

3 / *The Avoidance of Stanley Cavell*

STANLEY CAVELL, PROFESSOR EMERITUS of aesthetics and the theory of value at Harvard, though a philosopher by training and appointment, has sent to print in the last three and a half decades some of the most passionate and commanding essays on literary aesthetics and literary value to be found anywhere in the postwar critical canon. Over this achievement there is little if any dispute. Despite the accolades, then, why has this work been to a discernible extent overlooked in the discussions that stand most to gain from engaging it? Such was the broad question that led to my embarking on this essay. In the commissioning editor's more specific terms, I was asked to consider "any hesitancy in the literary response to Cavell's work, as well as what has really been useful." The more precise the formulation, the more disturbing the question.

Useful? Reason not the need? The trouble with any weighing of use value in the literary academy today is not a problem in the general "theory of value," much less in the free flow of ideas in a disinterested economy of exchange. Just because Stanley Cavell's stock has always been high does not mean that his ideas have been heavily traded. Right at the moment, multinational interests hold sway: postcoloniality, race, subaltern studies, globalization, cultural hybridity, pluralist identity politics. Before that, New Historicism. And before that, deconstruction. Just when Cavell emerged to wide notice in the late sixties with his monumental essay "The Avoidance of Love: A Reading of *King Lear*," which reminded us that philosophy might be the true interlocutor rather than the mostly silent partner of High Theory, the well-advertised cartel of Derrida, Lacan, and Foucault was beginning to monopolize the Anglo-American field— and at times seeming to swallow up Cavell's own premises, however dimly glimpsed.[1]

The passage of years has scarcely improved the situation for interdisciplinary exchange in this vein. Indeed, my essay lines up behind several others of the last decade on the regrettable undercirculation of Cavell's ideas. This alone may give pause. How many books and articles on the disciplinary nonassimilation of Stanley Cavell's thinking would begin to count as redress? But then that is not exactly the right question. The point is not to decide how much Cavell is appreciated, or not, or how widely, or even how deeply—and then to fill the gap. The point is to wonder (and so to ask out loud) why there persists a particular *kind* of "hesitancy"—or resistance—wherever the work is quarantined from serious consideration.

Michael Fischer has written a whole book to investigate the grounds of "neglect" in the specifically literary reception of Cavell—namely, the neoskepticism at its base.[2] Stephen Melville, surveying the full armory of Cavell's interests, launches a more recent essay by locating what we might call four avatars of disregard, with Cavell positioned as "a maverick figure within the American philosophic academy, an obscure resister of mainstream contemporary film theory, an odd man out with respect to the current literary theoretical orthodoxy, and, I imagine, a figure of retrograde enthusiasms to a community of Americanists largely in flight from New Critical canonization."[3] It is the last resistance that Melville confronts most directly when he draws out an implicit epistemology of reading from Cavell's account of Emerson's philosophical essays.

Two observations may deserve to interrupt at the outset this compressed resumé of response. The first has to do with the articulation, the second with the distribution, of resistance. First, what increasingly strikes a reader looking to assess the gauntlet thrown down by Cavell's work to reigning literary-critical models is that the complaints against him are best, and most often, phrased by his champions. This strikes me as close to unprecedented in the ordinary channels of academic discourse. It is as if the nuance, capaciousness, and candor of Cavell's thinking hold the seeds of dissent within the toils of their own subtlety, so that only his most devoted close readers can judge the pressure of counterargument from within the weight of original formulation. You have to be tuned in to begin with to imagine here the static might occur. Sympathetic readers of Cavell, that is, best pledge their allegiance by imaging an objection as if it were their own, so that even debate waits within testimonial as its true measure. And is not this (we may come to think with a little more evidence) no less than the very proof of the Cavellian method: a reading so intense as to internalize the shadow of its own alternatives?

The second preliminary observation has to do with the different cast of resistance to Cavell's enthusiasms depending on whether he is meditating on Shakespeare or on such favored authors of the now debunked "American Renaissance" as Thoreau or Emerson. Although the tragic humanism of Cavell's Shakespeare does not sit well alongside the latest postures of critique, it is the particular brand of American liberal humanism, namely heroic individualism, that makes Cavell's approach to certain American authors so uniquely unpalatable to the newer generation of politicized and materialist readers. The Cavellian problematic of self and other, however melancholy, is found to turn its back on materialism precisely where the given of the human spirit takes precedence over what is given to it as material subject. Socioeconomic readings of the capitalist American canon—and Emerson's reputed sponsoring place in it—feel obliged to resist what they see as Cavell's complicity in the elevation of the liberal free agent, emancipated by sufficiency to the leisure as well as the labor of spiritual contemplation. To borrow the title of Cavell's book centrally on Emerson, *Conditions Handsome and Unhandsome*, the most unhandsome facts of economic determinism would be found by its critics to disfigure his very topic, occluding a class- and race-based problem of other bodies as well as (and before) other minds.[4]

This distance from his supposed meliorist (or downright apolitical) tendencies in the assimilation of the Americanist Cavell has, since Melville's essay, been lucidly drawn out by Cary Wolfe.[5] In a separate but not unrelated context, Emily Miller Budick sees Cavell as the potential mediator between the excesses of Americanist New Historicism and those of Anglo-American deconstruction.[6] This mediation would be made possible by Cavell's salutary effort to break the deadlock of what Budick rightly detects as a "linguistic (and hence moral and political) determinism."[7] For New Historicism, words are so saturated with cultural weight and hence ideology that they block hermeneutic freedom, whereas for deconstruction they are so underdecided that they resist reading. Ideological critique forecloses meaning in the culturally foregone conclusion; deconstruction foreshortens meaning into a verbally unfixed and decentered skid of reference, flattening the sign to sheer signifier. Each, as Budick puts it, "may obliterate the space between ideology and interpretation."[8] Cavell's approach to reading would reoccupy that space, making it habitable once more. Here again two of the reigning movements of the last three decades in literary scholarship have stood to gain more than they knew from Cavell's sustained discriminations.[9]

The same parting of methodological ways attenuates the conversation around Cavell's Shakespeare studies as well. I will be turning to this "hesitancy" over Cavell's version of Shakespeare after considering a resistance more pervasive yet, bedeviling the reception of Cavell's work on *Walden* and *The Philadelphia Story* as much as on *Othello*. Cutting through questions having to do with difference of "opinion" in literary and philosophical circles, one writer has looked the problem straight in the eye. I refer to the question of Cavell's style and to its most searching defense in the work of Timothy Gould, a defense that intersects with the larger issue of methodological reception at another level. Brilliantly relocating the problem of style as a problematics of voice philosophically defined, Gould thus situates manner at the heart of Cavell's matter: a manner probing as it does the grounds of human connection, yet with a flourish that appears so self-involved, so "insinuating and domineering by turns," that its writerliness seems to undermine the very claims of "ordinary language" on which it stakes its chances of success.[10] Gould's allusion to Wittgenstein's "gaudy and painstaking modes of writing" would seem to apply in a different key to Cavell's.[11] That such extreme forms of expression should be mounted in Cavell to stage the possibility not of style's signature effects but of communicable voice as a condition of human intimacy is a "central irony" of Cavell's work, according to Gould, and a disabling one in some quarters.[12]

Cavell's diction is straightforward enough, no technical argot, and the syntax much of the time cadenced not unlike speech, but it all comes at us with a heft and velocity and wrought thrust that transfigures the ordinary (from within, perhaps, but often beyond recognition). At his farthest "pitch of philosophy" (from the title of Cavell's 1994 book of collected lectures), the high-flying periods have an unholy confidence and bravura intonation that put us in mind of prose arias, but only in mind—not in earshot. To think of this effect as a case in point for the everyday voicing of human expression is a critical stretch. Gould makes it into a philosophical leap. But the temper of the times would not let every literary theorist take the plunge with him, as Gould is well aware. One name for this refusal, though vestigial enough at this stage of post-theorical cultural studies, is deconstruction. This is the literary school which Michael Fischer's book had already joined a host of previous critics in teasing out as, in its own right, a form of skepticism: a skepticism on those overlapping fronts crucial to Cavell's problematic, a doubt about the availability of the world (through reference), of other minds (through expression), and of myself (through any inner voicing of the cogito).

Gould will not let the specter of deconstruction get in the way of what he has to say about Cavell's modes of saying, nor of their place in the "model of reading" that he incrementally educes from Cavell's hermeneutic as well as philosophic practice. Disentangling the suasive force of Cavell's writing from all mystified aura of "metaphysical voice," where self-presence is a grounding only because transcendental axiom, Gould attends instead to the pluralized and oscillating play of Cavellian voices in order to win them back, variously if not collectively, for a paradigm of conversible interchange with the reader: Cavell's reader, yes, but before that the literary reader whose recruited investments in a text have been so powerfully examined by Cavell himself.[13] To render this audition of voices a shade more hospitable to deconstruction, with its overthrown phonocentrism adrift across the flux of the signifying mark, as one might be inclined to do by putting quotes around the "voice" of writing, would be mostly meant to clear the air for a sharper registration of the true Cavellian tone rather than to plug our (otherwise duped) ears to it. But in doing so we are also beginning to track a more widespread reverberation of the deconstructive critique, one that collides with Cavell's Shakespeare essays precisely where such critique, following the likes of Foucault and Althusser, has widened its aim beyond human textuality to the human agent itself as quasi-textual assemblage. We thus cross the receding threshold from deconstruction to constructionism. This will take a little more space to bring out.

If my reflections had never been invited, there is already on record an essay that, as far as it went a decade back, serves expertly in this same line of inquiry: an essay staring over a paradigm brink when it still looked like a contested watershed. This is Richard P. Wheeler's "Acknowledging Shakespeare: Cavell and the Claim of the Human," whose title alone lodges two of its main points: Cavell's continued dedication to the textual integrity of authorship and his abiding preoccupation with the human condition and its inherent finitude, in both its given and its self-inflicted limits.[14] From the vantage of Wheeler's essay in 1989, these commitments were found at odds with the New Historicism's growing hegemony, as represented by such critics as Jonathan Dollimore, Jonathan Goldberg, and Stephen Greenblatt, each (with their deconstructively inflected posthumanism) arguing in different ways for the dissolution of authorial into social energy. Words are no longer determinedly those of the major author but rather discourses of the writer's culture dubiously funneled through the single strong work. And anyway words no longer express the human subject off the stage or page either; in being evacuated from that subject, they void it by definition. Cavell's passionate ear for "dialogue" (part of his commitment to conversation in Shakespeare, in Hollywood comedy, and in the circulatory energies of his own writing) would founder on this logophobic skepticism—if, that is, it were nearly so convincing an approach as Cavell's own. Wheeler certainly does not find it so.

But I have highlighted only two features of Wheeler's overview. For him, there are in fact five premises animating Cavell's work on Shakespearean theater that have fallen into fashionable discredit since the 1969 appearance of the *King Lear* essay: autonomy, unity, expression, intentionality, and human nature, each of which, as touchstones, can of course be seen passing between author and character—or constitutively denied to both at once.[15] As "an attribute of art, of a work of art, of a genre, of an artist, and of a human subject," autonomy has been decentered and diffused beyond (re)cognition—and with it the unity for which it strives, the intentional expressivity that fulfills it.[16] The Shakespeare text, as model of such expressive unity, such autonomous plenary authority, no longer draws students and scholars of the period in the same way as it did—and does—Cavell.

Wheeler takes us even deeper into the issue when he grapples more directly with Stephen Greenblatt's influential reading of *King Lear*, where the play's theatrical illusion of violence and its purgation can be historically located not just in Catholic/ Protestant debates over witchcraft and exorcism—debates that we read today, in hindsight, as passé, naive, and ideologically invested on both sides—but in the very retrofit of contemporary audience response.[17] Here lies, for Greenblatt, the continuing cultural viability of a theatrical violence that sustains wholesale, by locally extirpating, the illusion of lived fullness in a world otherwise recognized as that of self-presentation rather than self-presence. Catharsis is overturned as paradigm by constructionism, a variety of what Greenblatt would call cultural selffashioning. From his slightly removed seat in the balcony, the structuring of desire seems clear. We go to Shakespearean theater not to live through a death but to live through the illusion of a depth of identity worth dying to confirm—an illusion long-lost to the present-day viewer. Compared to this historical distancing and emotional withering of the play in more recent criticism, even Cavell's slips are, for Wheeler, the defects of an inestimable virtue. In Wheeler's specific arguments with Cavell's account of *King Lear*—in its purported underreading of incestuous sexuality in Lear's panic over a loosening grip on his daughter—Wheeler finds that Cavell identifies so completely with the tragic hero that he participates in Lear's own fantasy of unstinted reciprocation for a father's love. A passing comment in a footnote is revealing here, since "such may be simply one of the hazards his criticism runs, dependent as it is on his deep immersion in the texts he reads. It is, I hasten to add, a hazard well worth running."[18]

In a further effort to pin down the terms of Cavell's reading, its reason for never speaking the name of one of the loves that dare not speak its own, I need to mention two other orientations of Cavell's work—in Shakespeare and in film—that have fallen out of favor, or at least popularity, before drawing the renewal they might have in an encounter with just that work: namely, a psychologizing rigor repeatedly drawn back to the family romance as the structuring fundament of all desire; and, equally urgent and waning, a metatheatricality so constitutive that it rethinks the whole formalist mandate in the reading of such "performance" texts. To draw out the inferences of the first, in the teeth of Wheeler's critique, is at the same time to highlight a missed bridge to another of the most powerful literary thinkers of Cavell's day. This is René Girard, whose searing view of derivative passion in postromantic literature, its always mediated or triangular nature, is partly explained in terms of an Oedipal rivalry that never goes away, that poisons all desire with contest, that deforms every love object into a rejection of the original. Oedipus is the blind patron of all discredited romantic passion. Or put closer to home: the father's ghost hovers over all disenfranchised desire. In a passage to which Wheeler alludes (and from which he quotes a few phrases) in his argument that Cavell minimizes Cordelia's felt incestuous threat from her father, we might well take this to be just the point of Cavell's fine unfolding thought:

> I do not wish to suggest that "avoidance of love" and "avoidance of a particular kind of love" are alternative hypotheses about this play. On the contrary, they seem to me to interpret one another. Avoidance of love is always, or always begins as, an avoidance of a particular kind of love: Human beings do not just naturally not love, they learn not to. And our lives begin by having to accept under the name of love whatever closeness is offered, and by then having to forgo its object. And the avoidance of a particular love, or the acceptance of it, will spread to every other; every love, in acceptance or rejection, is mirrored in every other.[19]

This is not (*pace* Wheeler) to deny or even minimize Shakespeare's sense of incestuous anxiety in *King Lear* but rather to suggest that, in this play, the threat of incest lies not so much in looming abuse as in the disabusing of all illusions about love.

In fortifying Cavell's argument against Wheeler's otherwise revealing demurrals, I scarcely wish to blame Cavell for not openly invoking Girard, far less to ferret out an "anxiety of influence"—here or in the repeatedly thematized avoidance of an incestuous deadlock in the Hollywood remarriage comedies taken up in Cavell's *Pursuits of Happiness*. There is no retributive fantasy of poetic justice lurking in all these dramatic examples. It is not that Cavell is now punished by apparent neglect in some circles for what he himself commits in the case of Girardian triangulation: availing himself of a fallout so subtle and pervasive that it does not count as uptake. For even that would be an optimistic reading of Cavell's own legacy as widespread and indelible. My point is rather that even the "deconstruction" of autonomous desire in Girard—its displacement into a chain of narratable substitutions—seems too literary in its application, in part because too character-based, for recent schools of social materialism and cultural poetics. Girard is concerned, like the great ironic literature he probes, to denaturalize from the ground up a human autonomy whose nonexistence is now taken untroublesomely for granted. Like Cavell, Girard writes as if major literature were the lens under which the deceits of desire come into focus, whereas the most sophisticated recent criticism insists on seeing literature itself, in its very form of dissemination, as implicated in the artificial maintenance of such desire, such constructions of the subject.

In that second regard, if to a different end, the artifice of theatrical literature, with its complex lines of identification and distance on stage, has often preoccupied Cavell's metadramatic commentaries—and offers a direct link to his suggestive ontology of screen versus stage in *The World Viewed*.[20] The dramatic rather than cinematic side of these issues is never more fully articulated, however, than in his essay on *King Lear*, with its pressing investigation of theatrical presence and remove. For Cavell, the untraversable distance from us of characters on stage is a function of a skepticism activated but bracketed by the theatricalized conditions of spectatorship. If the skeptical withdrawal from the world can, in general, be depicted as the reduction of life to a drama performed at a fixed distance from us, then drama per se can be called a skeptical therapy. And less because we feel for a suffering not our own than because we embrace our outsideness to all real pain as temporary. This is the way the stage work does its work for and upon its audience. Theater keeps our distance for us until closure, when its silence leaves the rest up to us. Shakespearean theater, by "giving us a place within which our hiddenness and silence and separateness are accounted for," thus "gives us a chance to stop," which is to say a chance to start afresh, to take up with the world once more.[21] A chance and a risk. When the play is over, and our powerlessness to intercept its pain has been lived through, we can now elect our presence again to the world beyond the stage, can cease sitting back from it. If theater succeeds, its power is less to have suspended our disbelief in the fictive (a relatively simple matter) than to have openly and artificially suspended our belief in the real, thus releasing us back to it in due course. Skepticism puts the world at a fixed distance; theater puts just that withdrawal on hold for the scene of another sort of distance penetrated at once by meaning and by feeling. In sum, the complementary relation between the skeptical and the theatrical installed by tragedy becomes a corrective one.

The metatheatrical probity of this Cavellian dialectic is not calculated to win interest (forget credence) from those critics supposedly wised up about literary identification. Wheeler's essay, as I say, offers a finely judged plateau from which to view, in retrospect, a widening and unfordable gulf in Shakespearean studies. A decade later, prospects cannot be said to have brightened.[22] Beyond the early methodological fissures noted by Wheeler's essay, especially the break into decentered semiosis that drove all pre-Nietzschean philosophic considerations from the field of early modern (formerly Renaissance) studies, it must also be said that there are two further "schools" out of sympathy not only with the reciprocations of metatheatrical sympathy in Cavell but with the whole ideologically freighted notion of "love": the feminists and the Foucauldians. Cavell's reception has been ill-served by a sex-and-gender paradigm braced against the supposedly placid heterosexist norms in so much of his writing on theater and popular film. The feminist critic might well be so quick to see Cordelia's victimage, for instance, that any investigation of the play focused through Lear's skeptical deadlock might easily lose force. Unguarded asides of Cavell's like the following from *Disowning Knowledge* do not help much either, as regards the tenor of reception in this camp: "Then are we to conclude that the issue of skepticism does not arise for women? (I do not want this question now to expose the apparently more general question whether philosophy as such arises for women.)"[23] Fully justified in a context of a one-sided anxiety in *The Winter's Tale* about whether one's children are knowably one's own, the gendering of the skeptic's pain leads Cavell into apparently exclusionary waters. When his thinking takes a similar turn in his book on the Hollywood comedies—*Pursuits of Happiness*—where the male protagonist is repeatedly seen to assist in the "creation of the woman" by overcoming his own doubts about, if you will, the fullness of her company—the formulation can seem openly paternalistic, to say nothing of feminism's underlying doubts concerning the whole book's celebration of marital parity as a thing of wit rather than politics. For much of the misunderstanding that has attended such remarks, Cavell has sought not expiation but clarification in his prolonged engagement with feminism and queer theory in *Contesting Tears: The Melodrama of the Unknown Woman* (1996). But is the film studies (now cinema studies) audience he once unjustifiably lost even listening anymore?

The avoidance of love goes even deeper, deeper even than the deconstruction of sex itself, in the Foucauldian (via Althusserian) master plot. We can approach this from material already at hand. What I am suggesting is that the differences so well demarcated by Wheeler between Greenblatt and Cavell do not reduce to a narrow specialist debate about metatheatricality in Shakespearean drama. The presumptions—or at least the *moves* (mutual evacuation)—that render the elegant schematic reversals of Greenblatt's thinking so cleverly accessible were already at the time widely familiar to academic audiences well beyond the confines of early modern scholarship. They have to do less with the *theatrum mundi* rethought by Cavellian irony than with the private theatricals of identity-formation itself. From a perspective like Greenblatt's, the tragic exit scene of any one dying hero on stage, with all that is sensed lost by such violence, would seem to forestall admission of a greater and definitional loss. Enter, of course, Foucault. The imitated plenary beings that give utterance to themselves on stage are the undead of humanism, yes, but we are their vampires as well—nostalgically feeding our own comforting illusions of presence. Shakespearean tragic heroes, that is, die for our sincerities, which have everywhere else lost their savor and faith. Their deaths hide the foregone conclusion of a greater Death: not of Christ, or even of God, but of the Human.

Like sex, violence is the exception that proves the rule of integrated—rather than dispersed and transgressive—human agency. Foucault is everywhere the guru of this thinking—and the phantom sparring partner with Cavell, I suspect, in a widespread impatience with the latter's terms. But this is a Foucault who has withdrawn so far behind the curtain as to leave his arguments as the very ether of received wisdom. The issue is no longer, as in Cavell, the perceiving subject setting out to theatricalize existence as its only way to know it, in distance and hence obliteration. The deeper issue, we are now shown, is that the subject is itself theatricalized from within, a construct and an enactment, or—in that most vitiated (and hence, one assumes, inimical) borrowing from Cavell's own master, J. L. Austin—a "performativity": the cogito replaced by something like "I do myself."

Cavell's terms could only seem entirely backward, in both senses, to the Foucauldian initiate as posthumanist. Instead of love, there is violence in Shakespeare, yes, which we are to think, via Cavell, betrays all that any kind of love, sexual included, would affirm. But we have been smartened up since Shakespeare's day. Sex, as is all the more obvious with love, is a discourse not a praxis, an armature of acculturation rather than its private chaotic remission. With a capital *S* for Signifier, Sex has been reified by the apparatuses of culture into a category, where otherwise its activity would be all too palpable and nonabstract. So, too, with violence. Where sex unsettles, violence punishes the body or mind at the additional expense, but also as the only proof, of the human spirit. Violation is everywhere in Shakespearean drama, this thinking would suggest, if only so that we might be a little more sure that there exists something to violate rather than merely to manipulate. It is also there so that, in recoil, we might even harbor thoughts of the inviolable. Watching characters who are "made up" on stage—invented and given face—and then driven to the limit of their existence, we are put in mind of all that we take, also on faith, to make us up. Under humanist ideology, then, character and role on stage do not deconstruct personhood but shore it up from the underside (projected as the inside) of dialogue.

I continue to undo some of the inferential knots that bind up this thinking into a programmatic view, with the full knowledge that any summary of the position may harden to a cartoon. But so can Cavell be reduced to a caricature from the other side. In any case, some general outlines of the rift remain discernible. Tragic violence comes center stage in Cavell as a figure for a world-annihilating skepticism, a forced distancing of the other, a killing dissociation. But this is to pull up short, according to a reading like Greenblatt's. Looking harder, we are meant to shred the veil of such tragic sentiment. Posed against all that desperation, cornered or crushed by such violence, surfaced as inference only by its own effacement, is the otherwise unstageable human essence. This makes tragic drama the ultimate sop to the attending mob. As an extreme form of two ideological shibboleths, individuality and privacy, the strain of tragic isolation is the cover story of ideology, masking a lack ingredient to the self and reified as a deficiency outside it. In this way is skepticism itself a problem manufactured by ideology as the very supplement of selfhood. In this way does Doubt get reified, set off as a problem *for* rather than *about* the self. Over against Cavell, skepticism emerges on this view as a prosthesis of the human subject rather than its greatest danger.

This is to say that if the problem of other minds is the secular displacement of the problem of God, as Cavell shows, this same problematic, lodged at the heart of humanism as its negative image, is a tactical displacement of the problem of my own mind. Ideological interpellation depends on me thinking I know my own mind, and therefore knowing myself to have one, so that I can seem to choose what is already imposed upon me, what constructs me. If I can cordon off from self-image my annihilating doubts about the reality of other minds, then in my walled vacuum (which is actually my Althusserian state prison), I am still deluded into thinking myself freely empowered, if only in my disaffection and retreat. That is why, we are asked to realize, characters on stage suffering to their utmost do not, as they do (among other things) for Cavell, make me accept (rather than insist on) my distance from them with an empathetic clarity denied to me in the encounter with real others. Rather, so one version of the constructivist position would object, by the merest verbal signs, and however much othered by distance, these stage figments seem to bespeak a metaphysical inwardness which, once we credit it in them, we borrow by osmosis for our own thoughts, to say nothing of our own utterance. If selves can be known through the symptoms of their expressive trouble and doubt and endurance, then so may we be known, even unto ourselves. *Suffero, ergo sum.*

On this account, skepticism about others, for Cavell the ultimate threat to something we might have called humanism, is in fact its soundest bulwark. The retrenchment against the skeptic's repudiation of the world posits as a betrayal of the other what is in fact a reflex warrantee of the self. To remain locked within the problematic of skepticism as Cavellian philosophy (as well as bourgeois culture) does, we are told to see, is a way of underwriting the autonomous self that skepticism would seem to eviscerate. In other words, all that exercised anxiety about skepticism is a rather direct way of buying into the ideological lie of "unaccommodated man" as a "bare, forked," organic, self-present entity—when in fact the human being is a threadbare split subject held in place by the accommodating templates of the social network.[24] Skepticism, therefore, despite all of Cavell's florid angst, should be embraced, we are asked to realize, as the halfway house to a deconstructed modern agency rather than impugned as a lethal depletion of spirit: a case of epistemic lucidity rather than a cause for grief.

But slow. If such objections do not seem quite to rise to the occasion of Lear's howling desolation, Othello's maddened grief, Leontes' contagious paralysis, Hamlet's tormented emptying-out of desire, and Antony's lethal absolutism, then Cavell might be holding onto something in the plays that is worth not losing. If Lear avoids the incestuous intensity of his desire by driving away the other kind of love its human vessel offers instead, all so as to avoid acknowledging his own dependency and need; and if Othello avoids survived marital consummation for the same reason, trying to make love into death so that he will not have to live with never being sure enough of such love in the other to keep it going in himself; and if Leontes steels (or stones) himself against acknowledging the love of wife and child so as not to have to doubt, or even to live in the tolerance of such potential doubt, their legitimate relation to himself; and if Hamlet avoids love under interdict of the primal scene and its ghostly entailments; and if Antony knows love only as a foregoing of the world, and hence a fatality—if all this seems plausible precisely because moving, then Cavell has made his case that these self-assignations with a tragic fate offer facets of the same historically rooted crisis of epistemology: a skeptical turn from the otherness of the world and the minds that people it. Though we do not have in print Cavell's views on the massive acceptance of the Death of Man hypothesis in literary discussion, one can only guess that its unexamined manifestation in study after study would strike him as doing what Shakespeare's tragic heroes do, if without the pain or eloquence: turning skepticism into a fanaticism in order to render it invulnerable to inner doubts about the very logic of its outer ones. This is to say that the referential skepticism everyone sees in linguistic deconstruction extends to antihumanist social critique as well, which thus stands in need of just that continued challenge it is likely to eschew in Cavell's Shakespeare book, among others.

In light of that book's very title, this is not just a case of disowning knowledge but also of disavowing whole ways of knowing through words. I am not making this up. The most recent student teacher whose class I visited, a doctoral candidate in literature, happened to be teaching *King Lear* that period and led students through their responses to the scene of Gloucester's blinding without ever opening the play during the hour, quoting a single line or phrase from it, or once mentioning metaphors or symbols of vision, either by name or concept. Apprentice scholars have other things on their minds these days, and the craft of reading slackens. The effects are generational, which is to say exponential. Students who have read only a little Foucault, taught by younger professors who have read with full enthusiasm little in criticism before him, are as likely to carry a grudge as a torch. The consequences spread beyond any specific political agenda, less mission than attrition. A political distrust of "great" writers has devolved into a disuse of great writing.

Yes, the philosophic author of *The Claim of Reason* has his reasons, anathema to some, for seeing skepticism as the dead end of human reason; but, worse for the circulation of these ideas, in reasoning them out he also makes claims on our attention of an untoward (because so pointed) kind, claims to which increasing numbers of literary scholars have trouble cultivating a response. In nervous backlash, the charge of abstruseness becomes a euphemism for "old-fashioned"—or the slur word for "too beautiful." When Cavell is at his hardest he may sound soft. In writing, as if discourse could either retain or usefully invent a human voice, writing as if he would agree, for instance, with Timothy Gould's way of reading him—as if there were the idea of a self left to be spoken for in that way—Cavell can seem to undermine the acceptance of his whole enterprise among the second-generation rank and file of social-materialist critics, not least because he makes just such assumptions *on the reader's behalf.* Recalcitrance feels co-opted as well as impatient.

We are nearing the heart of the issue, I am afraid. In a 1993 Bucknell University seminar printed alongside his published lectures on Wittgenstein, Emerson, Austin, and Derrida, an unidentified appreciative interlocutor is met more than halfway by Cavell: "When one reads Lacan one looks for hitching posts which allow you to oversee what you have read. I do something similar to that when I read your texts. I look for places where you make your discoveries."[25] Cavell: "And you have trouble finding them? That of course might be a sign of my failure to write or to think well enough. But it also might be a sign of my best success."[26] This as opposed to Lacan, one assumes. In Lacan, what one oversees from the hitching post is the whole much-tilled (if still rocky) methodological terrain. Seeking respite from the undulations of ruminative detail in Cavell, looking to see where he has driven his wedge or stake so that you can call it a post, even a signpost, you realize you have already been ambushed by an intuition from the far horizon before recognizing it as your own. Cavell continues in this ad hoc response to suggest that "what I want in writing philosophy [...] is to show that whatever discoveries are in store, they are not mine as opposed to yours, and in a certain sense not mine unless yours."[27]

Note Cavell's telltale phrase "in writing philosophy," which is not to say not doing it, of course, or not living it, but which is more than to say, for instance, "talking philosophy"—or "thinking philosophically." Philosophy is a textual practice. That is the way Cavell treats its history—and that is the way he enters it. This is a point expanded upon in a closing essay to the Bucknell lectures by Richard Fleming, where he highlights Cavell's stress on philosophy less as a set of problems to be solved than as a set of texts to be read.[28] But read how? Philosophically? Literarily? For Cavell, of course, literary textuality writes philosophically, and should be read that way, when it tackles those crises in language or relationship to which, in its separate sphere, philosophy, when locating them as problems, has thought to propose solutions—where it has in fact been (like literature in its different way) simply generating texts about them.

The question remains: how to write—and read—such texts within what permissive (or transmissive) limits. In his reply to John Hollander's grandly appreciative review essay of *The Claim of Reason*, Cavell was moved—or should we say remotivated?—to find that the poet-critic Hollander was responding to something both poetic and novelistic in Cavell's prose, since lacking "such perceptions of the fact of my writing, of a reality to its ambitions, it would have no way to achieve the ground of conviction it aspires to."[29] The point is reprised in a more complex way a few years later, where it is clear that the "ground of conviction" is not external to the writing act, not a matter of audience but of immanent force. In a headnote to the reply to Hollander when reprinted in *Themes Out of School*, Cavell recalls his gratification by explaining "that I look for the conviction of others in what I say only to the extent that I can manifest my own conviction by it."[30] This could well seem inside out. Only if he meant what he said could he expect others to be convinced by it: that would be the ordinary road of argumentative cogency in philosophical or critical discourse, a one-way street. In Cavell's suasive circuit, though, other minds must fund or replenish the perception as if at its source. And what is this but the literary moment par excellence, intensively "voiced" so as to be the more readily ventriloquized by the reader's own participation? It was in the same year as *Must We Mean What We Say?* one recalls, that Georges Poulet famously said of reading and its transfers of consciousness that I become "the subject of thoughts other than my own."[31] Cavell would return those thoughts to us as our own after all.

And he would return them for the best of reasons, which is to say for reasons that go to the undernoticed crux of his entire writerly ambition. To admit to the fantasy of writing a prose that will be read by others as if they had thought of it themselves is not a rhetorical vaunt, let alone a sleight of hand, but rather the lodging of a phenomenological hypothesis—to be tested on the pulse of every new reading. It is therefore directly to the (missed) point here that Cavell's sustained contemplation of the image in Thoreau of "heroic books" as like "stars" in a textual firmament, so that "they who can may read them," has not been taken up either by the thinning ranks of literary phenomenology (or for that matter its critics) or even by such practitioners of a psychoanalytic narratology as Peter Brooks.[32] The invitation remains ripe. For what Cavell educes from this master trope in Thoreau is a sense that stars are the least impersonal of texts, since it is in them that we read our own fates. As the astrological figure becomes a philosophical paradigm, so might it have also deserved account in the proliferating work on literary transference and countertransference, since for Cavell, amplifying Thoreau, it is the truest work of a text, in the act of reading, to read and interpret us. Hermeneutics gets reversed to cognitive therapeutics. As argued into the open here by Cavell, and as infusing the very texture of his writing in many other places, this is nonetheless a philosophically grounded view of literature's reciprocal interchange gone unnoted by traditional reception theory as well as by the latest wave of psychopoetics—and left instead, in the best of hands at that, to the gripping last chapter of Timothy Gould's philosophical commentary.

So much for literary roads not taken. Lately, we are often faced with the more immediate problem of no one at the wheel. In my lingering over this, time has come for a disclaimer. It could never sensibly have been the burden of this essay to suggest that all lines of recent literary inquiry conspire to diverge from Stanley Cavell's unique intersection of philosophy and literature. A good deal of common cause has been lost, it seems clear, but this is no place for exaggeration or lament. Symptoms of hermeneutic decline hold the interest of these reflections only as they can help us, by default, to a clearer perspective on the operative logic of Cavell's whole program, its implicit and pervasive theory of reading. Indeed, given Cavell's abiding allegiance to the phenomenological grip of literary writing as bearing the potential for philosophical inquiry, he might well be among the first to agree that the risk of his own going unread is the least of the problems for so-called departments of English at this methodological juncture. It is the status of literary reading per se that is in peril, enervated by the very critiques that (in the first flush of New Historicism) drove reading to such voracious intake outside the literary canon. Let me make plain the sliding scale of negative associations that have attached to the literary object in whose spirited "profession" Cavell once helped instruct his academic neighbors. When read too brilliantly, a Shakespeare or a Thoreau may end up seeming inimical to all those who resist power in its every form, including the power of humanist eloquence. And not least because of the invasive power of such eloquence to render up images of ourselves. This is, however, a whole new level of retreat from the latent seductions of the literary signifier. Deconstructive reading, in its furiously literate heyday, used to be called against-the-grain reading. Rubbing literary texture the wrong way, exposing its weave and nap, roughening its surface, was at least a way of noticing that surface. But suspicious antihumanist reading is different. The ideologically compromised literary effect is now kept at arm's length, often hermetically sealed off from any detailed notice. The suspect becomes the distanced. And reading without closeness is the very rejection of what Cavell would mean by reading.

Over a decade ago now, and already looking back on years of wavering interdisciplinary response, Cavell wrote:

> I become perplexed in trying to determine whether it is to addicts of philosophy or to adepts of literature that I address myself when I in effect insist that Shakespeare could not be who he is—the burden of the name of the greatest writer in the language, the creature of the greatest ordering of English—unless his writing is engaging the depth of philosophical preoccupations of his culture.[33]

Leaving aside whether the "ordering of English" remains a shared concern at all for the newer "adept" of literary *qua* cultural study, how was one ever to write (as well as to think) that insistence on the "Shakespearean" from across a disciplinary border? Cavell further puts the question to himself this way:

> Is the issue of communication between philosophy and literature itself a philosophical or a literary issue? Something mannerly and no doubt something unmannerly in my prose is caused by acceptance of such a question and by my refusal to decide it prematurely, to decide it judiciously ('It is both'), or to decide that it is undecidable ('It is neither quite'), before closing with it, keeping it open, enacting it, experimenting.[34]

In Cavell's best moments, as in that last capping run of verbal apposition sprung from latent paradox ("closing" / "open"), syntactic structure "enacts" the drive of its own onrushing thought.

To write this way is to command reading closely—which is the answer to his own perplexity, once rephrased. If Cavell writes neither exactly philosophy nor exactly literary criticism, maybe what he writes is in fact literature.[35] I almost said just plain literature, but what I would have meant even then is literature in its most complex form, where demand and reward are interchangeable. And not, of course, literature as opposed to philosophy. Instead, Cavell outstrips all truisms about the wedding of form and content in any discourse to generate a mode of writing more keenly inductive (versus propositional) than most philosophic exposition—but no less conceptually pressured: a mode and a *mood* of writing where the ordinariness of language is estranged from within (the old formalist benchmark in a new philosophic valence). In Cavell's writing just as in literary prose, argument and articulation grow indissoluble *at the level of affect*—and hence of conviction. And if literature is thus one fair answer to the question about what it is that he writes, then this would be the first and most obvious reason why mainstream literary scholars will increasingly have a hard time with Stanley Cavell, not as an interloper but as a challenge for which the skills and the taste and the very aspiration have atrophied. In the epoch of cultural studies, discourse analysis, and the semiotics of social energy, what are called legible texts do not exactly require what we once called reading at all. And to set out merely to *decode*, rather than to encounter along the very contours of expression, the writing of a Cavell or, for that matter, an Emerson is to give up the game in advance.

After so jaundiced a view of the downhill slide in institutionalized literary study, I can be forgiven the need for an upbeat finish. Though undeniably providing litmus tests of our current academic malaise, Cavell's pages offer, more importantly in the long run, its tonic alternative. The year was 1971, and not being a Shakespeare scholar, I suspect I had not yet come upon the *King Lear* essay in *Must We Mean What We Say?* But I well remember the thrilling feel of a single reading moment three paragraphs from the end of Cavell's brief and inexhaustible book on film, just out.[36] This was *The World Viewed*, the play of its very title literary through and through. The moment in question was a response to the last shots of Carl Dreyer's *Joan of Arc* (1928), where the camera leaves behind a close-up of Joan at the stake for her own sighting of birds that "wheel over her with the sun in their wings."[37] *In* their wings, not *on*: a most Wordsworthian internalization. The literary is already in full swing, linked to the sense of cinematic epiphany. On view is film's indexical record of a world surviving death—as well as the marked symbol of a personal resurrection. From the immolation of one life arises the immanence of a larger life of which the martyr has until now been a part. And more—which mostly goes unsaid, intuited between the lines, between the words. In death, there is always continuance. As an immortality machine, film is the true medium of this secularized perpetuity. Those birds go on holding the attention of prose as well as camera in this tacit four-word ontology of all projected screen presence: "They, there, are free."[38] What is this but philosophy as criticism as poetry? The instantaneously eroded grammatical space between the nominative and the locative, between pronominal subject and its free and separate adverbial placement, arranges that one word should get phonetically detached from the other as the very microdrama of release in a monosyllabic theater of phrase. In the further swift gust of the verb across the cadenced swoop of "ey / ere / are," we audit on the underside of writing a pervasive "air," the subliminal breath of airiness itself, all but spelled out as the medium of uplift.

As those numbering ourselves among Cavell's captive audience know full well, this is the kind of prose flight that can readily be set loose, whether in a smiting brevity or a heady dilation, on any page of his work. As exactly a measure of his "best success," it is the kind of thing that takes your breath away with thoughts you did not know you had until they seem drawn forth, already worded, from the back of / your mind—and worded just ordinarily enough in their surprise to ring true. Even in this academic latter day and age, they still await the attuned reader. They, there, are free: yours for the taking, both in and up.

Notes

1 See Stanley Cavell, *Must We Mean What We Say? A Book of Essays* (New York: Charles Scribner's Sons, 1969; Cambridge: Cambridge University Press, 1976), 267–356.

2 Michael Fischer, *Stanley Cavell and Literary Skepticism* (Chicago: University of Chicago Press, 1989), xii, where Fischer notes of Cavell's apparent dim hearing among "literary theorists": "Despite Cavell's long-standing indebtedness to literature, not very much has been written about him" (ibid.). Reasons are sought in the remaining chapters on theory's refusal of "the ordinary," a concept central to Cavell's deliberations.

3 Stephen Melville, "Oblique and Ordinary: Stanley Cavell's Engagements of Emerson," *American Literary History*, vol. 5, no. 1 (Spring 1993): 172.

4 Stanley Cavell, *Conditions Handsome and Unhandsome: The Constitution of Emersonian Perfectionism* (Chicago: University of Chicago Press, 1990). Widening the circle of Otherness beyond human agency does no more to rope Cavell's thinking into recent debate. It is only the latest sign of methodological disconnect that when Thoreau is wrenched free from both literary and philosophical consideration in the interests of deep ecology and ecocentrist theory, he is entirely—and counterproductively—detached at the same time from a potential Cavellian model whereby rethinking precisely skepticism's defensive epistemological distance from the world might have helped, just might, to philosophize a nonanthropocentric rapport with the biological economies of the planet. The possibility would at least have been worth posing. Cavell's powerful writing on Thoreau in *The Senses of Walden* (New York: Viking, 1972), however, goes utterly unmentioned in the roughly two dozen cited studies, not all of them late-breaking by any means, that find their way into a two-part *New York Review of Books* overview of the current naturalist debate on Thoreau by Americanist Leo Marx, "The Struggle over Thoreau," June, 24 1999, 60–64; and "The Full Thoreau," July 15, 1999, 44–48. The story is not as full as it seems.

5 Cary Wolfe, "Alone with America: Cavell, Emerson, and the Politics of Individualism," *New Literary History*, vol. 25, no. 1 (Winter 1994): 135–57.

6 Emily Miller Budick, "Sacvan Bercovitch, Stanley Cavell, and the Romance Theory of American Fiction," in *Cohesion and Dissent in America*, ed. Carol Colatrella and Joseph Alkan (New York: State University of New York Press, 1994), 48–73. For appreciative readings of Cavell's Americanist thinking less immediately concerned to defend Cavell against tacit detraction, see Giles Gunn, who correlates Cavell's project with that of neo-pragmatist literary critic Richard Poirier, in *Thinking Across the American Grain: Ideology, Intellect, and the New Pragmatism* (Chicago: University of Chicago Press, 1992), 146–49; and Barbara Packer, "Turning to Emerson," *Common Knowledge*, vol. 5, no. 2 (Fall 1996): 51–60; whose own acquired taste for Emerson is traced out along lines of the conversionary experience—reading as the overcoming of resistance—detailed in Cavell's own approach to Emerson. See also Sharon Cameron, "The Way of Life by Abandonment: Emerson's Impersonal," *Critical Inquiry*, vol. 25 (Autumn 1998): 1–31, where Cavell's confrontation of philosophy with autobiography (28 n. 36) is correlated with her sense of Emersonian negotiations between the impersonal and the subjective.

7 Budick, "Sacvan Bercovitch, Stanley Cavell, and the Romance Theory of American Fiction," 59.

8 Ibid., 60.

9 It seems exactly right that one of the rare engagements with Cavell here and directly against Derrida, would come from the language poet and critic Charles Bernstein, with his own hypersensitive car for Wittgenstein's language games. In "Reading Cavell Reading Wittgenstein", *boundary 2*, vol. 9, no. 2 (Winter 1981): 295–306, Bernstein finds support in Cavell for his sense of Derrida's work as "the philosophy of paranoia" (304). He explains: "The lesson of metaphysical finitude is not that the world is just codes and as a result that presence is to be ruled out as anything more than nostalgia, but that we can have presence, insofar as we are able, only *through* a shared grammar" (ibid.), which is to say, via Cavell, only through keeping alive the possibility of reading, not only each other but ourselves.

10 Timothy Gould, *Hearing Things: Voice and Method in the Writing of Stanley Cavell* (Chicago: University of Chicago Press, 1998), 2.

11 Gould, *Hearing Things*, xii.

12 Ibid., 1.

13 Ibid., 108–10.

14 Richard P. Wheeler, "Acknowledging Shakespeare: Cavell and the Claim of the Human," in *The Senses of Stanley Cavell*, ed. Richard Fleming and Michael Payne (Lewisburg: Bucknell University Press, 1989), 132–60. For the engagement of a general literary theorist, rather than a Shakespearean scholar with Cavell's book, sec Gerald L. Bruns, "Stanley Cavell's Shakespeare," *Critical Inquiry*, vol. 16, no. 3 (Spring 1990): 612–32.

15 Wheeler, "Acknowledging Shakespeare," *The Senses of Stanley Cavell*, 136–37.

16 Ibid., 136.

17 See Stephen Greenblatt, "Shakespeare and the Exorcists," *Shakespeare and the Question of Theory*, ed. Patricia Parker and Geoffrey Hartman (New York: Methuen, 1985), 163–87, an essay which nowhere mentions Cavell's landmark reading of the play even though Greenblatt's later encomium on the back cover of *Disowning Knowledge*—and here is another symptomic disjuncture in the "use" of Cavell—celebrates the essays as "thrilling and essential reading."

18 Wheeler, "Acknowledging Shakespeare," *The Senses of Stanley Cavell*, 159 n. 28.

19 Stanley Cavell, *Disowning Knowledge in Six Plays of Shakespeare* (Cambridge: Cambridge University Press, 1987), 72.

20 See Stanley Cavell, *The World Viewed: Reflections on the Ontology of Film* (New York: Viking Press, 1971; Cambridge, MA: Harvard University Press, expanded edition, 1979). See also Garrett Stewart, "Assertions in Techniques': Tracking the Medial 'Thread' in Cavell's Filmic Ontology," in *The Thought of Stanley Cavell and Cinema: Turning Anew to the Ontology of Film a Half-Century after* The World Viewed," ed. David LaRocca (New York: Bloomsbury, 2020), 23–40.

21 Cavell, *Disowning Knowledge*, 104.

22 A recent book by Judy Kronenfield called *King Lear and the Naked Truth: Rethinking the Language of Religion and Resistance* (Durham: Duke University Press, 1998) makes this all too clear. Despite Cavell's probing speculations on the Christian subtext of the play, and, what is more, his project's overall sense of "the problem of the other as the replacement of the problem of god" (*Disowning Knowledge*, 11), Kronenfield makes no mention whatever of his writing in the

index or the voluminous list of cited works. This at least has the virtue of the naked truth. For, there is in fact no point of contact, in this self-avowed study of historical semiotics, with the reach of Cavell's thinking, even when it might impinge directly (but aslant) on the author's chosen material.

23   Cavell, *Disowning Knowledge*, 16.

24   Shakespeare, *King Lear*, 3.4.99.

25   Stanley Cavell, *Philosophical Passages: Wittgenstein, Emerson, Austin, Derrida* (Oxford: Blackwell, 1995), 85.

26   Cavell, *Philosophical Passages*, 85.

27   Ibid. [Ed.] Cavell continues: "Which doesn't mean that in writing I am not *doing* something, something for which, the better done it is, the less I should expect credit. No wonder I once or twice wrote about the pain of unacknowledgment" (ibid.; italics in original).

28   Ibid., 109.

29   Stanley Cavell, "A Reply to John Hollander," *Critical Inquiry*, vol. 6, no. 4 (Summer 1980): 589–91; reprinted in Stanley Cavell, *Themes Out of School: Effects and Causes* (San Francisco: North Point, 1984), 141–44; 142.

30   Cavell, "A Reply to John Hollander," *Themes Out of School*, 141.

31   Georges Poulet, "Phenomenology of Reading," *New Literary History*, vol. 1 (October 1969): 56.

32   For Cavell on this passage in Thoreau, see *In Quest of the Ordinary: Lines of Skepticism and Romanticism* (Chicago: University of Chicago Press, 1988), 16. For the complicities of invested and displaced identification in the reading act, as often foregrounded by frame narratives, see Peter Brooks, *Reading for the Plot: Design and Intention in Narrative* (New York: Knopf, 1984) and *Psychoanalysis and Storytelling* (Oxford: Blackwell, 1994).

33   Cavell, *Disowning Knowledge*, 2.

34   Ibid., 3.

35   This is a suspicion lent weight by Timothy Gould's thorough case (see n. 10 above) for the Cavellian task of language as deliberately "producing an illumination that is hard to capture in a paraphrase" (34). Not only do you have to have been there, reading along, but to just this extent Cavell's own writing rises to the literary standard whose chief violation in the axioms of New Criticism was indeed "the heresy of paraphrase."

36   [Ed.] Stewart initially encountered the first edition of *The World Viewed* (1971, which concluded with the chapter, "The Acknowledgment of Silence,"); "More of *The World Viewed*" was added to the enlarged edition in 1979. In a moment of enlarging his own critical attentions to the original ending of *The World Viewed*, Stewart has since elaborated upon a truncated allusion to "They, there, are free" in an interview for the journal *Philosophical Investigations*; see David LaRocca, "'It's All There in the Language'—A Conversation with Garrett Stewart," special issue, "Literature and Philosophy," ed. K. L. Evans and David Rozema, *Philosophical Investigations*, vol. 47, no. 3 (2024): 278–97. Invited to recall, in more detail, what had moved him so much about Cavell's phrasing in *The World Viewed*, Stewart expanded on its once and enduring power. He thought back to "what I might have called the self-aerated cadence of 'They, there, are free,' where, across the slide of the long-*a* note ('They/the[re]') and the othering distance it serves to enact from within this shifting differential—sounding out unspelled

the 'air' of their levitation—the birds, not in the same sense as the martyr in her imminent release from earth, are seen (and thanks to Cavell, all but heard) winging their way in the longer *ee* of freewheeling flight, this time without vocalic stoppage in a consonant." From philosophy to popular song, it is a similar kind of levitated mimetic syllabification that Stewart repeatedly audits in his most recent monograph, *Streisand: The Mirror of Difference* (2023), via high-note notations on the interpretive work of the singer's legendary vocal delivery, an "acoustic prism" in its own right—and, under which title below (chapter 4), he returns now to one of his home bases, nineteenth-century poetry and poetics, for the first of the new essays in Part II.

37   Cavell, *The World Viewed*, 159.
38   Ibid.

II

RENEWED VENTURES

4 / Returning to the aggressively granular rhetorical challenges, syllabically impacted, of Gerard Manley Hopkins' poetry for the first time since his 1990 book *Reading Voices: Literature and the Phonotext* (University of California Press), Stewart engages with the incremental phonetic density of both Hopkins' "sprung rhythm" and the pacings of his (somewhat) more conventional sonnets. What results is a rethinking of the famous inscape/instress circuit of ontological apprehension. Such thematics are explored here as model not just for the world's "pied beauty" in variegated recognition, but also for the transfer of differential optic contours to the *acoustic* prism of vocalization, the phonetic manifestation of which Stewart proffers as the intoned vehicle of written wor(d)ship: a resounding "inpress" that remains "markedly scriptive in the very grain of its spirituality."

4 / *Gerard Manley Hopkins' Phonetic Script*

"FIAT LUX" WENT THE WORD. And from the split prism of its infinite lucidity were spread out—and in poetic devotion separately *read out*—the divergent features and colors of the *made* world. That's one way to imagine the faith and aesthetic, at once and at one, of Victorian Jesuit convert and verse revisionist Gerard Manley Hopkins (1844–89). Well before an invitation to a 2024 symposium in Ireland, where he spent his last days, I had long been ready for a full-throated (even if mostly subvocal) return to the phonics of his "inscriptive practice." I call it that, so heavily, because, though its effects are "signature" in the extreme, "style" seems too light a word for his verbal exertions—and exactions. It would best apply only if the stylus is understood as a scalpel probing the integument of vitality's own shifting surfaces under his favored diagnostics of "instress," explicitly phenomenological before phrasal. Yet the linguistic sense of style is at the same time irresistible in what is, first and last, a "devotional practice" in words.

Decades back, my 1990 book *Reading Voices* came into close conversation, when briefly discussing Hopkins, with linguist James Milroy's chapter, in his book on the poet's verbal technique, called "Read with the Ear."[1] Borrowed from Hopkins' own injunction to poet, correspondent, and eventual editor Robert Bridges, the emphasis of Milroy's title (either way: assonant imperative or short-vowel descriptor) helped me put forward Hopkins' eccentric vocal calisthenics as exemplary (if not central) to my survey of the "phonotext" and its thematic fallout. The poet's mutating chromatic aurality—his graded, shaved phrasings realized in transit as what I now think of as discrete acoustic prisms—emerged as so obviously prone to the cross-word phenomenon I was auditing as to exhaust their own illustrative relevance well short of a fuller authorial appreciation. Given the flux of script's phonic activation in Hopkins, sufficient to the day seemed the cited lexical erosions and acoustic soak-throughs to which sounded script is prey—and in exactly those licensed slippages and blurs of literary writing mobilized with such abandon by Hopkins. If this way of saying so is noted to mix the metaphor of fluid dynamics with that of prismatic faceting, all the truer it might seem to the premium placed in Hopkins on pied perception, where variegation is one measure, one metered reflex, of complexity's divine(d) artifice. To mix again the collateral tropes of multifaceting and propulsive admixture with the language, this time, of tensile mechanics, one begins to sense how sprung rhythm, in its broadest sense as the torque and contortion required in giving the world a keener hearing, depends at base on the elastic slip-knots of this poet's intensified syllabic meshwork.

How should we listen to—and through—the launching word lists of a poem, one asks for instance, in which an ordinary evening sky, this from the opening line of "Spelt from Sybil's Leaves," is summoned as "Earnest, earthless, equal, attuneable, vaulty, voluminous, . . . stupendous" (the sprung accent taking its elliptical breath for the vault itself)? And then how audit in the second line—as if burst from the *lumin / stupen* gradience—a sunset energy (braced for the revved-up stress by comma and accent alike this time) that "strains to be time's vást, womb-of-all, home-of-all, hearse-of-all night"?[2] If the accentual stress on "womb," marked there at its onset, can't entirely prevent the apt cross-word anticipation of "hearse" in the faintly associated "vas*t womb*," then gradience may seem more narrowly ingredient to Hopkins' effects, cross-lexical included, than otherwise acknowledged.

Splintered and resutured lexemes are only the stress fractures—their syllabic shards instantly regrouped—incident to a broader acoustic "instress" (Hopkins' most mobile of coinages) as it stretches the nerve ends of attention in the molding of an embodied cognizance. Proposed here, then, is a disposition of reading more broadly transactional than narrowly sacral, concerned with instress as it seeks ex-pression through s/pied beauty's restless amanuensis in Hopkins. With regard to such phenomenological transcription, one fringe-benefit (or say prismatic edge-benefit) of this approach, especially when lending its keynote to the volume as a whole, comes from the phono/graphic optics of *refraction* in verbal form. The effects I'll be focusing on, under a variably raking light, are all familiar enough to the tantalized ear of a Hopkins reader. In accounts of the poet's specialized sonorities, however, they often (if it's useful to phrase it this way) tend to be heard at large without being really *seen*: registered on the undulant run rather than localized where—and so why—they are *legibly* taking place. Full recognition results instead from attending, more closely than usual, to the semantic inscription rather than just the metrical and phonetic folds of a ruffled line—where understanding is found (only when) engaging, rather than just discerning, the line's concentrated weft of echoes, its inner syllabic ligatures, its s/cryptic over-runs. Only then do the unmistakable aural slants and stratifications of Hopkins' poetics serve to pinpoint the thematizing work of a read *writing* under analytic refraction.

Stressed In, Read Out

TO RETURN TO HOPKINS now is for me to locate him even more directly—if never, in his phrasal vacillations, quite firmly—in the company of the earlier Romantic poets with whose pervasive phonic texture I had originally leagued his more drastic experiments. In this sense John Keats' little-discussed phrasing for subjective engagement with intangible phenomena—recently giving the title to Susan J. Wolson's searching and definitive treatment of his verse in *A Greeting of the Spirit*[3]—comes to literary-historical mind. The Keatsian principle can seem suggestively aligned—even along a different axis of welcoming address (poetry toward vocalizing audience in Hopkins; creative mind toward hazy idea in Keats)—with the later poet's even less investigated notion of "bidding" rather than "greeting." When scholarship goes, like this, to the personal letters of the artists for such provocative terms, the epistolary remarks can seem themselves posted directly to us as literary readers, orienting response. For Keats, as he writes to a friend in March 1818, the creative mind must reach out in a gesture (instress?) of its own so as to animate what might otherwise seem vaporous abstractions. Poetry in Keats can be understood, so Wolfson closely instances, as this greeting of the amorphous with verbal form—and thereafter greeting a reader with the text's materialized salutations in the sound of words. In Hopkins, the essential interface of poetic summons is located in a more direct and importunate "bidding": instress called up by phrasal involutions in transfer to the reader's intimate (because enunciated) recognition.

Here, then, is Keats to his letter-reader on the role of imagination and its language to vitalize the intangible—namely: "Things semireal such as Love, the Clouds &c" that "require a greeting of the Spirit to make them wholly exist."[4] Poetry provides the meeting ground of any such inferred solicitation. And no more explicit about any direct bearing of his terminology on the making of poetry, here is Hopkins in a late letter to Robert Bridges (November 4, 1882) on language reaching out to its audience in "oratory and drama," but also tacitly in a poetics concerned with an already greeted and God-given world. Being a thing of the "first importance" in oral art, according to Hopkins, of which we know he wants to include his own poetry and its sprung rhythms, "I sometimes call it *bidding*. I mean the art or virtue of saying everything right *to* or *at* the hearer, interesting him, holding him in the attitude of correspondent or addressed or at least concerned [...]."[5] Art in this sense as the greeting of our secondary attention—of which Victorian fiction's "Dear reader" is an alternate epistolary derivative; so, too, the typically displaced apostrophes of the Romantic ode: keeping the inferred reader—well within the circuit of rhetoric—at no more than one tightly leashed remove from hailed nature.[6] Hopkins continues his sentence on the power of bidding, of audience inclusion, in the work of such performed text: "making it everywhere an act of intercourse—and of discarding everything that does not bid, does not tell. I think one may gain much of this by practice."[7] And to vary this last sentence: gain much *by* this practice, even in other arts of the in-voiced. As for instance in the recitational theater of his "kaleidophonic" (prismatic by any name) lexicon, syntax, and metrics.

Extrapolating from these two very different nineteenth-century moments in Keats and Hopkins, neither pointedly about the drive of their own poetics, should nonetheless lay the foundation for a clearer and ultimately reflexive estimate of the "inscape"/"instress" coupling so much more central than "bidding" to the time-tested appreciation of the latter's writing. Yet those dominant tandem terms in Hopkins for the inwarding—the in-wording—of poetic witness take on a new perspective when heard filtered through his own version of an off-angle Keatsian "greeting"—of the elusive phenomenal world through secondary verbal apprehension—if only when fully actualized at the resulting scene of bidden reading. Always in its difficulty a bit forbidding–yet whose transliterated wordscapes, in all their over-runs, it is not likely one will "over read."[8] Time and again in Hopkins, the self-illustrative rhyming habit of a hovering "rove over" (rovover) principle would seem applicable to *in-jammings*, as it were, within (across) poetry's looped or knotted lines as well as between them: overovings that fashion unexpected ties (in the musical sense) that bind and build from within.[9] If this essay is interpretively unnerved by any one verbal freak of Hopkins' poetics, and thus tempted to register it as epitomizing, it is this: that his enjambments are by no means always a resistance to linear end-jam. In tracing the world's inscape, the poet's transcriptive instress fudges edges everywhere, between syntactic phrasing (and latent overflow rhyme) at line's end, yes, but also at the internal switch points of normal sequential wording, separable letters, phonic afterimages in the span of grammar. One result is that the internal gradience of forward-leaning slant rhyme often develops its own continuum with overrun echo, overhyme. Detached phonemes can seem hoved over or hovered over in the very shoves and latches of syntax. As further evidence should make clear, the conveyed instress of phenomenal inscape in evoking—evocalizing—the world's pied beauties can be described as a matter, often enough, of stressed *injambment*.

A further case in point is in order, moving beyond the gestalt alternatives (gestalterity) of the transegmental eith/or. To this end, the anagrams to which Hopkins gravitates (if only approximate for the most part) can be as suggestive as any transgram. Each is a scramble of language displaced from, in order to replay, the world's own mottled variation or inconstancy. Take the exacerbated phonetic evidence (pending next) in Hopkins' poem "That Nature is a Heraclitean Fire," with its slant match of onset rather than end rhymes, where the radical evanescence of the earth's surface is conveyed by double (or serial) effacement: first marked, before its blotting out, by weather-beaten damage and the crush of human trampling respectively, each soon expunged in turn by the literal wind of change. Here's a five-line sentence to this effect, where the thematic ephemerality unfolds in phonetics.

> Delightfully the bright wind boisterous ropes, wrestles, beats earth bare
> Of yestertempest's creases; in pool and rut peel parches
> Squandering ooze to squeezed dough, crust, dust; stanches, starches
> Squadroned masks and manmarks treadmire toil there
> Footfretted in it.

Not just sprung meter is "footfretted" here, but the rush and crush of syntax itself.

In summoning the leveling aftereffects of such windsweep, the poet's phrasing avoids (even while evoking) the fate of all things explicitly quashed or squashed in a shift from the oblique diction of "Squandering ooze" in one line (for the erasure of a "yestertempest" ravage) to the same effacing fate for collective human "treadmire" in the next line's even odder opening term, "Squadroned," for everyday human transit. Gradience, we may say, has here aggravated its commutational juggle across a cryptic distancing gap whereby, in front-rhyme rather than end-rhyme, the overdetermined and doubly unmotivated squandr/squadrn doublet seems anagrammatically strained to replay, in and between the syllabic underlay of an almost imponderable description, the ineluctable Heraclitean flux in question. So friable is Hopkins' phrasing in this evocation that the caking and flaking extends even to alphabetic structure. After the pulverization of "crust" to "dust," the parallel (*st*-ed) but non-assonant pairing "stanches, starches" has its way of enacting, in orthography itself, the crumbling surrender—beyond alliteration to *deletteration*—of the downstroked *n* to a broken *r*.[10] In this elemental vortex of upheaval, watered earth plus blighting wind figure in combination, under the poem's classic trope, the self-consuming nature of the title's metaphoric fire in an erosive dynamic that is more a raw force *of* (than *for*) change, molecular in implied scale. Generalizing further: in the commute between the ontology of form and the philology of its reinscription—exactly the route to be most traveled across the graduated aural mutations sounded in the coming Hopkins texts—anagram stands forth as a limit case of the phrasing's own *inscape* in demolition and stressed reassemblage.

Such phonemic shuffling is one of the stylistic options Hopkins wants to speak more categorically about—and does. Even by title, his "Poetry and Verse" implies—in regard to his continuing experiments in the sprung rhythm of accentual prosody—the subordinate place of traditional verse form in the capacious pacings of a more spontaneous, free-form poetics, as demanding as it is liberated.[11] But how, to this end, does that extra margin of phrasal inscape by which a more "natural" poetics exceeds the doctrinaire regularities of verse—how does this enhanced metrical vocation, together with its contorted vocables, become directly instrumental, for the linguistic ministrations of this devout poet, in leveraging immersive participation in such divinely sanctioned otherness as his writing takes as topic? For answers, I turn to individual poems with an ear to how the privileged dappled texture of evocation has organized itself for reception not just as devotional testament but as structured differential text: a thing whose instress is *heard* as pied as soon as spied. For it is in this way, and conveyed in a self-illustrative grammar of incremental apposition, that "repetition, *oftening, over-and-overing, aftering* must take place to detach it to the mind."[12] Not "detached" *from* its essence but freed "to" mental perception as such, the created is realized (released) in the creative.

And freed in this same way even when the text, by topic, seems under mimetic constraint to hold its tongue. Gradient sound play is so pressing in Hopkins that it can resound from the midst of its own thematic exclusion, an instress penetrating even quiescence. The result may best be appreciated as a mode of contra-pun-tal pacing. In a little-cited tribute to modest sanctification as opposed to bloody martyrdom, the sonnet "In Honour of St. Alphonsus Rodriguez" names in the sestet the perfectly phrased "trickling increment" by which God "Veins violets and tall trees makes more and more." So with certain modes of sacred heroism. Such accretion can be clocked even there—as hinted by that quintessential phrase's own acoustic knot—by the *tinkling* aggregates of the phonotext, as so palpably audited under erasure in the last line of the octave. Not for Alphonsus the ringing repute of crusading exploits or violent sacrifice. For, "be the battle within," such selfless devotion unfolds unheeded. Were it not, that is, for the urgent poetry of verse. "Earth hears no hurtle then from fiercest fray"—even while sounds of another sort reverb across the "ear" silenced in "earth" only to be dialed up in "hears" before "hurtle" plays against the un-*heard* in the self-swallowed clang of "*fier*cest." Embedded and tamped down, spiritually muted, still the drumbeat of such textual music plays on across a conjured selfless faith remote from the world's noise.

With the "trickling increments" of Hopkins' more colorful (or say chromatically scaled) sonnets, what we are to find is that the spin of unfettered lettering—rolling one hyphen-flared double-take of perception over into the next particolored combine—is a lexigraphic melange limned in tribute to a world myriad, brimming, mingled, glad with contrast. To recast this process in the kind of alphabetic enchainment by which Hopkins repeatedly envisages such cognitive linkages and alignments, a case of *instressed* perception can be held to name, by near-miss phonetic anagram, the defining *interest* we take in the in(fra)scape of being(s): the concentration bestowed under the auspices, and in the cadences, of awe. In the circuit of depicted inscape and our sympathetic instress, it is thus that the indwelling wells up in us. What we are bidden by are not just the poem's words in address but the phenomena whose shapes they often rush to inhabit in evocation. So, then: if the thronged instances to come from Hopkins' work—confirming his stated desire to have his poetry spoken out, not just inwardly read—make any generalization about its multitudinous phonic sensorium seem premature, it may nonetheless be worth distilling in anticipation a single main claim about the intent (and exemplified intensities) of this essay in regard to the inscape/instress crux. The purpose is not to sidetrack the question of ontology by shifting it to poetics, but to see the latter as the only textual manifestation of the former. If, in the poet's unabashed personification of his text, as we'll find, the page's very "paper" (not author) should be understood to chant its own litany of the worded world, in a function more medial than priestly, then the best lens for listening is the acoustic prism.

Syllabic ClaSP / RUNG Rhythm

IT IS IMPOSSIBLE TO READ the little songs of this Victorian hieratic sonneteer and not wonder—or, better, not guess—why so much palpable word*ing* goes, oftening and aftering, into finding words for nature's revelation: a wording syllabic and subsyllabic, intensively graphophonemic in the technical linguistic sense. Impossible not to hear how the effort amounts to conjuring— self-demonstrably—the integral form of natural forces, entities, and animated panoramas as citations from the open page of God's Book, textualized through and through. And thus impossible not to guess in such reading that poetry so corrugated and recursive, so tucked, puckered, and buckled, is one long onomatopoeia for the Logos in filtered intermittent manifestation across the sung things of existence. In pursuing the inscape/instress circuit of phenomenological (via phonemic) response to the world in Hopkins, one could do worse than cast it in a modern idiom. Each natural thing does its thing: tuned to its own divinely bestowed instress in performance and transmission.

> As kingfishers catch fire, dragonflies draw flame;
>   As tumbled over rim in roundy wells
>   Stones ring; like each tucked string tells, each hung bell's
> Bow swung finds tongue to fling out broad its name;

The quotients of similitude—"as" crosshatched with "like"—are as various as the evanescent self-insistence they bring out. One senses a sympathizing instress in verse action, in and beyond the gradience of *hung/swung*, meant to hear for us the undertone of "s-ung" in the clapper-like pendulous return of "each hung bell." So, too, a line later, this punning in-tone of the integrally self-same surfaces again in the clausal inversion "when tumbled over rim in roundy wells s/tones ring." Ring out, that is, from their own name as roundy noun.

Distilled there in this crispest of alphabetic slips is the overrim of Hopkins' phonetext, the overruns of its inner logic. It offers a heightened case of *linguistic* "inscape" here so preternaturally matched to its objects that the instress of "response" seems orchestrated for us in language alone. Even in etymology as well as phonic recursion, for no sooner is the bell's hung tongue *flung* out (the post-facto rhyming destiny of "fling out," unsung but pregnant) than the very name "bell" may be heard tolled in overtones of its "imitative" pre-Germanic derivation. The next two lines lift to summary: "Each mortal thing does one thing and the same: / Deals out that being indoors each one dwells." The definitive "in" is literally pivotal—model of inscape and its activating instress alike—as "indoors" swivels from a modifier of "being" to an elliptical version of "indoors [inside] of which." This is how the individuated entity, in the next line, "selves." Process rather than fixity, selving is honored, again and again, by a wording poised on the cusp of semantics but slipping over to an immanence too fluid for clear-edged discursive fluency.

After bird and insect on the wing, essentialized in their flashing out and past, have come the ontological distillations by which both mineral and metal object, in splash and clang, sound their nature. In the sestet, however, turning more abstract and metaphysical, sound is no longer an epiphenomenon of essence but a mode of responsive instress in words otherwise directed. This is an essential Hopkins move: staging the phonics indoors each phrase moves and lives.

> I say móre: the just man justices;
> 　Keeps grace: thát keeps all his goings graces;
> Acts in God's eye what in God's eye he is—
> 　Chríst. For Christ plays in ten thousand places,
> Lovely in limbs, and lovely in eyes not his
> 　To the Father through the features of men's faces.

The play in the octave between "as" as similitude versus parallel montage—each self-annunciation at once *like* and *simultaneous with* the other—gives way to the typical analogic sestet in Hopkins, description often turned almost prescriptive: in this case, with essence bespeaking itself in the human world by way of its derivation from the divine. The octave's matrix of vari(eg) ation and phonic refraction has been extended, that is, as explicitly as in any work by Hopkins, from natural ontology toward a theology of divine immanence. When created things become apprehended in their essence, they are heard to participate in the energy of the "Christ" who, by like saturation in the sestet, "<u>plays</u> *in ten* thous*and* <u>places</u>"—and five different phonetic ones right there (the recursive "-n" core spread to *sint/en/sand* in a vibratory micro-ubiquity framed by the instress of a divinatory play in *play*/s/ces).

Nowhere could this letteral crystallization of essence, this spiritual inscape, be more succinctly noted than in the self-confirming further "play" of the sestet's opening line: "I say more: the just man justices." Hard for the reader to assimilate any oblique fit of the rare verb form of "justice" (for "justify") to this convoluted phrasing before wording falls (apart) into the ontological confirmation (and dispersed syntax) of "just as is" if not the emphatic phantom punctuation of "just is, is." In either and any case, the inscape of virtue is manifested exclusively through the values it embodies, selved by self-justification. Reading is thus confirmed in retrospect regarding how the *metaphonic* keynote of the poem has come early and decisively with *tho/ se tones* of self-sounded plummet and annunciation. It is by association also that we may well hear the compression of "what in God's eye he is"—before its phonic if not ocular blur is parsed out again in the eventual cross-word rhyme "his"—as the existential distillate "what in *God's eye is*," where any and every "he" takes up its occupancy. (This insinuated subsumption of "he is" to the supervening "eye is" seems confirmed by the editorial variant actually given by interlinear insertion at this point, where the missing seesaw chiasm only tightens the phonetically tempting parallel—and audial equivalence: "In God's eye acts what in God's eye he is."[13]) By modeling sacred awareness on the work of art, reading in Hopkins lends instress to the inscape of otherness until that phrased prehension is internalized by the mind's own refashioned inscape as one of its enhanced cognitive powers. The hermeneutic circle is remade in the form of cognate sacral recognition.

And all under the assumption—in whichever of the ten thousand places in which its plied beauties are in play—of some such schema as follows:

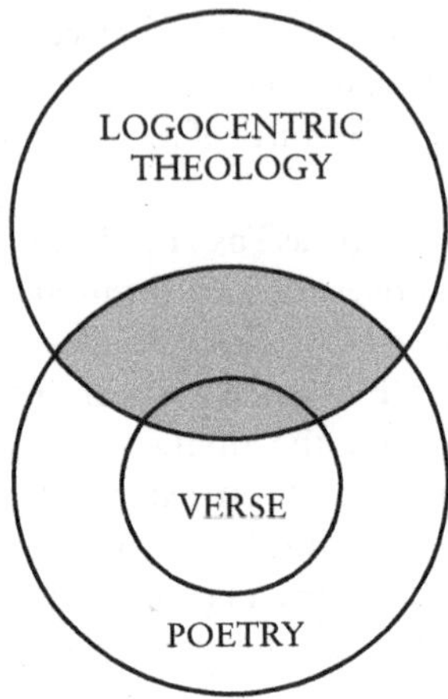

In logopoetics, the world's bestowed grandeur is met by a fresh ciphering. With traditional verse encompassed by a less routinized poetics, as charted there, part of each mode overlaps into the religious zone of notice, the latter more fully in its breadth of register. Whenever instressed by appreciative fervor, a truly poetic syntax pulses—beyond mere verse measure—with the hyperventilation of the world itself. For catching the spirit of this freshly realized world, any received vocabulary falls shortexcept in the flux of, the flex of, such lexical down-doubling and frenetic hyphenation as Hopkins lets loose in his surprise spurts of phrasing, with their eerie, earie freaks of overreach. What results is a polyglossia beyond Babel, a ritual of intuition in an untutored verbosity of approximation.

Under experiment is a grammar as well as a lexicon of awe. To predicate objects and to nominalize action, to dynamize and distill at once the featurings-forth of nature and its paths of motion, is to compass space and time, space in time, time installed in change: the *here-in-now* of linguistic inscape under the sign of self-performance rather than categorized existence, self-enactment rather than objective facticity. Nouns name the delved selving of phenomena, verbs the goings on(ward) of being. Ontology is logos and trajectory at once. Under pressure of this sustained experiment by Hopkins, and across the whole color and texture spectrum of his slant and glinting mimesis, the force of verbal immanence, beyond communing with the world, motors a poetics of transubstantiality. The material form of language waxes sacramental in its own right, tasting of participation and transferred embodiment. Deification finds its mirror in verbal reification. This involves no reductive short circuit in which Creation is lower-cased in a feedback loop with descriptive invention. Logopoetics unfolds, rather, as an homage to the mystery of creation in natural language's own sphere of operation, whose faithful (every sense again) figurings of the world delimit vital inscapes that language can both inhabit and dishabituate. In formalist terms, *ostranenie* is a strain so unremitting in Hopkins that estrangement and wonderment coincide.

On this model, what gauge of reading could be counted as too close? "Glory be to God for dappled things," begins Hopkins in his paeon to "Pied Beauty." And laurels to the powers of instress for dappled hearings. With enough of his intricate work in view, or say in mind's ear and eye alike, the admixture thus admired penetrates not just to lexical sutures like "skies of couple-colour" in the next line, but even to the English digraph itself (the unrhyming duple "ou," like the monosyllabic "ie" and "eu" in the poem's title). Scaled up to fuller lexical play in the sestet, this harmonized contrariety includes what the internal slant rhymes of syllabic infrastructure manage to evoke in "Whatever is fickle, freckled"—with the suggestion there of changeability as well as diversity, the fleeting and the streaked in a temporal as well as spatial blurring, rapid, patchy.

In another of Hopkins' most famous natural rhapsodies, "The Windover," offered up explicitly and by subtitle "To Christ our Lord"—one of his grateful benedictions for the answered prayer of living variety—language gauges, as well as celebrates, the maneuvered levitation of the avian cynosure in the aptly hovering gradients, over and above us, of assonance and phrasal escalation. So, in these refractive features, is the bird manifest to us. But with that dedicatory "To" is also implied a God's-eye perspective in delegation to the poet-priest.

> I caught this morning morning's minion, king-
> > dom of daylight's dauphin, dapple-dawn-drawn Falcon, in his riding
> > Of the rolling level underneath him steady air, and striding
> High there, how he rung upon the rein of a wimpling wing
> In his ecstasy! then off, off forth on swing,
> > As a skate's heel sweeps smooth on a bow-bend: the hurl and gliding
> > Rebuffed the big wind. My heart in hiding
> Stirred for a bird,—the achieve of, the mastery of the thing!

Right off, "this morning morning's minion"—with that internal chiastic hiccup floated by a transformative grammar (adverb to adjective)—a partial phonetic repetition also fuels a near-anagrammar cued, skewed, to release *min-ion* from *mo-nin-*. From there to the more obvious phrasal shove (the *d+* nudge) of "dapple-d*awn*-dr*awn* Falc*on*"—as if the bird's name took impetus and lift from its own strained epithets (more loudly sounded that the "fire" flashed across "fishers" in the shimmer of that other titular bird). Even hyphenation fuses as much as separates at a ligature like "*dapple-d*awn," ringing truer yet to the pied slide of graphonic possibility "drawn" out in the syllabic moment—as "dappled." After which the bird's levitated energy is further serviced by wording in the famously suspensive periodic warp of "his riding /

of the rolling level underneath him steady air." The whole vista seems striving (lurking third term in the *striding/riding* rhyme?) for the uncanny equilibrium of its internal palindrome "level"—as in turn leveled off four words later in the phonetic dapple, or ripple, of the homophonic comparative "steadi-er," plausible effect to the cause of "steady air." Indomitably airborne, the regal bird is then found—almost, by the surprising verb choice, heard ("rung" rather than "hung")—to hover "rung upon the rein of a wimpling wing / In his ecstasy! then off, off forth on swing." There, as actually written in the enjambed line, the fricative shove that impels "off" to a chiastic and cross-lexical "off forth"— as if in a single adverbial fusion at a blurred phonemic border—recurs in the sibilant audition of "on '(hi)s wing" flitting across the actually odder (though repetition-deflecting) scripted given of "on *sw*ing." Any idiom can be twisted into submission by the freed swerves of such riveted observation, its mode a contagion of instress from world to word. And not least when the octave's closing on the oddly nominalized verb in "achieve of the thing" takes on extra lunging thrust form the unspelled "heave." Even harder *not* to hear in such propulsion is the boosting *wind* rushing unsaid across the unwound phrasing "rung upon the rein of a wimpling wing."

And then the doubly grounding paired final tercets, earthborne and humanized:

> Brute beauty and valour and act, oh, air, pride, plume, here
> 　　Buckle! AND the fire that breaks from thee then, a billion
> Times told lovelier, more dangerous, O my chevalier!
> 　　No wonder of it: shéer plód makes plough down sillion
> Shine, and blue-bleak embers, ah my dear,
> 　　Fall, gall themselves, and gash gold-vermilion.

Notable that a critique in *TLS* of William Empson, in his reading of this passage a quarter century before (1930), comparing the lustrous force of airborne predation with the implicitly smoldering figures of human suffering, would have blamed the great virtuoso of glinting ambiguities for thinking, in anticipation of the gutted fire trope of the last two lines, that the agricultural blade indicates the "harrowing" (?) cause rather than effect when "sheer plod makes plough down sillion / Shine."[14] Rising to Empson's unsaid defense in his claim for the soil's own churned-up clay sheen is the transegmental re-grooving—like "*dapple-d*awn-drawn" in the octave—from instrument to result in the tacit hyphening of "Plough(e*d*)-*d*own sillion."

With so many various effects on call in "The Windover," a rough categorical census of Hopkins' word-splay can be proposed. His wording pushes to an outer no less than inner limit the distinction between verbal effects you hear without seeing (the sibilant swoosh of *ts* into "on swing," for instance, or the released "heave" of "achieve") and those you see without coherently hearing (the climactic "ash" in the "gash gold-vermillion" of inflamed "blue-bleak embers"). The poet's phonic inscapes edge up to this limit especially because he accustoms his reader to expect, at any moment, the gradient gashing-open of one such word to *fan the flair* of a phonetic alternative a split-second and split-word down the line. In comparable syntactic as well as phonemic rhythm, the sestet's own dramatic enjambment at "Brute beauty and valor and act, oh, air, pride, plume here / Buckle!" arrives with tightening emphasis (framed by the bold plosive alliteration of the front-loaded "Brute") on the transitional snap of "Buckle!" As so cannily tackled by Empson,[15] that hinge term is at once a blending latch and a bending out of shape, both clasp and collapse, as if enacted by a line break that falls and fastens at once. The linguistic buckling has been anticipated by the way that first line's loose sixfold list of celebratory nouns unbelts on the run, releasing (unmentioned by Empson) its last triad to three alternate verb forms as well (as if the raptor is impelled to *air* its essence by *priding* and *pluming* itself before precipitous descent). Under pressure of all such lexical (in)stress, one may spot (or "sight"-read) even unheard puns because—as with the blood-red embers that by echoic inevitability "F*all*, g*all* themselves" and then "gash gold-vermillion"—the radiant glow of such alphabetic g/ashes, such syllabic cinders, is never far, for the inculcated reader of Hopkins, from the explicit gradient buckling (each sense again, coupling and crumpling) of one enunciated syllable (in)to another. Or say one sounded word "ploughing" up its successor into a third term.

One pauses, at a point like this, to spot a certain abiding pattern behind the spotted, mottled patternings of Hopkins' natural inscapes in trans-script. Beyond the fresh sense of phrasal surprise, of perpetual nonacclimation to the lexis-nexus or its torqued syntax, my renewed attention has been met by one further overarching awareness. In thinking of Hopkins' ferocious originality, one readily remembers his vocalic soundings of the world, word by retooled word, but can easily forget how relatively few sounds emitted from the real— how few actual noises in described space—these molded instruments of registration attend to. One marked exception sings of nature's music, against the din of human decline, in "The Sea and the Skylark." Even its title seems unfurled from the more normative phrasal dichotomy of "sea and sky," just as the first line's "On ear and ear" must itself, as wording, be heard against the syllabic (if not the empathetic) grain of a proverbial "near and dear."

> On ear and ear two noises too old to end
>   Trench—right, the tide that ramps against the shore;
>   With a flood or a fall, low lull-off or all roar,
> Frequenting there while moon shall wear and wend.

Beyond the idiomatic shadowing that begins the poem, the turn of that first line is equally unstable in the skid of consonants at noises too old to end / trench."

Too old, sea and species, not to have "to[o]lled" their music here as well? And to have made it telling? As if in parallel "trenches" of cognition, below and beyond: where, via the fleetingly rendered lexical rather than just linear in-jamming at "end / trench," these aural glories have been perpetually installed? And, letting questions aggregate phonetically in this vein: where perhaps attention is *wrenched* in a figurative *drench* of sound? This would saturate a cresting motion—in watery tropes aligned with the sea swell—that, in a later overflow of enjambment, "pour / And pelt music, till none's to spill nor spend." Nor further mimetically to spell—and hence expend for poetic investment. Once make the ear the explicit subject, as Hopkins does in this sonnet, and the frequency modulation of his *auralterity*—the pied beauty of his soundings—is more salient than ever.

Certainly this poem exceeds the hum of human idiom by hearing "the *rash-fresh* re-winded new-skeinèd score" of the bird's music sourced invisibly off-shore and on high—where the graded return of "rash" in "resh" doesn't just phonetically lift the vocalic note, and tone, but teases the ear (in a "re-winded" energy of both breath and conveyance) with a syllabically inverted "re-fresh," thus re-stressing at once a renewal of airy intake and wind-borne transmission. In all this, the skylark's is a sound that rises above what has also been conveyed below it in the heard sea's surf—in a mix, there, of Welsh *cynghanedd* (recursive alliterative sequences crossed with internal rhyme) and a familiar phonetic gradience. Phrasing accomplishes its imitative mission in this regard by syllable-play's own ramping up in the pound of the "tide that ramps" against the shoreline: "With a flood or a fall, low lull-off or all roar." It isn't only the *flood/fall/off/all* cycle, propelled further by the supplemental orality of *or/roar*, that catches, on its own, the sea's sway. More carefully audited than this is the seesaw syllabic onomatopoeia of wave motion itself, lexically reversing course into the peak-and-recede mimesis of the self-valleyed chiasm at "fall lo(w l)ull-off." Hear, too, how *fah-lll-o*, in the outflow, is all but punningly "fahllo[wed]" in the near-perfect undertow of *u-ll-o-f*. In the phonemic clasp of this chiasmus (with its audible "Fahl … lahF" bracket), it is as if we audit the off/fall awe of the late Romantic sublime writ in water. And do so as a mediated gift, the poet not just validating but conveying in words a tidal "lull-off or all roar" that is indeed "for all."

But all this comes down, in the blistering sestet, to a gift apparently refused. Beyond such internalized phonemic rove-overs, it takes nothing away from the sonic meters of birdsong and oceanic undertow in the octave to note that the sonnet ends, given the usual shift of focus in the sestet, with the kind of sound play more typical of Hopkins, where words bleed over from within their own sequence less in echo of the pulsing world than in exacting response to it. And in this case lamentory, where no such unifying generosity as that "for all" shadows a grieved human decline in this "sordid turbid time"—whose very phrasing works there to extrude an intermediate third term in "torpid." (One may recall Wordsworth's warning about the spiritual environment in "London 1802," figured as a "fen of stagnant waters.") In Hopkins, the sky sings on, the sea throbs immortally in the octave, but here in the sestet, in a very different *falling-off* from that of the receding surf, degenerated human energy withers by comparison with its "past prime": "Our make and making break, are breaking, down / To man's last dust." Our kind ("make"?) and its creations, in the mimetic onrush of participial grammar, are tracked in collapse somewhere between verb phrase and its adverbial double (either breaking down per se—or decomposing [in]*to*). The octave's amphitheater of natural sound funnels down in these (fore)closing lines to the gloom of devolution, an enjambed and double-vectored deterioration where realms of value "break ... down / To man's la*st* du*st*, drain fa*st* towards man's fir*st* slime" across that stuttering, stair-step-tones of the *st* iteration. As if activating the watery sense of a first dead metaphor in the sestet's opening "*shallow* and frail town" (as synecdoche for broad social degeneration), the poem thus closes by flushing out, drowning out, the sounds of skysong and seabeat alike, under a disintegrating force that is found sluicing civilization away to a primal biological muck ("first slime").

So even with this most auditory of Hopkins' *topoi* in the octave of "The Sea and the Skylark," the typical dominance of stirred words over heard world, the latter's rhythms in this case primarily overheard at a distance, reasserts itself in the end. And especially in the erosive underwording of the poem's last line. In the anything but Edenic (de)Creationism of that final miring slide into slime, metalinguistics tightens its grip on poetics. For within the shamed "shallow(s)" of a human "town" edged and tacitly denigrated by sea and skylark, by better and bettering music far and wide, lurks in turbid meld the twin adulterated etymologies of "lime" (from Latin *limus* for mud) as well the proto-Indo-European *(s)lei* for "slimy," a condition to which pulverized limestone often reverts. Here, then, is a degeneration not just to an unfertile bath of protoplasmic algae but to something like the decalcified residue of "man's fir(st *s*) *lime*." In the transegmental ear of so intuitively philological a poet, etymon becomes metonym. Human animation—at this phonic splintering—is marked in descent to a lifeless terrestrial minerality, dust and ashes to pulverized fossil rock as well as organic slush: the travestied primeval clay of non-Adamic humus become a primordial morass more chaotic than inchoate in this etymologically "extractive" reading. Without enlisting the weary cliché of a "deep dive," anything plausibly surface-level does at times give way to the archaeolinguistic dig. Rimmed here by neglected aquatic rhythms and overarched by ignored song, the human slough of poetry's ground game is played out in the slippery rigors of regret.

Phonics over Sonics

IN "THE SEA AND THE SKYLARK," then, the natural music of air and sea are the counterpoint and the anomaly. Considering Hopkins' sonneteering at large, the cadences of musical inflection are overwhelmingly its instrument, not its subject. It is as if those stones ringing out their essence in the invisible depth of "roundy wells" were not just an exception to prove the rule, but already a trope for the self-disclosure of inscapes naturally unspoken, unsounded, needing to be sought and brought out. The material phenomena that Hopkins' sonnets filter so vigilantly for us, then, are predominantly visual: not the audible cadences of unseen songbirds in a certain Romantic vein, but avian motion sunlit-streaked—kingfishers catching fire in that ignited fuse of consonants themselves—on the wind and wing. Not lowing cattle but ploughed fields. Not Aeolian music whispering through a wind-brushed rush of leaves, but, as in "Binsley Poplars," the vacancy of the trees themselves and the barren ground their overpruned absence exposes. Surfaces, in short: variably reflective or bereft. Once our reading realizes this, a further sense of the poetics may well dawn. Hopkins' is an art of ingrained synesthesia—of found sights and fashioned sounds—that seeks no phenomenological synthesis. What results is a composite site (venturing on my part another integrated portmanteau) of *oculaurality*. Over against the outlines of the described, phrasing arises as a separate track (in cinematic terms, an acousmatic voice-over) running athwart the optic variety whose facets it traces—one enchained phrase, one phase change, one overlain phonic charge after another, lexiphonetic, auratic, oral-ecstatic. As if in the montage edit of some bedazzled soundtrack for a docudrama about the world's opalescent presencings, it is when seeking in inscape their probed terrain that we find in instress their inflected recognition.

So back now to the patterings and pleatings of such language under the auspices of this synesthetic realization, where a default instance of onomatopoeia in the matter of birdsong only goes to secure the norm of ocular dominance. The play between nature and culture serves, in another sonnet, to frame the more philosophical tribute to medieval theologian Dun Scotus as a presiding genius loci of Oxford. And as soon as the establishing soundscape of that fabled seat of written learning is dialed up, emphasis shifts to the more intangible aura of the place. Under the principle that all entities, when reaching the page, tend alphabetically to string out, ring out, their being in all but Adamic naming, it's not simply that the ubiquitous local "cuckoo" noted at the start of "Duns Scotus' Oxford" is mimetically named (according to etymology) for the notes it sings. Further, "Cuckoo-echoing" renews oohcooh (on the slant as "echcoh") at the head of an opening line where vowels are fast st/rung out in an atmosphere of concord that includes "bell-sw*arm*èd, lark ch*arm*ed." This last strong-armed phonemic seesaw then gives way (via another avian name, "origin probably mimetic") to the tighter gradient dyad of "*rook-rack*ed." Despite the dictionary backing for imitative etymology, these are word-sounds first of all. Then, too, deploying Hopkins' favored term ("dappled") for pied texture, the "dapple[-eare]d lily below thee" offers its own immanent if tacit gloss, not on the trumpet-like tubularity of vegetal form, but on the stipple-"eared" hearing, the marbled audition, to which Hopkins' abiding intricacies bid us.

And if the uneasy balance of nature and culture congregated at Oxford has "confounded" any monolithic focus in the variegation of the locale's "graceless growth," it has bestowed another spiritual grace in the process. In the aural reward for disparity, the landscape's "rural keeping—folk, flocks, and flowers"— foregrounds that near-anagrammatic twist of "folk" into "flo(c)k" as part of the flow into "*flo*w*ers*" that is hardly to be judged detrimental in its discrepancies to the meditations of philosophic theology. Where variegation is the stuff of life. And where the appearance of "flowers" confirms the suppressed third term in the opening phrase about a "Towery city, and branchy between towers": the (there unsaid) rhyme "flowery." Equally unsaid, the semantic play—the semic antic—of characterizing Scotus by syntactic inversion with an inescapably tendered (and immediately rendered inoperable) summative pun on the classic case of unravelling: "Of realty the rarest-veinèd unraveller; a{k}not / Rivalled insight." Just before, in this closing peroration, Hopkins' homage to place and personage is rerouted through the brief byway of a garden-path phrasing that closes the sonnet, under pressure from the initial "ah" (thickened to "air") of exclamation: "Yet ah! this air I gather. . . ." Beyond the "ah!" of sheer expressive breath, what about this air is to be gathered? Somehow that this variable air, this multifarious atmosphere, must have been part of the *inspiration* for Scotus that he provides now in turn for Hopkins? No, or not so simply. For "gather" does not take hold in this case as predicated speculation, but rather as the sign of direct intake in inverted grammar. Here respiratory presence is itself a mode of gleaning made clear when the sentence breathes out, in a corrected syntactic direction, its compound predicate of literalized breath: "Yet ah! This air I gather and I rele*ase* / *He* lived on." And hence, *lives on in* the motivated mind of his distant *in-spired* disciple, a legacy made easily feasible in the transfer of enjambment's own phonemic overhang. One hardly has to imagine phrasing's full lexical play to feel—across the suspension-bridge transfer of assonance— just how "ease / (H)e" it is for Hopkins to take up tenancy once the progenitor's spirit has been imbibed and—while "lived on"—revitalized.

Any such piebald espial of forked phrasal texture, whether in phonic or semantic over-rove, any such "dapple-eared" attunement to mutable poetic vocality, gets its fullest explication, perhaps, in the explicitly metatextual late work "Spelt from Sybil's Leaves" with whose ecstatic evocation of the night sky we briefly began. This is a poem, and as such a text, whose title signals from the first a transcribed oracular divination that returns through script to the orality of poetic performance—and to its prophetic (revelatory, if not predictive) phonetics. More than scribal transcription (the strictly "spelt") is certainly implied in this sense of the poet as intermediary, tracing out in English syllables a set of sibylline urgencies from "O óur oracle" (as if one dilated apostrophic "O"—marked in fact, above and beyond the sprung accent, by a drawn-in musical "tie" binding the first two words as one). This Sybil's omens are ones whose elucidation, at the receiving end, cannot be divorced from a voiced enunciation. Hopkins wrote at this point quite insistently for the audible voice, throwing visual lineation to the winds of contingency. About this poem in particular, he insisted that it elicits "not reading with the eye but loud, leisurely, poetical (not rhetorical) recitation, with long rests. . . . This sonnet shd. be almost sung: it is most carefully timed in *tempo rubato*."[16] The variable rhythm is at first keyed to diurnal pattern. Day wanes into night, so that light "wound to the west" in unravelment. Yet this night-and-day dynamic, the rule of black-and-light as it were, must be resisted as a too rigid sense of inscape in its coercive un-"wind"ing—via a curious (self-unwound) redundancy of phrase—"upon áll on twó spools."

Faced with such strained binarity, as the enemy of freeform multiplicity, one must stand one's guard, digging in like the accentual line that here (given this time with the manuscript's stress marks) drags out its cautionary length: keeping "wáre of a wórld where" (as dangerously self-contained as it sounds) "bút these | twó tell, each off the óther; of a rack / Where, *selfwrung*, *selfstrung*, sheathe- and shelterless, | thóughts agaínst thoughts ín groans grínd." In reading slowly and aloud, as particularly bidden with this poem (hence the cited markings), one might well fail to take instruction from that semi-colon in suppressing the sharply apt double grammar that alternately spans it: difference made *to tell* only *by* enforced contrast—in the process of telling further *of* the tormenting rack such *wracking* tension constitutes. This tortuous and rending syntax is its own kind of mental obstacle course. In the metagrammar of its di-splayed double pathway, its refusal of a grating either-or mentality evinces the plied composite—the split perspective—that makes for accentual poetry's own rout of rigidity. The model abides, even if it can't appease the depleted vital resources whose exhaustion seems carried by this emphatic exhale of unravelment: "Lét life, *wáned*, ah lét life *wind* / Off—hér once skéined stained véined variety," where again three digraphs and their last inverted syllabic variant in "*iety*" keep the issue of just such var*iance* alive from the thick of lament. Alive, if only in the alphabetic tissue of English orthography. Think of it, as think about it you must, as the lexical residuum of a lost existential breathing room.

Des/pairing Echoes

I've suggested that much of Hopkins' language seems "spelt" from a world whose scintillant stressed surfacings operate under auditory baffle, where phonetics does the weight-bearing work of hearing only in its own logocentric circuit. Even when seeming to denote an acoustic phenomenon in the habitable world, as with the double-voiced counterpoint between "The Leaden Echo and the Golden Echo," most sonic interplay is subsumed to the language of dialogic counterpoint rather than the acoustics of echoic duplication. In fact, this poem tacitly ironizes the playback mechanisms by which nature might be conceived to echo in return the voicings of the spirit in its wrestle with ephemerality and its sense of destitution. In frustration that there is no "waving off" the presaging wrinkles that arrive as harbingers of one's fate, three repetitions of "there's none" pivot after the second on the "O no" that alphabetically recycles the phonemes of negation (minus the silent softening schwa) before the curious forking grammar of the next line: "Nor can you long be, what you now are, called fair." Transliterating a choppy parallelism verging on syllepsis: "You are now fair *and* called so, but neither for long." After six repetitions at the first phase of the diptych—in leaden echo—of the two-syllabled "despair," a syllabic disparting of the ways bells/belts out its corrective: "Spare!" Not more emotional sparsity, but instead: Relent! Desist! In this word-world of Hopkins, where syllables take the pulse of possibility, despair cocoons its own renewal.

Such is the gradient degradation of one word into its misspelled and irrelevant, but suddenly redemptive, resident alien. The title that has cross-faded to the first line via the vocalic descent from "E*cho*" to the interrogative uptake of "*How*"—in worry over the mutable—now reverses direction with the phonetic backlash of a graphically flagged part rhyme. The overtones of all this are multiple and ravishing. Language alone, rather than any audible phenomena beyond it, is heard in this case wresting relief from grief, amelioration from lament, parting the "spared" from the despairing. Like Keats' "the very word is like a bell" ("*forlorn*") in the Nightingale Ode, the inscape of echo operates its own more welcome belling under the instress of intervention: chiming-in, resistantly, to break loose from despondency. The undulation of gradience reaches a flashpoint here in the flipped switch of lexically extricated defiance. All this despair, oh spare me! It is as if the first syllable of "despair" had been hiding there in plain sight as a negative prefix ripe for exorcism.

For such a sense of time slipping away, lost possibility, blocked spiritual hope, of the sort that oppresses the self's morbid echo chamber there, no comparable push-back, no redemptive dialectic, occurs in the "terrible sonnets" of the mid-1880s. In them, the speaker feels abandoned in his own un-relieved wilderness to morose self-contemplation and a frayed faith in God's conversation. "I wake and feel the fell of dark, not day," begins his titular hour-of-the-wolf lament—until next, after the downward phonemic gradient from "feel" to "fell," rhyming the cruelly night-postponed "day" with a telescoped and virtually synonymous phrase "light's d(el)ay." This distended lexical frame can seem performing its own woeful retardation, swallowing dawn in the very name of darkened prolongation. Phrased here is not a persistent and unremitting nightfall, but "fell" in the worse and more derivative sense of "fallen" as evil. Grieved thereby is a lapse into that sinister distress in which the cognitive "feel" plays against an internalized "the *fell*" in such a way as to elicit further, across the whole phrasal span, its pervading counterpoint in a synonymized (f)*ee*(l)-*fell*. In these terrible sonnets, the morose inscape of despair is uniquely matched by the instress that sustains and conveys it. Feasting on his misery as the "selfyeast of spirit" (with overtones of 'selfish') has become "gall" incarnate, a spiritual "heartburn," bitter and acidic. The effect is both alimentary and anatomical: a fate decreed by the God who "Bones b*uilt* in me, flesh f*illed*," where the phonetic containment of *ilt* is itself fleshed out, made full, by that inaudible graphic inflation to *illed*.

Comparably in "No worst, there is none. Pitched past pitch of grief," another of the desolate late sonnets, the "pitch" of grief—implicitly figured as a sonic wavelength as well as an extremity of mental pain—is also dragged along, as if emotionally down, by a rhyme scheme in operation as a kind of schematic plot arc. We are made almost to hear, by pun, the pangs that despair, from the speaker's racked mental frame, does "wilder w/ring." Clanging in chill rhyme against any absent "comfort*ing*," such false phrasal hope is countered by the sibilant hammer blows that, in the inward forge of despair, make its "age-old anvil wince and *sing*"—and thus deny, by rhyme's rove-over mockery, even any "l*ing*-/ering" between assaults. The speaker is so thoroughly wrung by the stings of his depression that the ultimate emergence of a rhyme with "w*ring*" in that new line's fragmentary "*ering*" only sounds a further spiritual dissonance that goes almost without hearing, without saying. For the speaker's audible "cries," unanswered by divine relief, have already been punned on—by a trope of elongation in an alternate spelling—as palpably un-"heard": "My cri*es heave*, *herd*s-long; huddle"—a congested desperation with no pain "sieved" through to a soothing deity. As quickly, as fleetingly, as "heard" is pluralized on the ear by the eccentric "herds," it is at once semantically cancelled, any deluded hope of audition re(s)pelled as instead the cued drove or pack or horde of pent-up appeal.

Elsewhere, resisting despair as a self-devouring "Carrion Comfort," the speaker refuses the elliptical (as well as truncating) defeat of a self-pitying "I can no more." And in an immediate rove-over with semi-colon latch: "I can; / can something. . . ." The speaker is groping for a predicate, from which resisted morass the idea of enablement rises as a momentarily freestanding intransitive, all transaction latent. Continuing vaguely: "can something, hope, wish day come, not choose not to be." In this aggravated, anti-Hamlet grammar of an all-too-fragile agency, the vow is to "Not untwist—slack they may they be—" the last sinews of his humanity, here mimetically twisted up in lexical overlap as the one-worded "lastrands of man." All this operates in an echoic self-recognition, wresting one phonetic cluster from another, when "a *wretch* lay *wrest*ling"—in a despair of salvation and its paired lexical irony—"with (my God!) my God." At the poem's blasphemous dead end, expletive and nemesis have imploded upon each other in the radical exhaustion of this inverted prayer.

Another of these terrible sonnets sounds the keynote of isolation per se—as almost a poetic deracination, where language itself is bled of efficacy. In the first-line-identified "To seem the stranger lies my lot, my life" (enjambed to "among strangers" and thus retrofitting the first noun to such a modifier as "all the stranger"), Hopkins, posted to a separatist Ireland, misses his English muse, "Wife / To my creating thought." That enjambment is followed by a rove-over that seems to be wearing away at human coherence altogether: "I wear- / Y of a being but by"—as if with a normalizing overtone of "put by"—"where wars are rife." In plausible human speech, the speaker is tired of "being sidelined," or in the vernacular sense of "but by," a mere "bystander." The extra notch of grammatical passivity in "put by" shadows the phrasing at its core. His current marginalization is as abnormal and vexing as it sounds. If only he were less tongue-tied, he imagines in the sestet that he could, if only opportunity allowed, give love and comfort, as well as receive it. What follows seems to begin as a question: "Only what word / Wisest my heart breeds. . . ." can I speak forth? But that's not the real undermining drift—as we instantaneously realize when that "what" comes to stand for "whatever" in a statement (rather than question) regretting that any such birthed "word"—getting beaten back here in the syntax of inversion—"dark heaven's baffling ban / Bars or hell's spell thwarts." Decades after "hell's bells" has entered standard colloquial English as an idiom for exclaimed frustration, its skewed homophonic respelling is indeed a cloven-hoofed lexical deviltry. (Recall the milder version of skirted phonetic formula in "O/n ear an/d ear" in "The Sea and the Skylark.") Certainly in this lamentory sonnet, language as comforting gift can't, in any case, find a way to "spell" itself out loud.

With the hereby enacted echo chamber of the persona's mind—laddering up toward the surface in its muffled efficacy—the poem groans grinding to a choked halt. For, in rhyme with the unreleased "word," the destitution of "to ho*ard* unh*eard*, / H*eard* un*heeded*, leaves me a lonely began." With rhetoric's proverbial word-hoard going unheard in all but this rued solitude—burying the "ear" in steady phonemic suppression (with -*heard* in its own homophonic reduction to a sublexical *ur/d*)—prosody releases its suppressed long *e* (of the unspoken *ear*) only to the further prefixed negation of "unheeded," reasoning not the *need*. Declined next into nonconjugation, as an ad hoc grammar might have it, the abusive use of "began" is toxic in its syntactic limbo. Swollen from its rhyme with "ban"—that diction of interdiction—"began" has become an abortive substantive, the always and already of a decidedly past-tense impetus, as if to say "leaves me a lonely has-been." And this by a radically inaudible anagrammatic association with the fuller spread of that anticipating rhyme "baffling ban" (gban/began). Cut loose in grammatical isolation from subject and object alike, such a "lonely began" may also seem to emerge as the virtual equivalent of a self-neutralizing "begone."[17] And if ever the knotted grip of such syllabic spasms in Hopkins, including their phantom undertones, once detached from all pulsing celebration of pied grandeur, has found its perfect subject, here in the cramped verbal blockage of this "instressed" sonnet is a quintessentially performed struggle for an eloquence strangled by circumstance.

Reckoning with "The Wreck"

I want now to tune my auditory return to Hopkins on the famous longer work to whose incremental structure his dappled phonic amplifications are dramatically paced to contribute. There is fearsomeness and grief in "The Wreck of the Deutschland," but unlike in those terrible sonnets, God is on hand as summoned redeemer—rather than absconded in the persona's despondence. It is notable that comparably gauged phrasal tensions, with the syllabic clasp and collapse of rhyme included, return in a later, sparer work on a similar mass drowning captured again in a roiling phonic saturation. In this subsequent "Loss" ("of the Eurydice"), rhyme is again not just a tolling but a uniquely telling pressure point where the formal impositions of verse upon language push through, in resolute Hopkins fashion, to the surprises of poetry—and can be seen in continuity with his stressed spectrum of lexical and syllabic interplay. Always the arcane, over-arcing enjambments of rhyme serve in part to exaggerate the internal fusions (injambments) of both syllable and sense. Turn, for instance, to such turns in the plaintive "wreck" poem that Hopkins particularly emphasized to Bridges must be read, not in a "slovenly" manner with "the eyes" only, lazily scanned, but "with your ears"[18]—as if the internalizing work of instress were coded there in the personalizing of "*your* ears" rather than merely "*the* eyes."

The power of inscription in "The Loss of the Eurydice" exceeds anything imagined by the term sight rhyme. In the process it is linked to other lateral play in the give-and-take of syntax. A sylleptic shift from material to spiritual cause in stanza 16, for instance, easily comic in another context (more Dickens than Dickinson), leads to a pure transegmental rhyme when, among the two survivors of mass disaster, "a lifebelt and God's will / Lend him a lift from the sea-swill." With that last phrase capsizing the normative expectation of "sea-swell," and thus evincing in transegmental rhyme the capriciousness of the "sea's will," the lexical and phonetic overlaps together (syllepsis and cross-word ligature) seem sprung to the verse surface from a shared principle in which violent disruption, as much as dappled profusion, registers in the time-based stress of juxtaposition. The energetics of such perception comes more grievously to the fore eight stanzas later, to sophisticate and darken the (again) almost comic rhyme of "crew in" with "ruin." There, the rove-over rhyme induces its own version of seasick dizziness in the coined condensation of these "daredeaths, ay this crew, in / Unchrist, all rolled in ruin. . . ." Rolled out by syllabic over-rove, as well as roiled nautically, the end-rhyme "in" spills over into the "Un" of ungodly tragedy, with a half-heard lurch into surging "*inun*dation," for a slant rhyme that further compacts the three-beat, brutally rueful return of "rew in un" in "in ruin." Instanced here must be some part of what Hopkins meant in urging Bridges to read this poem, like all his poems, as if the page were itself bidding for audition—or, in other (transmaterial) words, "as if the paper were declaiming it to you."[19]

Similar effects, their assonance and alliteration internally recursive, their rhymes even more mysteriously over-brimmed, characterize the more famous earlier poem of a nautical tragedy edged with transcendence, "The Wreck of the Deutschland." This, to follow, is the plot, and just to put it that way suggests how this epic work's unique mix of narrative and odic patterns will entertain certain descriptive oscillations exceeding the balanced rhythm—natural observation promptly recast as spiritual asseveration—in the typical octave/ sestet division of labor in Hopkins' sonnet formats. The plot, then. Escaping persecution on the continent, five Carmelite nuns have been reported among the many drowned passengers on the German vessel sunk in storm off the Cornish coast. When we finally arrive at this narrative kernel, internal rhyme marks the irony of a fatal liberation. For the voyage was of course launched without the passengers "ever as guessing" its destination: that "The *goal* was a *shoal*, of a fourth the doom to be drowned." One quarter of the ship's passengers have thus embarked on a fateful trajectory whose syntactically telescoped phrasing in "doom (ed)to be drowned" collapses noun and verb into the phonic knot of inevitability.

The poem builds slowly toward this nautical tragedy, however, with a framing gesture meant to transfigure the catastrophe to something more like sacrifice and intercession. To begin with, in address to his Lord, the persona, weighed down in his own mortality, acknowledges its divine origin: "Thou has bound bones & veins in me, fastened me flesh"—rather than the more predictable "fashioned my flesh." And bound it with that self-instancing entwinement of the ampersand in rare iconic appearance. On the way to stressing "flesh" as metonymy for the living being, the binding of bones with veins recalls the harbored "laststrands" of man clung to in "Carrion Comfort." The speaker of "The Wreck" who, in undaunted reverence still, says at the opening of the fifth stanza "I kiss my hand / To the stars, lovely-asunder," then adds—in a compound predicate whose parallelism, via another noun/verb flicker, it takes us a split second to catch up with—"Glow, glory in thunder." From that "glow," instressed not as fact but as refulgence in action, comes another gradient turn, whose radiating phonetics ignite the phrasal verb "glory in." The whole spiritual economy of inscape and instress seems condensed at this pressure point into the conversion of quality to affect: glow to the more subjective predicate of inward illumination.

In this tribute to the world-subtending God who, in further gradient extension from *asunder/thunder*, exists "*under* the world's s*plendour* and w*onder*," the next line insists—with unabashed over-emphasis—that "His m*ystery* must be *instr*essed, stressed." It is a phrasing that seems what it almost says at the dental/sibilant pressure point: *distressed*. There, in any case, in the phrasal infrascape of *yster* and *instr*—with the line's approach in that way toward a two-beat anagram—the entwined is disyllabically intimate with the mystic precincts it cryptically stretches to inhabit. Recalling one of the vaporous abstractions sensed by Keats to need a "greeting of the spirit," here Hopkins says, of this spur to instress in the matter of God's manifestation: "For I greet him the days I meet him, and bless when I understand." Bless—and a received blessedness it is.

Ultimately, when its gift is vouchsafed, it is this greeting of and by the divine, this meeting, that the persona projects as consummation for the "Maid," the collective virgin sisterhood, of the shipwreck. For when the storm clears, "jay-blue heavens" replace the "down-dugged ground-hugged grey" of the abating deluge, a phrasing weighted down in iteration by the echoic false past of "dugged" ("not a word in English," warns the Web, mistaken for the past-participial "dug"). That illicit past tense, with its self-enclosed "du—ed" bracket, is a mistaking that takes phonetic place twice over, first by open solecism, then in cross-word recursion in "ground-(d)hugged grey." Not just fading away in its grey fatefulness, this residual crepuscular dark, in lingering rov(e)over syllabification, "h*overs off.*"

At which point we "Grasp God, throned behind / Death"—as closely as those merged *d*'s of the enjambment would suggest. And lodged there "with a sovereignty that"—in this vocalized transcendental escalation—"heeds but hides, bodes but abides" (all predication subsumed to continuum). Disclaiming the lethal storm as a Miltonic assault ("not a lightning of fire hard-hurled"), not a brutal thunderbolt, but in its meaning—fitted to the world it irrigates—as "A released *shower*, let fla*sh* to the *shire*," the slant rhyme has freed cause to nurturant effect in the spirit's "dayspring." For here a plea for mediation sets in by apostrophe: "Dame, at our door / Drowned, and among our shoals," she is addressed in the request to "Remember us" in "the heaven-haven of the Reward," and, through God's transferred grace, sweeten the land(scape) on which, in drowning, she never landed. "Let him easter in us"—the ultimate predicated noun of kinetic resurrection—in the form of an irrigated "dayspring" sprung, for British "souls," from an otherwise mortal foreclosure on those lethal "shoals." In the nun's accident turned sacrifice, the tragedy of drowning seems almost to figure by proxy a second mass baptism. Nothing, however, is more characteristic of Hopkins than the way this consolatory closure should have been anticipated, from early on, by the open-ended inference of sprung rhyme. There God, before being seen as transcendentally "throned behind / Death," is figured, thrown lightning bolts and all, as the basis of a meaning beneath that turmoil. This transpires when all the pressure of "thunder" and the "splendour" of its "wonder" weigh upon the noun of its comprehension in that anticipatory fifth stanza, breaking apart its final rhyme to the self-enactively enjambed descent of "under/stand." It is there that one finds phono-graphically allegorized the divine grounding of all vicissitude in an undergirding faith, whose strophe tails off in its own strenuous mitigation of catastrophe.

Unhidden Being / Bidden Heeding: Inscape to Instress

IF VERSE LIKE THIS IS MEANT TO AUDIT some equivalent to the divinity that foreshapes our ends—as when reck(on)ing just above, by over-and-overing in the after-phrasing, the prismatic slants of "heeds but hides, bodes but abides"— that linguistic paradigm scarcely decides the issue. One wants an account of the consonance, so to speak, of such vocalic bracketing with a broader extratextual thematics. How does the beveled emphasis of internal echo point outside its own phrasal spans? That's one version of the question. Before returning to the climax of "The Wreck," it is therefore high time to pin down, precisely in its elusiveness, the reigning categorical duality in Hopkins. Any fresh sense of the adjusted division of labor between inscape and instress is one my argument has needed considerable verbal citation to prepare for. I bear down on this notorious terminological crux at this late point, and at the risk of anticlimax, because my contribution to it would have seemed overly schematic otherwise, less "evidence-based," an intervention more tendentious than linguistically self-evident.

Certainly I defer to the well-combed archive in grounding the extra "stress" this essay has set out to apply. A good deal of scholarship in previous Hopkins studies has been required to reach a point of even fertile uncertainty—verging on interchangeability—regarding Hopkins' deployment of those famous paired (but far from binary) terms, *inscape* and *instress*. In the nearly two decades of his most prolific "critical" writing, between 1868 and 1886, Hopkins used *inscape* and *instress*, along with its variants (indeed chronological precedents) *scape* and *stress*, two-hundred twelve times, we are told on the best authority— by the scholar who has thoroughly sorted, tracked, and mapped such mentions, searching for rooting assumptions (etymological and otherwise) and following out developing nuances in this vocabular quartet.[20] As Leonard Cochran's scrupulous tabulation of this terminological recurrence makes clear, after much dedicated culling and mulling, cause and effect do not divide around object and subject but are transfused from the instress of the one—the braced force field of its inscape in the maintenance of individuation—to the responsive reconstitution of this en-scapement by the attending mind. The distinction is ultimately between the world's immanence and its mental (hence phrasal) registration. Cochran's summary formulation of instress as in fact coextensive with inscape tacitly acknowledges the transference this allows. For to say that "all things are upheld by instress and are meaningless without it"[21] suggests that, outside the selved entity, any receptive mind grasping the "meaning" of the object before it—catching it in action or essence—must instress (sometimes a verb as well as noun in Hopkins) that apperception of the thing in question— and do so in the answering form of the subject's own mental contours, where "meaning" can be shaped and shared. Hence the vitalizing transit from cause to effect in what one might call (Cochran doesn't) the *secondary* inscaping of the other: its mentally (even before poetically) reformatted instress, which thus comes into play (according to my readings) as lynchpin or switch point in what is in fact a three-stage process resulting in oralized transcription.

But, no doubt about it, to transact any lucid shift in focus from ontological through phenomenological to inherently poetic terms is helped by some simplification of the coinages in play. Given the disparate mentions, overlapping usages, and freedom from definition in any distinction between inscape and its instress (inherent or induced, objective or subjective, noun or verb), it's no wonder that the Norton Anthology settles for a certain working distinction, an operable dyad—one having at least some statistical probability across the terms' variant evocations in Hopkins. According to the Victorian period editors Carol Christ and Catherine Robson, glossing the two keynote terms in their headnote to Hopkins, the "human being, the most highly selved, the most individually distinctive being in the universe, recognizes the inscape of other beings in an act that Hopkins calls *instress*, the apprehension of an object in an intense thrust of energy toward it that enables one to realize specific distinctiveness."[22] Add only: a distinctiveness braced in the first place by the object's own integral (and integrating) stress. But it would be much in the spirit of Hopkins' language for this engagement if we were to take that "realize" as a two-tiered verb, first for "acknowledge," then for "activate" in contemplation. With the result, in the Norton headnote: "Ultimately, the instress of inscape leads one to Christ, for the individual identity of any object is the stamp of divine creation on it." Ultimately, or rather say ideally, but the way is often labored, roundabout, and sometimes blocked. What is so useful in this responsible simplification, catching the main drift from object to subject before the return from individuation to creative source, is the way it allows us to see how the poet's own tendency to conflate and even reverse the terms of instressed inscape can seem productively to enforce—if not merely forcing it in some wish-fulfilment of the syllable—the necessary reciprocity around which any such distinction continuously swivels.

The "thrust of energy" (the Norton gloss again) that human perception brings to the world can be thought at such moment to coincide with, all but inhabit, the stress necessary—the force and pressured counterforce—that separates things out from universal matter in the first (fiat-ed) place. This is how individuation permits a glimpse of continuum and unity at the level of an almost literal, or say again reciprocal, *realization* of the differentiated world. To repeat Cochran's paraphrase alongside that of the Norton editors, about the inscape that upholds from within even while it is held up for perception: "All things are upheld by instress and are meaningless without it." Meaning is the sharing of the upheld as beheld—and internalized, though not in some thin sentimental circuit, recalling here the tacit liaison from st. 5 where even "God's mystery . . . instressed, stressed" seems burdened as well with the dentalized rove-over of "distressed." In the reach for meaning, or say the timbre of meaning, the goal isn't to be just moved by nature, but to be moved *toward* the inscaped force that fashions and sustains its individuated "grandeurs"—as well as its storm-battered terrors.

The Micropoetics of Inpress

THE PROCESS ISN'T CIRCULAR, but bipolar and ultimately dialectic, which is how it lends itself so readily, this essay wants to add, to an template for reading. To sum up under the aegis of a certain purposeful simplification: stress (or instress at this level), the formative pressure of inscape, is met more than halfway by the molded contours of human recognition, assimilating the that-ness of inscape as an internalized this-ness—here as well as now, in me. This takes place, claims place, via the interface of a mediating (rather than structural) pressure exerted upon the responsive consciousness. Instress, then, is both foundational and epiphenomenal: the object taut with its own ontology over against the mind's heightened openness to that tensile complexity in recognition. In this sense an original *stress* seems synonymized, in reception, with a sense of *emphasis* as well as foundational *tension*. The resulting instress becomes something like the impressed mirror of inscape. At which point, when captured in poetry's sympathetic vibrations, "realization" takes form as the tertiary imprint of inscape: again, the acoustic prism of internal difference under intensified vocal (and rhetorical) emphasis. And if all this terminological spiraling—descended from Hopkins' own shifting critical vocabulary—can bear another coinage as a mediating third term, we may identify this articulating literary interface as a textual *inpress*.

Even the immanent may need manifestation by an answering language. Poetry is the learned rather than native tongue by which inherence can be w/rung out in and by name. In the slant audial tautology of this essay's title, God's generative fecundity, streaked with difference, is only to be believed as s/pied—glassed by phrase in the unique grandeur of its glinting inward manifold. Where the admixture is heard stirred in words. Hence the sense of aural refraction not just as a mixed metaphor but an index of synesthetic deflections. Writing in process for Hopkins, eschewing the fixities of denotation, brings the otherwise still hidden to light, in all its defining contours, its gradations and shadings, often jarringly schismatic in its prismatic variations. Hopkins' advocated vocality, his reading by ear, his staggered earring of the word, is the reading *out* of inscape in the syncopated rhythms of pace and intonation. Verse, stretched past its limit into poetry, addresses the shading and gradations of the wrought world with the always fraught effort to meet its call, greeting it on terms that poetry can best enunciate. And to which it then bids our scrutiny. Wording is less a world-building materiality than, at one remove, a participant witness to revealed fertilities, vergings, and mergers that only such language has the inherent flexibility, not to mention the captivating fascination, to *mediate*.[23]

This condition of language is made available for a particular kind of devotion in Hopkins, of course. Divine unity, realized in multitude, comes worded into the world as the patchy and discontinuous: a thingness speckled and flecked, marled and mottled, tabby and dappled. Its secondary representation is in turn variegated, piebald, and multifaceted. All this we have seen, have heard. Including its scalar contradictions. For to elicit this interanimating multiplicity of the divine and revealed One requires at first the will to individuate—or, in the toggling and topple of Hopkinspeak, to submit impressions to the refractive staggering of slant and trace, where skewed lucidity is parsed in di/splay, layered, bent, blent, all glint lent out to significance. Every slice of mottled life, every cross-section of the mixed and diversified world, is in one sense, but rather abstractly, the synecdoche for Creation—divine fecundity in distribution, the parti-colored as *pars pro toto* of transcendental unity—and thus at the same time, more palpably, a metonymy for admixture across the broad spectrum of existence.

This emblematic metonymy deserves a moment more, and all but requires it in the interplay between natural observation and its creationist valence in poem after poem. If it is true that individual Hopkins poems are less microcosms of God's galactic handwork than metonymies for its proliferation in similar inmixed forms, the case isn't closed there. For metonym comes round to synecdoche again within the associational helix of the ontological system both girded and interpreted by sprung rhythm's filtering poetics. The internally composite and self-diversified essence of created objecthood ends up miniaturizing a universe of differends. What results is a sustained training ground for *reading*, whereby the world's blended densities are made malleable, and palpably so, only at the off-angle of gradient phrase under the instress of response. In the process, the ontological difference-within of inscape and its apprehending instress schools the reverent imagination in the *concordia discors* of subsumed multiplicity. In the specialized poetic *discourse* of such transcendent variegation and transcended *discord* (etymological false friends but true stylistic intimates in Hopkins), the skewing dazzle of ontological prismatics is transposed to oblique harmonics in the key of unity.

So it is that the bidden reading out loud of poetry's investments in life's pied beatitude ends up feeling in Hopkins, on the pulse of attention, more catechetical than categorical: a ritual recitation of poetic logos internalized. This is what I am calling second-order instress. Or *inpress*: markedly scriptive in the very grain of its spirituality. The circle is far from vicious. God's Word, become world, needs to recover its legibility as celebratory word in the form of interpretable text—whose mastery could never be facile, never transpicuous in depiction, precisely in deference to the ordained seethe and interplay of the created world's oscillating repletion. Answering the call, the bid, of such pied, plied density—such tensility, such flexed mercurial variety—is an act of faith as well as of interpretation.

Inscape measure, therefore, taken on inwardly by instress, can only be taken up for reading by the graphophonemic cast of inpress. This happens again, and in its own exploratory terms again and again, through that "over-and-overing" (both senses: iterative and overlapping) that participates, we might come to think, in the very duration of being—rather than simply stopping it in a name. To recall that notable prepositional phrase from "Poetry and Verse" about the netting of inscape, the effort is to "detach it," not from itself (in abstraction), but "*to* the mind" (in recognition) as experienced form (as if "dispatch" were the word). Every tangible appreciation, tactile or not, operates like the taking of an impression, stress refigured by mental impress on the path to transcription. Crucial for my analysis in all this is a devotion metalinguistic quite apart from metaphysical, still less religious. I've sometimes called certain moments of aural adumbration (almost unremitting in Hopkins)—moments surfaced in both prose and poetry—the flashing sites of *epiphony*.[24] More than merely ear-opening, the subvocal phonotext can serve in this way to refashion the very idea of subjectivity in reading. As illustrated here, such scriptive triggers take us (inward) from the immanence of being to the materiality of evocalized writing, whose pitch can vibrate with a meaning-fullness beyond semantic sense. For this is exactly the paradigm that Hopkins' experiments drive to their unabashed limit. There, writing's imprint on the page—and especially in the act of sprung rhythm, whether rung out loud or only shaped in sounded silence—is hyperbolically engaged with *vocality's own anatomical inscape*, its stressed pneumatic pressures emerging thorax-tongued, larynx-lunged, and everywhere breath-upheld in its transmitted bid for "in-spiration." Through the pulsional over-runs of enunciation, say then that inscape is met by instress—as if uploaded from the body's own voice-recognition software—under the phonic stylus of inpress.

One may stand by such a claim even while recognizing that discussion might best come to rest in a return from generalization to its germinating prompts in the throes of Hopkins' steady poetic surprise. To distill the writing effect of *inpress* as a thing of acoustic syncopation with and within script, one readily listens in again on the overoving, the overhovering, of Hopkins' rhymes and their internal, subsyllabic enjambments. For this dispelled lexical cohesion, there is no clearer example than the polemically audible "Spelt from Sybil's Leaves" ("not reading with the eye but loud"), which actually deploys its own portmanteau conflation (the rare form "throughther" for otherness in interwine) to name such eccentric blending in the process of exemplifying it. In the poem's opening nightfall, we see tracked in cursory fashion (have already seen, and cited, earlier) the "stup*endous*" scope of the evening starscape in the first line—and see now, in returning to complete the poem's opening rhyme, the sky's further encompassing (two-word) power to "overb*end us*." And just the "overing" of word borders is answered next in a counterintuitive dappling of syllabification in the eclipse of the earth's visible quilted patchwork. Under the dome of the star-risen evening, and in the loose-fitting third shoe-fall of the overstrained rhyme, earth's "dapple is at an *end, as-* / stray or aswarm, all throughther [thruther], in throngs." Hear then, if you can, against the spacing of script, the slant schema "stupendous" / "bend us" / "end as-." But hear it not as anything detachable *to the mind* as a descriptive inference, just as its own inherent flux of conjuncture and transfusion. In this respect I'm more than willing to credit Hopkins with the tacit last of this essay's metacritical performatives, a summary portmanteau for lexical admixture itself. In the syllabic meld of "through" with "other," under the stress of interpretation at least (dappled orthography in overdrive) inter*penetration* (in the druthers of its toppling momentum) spells itself out as one precision-tooled key to inscape's own *throughtherness.*

In this same spirit, to listen back in conclusion to the power of other such sprung rhymes is to get, through them, one last supersaturated litmus test of Hopkins' poetics in the renowned achievement of "The Wreck." Early and late intonations speak to each other, or call it audit each other, in this poem's arc of catharsis. The early "leeward" drift of the fated ship finds its eccentric "rove-over" forensics across the switchback gradation of the next two lines. It is there that "w—r-d" returns as the force—auditory as well as nautical, and cross-fading in this case to a single dental phoneme—that "drew *her* / *D*ead" to the shore (st. 14). This phonetic suction reads as if each sound frame were laying latent claim to homophonic enunciation as a metatextual pun on the very word "word" whose unitary status is under siege by this storming of lexical sequence. With the rove-over drift almost thematized there as the draw of a riptide, we read on toward the poem's climactic sprung leak in controlled lineation at the point of redemption, which begins as follows in the dramatic follow-through promised by the colon:

> Dame, at our d*oor*
> *D*rowned, and among our shoals

> Remember us in the roads, the heaven-haven of the rew*ard*:

Across four subsequent lines of sung restoration, including "Our King back," with the wish that such divinity might now "easter in us," the cascade of renewal descended from the colon after "reward" includes the emphatic nomination of a syllabic chime first sequestered in the enjambed slant of "door" / "drowned." One supreme reward in this life is, for Hopkins, to hear the divine presence everywhere, as enacted through thick and thin in the stanza's and the poem's own tongue-twisting, grammar-bending last line, final instance of the colon-prepared "reward" of this spiritually reclaimed calamity: "Our heart's charity's hearth's fire, our thoughts' chivalry's throng's Lord." Even from such a congested intensity of captured affect, this is the final echoic lift of instressed sound we've learned to recognize in Hopkins—and have been cued to yearn for, across this thirty-five-stanza case, as the redemptive order and ordination of the Lord's own Word.

The nun who "takes the veil" in Hopkins' brief undergraduate poem "Heaven-Haven," having asked to be "where no storms come," is fulfilled here—if only after a lethal storm—in the final half dozen lines of her author's masterpiece, where her martyrdom as implied bride of Christ is invoked to return the Lord's blessed husbandry to the English soil and soul. It is there that the drowned nun's consolatory "rew*ard*" slips into a rhyme (corrective of her "leeward" disaster in earlier wording) only if the quite metaphoric "door" is heard ajar (not just understood to be open) as the welcoming portal afforded by death's temporary closure ("d*oor d*/rowned" on route to rew-*ard*). Such a segmental over-ride is found operating internally—by ingrown enjambment— two lines later with the cross-word rhyme of "shoals" (under lisping license) with "[éngli]*sh souls*."

Enhancing the power of this final stanza by being mapped upon it from earlier in the poem, another long cathartic arc may be recalled here from our discussion of the framing fifth stanza. The "wonder" of muted "thunder" that pulled phonetically "asunder" the grounding substrate "stand" from "under" at the hanging finish (under/stand) of those summary lines may be recalled now, with the documented tragedy fully unfolded, as precedent for that even more defining phonic trajectory in the closing stanza—and its both embedded and distended final genitive grammar: "Our heart's charity's hearth's fire, our thoughts' chivalry's throng's Lord." Here is where an etymologically quickened under-standing catapults heavenward from the scene of natural violence. And where divinity has the last word. It is God's vastness that englobes, in any bravely attempted unpacking of that dizzying last nested syntax, the throngs of our chivalrous thoughts in realizing the fire of the hearth of our heart's charity. The poem's closing, self-ingested syntax builds to an effect that "has the last word" precisely as word, as Logos in elocution. For localized in vertical descent (and spiritual ascension) in the line-end rungs of this sprung rhythm, the telos of its inpress, is the fulfillment of a near-eschatological drive. In the earlier stanza, the etymological tropism of *ward* as "turned" (as, for instance, accompanying the *forth* rooted in "for*ward*") guides not just the obvious directional 'sidewards' of that drifting "leeward" but, here finally, (a)mounts to the forthcoming due of a future benediction. So that the overrun rhymes seem vectorized by a destiny anchored in, aimed at, and affirmed by the propulsive *towardness* meant to settle on the poem's final chiming in the resonant order of the "Lo*rd*": wholly the goal, as it were, the haven and home, of any and all open(e)d *oor/d* rew*ard*. In off-rhyme's economy of inpress, such notice is reading's own achieved recompense.

There's finally no missing, in its mediacy, the immediate lesson gleaned from such complex logopoetic transfers of verbal inscape in Hopkins. Offered up is that veritable motto for the mottled at divinatory work: again, if glory to God for dappled things, to art for their dappled hearings. To art we turn, that is, as a sphere of quasi-devotional practice—in its own almost liturgical formalizations. Sprung rhythm, together with its accompanying phonetic measures, manages throughout—and *througther*—a curriculum of keenly faceted audition. It does so across a set, and test, of mediating priestly orisons devoted in transcription, in inpress, to the verbal power of world-engrained worship. Such, for Hopkins, is the simultaneously babelized and redeemed *wor(d)ship* effected by poetry's acoustic prism. Reading, in turn, is for the influential if inimitable aesthetic of Hopkins' pied audition, a sounding of the world (a virtual unltrasound scan) whose blended phonetic entities rehearse—and rehear—the universe's sublime originary plural. So that, odd as it may sound to say about such audible oddness, Hopkins' method serves to generalize the power of literary inscription, of the poetic Word, even in his own most exceptional demonstrations. The outreach of "bidding," the virtual "declamation" of the page, passes to reader from transcription's felt world, inner as well as outer, through poetry's worked wording of its own awe and anxiety. In this transfer, inscape is upheld by displacement in the secondary stress of a wording, an evocalization, that quite openly *calls to mind* the intricacies of both spirit and world, bringing them, even when not fully together, to sounded terms with each other. And all the more ringingly when wrung from the ten thousand places of poetry's verbal play.

Notes

1 James Milroy, *The Language of Gerard Manley Hopkins* (London: Andre Deutch, 1977).

2 The cited lines from Gerard Manley Hopkins in this essay are widely available on the internet, including on the Hopkins Society website; all citations have been checked against the authoritative edition, *The Poetical Works of Gerard Manley Hopkins*, ed. Norman H. Mackenzie (Oxford: Clarendon Press, 1990) without ordinarily including (from here out) the rhythmic stress marks and other "musical" notations, like ties or holds, that Hopkins inserted as tags for recitation or declamation (see Mackenzie, liii).

3 Susan J. Wolfson, *A Greeting of the Spirit: Selected Poetry of John Keats with Commentaries* (Cambridge, MA: Harvard University Press, 2022).

4 Wolfson, *A Greeting of the Spirit*, 3.

5 Gerard Manley Hopkins, *Letters of Gerard Manley Hopkins to Robert Bridges*, ed. C. C. Abbott, rev. ed. (London: Oxford University Press, 1955).

6 Alluding to Garrett Stewart, *Dear Reader: The Conscripted Audience in Nineteenth-Century British Fiction* (Baltimore: Johns Hopkins University Press, 1986) in its debts to Jonathan Culler, "Apostrophe," *The Pursuit of Signs: Semiotics, Literature, Deconstruction* (Ithaca: Cornell University Press, 1981), 135–54.

7 Hopkins, *Letters*, 160.

8 Rhyme included, on the question of over-reading—particularly of one word over the edge of another (at the risk of over-ingenuity)—there is at least this much to say. It took me most of a second book on Dickens (*The One, Other, and Only Dickens* [Ithaca: Cornell University Press, 2018]) to demonstrate the overfull surge of the novelist's matured stylistic assonance as a potential reparation for the suppression of nuclear vowels in his days as Parliamentary reporter, with all syllabic sonority squeezed out by the reigning codes of phonetic shorthand before being laboriously reinserted by the keen ear of Dickens as transcribing stenographer. It is a much more economical (though, I fear, not a simpler) thing to cite any half dozen rich and orally overlapping single lines from Hopkins, with their graded syllabification, and ask whether it's likely that such wavelengths of enfolded and self-forwarded inner wording discerned elsewhere by the reader

would have escaped the author's own ear in the strokes of his pen—and hence slipped under all notice as nodes of potential interest. Better to take everything on faith: in the confidence, that is, of feasible pertinence.

9   Hopkins, *Letters*, 86, where rhymes that thus "rove over," straying into the next line for completion, contribute as "little grace notes" to the larger sense in this passage, when defending his practice to Robert Bridges, of an "over-reaving" structure in his stanzas—with "over-weaving" hard not to hear there in the trellising tendrils of such effects, clasping hold of the next line by the trespassing plunder implied in the verb "reave." But it's more, I suspect, what one sees and hears, by way of cross-gap auto-exemplification, in the collocation "rove over" that has made that term so much more frequently adduced in scholarship.

10   Hopkins can seem operating here on the near side of a hypertextual chasm whose experimental trajectory ends in the algorithmic mutations of John Cayley's work with "paraphones" and their complementary orthographic scrabble-play (where, say, **wor**d becomes **wen**d in a respective graphic remodeling, now slicing, now curving, of central vowel and consonant by aleatory digital drivers). See his essay and my response in *Bandwidths: Reading Across Media with Garrett Stewart*, ed. David LaRocca (New York: Bloomsbury, 2025).

11   Gerard Manley Hopkins, "Poetry and Verse," in "Lecture Notes: Rhetoric," *The Journals and Papers of Gerard Manley Hopkins*, ed. Humphrey House, completed by Graham Storey (London: Oxford University Press, 1959), 259–60, where poetry requires that the patterning (for its own sake) of verse, its sound figures, must reach beyond sheer composition (as in music) to meaning, rather than remain, for instance, just in the service of a mnemonic.

12   Hopkins, "Poetry and Verse," 289.

13   Mackenzie, *The Poetical Works* (n. 2 above), 141.

14   William Empson, *Argufying: Essays on Literature and Culture*, ed. John Haffenden (Iowa City: University of Iowa Press, 1988), 332, where one of the correspondents in a 1955 *TLS* exchange on this Hopkins poem, revisiting Empson's discussion of "The Windover" in *Seven Types of Ambiguity* from 25 years before, wonders "Why should Mr. Empson construe so strangely 'plough down sillion shine'? True, sillion may shine, but it is the shine of the plough the poet is considering. . . ." This is a point Empson returns to in his undaunted rejoinder on 336 without recruiting (typically enough) any *phonetic* wordplay to his defense.

15   William Empson, *Seven Types of Ambiguity* (New York: New Directions, 1947), 225, where his discussion of the double valence of "buckle" is part of the later debate in *TLS* above (n. 13).

16   Hopkins, *Letters*, 245–46.

17   Besides Milroy on gradience and Hartman (n. 19) on phonic juncture, another guiding light (or high-fidelity microphonic register) in this reading of Hopkins, as often in my previous work, is provided by the rich if elusive concept of the "anti-pun" in Christopher Ricks' *The Force of Poetry* (Oxford: Clarendon Press, 1984), 100. His term indicates the inescapable free association—deeply available in and to language—that can't quite be roped back into relevance, logical or grammatical, yet which colors the poetic line nonetheless. It hovers there as a scripted testament, in Wordsworth's phrase, to the "spiritual presence of absent things" (100)—and is first illustrated by Ricks with that poet's own phrase "*fleet* waters of the drowning world" (99–100), where the adjective of momentum calls up the

noun of an armada in a way strictly unusable (but cognitively unshakeable) by meaning. Related to this is the strictly phonic undertone—what I called "contra-pun-tal" in discussing "In Honour of St. Alphonsus Rodriguez"—that must be overridden by writing's own sequence. No stranger to these effects, Hopkins seems to introduce another freer association yet, unscripted but impinging, which I'm tempted to call the "arche-pun": potently (if only potentially) threaded into semantic resonance even when (unlike the anti-pun) entirely unwritten. So with many of the precipitant associations of the "terrible" sonnet at hand, "To be the stranger seems my lot, my life"—all "the stranger," so to say, for the way these lexical effects exceed any actual homophonic play (as, by contrast, in "hell's spell[s]"). Such arche-play involves not just extraneous but actually (actively?) unspelled formulations—ranging (never quite puns) from 'put by' (but by) to 'begone' (began)—that are related, at one further remove, to the kind of graphic anagrams in which Ricks elsewhere takes a revealing interest—though with cases never manifest in such encrypted cross-word form as in Hopkins' covert rhyme of "began" with "baffling *ban*." See Ricks, "Shakespeare and the Anagram," in Christopher Ricks, ed., *Proceedings of the British Academy, Volume 121* (2003), *2002 Lectures*, pp. 111–46. In contrast, any idea of the subliminal arche-pun— as close cousin to the inscribed anti-pun, though lying deeper in linguistic possibility than any one instance can "literally" trigger (as with that oddball "knot" suggested by Duns Scotus as "rarest-veinèd unraveller; a{k}not / rivalled insight") contrasts with the kind of half-said but fully verbalized d/rift of cross-word transegmental play, where its *ties that unbind* are only realized if they loose new semantic enunciations. Somewhere between a sounded junctural liaison in this mode like "la*st drain*" and the unscripted echo of an arche-overtone—the whole spectrum, of course, made available by Hopkins' porous sonority—is the impure phonetic dredging, also in "The Sea and the Skylark," of primal "lime" from "first slime."

18   Hopkins, "To Bridges," August 21, 1877. *The Collected Works of Gerard Manley Hopkins, vol. 1, Correspondence 1852–1881*, ed. R. K. R. Thornton and Catherine Phillips (London: Oxford University Press, 2013), 296.

19   Ibid.

20   George Leonard Cochran, O.P., "Instress and Its Place in the Poetics of Gerard Manley Hopkins," *Hopkins Quarterly*, vol. 6, no. 4 (Winter 1980): 152.

21   Hopkins, *Journals*, 127.

22   Stephen Greenblatt et. al., *The Norton Anthology of British Literature*, vol. 2 (New York: W. W. Norton, 2018), 1514–15.

23   Here, it might usefully be acknowledged, is the main difference between my earlier work on Hopkins in *Reading Voices*, as part of a speculative literary history of cross-word effects from Shakespeare to Vladimir Nabokov, and this new essay. In the years since, I became a "media theorist"—and so my emphasis inevitably arrives now at a seemingly oblique angle (a bevel) to the eponymous emphasis of my most influential teacher, Geoffrey H. Hartman, in *The Unmediated Vision: An Interpretation of Wordsworth, Hopkins, Rilke, and Valéry* (New Haven: Yale University Press, 1954). His is a study of a new secular poetics in the modernity of verse. No longer the dream of poet as priest, even though Hopkins was one. No requisite mediators, no prophets, no credentialed seers. One needs to view the world, God's or otherwise, through one's own eyes, feel it for oneself. That's

the new epistemology, so to say, but in the realm of poetics, one still needs words (to phrase as well as feel the world), and that's where sound mediates all (other) sense(s) of things. No critic in my experience knew this better than Hartman, even in this first book as well as in his stirring later work, but his earliest title may seem to play it down. His sense of the intricate woven filter of linguistic mediation in verse is certainly vouched for by the extended use I make of the shuttled voicings he elicits from syllabic juncture and its phonemic "zero values" throughout *Reading Voices*, repeatedly citing his famous essay "The Voice of the Shuttle: Language from the Point of View of Literature," (*The Review of Metaphysics*, vol. 23, no. 2 [Dec., 1969]: 240–58.)—with vigorous auditions uniquely attuned to the shunts of verse's phonemic loom. Furthermore, with the question of mediation in mind, one can better appreciate what is so slippery in the terminology of inscape and the matching phrasal instress that, on one construal, can be heard to shape such auditory registers in Hopkins. It is never as clear-cut, though, as finding the inscape of things translated to the instress of verbal emphasis, to soundscape.
But it is pertinent to think of *mediated vision* (contra Hartman's title) as a kind of translation into the synesthesia of cognitive apprehension—where sounding the world is both plumbing and utterance at once, musing and music. Anything like the so-called unmediated vision of secular revelation still needs the refractions of poetry's acoustic prism—which, by way of telling the truth "slant" (in the famous phrase of Hopkins' also posthumously published American contemporary), traces revelation by (again) phonetic bevel, only sometimes making for the outright mimesis of an aural mirror.

24   [Ed.] For more on epiphony, see Garrett Stewart, *Book, Text, Medium: Cross-Sectional Reading for a Digital Age* (Cambridge: Cambridge University Press, 2020) and *The Metanarrative Hall of Mirrors: Reflex Action in Fiction and Film* (New York: Bloomsbury, 2022). See also, *Attention Spans: Garrett Stewart, a Reader*, ed. David LaRocca (New York: Bloomsbury, 2024), 342, where the term is defined, in part, as "a moment of textual revelation sprung from the phonetic enunciation of a word or phrase not necessarily epiphanic in any other sense, as in many of the homophonic puns Stewart finds in literary texts from all periods."

5 / Motivated for the first time to bear down rather strenuously on the habits of punctuation in Stewart's favorite novelist, and in particular his favorite novel—full stop—Stewart builds here on an intriguing assignment to write about Charles Dickens' punctuation for the post-1800 phase of a three-volume philological treatment of the literary history of punctuation (marks and much beyond) forthcoming from Cambridge University Press. Closing in from his broader survey of Dickensian penchants in the matter of the "punct," the critic finds in the process unexpected new ways to appreciate the stylistic pacing, cadence, and parallelism of first-person report in *Great Expectations* (1861) as ironic *Bildungsroman*, tracked by its often punishing grooves of introspection. In this expansion and further refinement of Stewart's entry for the Cambridge anthology, the genius of that Dickens text stands forth with a newly delineated stylistic profile against the backdrop of the novelist's other volumes, "pointed up" here in part by the generative contrupun(a) tal interplay of commas and semi-colons as unexpected textual pressure points from the birth of the hero's consciousness forward.

5 / *Charles Dickens and the Plotting of Punctuation*

CHARLES DICKENS IS ALL PUNCTUATION. This claim is not the kind about prose intensity that, in the sense of sheer vivifying emphasis, could be restated with "is all italics," which anyway, in the spirit of the three-volume project that got me thinking along these lines, would speak—and merely in typesetting metaphor—only about one specialized mode of typographic punctuation, one (etymologically associated) manner of *pointing*. In writing about Dickens as master syntactician, I had meant to catch the spirit of this Cambridge University Press collection, and the weight of its philological history, by tracking certain effects of Dickens' both comic and melodramatic "periods" (his variable grammatic spans) by way of punctuation-marks other than the closing demarcations offered by the trusty on-line dot of a full stop.[1] Offered indeed by punctual recurrence itself, its own kind of pointed rhyming, phonetic or otherwise. As well as by gaps (not marks but marked absences) at every scale, from tethered sentence fragments like this and the last, through para/ graphic spacing and indentation, and back down to the cross-word calibrations of elisional word play. In all this, punctuation stands forth in broadest terms as a pointing (up more than out), a giving point *to*. And in expanding my remarks here beyond the borders of that survey, I am grateful all over again for what that invitation summoned to new view in my reading—especially with regard to the Dickens novel I thought I knew best (past tense duly noted). Yet what I came to see as the "point/counterpunct" of *Great Expectations*—notably in its play between commas and semi-colons, and they in turn with the underlying drama of narrative grammar—had its unexpected surprises, developed further here in their inflective function: a shifting indicial stress on inference over above reference. Dickens, as no reader is likely to contest, finds inexhaustible ways to press his rhetorical points.[2]

In the common keyboard understanding of punctual emphasis, the explicitly so-called exclamation-point is the clearest everyday instance of the case. In the broader sense of signaling promulgated by those Cambridge volumes, the work of *deixis*—from the Greek for pointing, showing—refers to a directed emphasis, an indicative accent, not narrowly confined to such differential linguistic orientations as I/you, here/there, etc.[3] The very term "punctuation-mark," we're alerted, would be a pleonasm if there weren't other forms of punctuation besides rote signals of a typeset-ready sort.[4] In the spirit of our editors lobbying those of *OED3* to think outside the mark, beyond the graphic point to the rhetorical and spatial pointer, this essay, too, seeks "to recognize punctuation *tout court* as a marked, spatial, deictic, & cognitive phenomenon that is part of the pragmatics of the written medium & praxis of the *mise-en-page*: a major form of hermeneutics."[5] I don't have the ear of the *OED* board, but I can, like the rest of us, bring an ear as well as an eye to bear on Dickens' punctuated page formats in all their adroit semantic channeling and leveraged emphases.[6]

In drafting my anthology remarks, I became so preoccupied with the comma's little "hook" that I've read on since about, and discussed with writing students, what one might call the striking pause given by the comma's strategic absence— as well as the stroked pace of its presence. In a brief article—from the April 1924 issue of *The Adelphi* magazine—called simply "On Punctuation," the novelist Dorothy Richardson is succinct and suggestive in her judgments. The comma is Richardson's special topic, and the advice is trenchant: "It is a good plan, in the handling of phrases, to beware of pauses when appealing mainly to the eye, and to cherish them when appealing to reflection." Thinking versus things taken in at a glance, the latter's seeing versus the former's cognition. Including an "appeal" to the ear as an intermediate feature of each, of course. "With sequences of single words, and particularly of adjectives, when the values are concrete [Dickens standing up to be counted here, first among equals], reinforcing each other, accumulating without modification or contradiction upon a single object of sight, the comma is an obstruction."[7] Never does Dickens occlude his best snapshots in this manner, so that the weighted phrase "accumulating *upon*" is just right for the pressure brought by his unalleviated and unsorted epithets: the very epiphenomenon of the single glimpse, that is, the slightest glyph. No better example than the second-hand impressions, still vivid in memory, item by item, of Pip's altogether unglamorous arrival to London in his new role as gentleman. Here a particularly negligible detail of the transit to Mr. Jaggers in the microcosmic "Little Britain" is seared directly onto Pip's mind (and recollection), as if brooking no reflection, no afterthought. For among the gaudy but seedy encumbrances of his transport was the time taken by his ancient coachman to take a seat on his box, "which I remember"—signal to our own deferred special notice—"to have been decorated" (false ironic lead, that past participle) "with an old weather-stained pea-green hammercloth motheaten into rags." Not nibbled *to* bits, but submitted to the more durational "into," the arriving noun itself folded over from "cloth" to the unhyphenated past participle "motheaten"—a notable compression after the previously sub-punctuated hyphenates accruing to this unified vision. The effect aspires as so often in Dickens to a kind of mimetic wording, here frayed and tattered at the phrasal level as depiction itself unravels before us—the (typo)graphical analog of onomatopoeia. My return in these pages to the topic and exemplification of my Cambridge entry has me more than ever alert, in this way, to the goings on without (short)comings of the dropped Dickensian comma and its fast-paced cognitive kin.

Discussion can well begin again where John Lennard does—in his "Introduction to Punctuation since 1700"—with Dickens' first novel, *The Posthumous Papers of the Pickwick Club* (1837), and linger further over the pointed editorial "mark ups" of its comedy. In the passage concerned with Mr. Jingle's scattershot volubility quoted by Lennard, the third twist of cricket lingo becomes a trope of fatality for the character who, unable to "bowl me out—fainted too."[8] This sporting argot is soon picked up again, and picked over, in Jingle's jangling wordplay. A close clang of different prepositional senses finds this same poor enthusiast, in Jingle's report, to have "bowled on, on my account—bowled off, on his own—died Sir." Two straightforward em-rules, rather than commashes (to use the favored Cambridge terminology)—first for the rush of precipitous action, then for appositive restatement—capture the almost punning *dash* of Jingle's cantering banter as the lingo of the cricket pitch in itself pitched over (and the monosyllable "on" bowled on in its own right) from playing field to a figurative play on death's exit stroke. The parallel commas serve further to parenthesize the difference between the spatiotemporal adverbs and the prepositional idiom "on account": a double ledger inherent to the comedy and its invited "hermeneutics." What we've heard in Jingle's slapdash rendering might in the narrator's own voice have been something more like the syllepsis of "he took his wicket, and his last breath, at once." Simultaneity can usually go without saying in such comic yokings, along with the grammatically irrelevant but semantically loaded commas, appearing even in the Cambridge project's General Introduction in a summary of the way W. B. Parkes' paleographic work "puts two millennia of ill-behaved grammarians to shame, and to the sword," where the comma helps in marking, pointing, the prepositional gear-shift from literal to figurative diction.[9]

And sometimes the down-shift is to an even more strictly idiomatic metaphor. Earlier in *The Pickwick Papers*, note the second, figurative descent when Mr. Pickwick, drunk on punch, "fell into the barrow, and fast asleep, simultaneously."[10] To paraphrase: "he passed the day in revelry, and then out." A similar transfer, this time metaphoric to literal, accompanies a different mode of transportation in the more famous (and differently punctuated) textbook example of such syllepsis from later in the novel, when we find the frustrated Miss Bolo carried away, as it were, by emotion and servants: "Miss Bolo rose from the table considerably agitated, and went straight home, in a flood of tears and a sedan-chair." The second comma there is a minor anticipatory drum-roll. But a sentence later, an extraneous stress on "simultaneously" closes the chapter with the parallel exit of Pickwick, who, "having soothed his feelings with something hot, went to bed, and to sleep, almost simultaneously." In this act of helping himself to some spirits and a needed rest, the comma-punctuated repeat of the prepositional "to" exaggerates the different quasi-spatial axes involved in lying down and dropping off. In all such wordplay, the league between comma marking and phrasal spiking brings the latter, too, into the realm of punctuation's deictic pointing. In which zone, as the Cambridge editors rightly insist (and were eager to have me help demonstrate), there are more puncta than are dreamed of in routine philology.

Including font shifts and differential typefaces. Even no punctuation at all, as on a title page a decade on from *The Pickwick Papers* in Dickens' career, can operate like a negative form of pointing. The blare of ALL CAPS can at times fall mute. An overarch of curved lettering—"DEALINGS WITH THE FIRM"—is followed by a modest "OF" on its own line, and then by another larger arch for DOMBEY AND SON, followed in turn, unpunctuated (otherwise), by a return to lineation with "WHOLESALE RETAIL & FOR EXPORTATION." This is masthead or billboard lettering, of course, but—without a comma after the embedded and familiar short title, merely identifying founder and commercial heir apparent. The question is thereby left open (where I left it as well in the "Foreign Offices" essay above, chapter 2) whether it may be our own narrative "dealings" (its plural in contrast to the more prosaic eighteenth-century chapter head "Dealing with" or "Concerning")—rather than the transactions of the colonial shipping firm itself—that are momentarily pointed (to) as "wholesale" in their mercantile satire. No question about it when the omniscient narrative, in the novel's second paragraph, has the senior partner and patriarch, alone and in isolation, conventionally enough introduced by surname. Followed—by noun fragment, after a punctuating gap—by the reduction of newborn child to the status of merely latent corporate figure/head and next-in-line: "Dombey was about eight-and-forty years of age. Son about eight-and-forty minutes."[11] No "and" to secure their strictly business connection as yet, the only thing of (going) concern to the former. Here, as everywhere in Dickens, the calculated sentence fragment carries its own quotient of often ironic punctu(r)ation.

Far from this ponderous mechanical binary in the polar bonding of Dombey and son, two novels later a sustained array of clausal fragments in the opening London overview of *Bleak House* (1853) evokes a kaleidoscopic chaos: "London. Michaelmas term lately over, and the Lord Chancellor sitting in Lincoln's Inn Hall. Implacable November weather. As much mud in the streets as if the waters had but newly retired from the face of the earth [...]."[12] On and on across three more complex syntactic arrests headed only by the detached nouns of "Smoke," "Dogs," "Horses," and "Foot passengers," the latter three's implacable urban stampede cementing the muck with a double mercantile pun (emphasis added, in fact added in their own terms by the focusing punctuation-marks): "adding new *deposits* to the crust upon crust of mud, sticking at those points tenaciously to the pavement, and accumulating at *compound interest*."[13] Such is the crud and squalor of an acquisitive and obscurantist social scene even as Dickens "points tenaciously" to evoke their qualities. Similarly: "Fog everywhere. Fog up the river [...]; fog down the river [...]." No full stops, because that river-fog never does. As capping allegory of the passage in emphatic rhetorical parallelism: "Never can there come fog too thick, never can there come mud and mire too deep, to assort with the groping and floundering condition" of the legal scene (unseen unless pointed out).[14] "Thus, in the midst of the mud and at the heart of the fog"—a chilling bureaucratic mist in the midst of it all—"sits the Lord High Chancellor in his High Court of Chancery"—addressed finally by lawyer Tangle, who, for all we know, has been namelessly introduced a few paragraphs before, with punctually deflating commas, across the lightly sylleptic triplet and final terminological oxymoron of "a large advocate with great whiskers, a little voice, and an interminable brief."[15] Tangle designated there or not, in any case his is eventually an address to "My Lord" as "Mlud,"[16] where the absent orthographic apostrophe lends its own punctuational subversion, becoming, beyond another deposit of "mud," a deconsecrated anagram of "muddle" in a slurry more than syllabic.

This is the world of capitalist furor and bureaucratic dead-ends on which, two novels later, *Little Dorrit* (1859) will close, with as clear a case of anaphoric iteration—as punctuation—to be found anywhere in Dickens' prose. The marriage register has been signed, and a double compounding by "and," clausal and phrasal, relaxes us toward conclusion: "and Little Dorrit and her husband walked out of the church alone. They paused for a moment on the steps of the portico, looking at the fresh perspective of the street in the *autumn morning sun's bright rays*, and *then went down*" (emphasis added, italicizing the existent "punctuation").[17] At his most metrical in that participial phrase of overview, pointed by the counter-graphic hinge at "mn/m" in "autumn morning's" (as if the phonetic chiasm were fusing a lexical portmanteau), Dickens' prose then gives way to the evened-out three-beat stress of "then went down." This concentrated downbeat yields (to) an already cadenced descent immediately given further point—via linguistic and bibliographic codes together[18]—when the iterative verb phrase is matched, in a kind of meta-deixis, by the downward drop of paragraphic blocking itself: "Went down into a modest life of usefulness and happiness. Went down to give a mother's care [...]. Went down to give a tender nurse and friend [...]." Theirs is the gift that so insistently keeps on giving that it twists the idiom of being ("be a friend") into that of bestowal ("give" [over] oneself as). On its third return, the fragmentary verbal iteration ("Went down") is renewed in its legitimized full grammar for the novel's last sentence, repositing the pluralized marital subject in this litany of selflessness: "They went quietly down into the roaring streets, inseparable and blessed; and as they passed along in sunshine and shade, the noisy and the eager, and the arrogant and the froward and the vain, fretted and chafed, and made their usual uproar." The syncopated phonetic sensorium of the effortlessly melded phrase "inseparable and blessed" is hard to miss, but a punctilious grammar—less rhetorically punctuated—would have set it off earlier, rather than with the risk of false modification in proximity to the bustling "streets." And yet what we might call this ungrammatical pointing has cordoned off the couple further yet from the contaminating fray of life's usual traffic, where the remaining rasp of fricative phonemes (*f*orward/*v*ain/*f*retted/*ch*afed) rubs against the grain of the rhythmically comma-marked polysyndeton of this final horizontal panorama. The whole palpably stair-stepped effect of this last paragraph—after the deictic prepositional pointing (an almost topographic signposting) from "down into" to "along"—culminates with the damped-down vertical etymology of "uproar." In resistance to which a contrapuntal linguistic rhythm has traced the couple's fivefold immersive move into and across social and page space alike.

Useful to recall here Soviet director and screen theorist Sergei Eisenstein's famous sense of Dickens as the virtual inventor of cinema (in what we might call his kinetic visual punctuation, in everything from close-ups to tracking shots to dissolves).[19] If the jump-cut scenario of mud and fog at the start of *Bleak House* is (though unmentioned as such by Eisenstein) a classic prose example of montage, here at the end of *Little Dorrit* is a loop edit, recursive even while incremental, circling back to rehearse and expand a grammatical template of period-broken sentence fragments. Retaining the proto-cinematic model in looking back to *Dombey and Son*, a more unhinged kinetic grammar of jump-cuts and reversible POVs (that is, here, *points* of view) can be found to characterize a climactic scene of violence far from the staid and complacent antimonies of commercial patriarch versus neonate (and partner in embryo) from our glance at the opening page, with its continuing alternate closeups of parent and child. The Son of the titular firm is by now long dead, and Carker the Manager has betrayed Dombey in supposedly managing to abscond with his second wife. Betrayed by her in turn, he has been tracked down by Dombey across France in a revenge now literalized in the vicinity of actual railroad tracks, along which a monstrous express train regularly tears its way. Its barreling past is first conveyed in spaced-out noun fragments too fast for standard grammar, yet personifying, with its own version of jump-cut closeups, the feared engine of Carker's nemesis: "A trembling of the ground, and quick vibration in his ears; a distant shriek; a dull light advancing, quickly changed to two red eyes, and a fierce fire, dropping glowing coals [...]."[20] An otherwise inert repetition rare for Dickens (the undramatic "quick" before "quickly") may alert us to the way the past-participial insertion "quickly changed" entails in transit what might, unpunctuated, have anchored this spectacle in an intransitive predication, rather than an assault of fragmentary phrases, but instead traces in raced passing a fleeting figurative glimpse of the engine's demonic stare.

Pitting the quick against the pending dead in this first major Victorian railroad-novel, Dickens, building on similar passages of this kind earlier in the book, is at work inventing a new punctuational system for locomotion's time-space ratios. Carker's premonitions are confirmed when the locomotive next fixes its "red eyes" on him in the line of Dombey's own horrified (counter) stare. It is here again that a "bibliographic" punctuation, as with the serene rather than violent paragraph break at the end of *Little Dorrit*, sets off the villain's mutilation in the *tour de force* of a single-sentence (and brutally em-ruled) paragraph that is wrenched into reorientation at the swivel point when villain, now victim, in becoming aware of the locomotive's advancing anthropomorphic glare, "looked round—saw the red eyes, bleared and dim, in the daylight, close upon him—was beaten down, caught up, and whirled away [...]."[21] If punctuation typically disaggregates by marked pause, it does so here by an ingrown pointing that is actually a two-pronged grammatical forking invisible to orthography: not the conjunctive fun of syllepsis, certainly, but nonetheless a kind of syntactic pun. Where "quickly changed" (discussed in the paragraph above) turned either, and almost incidentally, on a finite verb or a past participle, the division of syntactic labor in this present case—between adjective and past-tense verb—is final and fatal: the locomotion no sooner close upon the villain than closing in and down on him. Pun? Double-taking or twinning? At speeds like these, there's of course no time for a sylleptic breadth (or breath) of phrase, no grammatical second wind, just an annihilating version of *Pickwick*'s "simultaneously." The delta function of imp/ending impact in the split-second deixis of Carker's fate is a joyless double meaning riding in on non-homophonic wordplay (the sibilant pointers passing from unvoiced to voiced in "cloz/se") under a notice too fast for enunciation, open only to recognition, as we read. One remembers that pun, via *punctilio*, rests at the root of punctuation—especially salient when separate emphases are lodged at once in the slamming shut of lethal articulation.

In the spotty roster of examples so far, we've seen punctuation linked to syntactic comedy and bibliographic mimesis, toying with the codes of lexicon and compound grammar as well as those of paragraphic space. And there's another space at stake as well, calendrical rather than graphic: the gap between monthly numbers that turns suspense itself into its own kind of punctual stress. But the broadest issue for Dickensian prose is anticipated by the distinction from the Cambridge editors' General Introduction: "When the primary display using marks & spaces is of grammatical structure punctuation is *syntactical*, when of phonetic & oratorical cues *elocutionary*," depending "largely on whether one is reading aloud or silently."[22] Hence it follows, regarding the valence of punctuation, that "the greater stress on syntactical [marking] since the Seventeenth Century is because more people were & are reading silently, deprivileging the elocutionary."[23] But the disjunctive "or" of "aloud or silently" can be taken to beg the question of what I have wanted in my own stylistics to call the "secondary vocality" (non-technological variant of Walter Ong's "secondary orality") in the silently auralized activation of graphophonemic language.[24] Yet the waver of silent|out loud doesn't finally strain any reasonable claims for Victorian reading aloud in the heyday of prose fiction—as taken up later by Lennard in connection with Dickens' character Sloppy and his reading of the "police in different voices."[25]

My counterclaim is first of all linguistic, not historical—or not the latter once, over a millennium ago, the introduction of word-break spacing allowed for the disambiguation of word from word without manuscript interpuncts. Nor, biographically, is the main point that Dickens performed his own texts aloud, or that they were, like much other Victorian fiction and poetry, read aloud in the home from single copies. Of more stylistic note is the kind of pointing that Dickens' language builds into the tenor of diction and phrase—and channels there by the guardrails and turnstiles of actual punctuation-marks and their kindred phrasal and phonetic arrangements.

Here indirect light is shed by the only essay centrally concerned with punctuation-marks in a recent collection on the style of Victorian fiction. Under the chapter title "Kipling; and," Daniel Karlin defends Rudyard Kipling (1865–1936) against critics of his early colonial fictions on the score of a condescending tone, which Karlin finds notably symptomatized in the writer's breaking with Victorian standards in the serial use of semicolons.[26] Kipling adds a "superfluous element"—in what amounts to a consequential rather than just sequential "and," not openly hortatory but knowing and conclusive.[27] Karlin cites J. C. Nesfield's *English Grammar: Past and Present* (1898) on the need to relate clauses cordoned off by semi-colons, when not standing by themselves as elements in a list, by "some Alternate or Illative conjunction."[28] That second specialist term is soon glossed by Karlin—in contrast to the obvious disjunction (or "alternative") implied by "; neither" or "; nor." Illative linkage is instead a matter of inference or consequence ("therefore," "then," "so then," "for"), often implicit in Kipling's capping "; and"—with its superior inference of "and thus obviously."[29] In the tactical use of this pointing—beyond "'braking' the pace of the sentence" for emphasis—the effect for Karlin is all but metalinguistic: "In replacing the colon, which stands above it on the punctuation ladder, the semicolon also replaces the comma, which stands below."[30] Rung-rank is a trope for a heightening of point, of emphasis, of assertion itself. Its force "belongs not to the rhetorical effect, but of the rhetorician; it interpolates him into the sentence, draws attention to his knowledge—his knowingness"—and this as part of the stylistic innovation that made Kipling's "a genuinely new voice" in English literature, often dismissed in his debut works as vulgarly self-assured.[31] A succinct (though non-serial) example, from the story "Thrown

Away," and characterized as "aggressive" by Karlin, operates in the prescient mode of "naturally" or "in short": "There was a Boy once who had been brought up under the 'sheltered life' theory; and the theory killed him dead,"[32] with the speaker's confidence as if bolstered by phrasing's final overkill, the "to death" as gratuitous as is the "and" that finds it inevitable.

Quite different, as we turn back to Dickens for a longer look at *Great Expectations*, is the case of a sequenced "; and" that operates as a force more introspective than rhetorical. The novel's guilt-beset hero lapses at one point into a self-knowledge he keeps trying to ward off, so that Pip's ill-at-ease "illative" in a chapter-capping sentence delivers the sting and wince of unwanted awareness. Dissatisfied, unsated, the boy has been caught up in the fetid glamor and lies of Satis House, only to be thrown back on his home at the forge with Joe: "Looking towards the open window, I saw light wreaths from Joe's pipe floating there, and I fancied it was like a blessing from Joe,—not obtruded on me or paraded before me, but pervading the air we shared together."[33] After that perfusion of assonance: "I put my light out, and crept into bed; and" (there it is, Kipling's favored format)—"; *and* it was an uneasy bed now, and I never slept the old sound sleep in it any more."[34] As prideful expectations have begun separating Pip from his friend and protector Joe, the word "crept" suggests the abject and stealthy, even while—after the more-than-merely-serial precedent for the "; and" transition—a return to another normative comma simply drives home the chastening recognition in a vitiated cognate object ("never slept the old sound sleep").

Normative is the name for Dickens' typical disposition of commas. This deft grammarian rarely lets the guard down so routinely provided by semi-colons. The demotic comma splice (two clauses bonded as if they were only phrases in a single differential syntax) is rare in *Great Expectations*, as elsewhere on Dickens' watch, and is easy to forgive for its intuitive logic when it does pop up, as when Pip can't repress laughter at the absurdity of Mr. Wopsle's misbegotten *Hamlet* in a sentence lucidly inverting a more immediately explanatory syntax (because of x, I did y) around the comma: "I laughed in spite of myself all the time, the whole thing was so droll [...]."[35] It is a performance as shot through by absurdity as is this sentence by the punctual echoing phonics of "whole . . . so droll." In a memorable exception to Dickens' authorized comma usage, there is of course the radically punctuational splicing at the logically unhinged launch of *A Tale of Two Cities* (1859), merging all of pre-Revolutionary chaos in the blatancy of its contradictions when couched in "the superlative degree of comparison only." To wit: "It was the best of times, it was the worst of times, it was the age of wisdom, it was the age of foolishness, etc., etc., etc., etc. [...]."[36] It is this opening barrage that makes the novel's last move so movingly *pointed* in its reach for quiet poignancy, settling for "better" rather than straining after "best" in the closing inner monologue of Carton's sacrificial death: "It is a far, far better thing that I do, than I have ever done; it is a far, far better rest that I go to, than I have ever known."[37] The final sentence lodges four commas—alternately prenominal (debatably mandated by grammar) and strictly elocutionary—with the last turning also on the further pointing, after the "do" / "done" eye rhyme, provided by the assonant chime harmonizing "go" with the more metaphysical "known."

In regard to standard-issue punctuation-marks, mastered before any telling departure from them, it is part of Karlin's case about Kipling that he was "not simply a journalist but an editor, a proofreader, a compositor."[38] Add stenographer to such a list and one has tallied Dickens' credentials—as we can distantly hear in reauditing his build-up to that "; and" syntax about troubled, guilty sleep. Listen again, amid Pip's restlessness over Joe, to that fourfold assonant and alliterative clustering—the *pointed* permeation—of "not obtruded on me or p*arade*d before me, but p*erva*ding the *air* we sh*are*d together." Call it a mimesis of atmospheric suffusion, in contrast to the "airs" which Pip has begun to put on—and, worse, internalize. But recognize it as well as the literary hay made of a once traumatic wrestle on the part of the young Dickens, as Parliamentary reporter, struggling to master the "brachygraphic" ("short-writing") method of his day.[39] The elision of medial vowels in this technique of phonetic compression—with its reliance in later transcription on coded consonant brackets for filling in the enunciable sound forms—left lexical scars, I've argued, on the apprentice stylistic imagination for which Dickens' later prodigal sound-play can be understood as a lifelong therapy and compensation.[40] On this considered hunch, we can reverse-engineer some semblance of his nonalphabetic shorthand code (transcribed into lettered language) for such a contrast as "not paraded" versus "pervading." Cramped notations not unlike "n prdd b prvdg" would have been the high-speed prods to later reconstruction. A just-add-water approach to the compressed density of vowelless avowals. Although Dickens' famous early bout with stenography has often suggested to commentary one source for the breathless gait of his dynamic narrative phrasing, such an effect is one I would associate more with Mr. Jingle's *telegraphic* style.

The stenographic impact seems to me more like the recoil from a stunting of language endured by the young Dickens (devouring Shakespeare by contrast at the time)—especially in regard to the phonic timbre of wording's vowel sounds. Here was a deprivation of sonority that led him ever after to force feed his lexicon with an unjingling vocalic density across the onward drive—and frequent consonant clip—of syntactic action. I had this sense of stenographic backstory in mind, as it happens, when speaking of the syncopated phonetics of "inseparable and blessed" (nsprbl & blsd) at the end of *Little Dorrit*, a phrase rounded on itself in its grammatically displaced comma-marked isolation. But *Great Expectations* is more punctuation-mark heavy throughout, and certainly more pointedly so (any trivial comma-splice aside), than the earlier *Little Dorrit*—and more inclined to parallelism by decisive semi-colons than anywhere else in Dickens' work. We're on complex lexigraphic ground right from the start. First there is the narrator's lisping together his given two names

(Philip Pirrip—as if via a shorthand Phlp Prrp) into the more than stenographic collapse of "P(i)p": not just a pun on the seedling he is, or a fumblingly scrunched portmanteau, but a palindrome from which a genuine (more than lower case) *I* has a novel-length difficulty in piping up—or out. Then, the second paragraph begins with the grammatically needless but rhetorically heedful comma setting off, with a little arrest of breath, a very mild syllepsis quite in keeping with the cowed imagination of the young boy: "I give Pirrip as my father's family name, on the authority of his tombstone and my sister,—Mrs. Joe Gargery, who married the blacksmith," where the commash (antequated comma before em-dash) appends the essence of an "authoritarian" family psychodrama soon to unfold.[41]

Usually more striking and comic in Dickens, as we've seen, syllepsis, however marked by internal punctuation, is a kind of decontracted pun, a phrasal byplay—two divergent senses bonded in a single wording (a double transport, say, in the *Pickwick* instance, of tears and by servants). As in itself a mode of semantic punctuation via split deixis, a cleft in grammatical directive, the effect depends entirely on readers *getting* the two-pronged point. Repunctuating this sense of a word's play as *word splay* can help identify other related moments crossing between two adjacent words, redefining each in terms of the other or eroding their shared boundaries by lexical friction. In this vein, the illiterate Mr. Boffin in *Our Mutual Friend* (1865) wonders why he should seek out Dr. Scommons (misheard by aural "punctuation error") in the recommendation of Doctors' Commons.[42] Just as easily, the ghost of an apostrophe, rather than its burial, can inflect a meaning. This is the case, in returning to *Great Expectations*, when, in one of the novel's many nervous pointings of identity as a guarded frailty, the italicized *I* puts Pip in rhyme with his paranoia over the boorish Pumblechook's aggressive surveillance: "But he eyed me severely—as if *I* had done anything to him!"[43]—where the phonic contraction "I'd" hovers dormant there to tighten the rhyme with "eyed." Indeed, in the matter of obstreperous lettering, one can well imagine Dickens, as former stenographic slave battered by cryptic pictograms, seeing in his own phrase, via graphic rebus, a hint of the (cur)tailed palindromic eye (the amputated *eve*) at the core of *severely*. Short of that, the very fact of being "eyed" all but spells out in advance, in the recoil of its punctuating italics upon the passive subject as object, the inchoate guilt of whatever "*I* had done." One can't read too closely in seeking the "hermeneutic" valence of pointed wording in the thick of Dickens' linguistically self-conscious turns.

Nothing contrasts more obviously with the heavily cadenced, semi-colon braced checklists of recognition, channeling Pip's consciousness from the first chapter on, than his borrowing, as if out of character, the grammatical wit of his author. Such recourse to syllepsis is likely, even when muted, to seem pompous and self-incriminating on his tongue. "I was for London and greatness," Pip boasts to himself, pre-positing a topographic destination and a personal destiny at once. Or lax, sad, as when living in London only off the crumbs of Estella's limp intermittent politeness ("she gave me her hand and a smile"). Or otherwise whiling away stray hours in a crosstown journey ("Mr Wemmick and I beguile the time and the road"). Or finding himself tediously "busy with my books and Mr. Pocket." And before London, though eventually funding it all unseen, is Magwitch, not entirely surprised that a young boy would have sympathy for a "warmit" so obviously "hunted as near death and dunghill"—driven, that is, no wit intended, to the mortal convergence of cause and material effect, fate and ignominious burial—a varmint without remit. Certainly no comma there, since like "London and greatness" they—degradation and death—go hand in hand in the "warmit" sphere. This is the same Magwitch who first appeared to Pip like a spectral pirate freed from the gibbet—in that case the sylleptic twist punctuated as part of a tripartite series, idiomatic before literal, when the figure seems "come to life, and come down." Later in London, Pip's more sophisticated roommate Herbert Pocket has these sylleptic effects quite credibly up his sleeve. In the backstory of Miss Havisham's jilting, the rare comma is used to punctuate an equally rare contrast, rather than the usual even-handed yoking, in Herbert's ironic report: "the day came, but not the bride." Usually the "and" glides more smoothly from one register to the other, literal over against figural, as when Herbert admits to knowing all too well, even without confession, of Pip's obsession with Estella, summoning its inescapable evidence with a further comma punctuating (both senses) the dyad: "You brought your adoration and your portmanteau here, together."

In the mantra of the Cambridge history of such pointing, where punctuation is as much a matter of blanks as of marks, of breaks as of ligatures, it is clear from Dickens' practice alone that marks, spaces, and typefaces all operate together in the register of sorted and inflected legibility. Recall the famous play of typography and alphabetic default in Pip's remembered first letter to Joe, with the extra edge (at letteral borders) of deciphered irony in its sign-off: "BLEVE ME INF XN PIP."[44] Twin pointings—in punctuational shifts of scale and inter-word spacing alike—combine to spell out, even before the poison of Miss Havisham has begun setting in, the "inF[E]XN" (two slurred syllables: "infex(sh)n") broken loose from the rebus lexeme along with that intended affectionate valediction in trisyllabic enunciation: the innocent "in[A]FXN." Writing less well than he thinks, in this pride that cometh before the fall, Pip says more than he yet knows. Differential fonts can be the founts of ironies as yet untapped.

But long before such an accidental pun in inept caps, there was the patient introduction of Pip's childhood world—to himself and us at once. After a brief opening paragraph in which he nicknames himself as a kind of post-stenographic "Pp"—fill in the "I" that puns with seedling and self—and after making erroneous pictograms out of the lettering on his parents' tombstones, he continues in this vein with the sidewinding commas of a decidedly mimetic punctuation: "Ours was the marsh country, down by the river, within, as the river wound, twenty miles of the sea." Syntax next opens, uninterrupted, to the breadth of its both topographic and ultimately psychological subject: "My first most vivid and broad impression of the identity of things seems to me to have been gained on a memorable raw afternoon towards evening," where the phonetic chiasm of "*seems* to *me*" is pointed up—as if already internalized by reversal—at the head of "*mem*orable."[45] What ensues is an exacting grammar of retrospect and recognition—schematized by semi-colons—in processing the comma-suspended adjectival mimesis of a low-lying uneventful landscape (Dorothy Richardson applauding the unpunctuated roll-out from the wings). The flatlands of a rural expanse are compassed by punctuated expansion in the measured scope of recognition, a tight mesh of topography and epistemology.[46] The format of such parallelism, with its subordinating "that" and unfolding bullet points, recalls the shorthand fill-in-the-blank procedures of codified stenographic notation as, for instance, in a format like "Be it resolved that a; ____ b; ____c." Transfiguring again his early reportorial ordeals, Dickens has turned checklist rhetoric to cognitive revelation, as pointed by the very absence of epithetical punctuation: "At such a time I found out for certain that this *bleak place overgrown with nettles* was the churchyard; [...] and that the *dark flat wilderness* beyond the churchyard" [commas only when breaking into the horizontal: "intersected with dikes and mounds and gates, with scattered cattle feeding on it,"] "was the marshes; and that the *low leaden line* beyond was the river; and that *the distant savage lair* from which the wind was rushing was the sea [those paired modifying triads again perfectly anticipating Richardson's advice about the all-at-a-glance freeing of epithets from comma partitions]; and that the small bundle of shivers growing afraid of it all and"—the gulp of a syntactically gratuitous comma coming—"beginning to cry, was Pip."[47] Not a colloquial "me," let alone "I," but instead the objectification that precedes, if only by a split second, inhabited identity. With a landscape panning-shot fenced in and stepped off by semi-colons until now, the elocutionary comma after "cry"—a kind of musical notation in this stretch of prose as a performance score—catches the held breath of self-expression per se and delivers the boy to the end of the sentence, safely, if sad.

Like the "cry" of a birth pang, Pip's weeping is answered with what becomes a pending death threat: "'Hold your noise!'" cried a terrible voice, as a man started up from among the graves [...]."[48] What has "started up" is now dropped down by jump-cut bibliographic code into a paragraph of roughly punctuated sentence-fragments in which capitalization is itself the deictic pointer of uprisen aggression: "A fearful man, all in coarse grey, with a great iron on his leg."[49] And after another such fragment, the upstart indefinite article again: "A man who had been soaked in water, and smothered in mud"—that second past participle making for a mimetically clotted assonance—"and lamed by stones, and cut by flints," etc. But Pip survives Magwitch's threat and nearly dies (dozens of chapters later) laboring to save him. After which, and the convict's own death, it is the deserted Joe who, by proxy, returns the favor by tending Pip in his own near death, whose grinding fever evokes, in reverse, the novel's opening anaphora of consciousness under consolidation ("I found out for certain, that [...]"). What is later found out, evacuating the foundational, comes only under duress and long periodic inversion: "That I had a fever and was avoided, that I suffered greatly, that I often lost my reason, that the time seemed interminable, that I confounded impossible existences with my own identity; that I was a brick in the house-wall [...] a steel beam of a vast engine [...]."[50] After these two dehumanizations, another semi-colon and summary clause with oratorical comma, merely for emphasis: "; that I passed through these phases of disease, I know of my own remembrance, and did in some sort know at the time." First and last among the hallucinated friends and enemies peopling Pip's troubled brain, we are told, in emphatic repetition after an em-dash: "—above all, I say, I knew that there was an extraordinary tendency in all these people, sooner or later, to settle down into the likeness of Joe."[51] Even that last verb phrase, the idiomatic "settle down," is pointed up and out against the dead metaphor of "above" in the ranking of priorities. Here (under Eisenstein's influence again) we might read "settle down into" as the equivalent of the cinematographer's "focus in on" or the film editor's "cut in on," the true face of affection only slowly emerging from a hazy blur, which happens to be exactly the way director David Lean filmed the scene by way of the in-camera punctuation of his 1946 screen adaptation.

And if this passage of cognitive parallelism recurs to the moment of Pip's dawning consciousness on the marshes (again "that the bundle of shivers [...] beginning to cry, was Pip"), so does that early comma-hesitant mimesis of inaugural self-surprise return at the novel's denouement—at the forge-become-hearth of Joe and Biddy's marriage (and hence in cold comfort for the friendship and desire the man of expectations has squandered). What is revealed to Pip is that "there"—in the person of his namesake, but in a first-person linking grammar that the adult Pip is now able to bestow, if only by displacement—"was—I again!"[52] He has been given a disembodied and entirely symbolic new start after an illness ironically derived from the violent strain entailed in showing his returned criminal benefactor, Magwitch, the devotion he had for so long withheld from Joe. At the climax of the melodramatic escape plot that results, Pip realizes that a trap has been set for him by Magwitch's arch enemy Compeyson, and a capped three-word warning note penetrates his nocturnal worries and erupts out of the page: "Whatever night-fancies and night-noises crowded on me, they never warded off this DON'T GO HOME. It plaited itself into whatever I thought of, as a bodily pain would have done."[53] To evoke the paranoid braid of the "plait" (where the monosyllable's own off-chime with "pain" or "plaint" is, as rhetorical punctuation, part of the figured intertwine), the studied and ready grammarian Dickens orchestrates a drumbeat of lesson-plan punctuation, varied between commas and semi-colons, on the way to the sylleptic fork between idioms of literal and figural transport (go not / go mad): "When at last I dozed, in sheer exhaustion of mind and body, it became a vast shadowy verb which I had to conjugate. Imperative mood, present tense:

Do not thou go home, let him not go home, let us not go home," and so on. The impetus of the barrage extends beyond the imperative to a further grammatical category: "Then potentially: I may not and I cannot go home; and I might not, could not, would not, and should not go home; until I felt that I was going distracted, and rolled over on the pillow [...]."[54] Pointed and parsed by the split between the negatives of going home and going crazy, the effect is not just a metagrammatical torture but a metanarrative underscore—associated, by symbolic metonymy, with that other and earlier home he has foresworn.

There was, to be sure, room for comedy once, early on, in the pretensions of his upward mobility—in one case a sylleptic fantasy, framed by an extra comma to bracket the joke, in which Pip imagines the high-handed fun of "bestowing a dinner of roast-beef and plum-pudding, a pint of ale, and a gallon of condescension, upon everybody in the village."[55] In the next paragraph, in a further wordplay noted above as at first mildly sylleptic, then cross-syllabic, he apostrophizes his past with an unusually sloppy comma splice that suggests the inevitability of his destination, lifted to emphatic glory by the delayed exclamation "point" postponed until after the contemptuous apostrophe: "farewell, monotonous acquaintances of my childhood, henceforth I was for London and greatness; not for smith's work in general, and for you!" One perks to the missing verb in an implied "bound for" as it may seem implicitly swallowed up in the long-standing negative motif—enchainment rather than destiny—of being "bound apprentice" to Joe and the forge. But there are other shackling desires, admitted in this very paragraph, to which he is eager to submit, even if mocked subliminally in their cross-word dreaminess by his own wording: "I made my exultant way to the old Battery and lying down to consider the question whether Miss Havisham intended me for Est*ella*, *fell a*sleep."[56] A fella duly overtaxed by circumstance, if not circumspect about his prospects.

Despite the sing-song travesty of this fetishized, comma-earmarked siren call, he can still imagine himself Estella's "intended" on the novel's last page, clinging to that fantasy in the famously revised and notoriously "happier" ending that Dickens drafted to replace his original somber conclusion. Now, in returning Pip to the ruins of Miss Havisham's estate, Dickens has recourse once again to that elisional parallelism mastered as a Parliamentary reporter, though here without filling in all the blanks: "I could trace out where every part of the old house *had been*, and where the brewery *had been*, and"—as if ontologically dismissed in their very recognition as missing—"where the gates, and where the casks."[57] Their very "where" is eerily cathected as *nowhere*. In inventorying these absences, he is surprised by Estella's presence, characterized for him still by an "indescribable majesty and indescribable beauty." But a new allure is immediately pivoted around a chiasmatic semi-colon: "Those attractions in it, I had seen before; what I had never seen before, was the saddened, softened light of the once proud eyes [...]," with those tandem epithets of "light" comma-bonded as if by apposition, the latter a metaphor for the former.[58] Without a concessive "but" after the semi-colon, punctuation all by itself offers hinge and swing. And Pip still keeps straining to see what there is to see. In the supposedly "de*mist*ified" last sentence after the dissipated haze of evening, four quietly mounting "and"-links try hard to capture the cadence of the inevitable, but the fourth clause is trouble: "I took her hand in mine, and we went out of the ruined place; and, as the morning mists had risen long ago when I first left the forge, so the evening mists were rising now, and in all the broad expanse of tranquil light they showed to me, I saw the shadow of no parting from her."[59] Especially without a pointing first comma before the climactic "in" clause, and despite the lulling effect of assonant nuclear vowels and liquid elision (*anse/ anquil/ ligh*), we expect a normal grammatical object (they showed to me x or y) where instead we get a willful independent clause of potential further blindness. All is pointed by double negative and spiritual litotes, with the absence of atmospheric occlusion making visible nothing but the light thus shed.

Syntax may well throw us off in this cadenza, partly because we so recently encountered "showed," with no ghostly expanded "shadow" so near, when the unidentified figure of Estella in the garden—via a transitive verb in ungendered reflexive aspect—first "showed itself aware of me."[60] But now, what is being showed to whom? And what still occluded in the twilight gloom? Toward a fuller answer, an experiment.[61] If Dickens could rewrite his own finale, so can I, with the ironized aid of ChatGPT. Prompted to repunctuate the input passage for clarity, robotic normativity chose to recast it in three sentences, dropping the "; and" along with the sentimentally more effortless, relaxed, and comma-spurred ", and in all." The final adjustment is a perfect litmus test of the oddness of the original. With all its Large Language Models to draw on, the Chat stylist had every reason to impose some causal/clausal order, however awkwardly circuitous: "In all the broad expanse of tranquil light, they showed to me that I saw not a shadow of another parting from her." Just so, if only in an AI translation so different from the lingering erotic equivocation of Dickens' strenuous revision: they, the lifted vapors, revealed only what was already in Pip's mind's eye, the still misted mirror of his own desire. What linguists call a garden-path sentence is in fact Pip's only way out of the despoiled Havisham garden, with syntax's false lead corrected by punctuation-mark only grammatically, not emotionally.

You heard it here first: Dickens is all punctuation. And across broad arcs of recurrence. If we remember, along the particular route of this essay, how the semi-colonnade of "that" clauses, sorting the world for Pip on the opening page, has returned inverted for the reassemblage of consciousness after his fever, we are likely to remember an even more exaggerated anaphoric passage that impinges, by unnerving reverb, upon the novel's last sentence. In the earlier moment of half-candid disillusion, a long-smitten Pip is watching Miss Havisham revel in Estella's checklist of victimized men stung by her teasing and rebuffs: "I saw in this, wretched though it made me, and bitter the sense of dependence and even of degradation that it awakened,—I saw in this that Estella was set to wreak Miss Havisham's revenge on men, and that she was not to be given to me until she had gratified it for a term" (another commash to stutter the see/saw-ings of Pip's self-aware and savvy stock-taking).[62] The ingrained new rut of grammatical reboot, as if fixing the impression, passes through three more iterations of this base clause, in its extra-grammatical abjection, until a sixth iteration, with another then beginning in summary distillation: "In a word"—and the exact word here, idiom for "gist" aside, is the verb of limited perspicacity in "saw"—"I saw in this Miss Havisham as I had her then and there before my eyes, and always had had her before my eyes; and I saw in this, the distinct shadow of the darkened and unhealthy house in which her life was hidden from the sun."[63] What the past perfect stammer of "had had" marks is the traumatic stain of debasement that has, always already, been imprinted—far from the garden—by Estella's guardian and false mother. In her a Miltonic darkness visible (a living "shadow") is to be glimpsed even through the fog of Pip's continued delusions about "the prize," however devalued by then, being "reserved for me." This compromised (itself benighted) vision can well be found operating in the novel's last ambiguously punctuated sentence—and in fact anticipated by an unorthodox ap/positional comma at the beginning of the earlier passage just cited. For the "this" in which Pip sees what he should, amid the psychological debris, closes the preceding paragraph with the image of Miss Havisham's "wan bright eyes glaring at me, a very spectre."[64] The free-floating appositive has no secure antecedent; in grammatical legality, Pip hovers there as the proleptic ghost in this machine, subdued to the material he eventually dreams in. And chronically contaminated, to be sure, so that even when he "saw" so insistently and irreversibly, in her vindicative manipulation of Estella, "the shadow of the darkened and unhealthy" world they shared, he could still, refueling his false hope, "see the shadow" of no such thing at the end—only a dim and indeterminate continuance.

Such moments of explicit subjective impression (and equally ambiguous information) accrue across the ironic armatures of Dickens' plotting, punctuate each other, point up and point forward. Not least within the motif of visual recognition—where blinkered vision may still be operating in the residual irony of the revised conclusion. Pip's instincts knew better once, apprehending the repellant on its own overt terms. In another ferocious anaphora on first entering Satis House, and with Estella not yet in the picture, he was seeing more clearly the ghastliness of Miss Havisham in her sepulchral lair, his own desire not yet manipulated by her plans. Aspects of her living tomb assault his gaze and even his incipient understanding. "It was not in the first few moments that I saw all these things, though I saw more of them in the first moments than might be supposed."[65] Three more sentences focalized by the transitive grammar of "I saw" then take a turn into phantasmagoria (Eisenstein's cinematographic Dickens again) with a stunning double flashback (via superimposition) that is *pointed* (all but skewered) by grammatical parallelism as much as by punctuation-marks: "Once, I had been taken to see some ghastly waxwork at the Fair, representing I know not what impossible personage lying in state." And recalled in the same moment, enforced by another extraneous comma after the retro adverb: "Once, I had been taken to one of our old marsh churches to see a skeleton in the ashes of a rich dress that had been dug out of a vault under the church pavement. Now, waxwork and skeleton seemed to have dark eyes that moved and looked at me."[66] Later, too often, Pip looks away from what is there to see. But, as in that passage's own compounded triad of parallel, comma-marked openers, it is punctuation that is often staged to aim the camera at the right angle of vision—whether accepted or deflected within the first-person discourse.

Having once reciprocated looks with this madwoman in the parlor, Pip afterwards, and sadly, sees himself differently. The pause before ", was Pip"—in that uncertain objectification of himself that begins his conscious life in the novel's third paragraph—is gone, along with the inverted grammar of the punctuating personal moniker, in the straightforward anaphora of self-recrimination when he walks home from his first visit to Satis House. By then he is found "pondering, as I went along, on" (the prepositions going forward and back at once) "all I had seen, and deeply revolving"—the perfect formal participle for "turning over" in *revulsion*—"that I was a common labouring-boy; that my hands were coarse, that my boots were thick; [...]." Here, and in the rest of the "that"-emphatic list, semi-colons compartmentalize separate facets of a degradation that internal commas further itemize. Next, the diction of original sin in regard to humble lingo: "; that I had fallen into a despicable habit of calling knaves Jacks; that I was more ignorant than I had considered myself last night"—with the quasi-prosecutorial subdivision of semi-colons now succeeding to a mere comma, in wrapping things all too obviously up, as the chapter is choked off in a total foreclosure of self-esteem: ", and generally that I was in a low-lived bad way." A grammar subordinating everything to shame—from identity ("that I was") through telltale attributes ("that my") to resulting condition ("that I was in a ... bad way")—has been so far internalized that on Pip's next visit, when allowed to kiss Estella's cheek rather than be kissed by her, the diction of transaction rather than idiom (normally "give a kiss") sets up the further irony, carried across two less-conspicuous *that*-clauses. Having by now ingested her contempt via third-person free indirect discourse, he who "was Pip" can only now see himself abjected through the eyes of the other: "But, I felt *that* the kiss was given to the coarse common boy as a piece of money might have been, and *that* it was worth nothing." All such anaphoras of recognition or identification, swift or sustained, seem exaggerated, reversed, and cured by that final fever that hallucinates further—and even more dehumanizing—reductions across an eightfold inverted grammar of delayed subjectivity (again, by inverted openers, "that I was a brick in the house-wall ...; that I was a steel beam of a vast engine ... "). All this Pip confusedly "knew" through the phases of his delirium—before in the end, when finding *that* it is trusty Joe who is there at the sickbed, Pip in the better sense *knows* him again for who he is.

To have lingered on our part (as the device itself tends to protract attention) over Dickensian anaphora is to see how the deictic or pointing force, the ostensive (or "showing") valence, of such "punctuation" can betoken a rhetorical as well as grammatical stress at the level of narrative—even while generating its rhythmic uptake in the silent aurality of reception. My common cause with that Cambridge editorial project on punctuation *tout court* (out of which the present essay evolved), widening our sense of the *marked* to extra-lexical pointing, ends up cultivating critical scrutiny, finally, via an extra-deictic (because extra-diegetic) orientation that looks beneath the text itself, however ingenious its specificities, to a culturally formulated intertext: some received truth that literary writing estranges, or tries to originate afresh, by not quite spelling out. Beyond mark, font, face, or any other aspects of such punctuating force, though sustained by them all, this mode of subtextual deixis points outside and before the text—according to the semiotics of Michael Riffaterre—to the always and already preformulated worldly wisdom it labors to rephrase.[67] Subtexts thus recur as the punctual variants of a prefab matrix activated but not surfaced in the text. One such remotivated commonplace is overridingly—or underpinningly—clear in *Great Expectations*. The dream-invading trauma of the "Don't Go Home" note (typeset in CAPS), especially conjugated negatively in the "potential" mood of the verb, becomes the compressed iterative "model" (Riffaterre's recurrent term), unmistakable at last, for the "can't go home again" melancholy of this novel. Don't go, because, in the larger sense, the futility of trying will end up defrauding your best instincts. Which is to say that despite Pip's return to the ruined garden from the foreclosed family hearth, in either zone the exclamation-marked uncanny of "—I again!" is only a pointedly impossible figure of speech. In the very graphics of punctuation, its transmigrated first-person vertical (as if borrowed in exclamatory uprush from the squeezed "I" of a here unsaid "PIP") recalls the narrator's original self-nomination, its twin consonants imploding on a timid inner "i." No wonder the astonished em-rule pause for the protagonist who long ago (among the inventoried "identity of things") ", was Pip" when brought now into face-off with his depleting double at "was—I again!" Punct/counterpoint: scaled up from mark to the whole mordant story in diagram.

Notes

1   With title and subtitle adjusted for yet more "point" upfront, the present essay is a considerably revised and expanded version of my contribution "Punct/ Counterpoint: Managing Syntactic Expectations in Dickens" in *The History of Punctuation in English*, ed. Jeffrey Gutierrez, Elizabeth Bonapfel, Mark Faulkner, and John Lennard (Cambridge: Cambridge University Press, forthcoming 2025).

2   [Ed.] The temptation to map this pointing by punctuation against the famous *punctum/studium* division in Roland Barthes' *Camera Lucida* (1980), on which Stewart has elsewhere written (especially in *Between Film and Screen* [1999]), is

not easily gratified, since Barthes' "punctum" (so private and subjective as to seem the opposite of rule-bound, even loosely so) stabs out at you from the otherwise objective "study" constituted by the photographic image. In the general taken-for-grantedness of literary punctuation marks, their *puncta* are ordinarily neutralized by the expected ruts of grammatical "objectivity"—unless, under a specialized analytic agenda, like that Cambridge project to which Stewart was recruited, they are called to the very *topos* of attention. At which point, for Stewart, one might say that the syntactic *studium* was no longer flattened to rhythmic background, but rather thrust forward in one stressed punct after another. Bringing Barthes' terminology to mind here can, after all, add to our sense of the figure/ground oscillations of Dickens' punctuational system.

3　See "General Introduction," *The History of Punctuation in English*, 8.

4　Ibid.

5　Ibid., 22.

6　[Ed.] Recalling how Stewart's fascination with punctuated syntactic inflection (though the critic accuses himself of paying too little heed to it before in his treatment of *Great Expectations*) actually goes back to his earliest writing, on Dickens and Keats among others, with his mentorship in William Empson's modes of comma-dependent ambiguity and double grammar. So deeply engrained—in Stewart's evolved sense of medial articulation—is the *punct* (comma or fade, period or cut) that in introducing his "narratographic" method to the field of cinema studies, in the opening chapter of *Framed Time* (2007), he analyzes the late prose of Henry James in translation to the camerawork of the Merchant-Ivory adaptation of the *The Golden Bowl* (2000). Stewart finds in the claustrophobic clausal tension at novel's end a virtual shot/countershot exchange in the syntax of the couple's cryptic last dialogue, inflected at first by the manipulative heroine "to point further her moral." Punctuational pointings, and slippages, in the subsequent prose edits (as spatially "graphed" by Stewart) develop at one point in James' taut, uneasy prose a skewed mirror shot across the period-punctual but nonetheless syntactically overlapped and comma-enjambed stutter—call it pause/counterpunct—when framing of the cornered hero: "trying to" / "tried, too"—the jarring echo, at awkward close quarters, marking his throttled attempt to embrace the deadlock of a coercive union.

7　See tinyurl.com/e9hrkrdf; Richardson thus prefers "huge, soft, bright, pink roses" without that extraneous bouquet of commas, and no doubt relishes Dickens on Mrs. Skewton having her portrait taken by reflection in the Veneering mirror, in the second chapter of *Our Mutual Friend* (1865), boasting four fewer commas than a lack of mimetic feel for the passage might have inflicted on it: "an immense obtuse drab oblong face, like a face in a tablespoon." Whether in action or description according to Richardson, we are "sensibility near to sharing the incident" if commas are kept out of the way.

8　John Lennard does—in his "Introduction to Punctuation since 1700," *The History of Punctuation in English*, 23–24.

9　General Introduction, *The History of Punctuation in English*, 45. See W. B. Parkes, *Pause and Effect: A History of Punctuation in the West* (Berkeley: University of California Press, 1993), with those (cumulatively "space-saving"?) ampersands mandated across all three volumes.

10　This and the following examples of syllepsis cited from *The Posthumous Papers of the Pickwick Club*.

11   Charles Dickens, *Dombey and Son* (London: Bradley and Evans, 1848), ch. I, 1.

12   Charles Dickens, *Bleak House* (London: Bradley and Evans, 1853), ch. I, 1.

13   Dickens, *Bleak House*, 1.

14   Ibid., 2.

15   Ibid.

16   Ibid., 4.

17   Dickens, *Little Dorrit* (London: Bradbury & Evans, 1857), ch. XXXIV, 625.

18   Lennard, "Introduction to Punctuation since 1700," *The History of Punctuation in English*, 69.

19   Eisenstein, "Dickens, Griffith, and the Film Today," in *Film Form: Essays in Film Theory*, ed. and trans. Jay Leyda (New York: Harcourt, 1949), 195–256.

20   Dickens, *Dombey and Son*, ch. LV, 552.

21   Ibid., ch. LV, 553.

22   General Introduction, *The History of Punctuation in English*, 14.

23   Ibid.

24   [Ed.] See Garrett Stewart, *The Deed of Reading: Literature * Writing * Language * Philosophy* (Ithaca: Cornell University Press, 2015), chapter 2, "Secondary Vocality," 41–75, developing an argument laid out earlier in Garrett Stewart, *Reading Voices: Literature and the Phonotext* (Berkeley: University of California Press, 1990). See also *Attention Spans: Garrett Stewart, A Reader*, ed. David LaRocca (New York: Bloomsbury, 2024), 11, 145; "building on Walter Ong's (1912–2003) famous supplement to his transhistorical divide between orality and literacy, whereby post-print technologies such as phonography and sound film provide 'secondary orality,' Stewart stresses the inbuilt vocality of silent reading itself in its graphonic basis" (345).

25   Lennard, "Introduction to Punctuation since 1700," *The History of Punctuation in English*, 29.

26   Daniel Karlin, "Kipling; and," in *On Style in Victorian Fiction*, ed. Daniel Tyler (Cambridge: Cambridge University Press, 2022), 278–95.

27   Karlin, "Kipling; and," *On Style in Victorian Fiction*, 280.

28   Ibid., 279, citing J. C. Nesfield, *English Grammar: Past and Present* (London: Macmillan, 1898), 134.

29   Ibid., 280.

30   Ibid., 281.

31   Ibid., 283, 278.

32   Ibid., 287, citing Rudyard Kipling, *Plain Tales from the Hills* (London: Macmillan, 1888), 15.

33   Charles Dickens, *Great Expectations* (London: Chapman & Hall, 1861), ch. XIX, 312.

34   Italics added.

35   Dickens, *Great Expectations*, vol. II, ch. XXI, 220.

36   Charles Dickens, *A Tale of Two Cities* (London: Chapman & Hall, 1859), Book I, ch. I, 26.

37   Dickens, *A Tale of Two Cities*, Book III, ch. XV, 254.

38   Karlin, "Kipling; and," *On Style in Victorian Fiction*, 290.

39   Garrett Stewart, *The One, Other, and Only Dickens* (Ithaca: Cornell University Press, 2018), see esp. chapter 2, "Shorthand Speech / Longhand Sounds," 29–65. With an expert treatment of Dickens' shorthand training and its later novelistic ramifications, though without the stress I place on phonetic compensation,

see from the following year, coincidentally, Hugo Bowles, *Dickens and the Stenographic Mind* (Oxford: Oxford University Press, 2019).

40   [Ed.] In addition to revisiting Garrett Stewart's two books on Charles Dickens—*Dickens and the Trails of the Imagination* (Cambridge, MA: Harvard University Press, 1974) and *The One, Other, and Only Dickens* (Ithaca: Cornell University Press, 2018)—also consult his own recent revisitations of those earlier monographs in *Attention Spans*, "Trials—and Test Sites" (53–60) and "The Dickens Page, In and Out Loud" (163–70).

41   Dickens, *Great Expectations*, vol. I, ch. I, 1.

42   Dickens, *Our Mutual Friend* (London: Chapman and Hall, 1865), ch. VIII, 75.

43   Dickens, *Great Expectations*, vol. I, ch. XI, 116.

44   Ibid., vol. I, ch. VII, 93.

45   Ibid., 2–3.

46   It is a very different spreading out achieved in the streaming consciousness of Virginia Woolf, as discussed by Lee Clark Mitchell in chapter 5, "Expansion: Woolf's Semicolons," in *Mark My Words: Profiles of Punctuation in Modern Literature* (New York: Bloomsbury, 2020), 65–76.

47   Dickens, *Great Expectations*, 2.

48   Ibid., 3.

49   Ibid.

50   Ibid., vol. II, ch. XVIII, 296.

51   Ibid., 297.

52   Ibid., vol III, ch. XX, 335.

53   Ibid., ch. VI, 90.

54   Ibid., 90–91.

55   Ibid., vol. I, ch. XIX, 314.

56   Ibid., 315.

57   Ibid., vol. III, ch. XX, 340.

58   Ibid.

59   Ibid., 344. Since, after the first printings of the novel, Dickens changed this adjusted ending one more time for the 1868 edition to "saw no shadow," rather than "saw the shadow of no," it is to this now canonical version that I return in chapter 8 below, with the interposed long *o* in "no" marking the resisted drift of "aw" into "ow."

60   Ibid., 340.

61   [Ed.] It is another kind of rhetorical "experiment" to which Stewart submits this vexing passage in the closing chapter (on closure) in this collection, where without the aid of AI he imagines what a readerly intelligence might do by way of filling in the blank of a conclusion so much, in connubial terms, cut off *in medias res* and under the spell of a kind of double negative. For Pip to see a "shadow" in all that final mist-lifted light, but, wait, only that of "no parting," also aligns his reading, in verbal rather than visual terms, but conceptual either way, with the aesthetic "negaction" calibrated in chapter 6 below ("Negative Imprints in Conceptual Art").

62   Dickens, *Great Expectations*, vol. II, ch. X, 305.

63   Ibid., 306.

64   Ibid., 305.

65   Ibid., vol. I, ch. XI, 121.

66   Ibid.

67   Michael Riffaterre, *Semiotics of Poetry* (Bloomington: Indiana University Press, 1978).

6 / In the prolific wake of John le Carré (1931–2020) even after his death, including several posthumous publications from his own hand and a spate of international commentaries on his heralded achievements, his (often-filmed) novels are considered here, in their characteristic prose, for the inner drive of their kinetic visuals. Regarding two of his most powerful narratives—the lionized *A Perfect Spy* (1986), a quasi-autobiographical work that Philip Roth, no less, anointed "the best English novel since the war"; and the underrated *Absolute Friends* (2003)—this exploration by Stewart into the optics of prose includes the way photographic ekphrasis serves early on, in both books, to anchor a dynamics of stylistic evocation more cinematographic in texture than, lamentable to admit, many of the high-profile films adapted from le Carré's fiction. Here Stewart's fine-grained sense of cinematic textuality is manifest through such prose analogs as jump cuts, cross dissolves, flashbacks, telephoto zoom-ins, and reversible POV.

6 / *John le Carré's Cinematographic Style*

THIS NEWLY DECLASSIFIED DOSSIER CONCERNS—or say regards—the cinema, rather than the films, of John le Carré, who died in 2020 leaving one since-published novel to add to a legacy already burnished by his being one of the rare living authors to see his collected works taken up under the Penguin Classics umbrella. This essay's appreciation looks to his audiovisual kinetics on the page, not the many screen adaptations of his books. Its title is a fan's claim. But a fan not of those popular films made from among the just over two dozen best-selling novels of this towering postwar storyteller and political ironist—the books all international hits once he himself (born David Cornwell, alias *le Carré*—a new twist on the semiotic "square") hit his stride, and upon his true topic, in the espionage plot. A fan, rather, of what I will "rerun" selectively here, on criticism's small screen, the page, setting down in black-and-white the intricate action thrills of his prose alone, its wrought (-up) syntactic stress, its restless shot plans, its sudden cuts, overlaps, and zooms, its swift dissolves and dilated flashbacks, its discursive voice-overs and other soundtrack manipulations, including even the assonant matches on grammatical action that often clock the unreeling of prose in a phonetically captured traction.[1] All this within the "old-fashioned" verve of his melodramtic lucidity in its routinely celebrated "classic" storytelling.

Le Carré is a detailist, his observant prose close-knit and exacting in both its local texture and its tight segues between layered plot strands. The movies of his books tend to operate at another scale altogether. In them, plot and character get regularly extracted from the syntactic timing that makes them tick. They are peeled away from the character and drama of the prose itself—and thus from its particular kind of cinematic snap: a tension penetrating to the echoes and cross-fades, the recursive loops, within and between sentences as well as paragraphs, clocked throughout by the tensed scenarios of syntax in action. There is a paradox here, though not a new one. In the case of the Victorian Dickens, dead before movies were born, what has long been noted as proto-cinematic in his operational *narration* (close-ups, tracking shots, flashbacks, dissolves, and so forth—all first highlighted by Soviet filmmaker Sergei Eisenstein[2]—and discussed in the previous chapter) is lost in screen adaptation by an emphasis on the plotting and peopling of his *narratives*. The paradox is only sharpened for a contemporary writer whose own books have been increasingly filmed, and in whose plots—under the influence of, as well as under option by, the screen industry—audiovisual machination is often an engine of story event as well as of its cinematographic depiction, each "fast-paced" in their interdependence. But at different levels of calibration. And along with the paradox, the parallel: for if le Carré is arguably the greatest "popular" novelist in English since Dickens—weathervane, like him, of an entire age—the comparable intensity of his social vision is equally conveyed along the inner lining of his sentences, so much less extravagant, mannered, and allegorical than Dickens' writing, but no less closely gauged in the mobility of its quick-cut camera eye.

So the issue on that score, again, is a matter of prose (style) rather than plot (points). There are, of course—especially in le Carré's more recent high-tech thrillers, as for instance with the CIA-backed aerial surveillance mobilized at the withering denouement of *A Most Wanted Man* (2008) or the infrared filming of a paramilitary night raid at the opening of *A Delicate Truth* (2013)—many explicitly "cinematic" scenes, including overt stratagems of mostly invasive filming, which on screen would read as metafilmic touches. But in that former novel, when it was adopted in 2014 by Anton Corbijn, there was nothing so emphatically optic as, for instance, a visual detail on the first page of the latter (and so-far unfilmed) book—centering its mediated espy-ing, its "eye's-on" video feed, amid the "vying" for focus (a vantage v-eyed-for?) by the aerial relays of the remote-controlled opening optical stakeout.[3] Nothing so cinematic or visually evocative, that is, as the three-notch paragraph whose telescopic syntax—ratcheted from perfect tense grammar through present tense to a mere recursive fragment—executes the prose counterpart of a video rack-focus in a precipitated iambic close-up all its own: "The camera has closed on it. The camera enlarges it. Enlarges it again."[4] Only then do we get a description of the suspicious black bag in question, potentially loaded with explosives. Where Hopkins' discerned mottling of nature'/s pied beauty put a premium on oculaurality in chapter 4, style in le Carré is a roving node of a cri/ sp-eyed hypervigilance.

Before turning further pages in *A Most Wanted Man* and *A Delicate Truth*, I think back here to the paradoxical opening shot, and then a literal one coming at the end of the same first chapter, of 1999's *Single & Single*. In a cold-blooded murder meant as warning to his employer in the form of "exemplary punishment," as we soon discover, the shady lawyer Winser—about to be assassinated on a sun-baked Turkish hillside, and on camera, high above the Mediterranean—lends his panic and denial to free indirect discourse in the novel's first sentence: "This gun is not a gun (there being, of course, two legalistic sides to any question)."[5] As the chapter—fueled by this refrain of denial—lingers almost intolerably over the recorded interrogation and inflicted agonies of the victim, a knot of idioms tightens around the lawyer's last moments in an obliquely punning form of gallows humor. With Winser's "arms and shoulders *screaming bloody murder*," his own actual "shriek" of pain, of externalized hurt, "*hurt*led from one hilltop to the next on the way *to extinction*."[6] Just before, wrenched toward the "scalding" sun, his closed eyes have become, in a sudden filmic trope, a "screen suffused with a vibrant yellow wash": the optical apparatus of a strictly figurative cinematics.[7]

Answering to this metaphor of the "screen"with the anticipation of actual camerawork, POV narration has the lawyer eventually notice a "surveyor" (the lawyer still in denial) waiting uphill, "wearing earphones and peering through the sights of a movie camera"—sights, like a rifle's—"with a sponge-covered micropohone fitted to"—yes, its "barrel"—rather than lens.[8] "Surveillance" weaponized. Until now, Winser has tried to drown out the drone of his accuser's voice by tuning-in to the ordinarily ignored sounds around him of the now-coveted living world, including, in a kind of acoustic montage (familiar in cinematic counterpoint to Coppola's *The Conversation*, 1972), the screech of gulls, the whisper of the breeze on waves, even the onomatopoetic "tink-tink of pleasure boats in the bay as the geared up for the season"—anything to dial out the "awful voice booming out his death sentence."[9] With his pending execution a *fait accompli*, suspense is distilled to sheer tension, prose tightening the screws. After many interior flashbacks in his "reckless flight down memory lane," but with no escape from the present—images erupting like a prolonged death-moment firing of memory's synapses—the lawyer is again up against the "non-gun" at his temple, while the video cameraman "made ready, in the best tradition of photography, to immortalize this very special moment."[10] Cut away to the condemned man's POV glimpse of a last and wholly displaced embodiment in the form of an virtual younger self, "a smear-faced boy" looking on surreptitiously at the proceedings, whose returned view of the killing is never recorded at the chapter's truncated end: "He had big brown unbelieving eyes, like Winser's when he was the same age, and he was lying on his stomach and using both hands as a pillow for his chin." Drama drained to banality. *Finis* chapter 2. Only later do we learn that this boy is a plant of British

Customs. In the moment, without suture or reverse shot, we have stared into the very gaze whose bloody last image prose has spared us. With an elliptical violence all its own, of course.

And then there's a similarly elided bullet-firing finale in *The Constant Gardener* two years later, whose hero, at sunset at the edge of an isolated African lake, knows the game is up when seeing "the fast-moving shapes of fit men in bulky clothes crouching on the run behind him."[11] Darkness "grew suddenly deeper"—in an ocular figuration of sheer contrast—from the onslaught of high-powered lights, the brightest of which "picked him out, and held him in its beam."[12] This is more like anti-cinema, given the next and final one-sentence (and obliquely synesthetic) paragraph: "He heard a sound of feet sliding down white rock"—enough said of the coming assassins—as if the blankness of white is part of this last hearing.[13] When the novel actually comes to the screen (by Fernando Mereilles in 2005), it is without that high-wattage metafilmic "beam." The hero, though still in gloomy half-light, instead turns around to be sure of his assailants, looks back at the quiet water, and closes his eyes while whispering his murdered wife's name—as the camera cuts away from the coming gunfire to (again) "gulls," implicitly disturbed by its unheard bursts, flapping their way toward fadeout across the lake. With its recurrent mortal syncopes, the inner cinema of le Carré's prose tends, instead, to make hiatus alone—with no distancing or figurative after-image—the trigger-stroke of fatality: the resonant but soundless caesura of its own annihilating quick cut.

To catch the drift of le Carré's grammatical montage, one has to do exactly what his heady narrative momentum tends to forbid: slow down. That's really what I mean by this being a "fan's" essay: *for* the admirer as well as *by* one. Such is its fantasy at least: to give, among whatever other audience it finds, certain inveterate readers of le Carré's often headlong narrated disasters, as *narrational* triumphs, that extra time—time his own pacing typically overrides, if not tramples over—for pausing to admire the gut punches of his unsparing reversals and killer endings. After the release of the final "le Carré novel"— last of a genre in itself—the time seemed right to pick out (by only the most selective of demonstrations, of course) what has always for me stood out: the canny mesh between turns of phrase and of plot, the synching of style to the pace of events that his coiled language doesn't just report on, but executes. And always with an unholy economy of verbal effect. Yet one needs to stand back a bit before closing in again, the better to throw the pending stylistic details into relief against the blanket of received opinion about the "dark art" of this acknowledged verbal master.

I allude there to the "dark arts" of the Security Service (MI5) and the Secret Intelligence Service (MI6)—he worked for both—their tradecraft so dubbed in the hindsight of 2019's *Agent Running in the Field* (2019). That "dark" is to my mind a more accurate description of his prose than the "gray" bleakness often adduced in reviews (make that "grey," if they are British reviews).[14] Yet in the novels there's no missing, in or out of dialogue, the polished ease of le Carré's class-signature phrasal cadences on the long downside of empire, the wry flair of his elite "voice," a tone of muscular eloquence well short of toniness, in his case to the Oxbridge manner bred rather than born: a privileged loquacity never more effortlessly scintillating than when in the mouth of manipulation or outright villainy. The writing is everywhere acknowledged for its branded stylishness even when not submitted to any close stylistic attention. But one can't settle for this unmistakable class *langue* without more attention to its unique historical *parole*, with its abiding gloom over political wrong turns and moral shortcuts. Any detected grayness in the prose, certainly seldom leaden, was shrewdly suited in his early work to the decline of British power (political, ethical, and otherwise), the fog of geopolitical intrigue beneath the radar of public diplomacy, the whole deadening chill of Cold War espionage, with its murk and coercion. And shadowed since, in his disheartened art, by a palpable dismay over British political corruption, international criminal conspiracies, wars of convenience, eroded democracy, and the rifts of Western European solidarity—every miserable decline of social cohesion down through the nationalist retrenchments of Brexit and (from further shores) Trumpism. Even when prose is at its drollest, one audits the lurking defeatism that fuels it, running not on fumes but on righteous fury from novel to novel.[15]

Gray maybe in aftertaste, the prose, but not in delivery. Of if gray, only with the pallor of skepticism when pitted against the bland moral complacencies and administrative sell-outs to which it refuses to capitulate. Steely gray— often as sharp as a biopsy scalpel—and certainly punctuated by black if not white: strokes of violence and rage that slice through effect to cause, disaster to political exposure. Apart from any particular cinematic effects in the mode of verbal montage, more *film noir* than *film gris*—since le Carré keeps the narrative contrast set high, even while ethical nuance gets washed out. Better, then, to say a *stark* rather than a gray prose, steeled against what its protagonists can't finally fend off, with sentences brittle, nervous, fragmented, but mercilessly aggregate in their twists, turns, and double-crosses, shifting their own field of para-cinematic focus as they go, latently wary in every insistent detail. Focus, then, first of all: guiding an audiovisual epistemology of threat and caution, with any native suavity of phrase set continually on edge from the vigilance of its own noticings. Yet the narrator's sardonic posture of voice is often the only stabilizing force, a tone to be consciously reckoned with in the various facets of its own narrative reconnoitering, including an almost unruly genius for free indirect style. When the tonal and focal come into their tightest structural rhyme, into full plot-synched alignment, we get the lens adjustments of le Carré's most characteristic mode: a branded *melodrama of understatement* precision-tooled in its ironic exactions. That's the kind of prose this essay has started to bring into focus and will ultimately be bearing down on. For it is in just this laconic and saturnine vein, in parallel deadpan moments of an unnervingly dry—and desiccating—wit, that the writing zeroes in on the zeroing-out effected by the closing death scenes of the two densely plotted novels ahead. These are books paired here for their comparable arcs of characterization (each protagonist betrayed by himself first of all) brought in each case to such endemic dead ends—and for the verbal force uncannily leveraged, just there, with so minimalist and tongue-in-cheek a rhetoric of climax. Questions always follow in the immediate wake of these high-stakes let-downs. How in the world does he do it? And what, exactly, is he doing?

I'll be querying in this light what strike me, though hardly me alone, as two signal triumphs (and indeed career bracketing landmarks) of le Carré's "middle" (and most ambitious) period, beginning with one of many telling threads between them. Whatever their uneven favor with reviewers, the quasi-autobiographical, highly lauded *A Perfect Spy* (1986) and—recoiling from a new century's variant but inherited political threats—the kindred *Bildungsroman* form of *Absolute Friends* (2003), less widely celebrated, share a pointed common denominator near the start of each plot's separate spiral toward mortal closure.[16] Filtered through their permeable modes of third-by first-person perspective (calling all unreliable narrators), each story is set in psychological motion by parallel episodes of narrowly subjective photo-ekphrasis on the way to a now subliminal, now flagrant cinematics of defeat and narrative effacement. With those parallel ocular scenes of studied image at the launchings of plot, where omniscience burrows with the hero into an imprinted visual trace of the unrecoverable past, we need to begin, oriented as always by the "focus-pulling" rhetoric of free indirect discourse.

First Person, Third Person, Split Person

THE WAVER BETWEEN point-of-view registrations is what regularly manifests a hero's inner rift in le Carré: a split from himself into dubious interrogator or repudiated object, subjective force or abjected other, agency or its evasion. And certainly never more than in the natural pairing of those two biographically curved—and psychologically bent—novels I'm singling out for the kinetic microdrama of their predestined finishes. So there's no postponing any longer the difficulty of plot summary for the looped timelines of their backtracking trajectories and the porosity of their unstable omniscience, open to an indirect discourse so free as to seem anarchic and derailing at times, almost schizophrenic. In each book the gap between narrative vantage and internal motive is exacerbated to the point that it invades the subject himself as an agon of identity adrift. One unique brilliance of le Carré's style in all this is that free indirect discourse often serves to overhear the secret agent thinking *of* as well as just for himself in third person.

In the titular (at once avowed and doubly clandestine) role of *A Perfect Spy*, Magnus Pym is the son of a withdrawn and eventually disappeared Dorothy and her philandering con man husband, Rick. A clever boy of minimal nurture (and stature) raised on the lamb by the criminal parent and his inner circle, schooled in the life skills of rhetoric and deception, Magnus comes into his own as title figure when his seasoned childhood gifts for anecdote and mimicry (read: cover and impersonation, Ripley-style) render him—during his exiled college days in Bern—a ready candidate for recruitment into the British Secret Service by a man as if named for the network of this covert society, one Jack Brotherhood. In a gathering mix of lapsed patriotism, political cynicism, and vestigial ethical idealism, Pym is cornered and politically seduced in turn by a charismatic Czech agent who keeps up a career-long liaison of exchanged secrets all through Pym's marriage of convenience to fellow British spy, Mary. This counterpart and seditious double, Axel, with his prominent limp, seems himself named by homophone for the bent axis on which the careers of the two men spin forward—and finally out of control: lives powered in tandem by the drive shaft of subterfuge, political futility, and addictive risk. Only the eventual death of Pym's manipulative, long-clinging, and eventually abject father releases Pym to flee his Viennese post, further "secrete" himself incognito at a modest boarding house on the British seaside, lands-end in a figurative sense, and finish the novel he, as it were, has *in him*. This last-minute reveal is an epistolary confession, in effect, that we now realize we've all along been reading in the bits and snatches of interior monologue compulsively shunting between first and third person in the narrator's incremental self-detachment. It amounts to a final testament of explanation addressed to his adult son Tom, alternately to Brotherhood, for a life that has now to end in a suicidal escape from the shame of a traitor's life (and thus death) sentence. Missing a mother and her influence, shaped to the core by the crooked charms of a both loved and loathed father, this secret agent has become double even to himself, as emblemized—once his manuscript is sealed and addressed—by his espying with curiosity his own self-murder in the optic frame of the bathroom mirror; and by the aforementioned twin register of voiced effect in the direct affect of first- and third-person discourse.

A comparable ballistic fate—after similar parental losses both real and symbolic—awaits the hero nearly two decades later in *Absolute Friends* (2003), even the title half evoking (and ironizing) its status as companion volume to the earlier book. In flashback to colonial India, we find that Ted Mundy was birthed posthumously into a shapeless life to which his mother's own life, and his stillborn twin sister's, were as if pointlessly sacrificed, with the son next separated at boarding school from his military father once the Major has been repatriated in disgrace from his British outpost. In giving birth to only one surviving twin on the very day of Pakistan's ouster from India, his mother's lethal division of that labor has coincided with the violent separation of, say, brother from national sister: parturition as Partition, in a nod no doubt (hard to imagine it accidental, and this well before their long-standing feud in the editorial columns) to a similar allegorical treatment of the title characters in Salman Rushdie's *Midnight's Children* twenty years earlier (1981). With le

Carré's very different child of fate, internally as well as geographically displaced, Mundy, our fallen man-of-the world hero—reduced to mundane cultural work (tour guide) when we first meet him—comes over the course of the novel, irresistibly, to embody (*nomen est omen*) nothing less than the doomed *spiritus Mundi* of geopolitical violence in the New World so-called Order.

Pakistan behind him on his way to the University of Oxford, Mundy is soon altogether orphaned by his father's death—and set further adrift, until, studying German abroad like Pym, he is swept up in protest movements in East Berlin. Like Pym, too, under the pall of family damage and emotional isolation, he seeks the brother he never had (or more to the point the surrogate twin sister) in the radical alter-ego of an offered "absolute friend."[17] This is the brilliant and charismatic Sasha, ringleader of the student protests: Axel redux, complete with a limp of his own as a kind of political Achilles heel. We learn all this in hundreds of pages of an extended flashback, long after Mundy's recruiting by MI6, when two phases of his European career have come crashing down. First is his role as spy under disguise as cultural attaché of the Arts Council, in trips to Eastern Europe, over whose secrecy and distance his marriage collapses. But on one of the covert junkets he again connects with Sasha, now a double agent working against what he sees as the neo-Nazification of his native East Germany. This second collaboration, too, is short-lived, violently broken off by Sasha's interrogation and torture. Aimless for a while, severed from the Service, Mundy's next impasse comes when the English language school he founds in Heidelberg is ruined by an embezzling partner.

This lands him (literally and figuratively) where the novel opens, before its long definitive backfill—in his feckless role as charming, voluble docent at Ludwig's castle in Munich, where again Sasha crosses his path like a "ghost"— and not just of the past, but as a spectral foreshadowing of their doom ahead. What follows is a replay of Pym's dangerous bond(age) to Axel's subversive vision—verse below the surface of prose, revolutionary poetry in motion, cinematic in scope and intensity. This time Sasha's idealism has gravitated toward the magnetic rhetoric of a reformed arms-dealing billionaire and now leftist firebrand, one Dmitri, bent on renovating Mundy's deserted school as a center for radical free thought in resistance to the Americanization of Europe. It's a cause dear to Mundy's heart in his current rage against British complicity in the Iraq War (an all too up-to-the-minute bit of world weary commentary). Our wary hero is naturally dubious about the improbable scheme, even when money starts flowing for the luxurious renovation of his school building, but goes along with Sasha's fiery enthusiasm until, as warning signs mount, the double-cross is finally revealed. Dmitri, it turns out, is a mere pawn of underground US interests. The plot is to tar the left with a radical brush by planting terrorist material—and *materiel*—on the school's premises in order to justify a staged purge. What results from ersatz *kompromat* is a paramilitary attack in which both principal characters, Sasha and Mundy, are shot dead many times over, for maximum press effect. Only in their separate burial sites, we will find, do the "absolute friends" (in a relation as internecine as if they were truer to the more idiomatic "absolute enemies") return to that original maternal void—photographically indexed here, as before in *A Perfect Spy*—that has rendered these deracinated idealists so dubious about all motherlands.

Ekphrastic Action, Narrative Matrix

So matrix in the etymological sense (*mater*, womb)—with the arrested photographic frame of lived motion also a case, for each novel, of prose cinematics in embryo. At one foundational moment in both storylines, that is, le Carré gives over the forensic sensibility of his protagonist to the decoding, and hence ekphrastic description, of a long-absent mother's sole photographic remains. Given the English publication of Roland Barthes' *Camera Lucida* six years before *A Perfect Spy*, with Barthes' famously unseen Wintergarden photograph of his mother as well as his rumination on the private "punctum"— the poignant piercing node of certain photographs in subjective uptake— Barthes' book may well seem the prototype of both scenes in le Carré.[18] (And for close listeners to this collection of syncopated essays, restart the album one track back to hear more about the "punct" as pun, punctuation, and point—in chapter 5). In any case, these two scrutinized planar fields of arrested motion— narrativizing the still image as mourning-work—answer to each other in revealing fashion. And anticipate the *tour de force* closing moments of each book: not for the way that, at the medial level, the still imprint is recognized to inhere at the spun base of all cinematic flux, but rather for the moment of visual scrutiny itself in its stylistic activation by a secondary ekphrastic "camerawork." What stands out are the specific prose means by which these particular iconic objects for the orphaned spirit of each protagonist are virtually cinematized, in the very moment of depiction, under the detective gaze of apprenticed spycraft: not brought back to an irretrievable life and motion but dynamically scanned in the throes of epistemological deficit. Elicited by turns as foreground and recessive optic depth, the image plane is ultimately, in each early episode, both sectored and vectored as if by the intervening close-ups of psychological fixation itself.

In an internal monologue taking shape as a letter to his son and doubling for a primal episode in the autobiographical novel we find him to have been writing, Pym laments having only "one photograph of her," discovered tucked in a scuffed Bible. "One in all the world. One spotted sepia-brown photograph is all, taken like a pause in flight as she steps down from"—not "a," but "*the* taxi," previously unmentioned, so that the photo's frame is now subtly coincident with narrative perspective in process.[19] After a parenthetical "license number not in frame" set off only by commas—wholly extraneous, unless to suggest a route untraceable even by the keenest covert observer—standard participial modification takes over momentarily in a frozen progressive tense: the mother "clutching a homemade posy of small flowers that could be wild," at once compounded with a new clause that seems even more immediately to inhabit the vanished scene: "and her big eyes have too much behind them"—history internalized by preposition and a subsequent plural—"for our comfort."[20] Either for her own peace of mind or for that of her surviving son, in the grip of transferential identification. "Is she on her way to a wedding? To her own?"—approaching a ceremonialized bond that, effacing her, she must eventually flee? Pym ultimately reads it differently in his photo inquisition, as if she is already on the run: "Where is she escaping to this time?"[21] And in a spy's incognito at that: hiding beneath a bonnet that "throws a shadow like a mask across the scaring eyes." Not explicitly "scary," though they are that, to be sure, in their discomforting hidden depth, nor just "scared," but eyes caught in the act of their own mounting fear ("scaring")—and thus piercing the protective front, the "mask," hovering at the phonetic level across the slide into "guise" of her withdrawn gaze ("scaring *eyes*").

Pym's analysis continues like a study in geometric composition, but whose objectivity collapses through fetishism to identification as attention continues dollying-in on this frame-within-the-narrative-frame. While her "forearms form a vertical line from waist to neck," an abstraction of pose, the linearities of her stance become more precarious: "Shoulders on a slant, as if she is on the point of losing her balance, and"—a quick further detail in this *cap-à-pied* blazon, "one tiny foot tipped sideways to prevent her."[22] And not just head to foot, but head to toe with those shoes in which, as it were, the son seems involuntarily standing, "patent leather, pointed, buttoned"—just as the prose itself is cinched up in this final sharp punctum: for "somehow I know they pinch her, that they were bought against the clock" in one of her husband's flights from his creditors. Nothing more to reveal. She is not hatted for depature so much as shod, if not for any real escape. And the pinprick pointillism of this low-definition dot matrix photograph, encroaching just here on the narrator's fuller story, seems in synecdochic keeping with her own nickname and the dot-dash signals it precipitates: "Enough. I'm running out ahead. Dot, a.k.a. Dorothy . . . An abstraction. Mine."[23] A lonely possessive claim, followed now by another freestanding grammaical fragment in response to this lone optical document, where origin is no more than its own lingering image in the son's mind: "An unreal, empty women permanently in flight." Both the vacuum and its continuance linger in off-rhyme—with all the *empty*-ness echoing there in the phonetic weft of its *permanentcy*—until the image itself grows irrelevant, the absence wholly internalized: "If she had had her back to me and not her face, I couldn't have known her less or loved her more."[24]

But that antithetical parallelism, "I couldn't have known her less or loved her more," is not all in this plot's nexus of voided maternal presence—and the compensatory course of a perverse nurture and erotic maturation. That material photo of the primal woman in flight, that image of arrested liberty, is matched later by a secondhand vision of the suicided mother-substitute,

Lipsie, one of the mistresses in his father's entourage—and the son's first preteen erotic fascination. When she mysteriously kills herself in a leap from Pym's boarding school tower, the report of her smashed body in the quad has, for him, the hallucinatory feel of motion in a horizontal freeze-frame, another index of withdrawn affection in yet another photograph-like glimpse of a scared woman in flight: "a mind's picture of her [...] in a running position, sideways on the flagstone, her forward hand punched toward the finishing line," her broken "rear foot pointing the wrong way." The schoolmate who first saw her—and whose report was imprinted in bloodless form on Pym's memory—actually thought at first that "she was running [...] until he saw the wonky foot."[25] Not running upright, but in a skewed plane, like a photo of motion laid flat: "He thought she was doing a special exercise on her side, a sort of kicking, bicycling exercise."[26] Only a further stasis spells the truth. This first witness "had assumed the blood round her was a cape or a towel that she was lying on until he noticed"—in nature's displaced arrest from corpse to other fallen matter—"how the old chesnut leaves stuck to it and wouldn't blow away." As if chemically embalmed in their own right. These are linked freeze-frame moments—the halted stride of the actual mother's photo and the cemented thrust of motion for this later substitute beloved—that work to punctuate an ongoing flashback structure that is explicitly figured elsewhere, for Pym and his wife separately, as inescapable film footage. For him, there is "a clip of film running forever in my memory," while for life has become in review "a nightmarish film that she dared look at only piecemeal."[27] In the latter case, such guarded clips of any cautious mental rescreening could easily get snagged into traumatic single frames—as will happen, in fact, when she looks on as interested bystander at the scene of Pym's death.

Another postmortem maternal ekphrasis sets the scene—the biopsychic scenario—in *Absolute Friends* as well, but limning an even more primal absence coincident with the hero's birth. Precipitating the earliest phase of the novel's flashback structure, we learn of Mundy's Indian childhood from a stash of his father's papers secreted for safe-keeping in a locked basement room on the Ludwig property for which Mundy is the affably comic tour guide. On first mention, there is a photograph given only a "curt"—for cursory—"acknowledgment": one "ancient group photograph of an Anglo-Indian family with its many native servants posed on the steps of a grand colonial house"—this, among sundry other mementoes and odds and ends, along with "one twist of a woman's hair, dark brown, bound round a sprig of dried heather."[28] The sudden euphony of that phrase, with the assonant syllables loosely twisted round and bound up in each other, is its own give-away, first time through, that any related index of an absent body, as in that photograph, is of special note. As certainly the return mention of the photo will make clear—this in a flashback to the much earlier period of the father's death, to whose Surrey bedside Mundy has rushed in time to hold the ominously phrased "sweated head" of the dying man.[29]

Soon introduced again in the wake of this second parental loss, the photo is evoked by a just slightly expanded repetition of the initial "curt" phrasing, here on the brink of being studied far more closely. Details emerge as they had once commanded the son's notice: "One sepia photograph, quarto size, on presentation cardboard mounted with gilt surround."[30] Just slightly more expanded in its description here at first, the gist of the image as household portrait is given this time in a present active tense, the figures not just "posed" but caught in the moment of their clustering (in the form of an active verb) against a now more fully receding landscape and its visualized architectural "set." Mundy had once been looking more closely, the reader now with him: "An Anglo-India family and its many servants cluster in a rigid group on the steps of a muliturreted colonial mansion set in the foothills of upper India amid formal lawns and shrubberies."[31] Ensuing close-up of an entirely unanswered look: amid the "many servants," one in particular—the tall girl with her eyes closed against the bright sun, whose self-gloss to that effect on the back of the uncaptioned image matches the semi-literate handwriting on the accompanying note written to Mundy's father, then her lover, about the "fockin twins" whose "heartbeats" she hears because of him.[32] Amateur detective work on the part of the future spy has thus exposed the truth, from within this overbright photo exposure, of a lifelong lie. The barely literate Irish girl who had repeatedly been described to her surviving son as an aristocratic paragon of erudition and colonialist elegance stands revealed as a mother he had actually rather have known.

Every turn of phrase has abetted the temporality of this posthumous disclosure—beginning when, peering back before his birth, he misguidedly "scans the ranks of the female members of the family for the tall, polyglot Anglo-Irish aristocrat who will turn out to be his mother": in the double timescale of "turn out," both in gestation and in subsequent revelation. And once looking for her squinting eyes instead of for her posh bearing, he finds she "isn't hard to spot." For "if Mundy ever wore a nursemaid's drag and a black wig and squeezed up his eyes against the Indian sun, this is what he'd look like, because"—noted with the hint of an extra unnerving twinge—"she's the same age as I am now, and the same height, he thinks."[33] She lives on in him, duplicated in his own double self, and not as the aspirational Oxford intellectual and Germanist but in the residue of her gangly life force itself. And she is brought into quasi-cinematic close-up now through a handheld viewfinder, wearing the same "damn-fool all-weather grin" that Mundy knows himself to be precisely mirroring (inheriting)—in this shift to the idiom as well as POV of free indirect monologue—when "I gawp at her through the magnifying glass, which is the closest I will ever be to her": a strictly optic intimacy of telescoped spatial as well as temporal distance.[34] Explicitly seeing himself in the maternal photograph—the punctum as mirror—is, of course, only an exaggerated version of the cathexis involved in the harbored maternal image dwelt on in *A Perfect Spy*. In that case, too, the verbal irony of an early Jackson Browne lyric would come pertinently to mind, both in and beyond its erotic context: "I was taken by a photograph of you" ("Fountain of Sorrow"), where the song's persona turns out to have been *mistaken* about the woman's pictured look, his own verb thus carrying the further sense of being not just riveted but *taken in*— and even there in the double sense of invited and duped. In the case of *Absolute Friends*, Mundy's magnifying glass, correcting a longtime maternal cover story, offers an extra measure of prosthetic "familiarity."

Nor does Mundy's identification with the mother come cleansed of desire— or come clean about that erotic investment either, for that matter. Inferences nonetheless impinge. Speaking back to the image, he senses "there's something of the wild spirit about you too," and in this he imagines her to resemble his first puppy love for the Pakistani girl he was so miserable to leave when his father was drummed out of the service: "something" in the mother's image— as caught by the freeform unpunctuated compounding of her "spontaneous and trusting and joyful" look—recalling "that of a tall white Rani full-grown." Along with the sublimated eroticism of this maternal projection, what goes unsaid in this recognized female version of himself "in drag" is the yet more saddening resemblance to his stillborn twin sister, who would also be the mother's premarital age now—and thus the potentially fuller inheritor of the maternal resemblance. Without a word said in this moment of tacit repression, loss crowds on Mundy from two directions.

And part of the irony in all this photo-descriptive spade-work, given its symbolic depth charge, is the pressing intertextuality of the model. Whether or not le Carré had *Midnight's Children* in mind, with the fatality of his own natal twinning in the political context of Partition, it's clear that the orphaned Irish Mundy is modeled on Kim the Irish colonial spy in Kipling eponymous novel from 1901. It's not just that Mundy's father used to read excerpts from *Kim* aloud to his son between sips of whiskey night after night, about "a boy called Kim who became a spy in the service of his Queen and Emperor, though what happened to him when he had become one, and whether he won or was caught, were matters not divulged by the extract."[35] A truncated storyline leaves the son "puzzling his unfulfilled way" through such an abridgment, as he must later muddle through his own spy's life.[36] More than that, though, by unspoken link on le Carré's part to a scene that may or may not be included in Major Mundy's beloved volume of anthologized *Readings*, it's also the case—in the full Kipling—that when we hear in chapter 5, with Kim under informal interrogation, how his dead father is "gone-out," this strikes his interlocutor as an "abrupt way of putting it." As abrupt as the fact of death itself. This cancelled paternity is then accompanied by the more striking intertextual fact that, as in Mundy's case, Kim's mother (and this time the hyphenated past participle, "gone-out," is transformed by Kipling to a main verb) "went out when I was born." Here, then, are two senses tacitly summoned in turn for le Carré's absconding or deceased mothers: a going out that, for the surviving boy, means both departed and extinguished at once.

Toward the Stylistic "Finishing" Line: Prose as Curtailed Cinematics

MUNDY'S IS NO MORE AN UNMOTHERED LIFE than that of his precursor Pym, who takes in the end to some gentle compensatory fondness for the elderly landlady, Mrs. Dubber, at his final hideaway. When Pym's first erotic fixation, Lipsie, ends in her own petrified flight with her "forward hand punched toward the finishing line," the last modifier offers one of the author's familiar mortal ironies in a single truncating turn. "Forward . . . toward": such, too, is the thrust of fatal inevitability in the novel's broader plotting. The build-up to Pym's suicide is larded with verbal irony in dialogue before it unfolds its constrained cinematic effects in the cut-short prose. Explaining to Mrs. Dubber that he can't accompany her on the vacation he wants to fund for her: "I told you! I've run out of leave"—and out of all leeway and allowance, all freedom of movement, under a state dragnet that is closing around the boarding house as they speak.[37] In his taking what he knows to be final leave of her after she wishes him "a nice rest" ("from what?" he asks with a smile), he reverses the idiom by saying that he will "put myself to bed and give the world a rest."[38] It is not, however, the disgraced and defeated turncoat who climbs the stairs one last time but—flashback, and by scenic inference only—a unsullied and fresher self, captured in the most passing of details: "The stairs belonged to the houses of his childhood so he skipped up them light and forgot his aches and pains."[39] No memory is adduced, just a present occupancy of past locales, call them rear-projected: generic, impersonal, as if relieved of self. And after a postscript to his son, appended to the epistolary novel that has been passing in and out of address to him all along—a departing note about Pym being a generational "bridge" ("I am and what you must walk over to get from Rick to life"[40])—it is then a narration no longer his own that takes up the further burden of objectifying his body in a reflexive grammar as well as a visual reflection: "Placing himself for the last time before the shaving mirror," our now third-person secret agent arranges towels to minimize the blood: "Then he held the gun"—not "to his right ear," as might have been expected—but with almost clinical precision "to where his right ear was" (with the extra morbidity of tense for an ear soon to be no longer, blown to bits). In the process, with a typical fillip of neutralizing colloquial generalization, he finds himself "forgetting, as anybody might in the circumstance, whether the trigger of your Browning.38 automantic has two pressures or just one."[41] Might find oneself forgetting "in the circumstance"—what a phrase! After which that ironic idiom of a generic second person further widens the remove of subjecthood from its own catastrophe. On top of the subsequent casual possessive "your," at the very same and final instant, in the least incidental of glimpses, "he noticed how he was leaning"—not just "that he was," but precisely "how"—"not away from the gun," in anticipated recoil, "but into it, like someone a little deaf, straining for a sound."[42] Will it come with one pressure-point squeeze of the trigger or two? In either case, given the coiled spring of this simile alone, a wide circle is closed. In the opening event of the novel's chronology, in the protagonist's pre-partem tryout for a life of covert surveillance, the as yet unperfected spy is a "deaf microphone" in his mother's womb—"planted but inactive in any but the biological meaning."[43] Pym in embryo waits in abeyance there as a "mute and foetal spy"—turned off for transmission but still, as genetic "plant," recording for us and his novel one of its primal scenes: overhearing, that is, or under-hearing, the first of his father's rhetorical shell games in avoiding legal action and punishment.[44] Hundreds of pages and dozens of years later, it is as if he returns to that womb in death—to that condition of the unborn—in the form of just such an embodied microphone, gone deaf on the instant. Paragraph break, with a shift to our acoustic proxy in his nearest survivor. "Mary never heard the shot."

Typographic break; perspectival gap; scene change; dramatic rather than optical reverse shot to the wife in stand-by mode.[45] Whether or not death leaves time for the audition of its onset in the perpetrator's straining ear (soon foresaken, as entry point for the bullet's pulverizing projectile), outside in the car the moment goes unnoted—lost in the white noise of that space between paragraphs as well as in the surreptitious hubbub around her. The elision is absolute: leaving no room, as the rest of the scene does by contrast, for future embellishment. Not "Mary didn't hear," but "never heard" the retort, then … or ever. What she never forgets, though, at least in their unconscious returns, are the flashings of fantasy's audiovisual traces that she is all the while both shoring against the horror of the moment and storing up for its replay. Despite what she loathes as the "theatrical nonsense" of the scene, with whispered contingency plans about protecting "non-combatants" and a quartet of "shock troops" on the roof in "classic postures of stealth," these assaulting impressions are rendering themselves indelible, registered in the traumatic grammar of the future perfect in its present (tense) foreshadowing: "All those things in her memory were taking place and had just done so"—a telltale overlapping slide from progressive to pluperfect in the heat of a distended moment—"had just done so as Brotherhood" (as if he has in fact either heard the shot himself, or heard about it from the attending policeman) "shoved open the driver's door, sending the superintendent flying to one side, one boot forever frozen in the window frame."[46] What might have been an incidental and passing evocation, seared into the wife's memory, of a shocked visual fixity in the restricted frame of a car window (as caught in that apt last absolute construction, no finite verb involved) turns out to unfold instead as the trigger ("frozen forever") of a full-scale cinematic trope for the psyche's optical imprint. The effect develops across the immediate return to motion—but with what we discover, in turn, is merely a fantasized fast-forward, summoned like a flashback from the mentally unfaithful wife's own dream backlog: "After that she had a forward image of Jack pelting toward the house at a young man's pace because sometimes she had a dream of him doing exactly that [...] coming to make love to her."[47]

Not so here—but instead moving in the opposite direction, with his own "forward image" as if permanently frozen in facing away from her. Typical of a certain dazed frenzy in the climactic moments of le Carré's otherwise scrupulous realism, these last-minute confusions of focus and framing mark the breakdown of any normative descriptive protocol. Just as Pym strides with boyish gusto up long-lost stairs to his death, so Brotherhood, the handler tracking him, races to the scene—in Mary's now-widowed eyes—too late for rescue, but with a displaced lover's enthusiasm. Only to be petrified on the spot, fossilized. The fleeting "forward image" is compensatory even before its arrest, fending off the inevitable. For it is now clear that "with the clamour all around him he was"—in fact, and in the novel's last sentence—"standing still." Yet that participle is immediately rephrased by apposition, along with a ceremonial militarist idiom, like a cognitive snag in the onlooker's reeling mind—or a jam in our mental reel. For it is at this point that the surviving secret agent, not just holding still, is recognized to be "standing to attention like a dead centurion at his post." In Wordsworth's sense, we can "murder to dissect" even with a brief simile, given here its word's reinvested worth in converting a dead metaphor like "dead in his tracks" into the very figure of petrified corporate agency in prose's own arrested track. In short, called up short, a narrative freeze-frame offers the self-arrested legal aftermath of plot's last violent spasm.

In a late explanatory turn of his epistolary novel-within-the novel, in a double inversion of omniscience and free indirect discourse, Pym speaks in the third person, without quotation marks, about talking to himself as such, as other—yet in the fatally inherited idioms of his dead trickster father: "That's how it was, Tom. [...] Just one more con, Pym kept saying to himself, one more con will see me right." A comparable psycho/logic in *Absolute Friends*—again filtered through the split from (and within) omniscience to divisive free indirect—gains access to the hero's serial identity as, in his own self-conception, Mundy One, Mundy Two, and eventually Mundy Three: first patriotic teacher and major's son, then deceit-steeped spy, then vestigial washout on the skids.[48] The sordid political maneuver by which these tripled selves are succeeded briefly by Mundy *redux*, under the false pretenses of leftist backing, is also subject to the rule of three—and developed, he realizes after the fact, in a metafictionally phrased trio of artificial "set pieces" luring him on toward the final staged mayhem.[49] As with the syntactic nub of Pym's short-circuited grammar in the earlier novel ("kept saying to himself"), all of this self-trifurcation may seem sprung, as characteristic of le Carré's colloquial ear, from an initial idiomatic word-splay. For the "man of parts," as the multifaceted Mundy might be described, the man of composite talents, finds any such idiomatic idea of "part" warped to its theatrical sense when we read, earlier in the downslide of plot, that "Ted Mundy in his many parts turns out to be a master of prevarication."[50]

Again and again in the novel, as Mundy moves inexorably toward a doomed future, the past keeps dragging him back to the present. Such shifts happen nearest the end, in a visit to his abandoned school after billionaire Dmitri's promise to refurbish it with new purpose, where he sees his long-forgotten writing on the blackboard. As if it were a figurative writing on the wall, it concerns a grammar that doesn't parse. It thus serves to insert our own reading lesson for what's coming in the deception plot. In private voice-over, Mundy overhears his past self in the process of intoning the grammar lesson, with its bad object exactly the kind of dangling participle that will blisteringly return in his son's obituary remarks after his killing. First time around, in commercial claptrap: "As a valued customer of British Rail, we would like to apologize to you for […]." Amid his chalked list of cross-examining queries: "Who is the subject of the sentence?" If we suspect here an underlying irony about the genuine elision of the subject in British institutional functions, rail and Secret Service alike, that too will come home to roost in the narrative's climax of treachery. But for now: "End of reverie." And in this mode of inward self-command borrowed by omniscience: "The past isn't what you came for."[51] Trouble is, the future is a subterfuge.

The past returns as well in his last interview with Sasha, where Mundy is hoping to smoke out potential terrorist sympathies in the Dmitri scheme. The two absolute friends are riverside for a picnic, as they were riverside in a hotel when, years before, they last parted company and ideological ways. In his equally heated exchange much later about the pending venture, setting is the objective correlative of their shared gamble: "On the river, earnest oarsmen wrench themselves a path against the current."[52] But the ominous present is itself encroached upon by the past, for as they continue to argue about what's coming, the scene reverts: "It's the Dreesen Hotel all over again, Mundy thinks […]. It's the same bloody river going by, and the same impossible gap between us," the hopeless idealist and the hope-depleted realist.[53]

The audiovisual superimposition is smooth enough, since the scene to which he adverts was all but allegorical the first time around—and not readily forgotten in its evocative strain: life's river of no return, styled into parable by sound play and metaphor. A hundred pages before, but present in a tonal return of the repressed channeled by the felt residuum of style's original force: "They fall quiet again, but the Rhine is never quiet."[54] When later narration is thrown back by triggered memory into that divisive hotel encounter, inner and outer world are in a similar contrapuntal flux—with only direction and no destination: even then an upstream "path" they must "wrench" against a "current" more than literal. Back then: "Though it is nighttime, chains of barges charge ceaselessly past the windows, and by their din they could as well be passing through the room."[55] In a second refrain of the previous corrective seesaw about the never-quiet Rhine: though he and Sasha are sitting "in darkness, the Rhine is never dark." This is because the "sodium lamps that line the towpath shine upward onto the oval ceiling."[56] But no path is illuminated, made clear, for Mundy and Sasha, nor any pleasure, despite the fact that—in a discharge of internal echo more delicate than the "charge" of those "chains of barges"—the alliterating "lights of the pleasure boats flit at will across the pilastered walls": *li / li / ill / il* [uhl] / *all*, a liquid-like coruscation in which the last descriptor is indistinguishable in sound from the plaster that is likely to compose it.[57] Or call this iterative syllabic rhythm the intrinsic flicker effect of prose's inner cinema—in mockery of the heroes' stasis and deadlock. After Sasha once stormed out, as he will break away again in the present, an importunate audiovisual association had closed in even further on Mundy from off-screen space, so that the metaphoric "chain" for that nexus of barges, a suspected metonymy at the time, is now brought explicitly forward, if ambiguously, in the mode of a personifying synecdoche, mooring part from the mobile whole: "An anchor chain shrieks and drowns. A ship's horn laments its passing"—as it ceases its own passage.[58] The pall of demise is as amorphous as it is contagious, with Mundy stuck "listening to the clangor of a world he is no longer part of [...] wondering what's left to him now that his past has walked out on him."[59] No Mundy *redivius* there. Nor when the absolute frenemies relive their Rhineside debate years later—and nearer the end. Within the idiomatics of "left," the figuration is like a chiasmatic reversal of Pym, who has "run out of leave"—any leave except exit.

But Mundy still clings, against his better judgment, to a recovery of his ghostly past in the person of Sasha. And after the "set pieces" that have set them up for disaster, the fourth act of this charade is ominously foretold by a typical slick switch into sarcastic free indirect at the treacherous return into the plot, from his previous liaison with MI6, of Mundy's "old friend and confidant Orville J. Rourke—call me Jay—of the Central Intelligence Agency in Langley, Virginia—and dammit, Ted, you don't look a day older than when [...]."[60] And won't look any older yet when I'll soon have slain you at point-blank range. At the narrative level, the double-cross is almost allegorical. The leftist writings Sasha has supposed himself collecting in Paris and shipping back to Heidelberg constitute, almost by pun, the "crates of inflammatory literature" whose packaging actually contains planted explosives meant to incriminate the heroes in a terrorist plot.[61] This Mundy discovers way too late. In his exhaustion, a slack second-person address has him trying half-heartedly to talk himself into an escape route: "Then maybe you're too tired to face the microphones tonight, Edward," an idiom twisted from "face the music" for a building he knows to be thoroughly bugged. But the show must go on, its maestro and ringleader— and now more like ringmaster—Rourke very much at the ready, awaiting only Sasha's approach. If le Carré has wanted us to bring Joseph Conrad's *The Secret Agent* (1907) explicitly to mind, where an anarchist bomb is hidden in a satchel of books by a seditious bookseller specializing otherwise in pornography, the intertext couldn't have rendered any more effectively reflexive our sense of the present book about to explode as well—and in a phantasmagoria of premeditated violence.[62]

Son, Lumière, *Silence: Closure's Cutaway*

Mundy is himself under attack quite literally before he knows it—or before we have heard report of it. Not realizing in a heavy numbness the extent of his first wounds, this eventually reported terrorist and Islamist sympathizer, after stumbling upstairs in flight to the school's attic, "discovers he is on his knees, mosque style, with his arse in the air and his face in his blood-caked hands"— cartoon of the jihadist fundamentalism to whose ruse he is being sacrificed. Yet "he can still crawl to the dormer window and crank himself up high enough to see over the sill," where the mechanics of the crank is transferred from a likely tool of fenestration to the robotic reduction of a damaged anatomy.[63] From the frame of that dormer aperture he surveys, in the delusional confusion of injury and excessive spectacle, the gathering panorama of ambush and overkill as a literal "show" of strength. And "what he sees in truly amazing, the sort of *son et lumière* show you'd travel miles for."[64] So he did with his child Jake, as he recalls by mental and visual superimposition, in a last (and too vividly induced) memory of a rare good outing after his divorce: a kinetic medieval tableau, only partly updated in its brutality, complete with "cannon and pikemen and halberdiers and siege towers, and chaps pouring very lifelike boiling oil from the battlements." The present show is "just as impressive: spotlight and floodlight and arc lights and searchlights, lights tucked up on cherry pickers and flashing lights on the police vans"—on and on, all aglow "except in the blackened windows of the surrounding houses, because marksmen like their privacy."[65] With a design (upon us) no more than subliminal, we are cast back as well to the sound and light show of that fateful Rhineside hotel (the river "never quiet" in its traffic, "never dark" in its glare).

Yet with no other memory explicitly recorded than Mundy's outing with his son (in English this time), the next present-tense paragraph panders further to "our" taste in spectacle in this last great cinematic heave of plot: "And costumes?" In such a palimpsest of carnival and menace, the typical overlap and cross-penetration of episodic recurrences in the hero's story has produced a temporal pastiche—or more like implosion—so that the whole history of state violence is circulated in dizzying anachronism from the earliest anti-Muslim crusades to this spectacle of anti-Jihadist intervention. Costumes, you ask? "Well, if you don't mind mixing ancient and modern" in the dress department, as in some trendy stage version of a classic play, these are "unsurpassed," including "frogmen rubbing shoulders with King Richard Crusaders in balaclava helmets, blackamoors with battle-axes, maces and witch's boxes lashed to their belts."[66] And in a more recent conflation of terrorist regimes across the roving zoom closeups of this satirized melange: "West Berlin police in Prussian-style helmets, firemen like Nazi storm troopers, paramedics in tin hats and laundered white coats adorned with red crosses"—as if in some further resurfaced insignia of the Knights Templar off to defeat the heathen.

Lights, costumes, action. And again like a circus barker hawking the sonic ingenuities of this *son* and *lumière* display in a button-holing second person: "And for your sound effects, instead of the usual tattoo of music and spotty rumble of cannon fire, we have the sergeant major form the parade ground at Murree, no less"—flashback to Mundy's colonial boyhood—"barking orders in English, German, or, for all Mundy can hear, Pujabi."[67] The reversion to a long-lost acoustic memory, a mere sideshow from the wings, cannot detract from the feature attraction on the over-lit main stage. For "the unquestioned star of the show, the man everyone has come from miles around to see"—in this bitter dribble of hyperbole—is Sasha, his congenital limp almost corrected by the loss of a sneaker as he speeds across the courtyard, wholly unwilling for the barrage of attention bestowed upon him, "waving one hand in the air, saying 'No, no,' the way a film star says to the paparazzi, please boys, not today, I haven't got my makeup on." In this pre-choreographed dance of death at the *son et lumière* climax, it is "probably the bullets that are keeping him going rather than his own effort." The machine-gun fire is "mauling and disfiguring" his carcass in the process, shredding him like a "rag doll" that Mundy is powerless to lift and carry away to safety—as he had once before done, and now in a last vanishing moment remembers, during their radical student days in East Berlin. For here in the attic, the show is over for good with his own assassination: "But not before Mundy has filled his lungs for one last attempted yell of *Hang on it's all right, I'm coming*, to his dead friend lying in the square." Coming not to the rescue, but to join his "absolute friend" in a twin finality.

Just before—recruiting the full mordant irony of le Carré's darkest, but hardly gray, prose—Mundy's POV is riveted to a "sophisticated rifle with sights so big that an uninformed and recumbent person at the receiving end—such as Mundy—might not know which hole to watch when he is being shot."[68] The "such as Mundy" is a devastating touch, like the phrasing "as one might [wonder] in such circumstance" in the matter of the Browning pistol's discharge mechanism for Pym's last moment in *A Perfect Spy*. Yet here the free indirect style has freed itself so completely from identification—as has the hero from his own last (split) second of identity, becoming just a case in point, yet again, for an inevitable ballistic uncertainty—that the scene now transpires, unspliced into any cinematic suture, across the instantaneous evacuation of consciousness. The optic black holes of barrel and viewfiender are in fact interchangeable, once the fall guy has been targeted. With a "studied deliberation" visible to his prey, Rourke, the former CIA agent and now rogue provocateur, having set up his victim as a falsely suspected terrorist, now backs himself rather than Mundy "against the wall, in fact" in order to steady his aim (in an inversion of standard execution lingo and its figurative derivations). At which point, still at point-blank range, he sends "three high-velocity sniper bullets into Mundy, one straight through the center of his brow and two more at leisure into the upper body"—only a body now, a corpse in the moment of brain death: "one to the abdomen and the other to the heart"—fake signs of precaution, no doubt, in this supposed confrontation with a ruthless terrorist. Followed by the further piercing irony of modal grammar in the perfect (rather than standard past) tense, building on the "leisure" thus afforded: two more shots, that is, "though neither can *have been* strictly necessary." Not when private time, shunted here across the grammar of temporality, is already up—subsumed in the "But not before" of that last drawn breath for Sasha, life's literalized last gasp. With Mundy, as with Pym before him, the orphaned loner has sought more than a brother, instead an empowering alter-ego, in this spy's game of redoubled agency. But the later novel has taken the logic even farther in its stringency, rendering the resulting fatality inherently mutual, each "absolute" friend now—and without emotional absolution—fulfilling the role of "secret sharer" (this time an unmistakable Conradian allusions, with the extra overtone of "sharers of secrets") only in the leveling partnership of death.[69]

However "cinematographic" we might consider the elided subjectivity of Mundy's death moment and its immediate white-out at chapter's end, the hero's previous view through the upper window, in framed dazzlement and horror, has offered this phase of Mundy *redux* its own extra and final "set piece." And indeed the *son et lumière* display, the staged audiovisual extravaganza, has actually been filmed—and this under direction of the murderer and security entrepreneur, richly remunerated by the results. Not only did Rourke fabricate a terrorist plot to bolster anti-Muslim propaganda for the Western right wing, a lucrative commission in itself, but, as we learn from the exposé of the closing chapter, amidst the cover stories blandly circulated by the press regarding the publicly dubbed "Siege of Heidelberg," he was able, "by means of a sophisticated smokescreen of proxies" to become "sole shareholder of a security company" that also "owned the copyright in the only piece of video footage of the siege ever to appear."[70] And a clip from the action thrills enhancing its *mise-en-scène* is replayed for us now, with its parade of "unidentifiable heroes in full antiterror rig storming through clouds of Hollywood smoke"—the complot's whole typified smokescreen—"across the roof the school building"[71] The prime victim is a mere bit player in this thriller staging, since only "in the background, just distinguishable between the chimney pots, lies"—in this hierarchically inverted grammar of a deep-focus shot—the almost incidental "body of the Euro-terrorist Sasha, shot dead in the very act of flight."[72] Like 9/11 footage, or the Zapruder film of the Kennedy assassination, but here funded in the first place for return profit by its executive producer, this "clip, run and rerun on every television station in the world, had earned millions of dollars for its owner."[73] Propaganda doubles as commercial property: no political news there.

Not exploitative video shots and its fake inferences, however, but prose's own shifting *foci*, even after the slaughter, get the last word in this narrative—once transferred to fiction from the objective journalism of an enterprising reporter, whose findings seem every bit as allegorical as those explosive-stuffed book cartons masquerading as incendiary literature. The final subsiding wave of coverage for all this newsworthy violence and its supposedly aborted scheme concerns the last resting places of the terrorists, with father-despising Sasha, sired by a Nazi turned Lutheran German dignitary, matched at a distance by Mundy—both discovered, that is, to be "buried alongside their respective mothers: Sasha the German in Neubrandenburg, and Mundy the Englishman on a sun-baked hillside in Pakistan."[74] The latter setting is an emblematic post-colonial site in an archaeology of empire and disillusionment—at once in terrain and atmosphere—with its foggy ruinesque vestiges of Western faith as well as the continued war games it both facilitates and trivializes. The novel's splendidly simple and epitomizing last sentence, cited from the journalist's account: "The mist, she reported, never quite lifts"—never has, never will—"but the broken Christian masonry makes it a popular place for children to stage their mock battles"[75] Never quite clear, the scene of this final fade-out: its perspective misted over with the continuing fogs of war, a larval violence waiting not just to be staged but to be played out in the real.

In another kind of closure earlier in this shattering final chapter—entirely verbal (linguistic) rather than pictorial, and stinging in precisely its lapse of literacy—the tearful remarks of Mundy's increasingly estranged son Jake before the TV cameras are obliquely fit in their sloppiness, the logic and texture of syntax pried asunder like the chasm of loss it mourns. For "in a grammatical solecism that must have had Mundy spinning in his grave" (he whose one recorded schoolroom lesson exposed an earlier dangling modifier), the son utters this pained and hapless lament: "As my natural father, I shall always feel there is a hole in my life I can never fill."[76] Seemingly inherited there: a parallel absence to the one that yawned for Mundy in the lifelong absence of his own mother—and bearing traces as well of Pym's notorious father, Rick, whose inverted responsibility was broadcast in repeated ingratiating address (paradox rather than solecism) to Pym as "old son." In the later novel, with that climactic misplaced modifier, we're reminded again that narrative grammar, bad as well as good, has its own shot sequences, its own deliberate slips in continuity editing, its own balked sutures, dropped stitches, incoherent ligatures.

The double trouble with the son's syntax of trauma in Mundy's case—with its stark dangling participle, its abyssal gulf of failed reference—is not just that the son must father his own future. It is also that the man he mourns has disappeared altogether from the intended phrasing of this human equation. Here is the black-comic melodrama—rather than mere gray lapse—of grammar itself: screened for the slip-geared kinetics of its irony. No narrowness of scale or lack of imagery need prevent the filmic analogy for this emblematic verbal disjuncture, this failed, jagged splice. En route to a not just obscure but optically hazy burial ground marked for us by cited prose alone, phrasing has stumbled on, and over, a precipitating ironic instance of le Carré's verbal "inner cinema"— and, so to say, the pathos of its marked continuity error. At the narrowest compass of prose's jump-cut elliptical editing, burying its own syntactic subject on the run, style serves in this way to visualize the raw solecism of the son's withered tribute, its gaping logical elision under self-referential pressure. It does so as if graphing a tangible "hole" in the very fabric of narration—hollowed out by an unsaid play on generational *antecedence* all told, the *decedent* gone and all but already forgotten.

Notes

1   [Ed.] Part of the irony of Garrett Stewart calling his stylistic notatations a "dossier," though "declassified" here by going public, as he says in his opening sentence—resides in the fact that these effects, to judge from previous criticism on the spy-novel master, John le Carré, have seemed secrets well kept regarding the seemingly effortless propulsion of the novelist's prose. But the close-focus calibration of such notice is no secret to readers of Stewart. Indeed, two chapters of *The Ways of the Word: Episodes in Verbal Attention* (Ithaca: Cornell University Press, 2021)—"Threading the Read" (chapter 4) and "Fframe-Advance" (chapter 5), with latter's duo-scale typography evoking the screen *Frame* and photogram *frame* simultaneously—are given over, with Stewart's typical relish and rigor, to "cinematographic" grammar in writers from Alfred Tennyson, Charles Dickens, and Herman Melville through Henry James, Thomas Wolfe, and Virginia Woolf to William Faulkner and Vladimir Nabokov, including as well such contemporary novelists as Salmon Rushdie, Don DeLillo, Richard Powers, and Jonathan Franzen.

      Consider too, here reproduced for convenience, a glossary entry for "Fframe-advance prose": "by analogy with the double sense of 'frame' in celluloid cinema—the image cell on the strip and, simultaneous with it at a different scale, the rectangular field of the moving image in projection—the F/f model applies as well to the gap between syllabic matter and syntactic momentum in the kinesis of the 'cinematographic sentence,' as when at the end of D. H. Lawrence's *The Rainbow* (1915), long before the Ken Russell film's special effect, the titular 'arch'-itecture of hope layers its chromatic striations via the overlaps of a twofold comma- spliced grammar, the rough verbal equivalent of serial cinematic cross-fades: 'Steadily the colour gathered, mysteriously, from nowhere, it took presence upon itself, there was a faint, vast rainbow.'" That glossary notation closes in sum, in allusion to a previous Stewart book title: "Cinematographic prose as one of *The Ways of the Word*." From *Attention Spans: Garrett Stewart, a Reader*, ed. David LaRocca (New York: Bloomsbury, 2024), 342–43.

2   See Sergei Eisenstein, "Dickens, Griffith, and the Film Today," in *Film Form: Essays in Film Theory*, trans. Jay Leyda (New York: Harcourt, 1949), where Dickens is found to "give to cinematography far more guidance than that which led to the montage of parallel action" (211), including "cinematic 'optical quality,' 'frame composition,' 'close-up,' and the alternation of emphasis by special lenses" (213), "even . . . a 'dissolve'" (213)—as well as a pattern of cumulative detail "intercut" (218) into a bustling street scene and the travelling shot that negotiates it.

3   John le Carré, *A Delicate Truth* (New York: Viking, 2013), 30.

4   John le Carré, *A Most Wanted Man* (New York: Scribner, 2008), 37.

5   John le Carré, *Single and Single* (New York: Pocket Star, 1999), 1.

6   Le Carré, *Single & Single*, 6; italics added.

7   Ibid., 5.

8   Ibid., 18.

9   Ibid., 13.

10 Ibid., 18.

11 John le Carré, *The Constant Gardener* (London: Hodder and Stoughton, 2001), 504.

12 Ibid.

13 Ibid.

14 John le Carré, *Agent Running in the Field* (New York: Viking, 2019), 12. As to the valence and shades of "dark" as a descriptive of his style, discussion continues. In full appreciation of the fact that, despite le Carré's renowned spy coinages, it is "the prose more than the terminology" that one notices in rereading him, Siddhartha Deb, in a retrospective assessment for *The Nation* (December 17, 2020), sums up the writing's stylistic tone as "a gray prose for a gray world perpetually somber with memory," yet this in an article entitled "The Blinding Clarity of Genre le Carré," where in fact the incandescent is stressed over the crepuscular. https://www.thenation.com/article/culture/john-le-Carré-imperial-decline/ In a more detailed career re-estimate from *The New Statesman* the next year (January 6, 2021), novelist—and, as it happens, screenwriter—William Boyd, arbitrarily focusing on two novels decades apart, *The Honourable Schoolboy* (1977) and *A Delicate Truth* (2013), explores, beyond le Carré's preference for a highly mobile omniscience, certain "tics" (or "tricks of the trade"), including the exacerbated suspense generated by unanswerable rhetorical questions, about human movements and motives, posed within the discourse—but on the reader's puzzled and antsy behalf. Of these broadly defined tics, the most cinematic (unmentioned as such) is dispatched by grammatical fragments (ditto) in what Boyd calls a characteristic "staccato" (more frequent, he rightly claims, in Carré's later work), as for instance from *A Delicate Truth*: "Footsteps approaching, faint but getting louder. Party the first [of two expected conspirators] is arriving . . . The footsteps approaching the anteroom. One pair only. Hard soles. Leisured, nothing stealthy." These and other instances are lifted from a single passage that, with its nervous mode of zoom acoustics (as I would want to put it)—and resultant quick-cut succession of action and inference—recalls the automatized prose focus earlier in the novel, as noted above—breaking into it is own staccato fragment of reflexive videography at "The camera enlarges it. Enlarges it again." See Boyd's article at https://www.newstatesman.com/culture/fiction/2021/01/prose-style-john-le-carr. And his earlier: "Why John le Carré is More Than a Spy Novelist," *The New Statesmen*, October 21, 2015: https://www.newstatesman.com/culture/2015/10/william-boyd-why-john-le-carre-more-spy-novelist.

15 [Ed.] Keeping track of the decline, we register the ongoing pursuit of lose ends and their aftershocks in Mick Herron's *Slough House* series (2010–), subsequently animated into shape as *Slow Horses* (2022–) by AppleTV+ with the sometimes le Carré spy, Gary Oldman, as the anti-Bond Jackson Lamb, performing his spycraft expertly if amidst radical dishevelment while being the sometimes keeper of a band of losers.

16 Amid the whiplash contradictions of the journalistic record in the matter of reviewers' judgments (sampled novel by novel in Adam Sisman, *John le Carré: The Biography* [New York: HarperCollins, 2015])—with almost every novel being pegged at once in different venues as "vintage le Carré" and its "pale shadow," "the best since . . .," and "a forgivable falling off from"—it may rightly take the estimate of fellow novelists to tether the random hyperboles to a more persuasive view, with blurb-worthy Philip Roth finding *A Perfect Spy* "the best English novel since the War" and novelist-biographer A. N. Wilson singling out *Absolute Friends* as the author's "finest novel" ("Le Carré: Old Wars on New Fronts," *Daily Mail*, December 26, 2003): a genuine *piece de resistance*—despite frequent resistance elsewhere to the author's strident anti-American bombast as the thinly disguised animus of his lead character. Countering such complaints, as if the anger warped the plot and sabotaged the author's seasoned realism, Terrence Rafferty delivered a laudatory review of *Absolute Friends* in *The New York Times* under the Conradian title "One of Us," and with the opening assurance that, unlike most best-selling novelists, "John le Carré never, ever phones it in—not even on a secure line." Rafferty admired the novel's daredevil flashback structure and, though caught up in the indisputable excitement of an apocalyptic ending he nonetheless felt gratuitous, found no fault with the "plausibility" of its premise in *ex officio* American treachery and betrayal. https://www.nytimes.com/2004/01/18/books/one-of-us.html.

17 John le Carré, *Absolute Friends* (London: Hodder & Stoughton, 2003), 128.

18 Roland Barthes, *Camera Lucida: Reflections on Photography*, trans. Richard Howard: (New York: Farrar, Straus, and Giroux, 1982).

19 John le Carré, *A Perfect Spy* (New York: Scribner, 1986), 30.

20 Le Carré, *Absolute Friends*, 30.

21 Ibid.

22 Ibid.

23 Ibid., 31.

24 Ibid.

25 Ibid., 81.

26 Ibid.

27 Ibid., 106, 145.

28 Ibid., 27.

29 Ibid., 51.

30 Ibid., 54.

31 Ibid.

32 Ibid., 55.

33 Ibid., 57.

34 Ibid.

35 Ibid., 39.

36 Ibid., 42.

37 Ibid., 583.

38 Ibid., 584.

39 Ibid., 587.

40 Ibid., 588.

41 Ibid., 589.

42 This is a stray optic detail, clinically inflected by style, whose weird rightness and power—in its return from ballistic speculation to mirroring POV—can be

measured by its regrettable deletion from the abridged audiobook version of the novel recorded by the author himself in 1987, the sentence pared away perhaps to make an even more melodramatic leap from trigger action to unheard "shot" on Mary's part.

43 Le Carré, *Absolute Friends*, 26.

44 Ibid.

45 [Ed.] Note here a perfect illustration, in the dramatic pace of such sheer paragraph spacing, of that expanded definition of punctuation urged by the Cambridge editors discussed in chapter 5 and pursued there as part of the punct/counterpoint rhythms tracked by Stewart's analysis.

46 Le Carré, *Absolute Friends*, 590.

47 Ibid.

48 Ibid., 248, 264.

49 Ibid., 302, 347. This Mundy multiplex—at first triadic, then fourfold in its deceptive resuscitation—might readily seem to support a resistance to "narrative identity" in theorical debate, given its virtual parable of what philosopher Galen Strawson posits instead as the less determinate and linear "episodic self." But of course Mundy's fragmented travails are nonetheless, in le Carré's typical weave of psychodynamics and story, all part of a tripartite narrative in their own right. This is a bioplot, as it were, in which disjunction and rupture *are* the self's recursive story. As if combining the alternate "diachronic" and the "episodic" models of Strawson's antinomy, Mundy, certainly after Pym, is the clearest instance in le Carré's fiction of what we might rather call the *periodic self*: functioning in its fated turns like a narratological return of the repressed. See Strawson, "Against Narrativity," *Ratio*, vol. 17 (2004): 428–52. http://lchc.ucsd.edu/mca/Paper/against_narrativity.pdf

50 Le Carré, *Absolute Friends*, 235.

51 Ibid., 353.

52 Ibid., 395.

53 Ibid., 399.

54 Ibid. 289.

55 Ibid.

56 Ibid.

57 Ibid.

58 Ibid.

59 Ibid., 293.

60 Ibid., 371–72.

61 Ibid., 441.

62 [Ed.] Beyond discussion below of *The Secret Sharer* as explicit Conradian interetext at the close of *Absolute Friends*, for more on the political Conrad much admired as forebear by le Carré—and on the former novelist's own cinematic prose of chiaroscuro superimpositions as they are transposed to the screen—see chapter 1; and on what we might call the iris-out conclusion of *Heart of Darkness*, in turn chapter 8—where the British imperial river that "seemed to lead into the heart of an immense darkness" is mapped further under ghost-read f(ol)low-through.

63 Le Carré, *Absolute Friends*, 434.

64 Ibid.

65   Ibid.
66   Ibid., 434–35.
67   Ibid.
68   Ibid., 436.
69   Ibid., 276.
70   Ibid., 449.
71   Ibid.
72   Ibid.
73   Ibid.
74   Ibid., 453.
75   Ibid.
76   Ibid., 445.

7 / Garrett Stewart's appreciation for the ekphrastic finesse of John le Carré's photo evocations in the preceding essay gives way now to the strenuous labors of ekphrasis on Stewart's own part in bringing intricate museum images to the reader's "conceptual" view. Film returns in selected experimental modes in this essay with a panorama of negative imagining as medial disclosure. Author of *Transmedium: Conceptualism 2.0 and the New Object Art* (2017) and theorist of "demediation" (*Bookwork: Medium to Object to Concept to Art*, 2011), Stewart moves here to survey, across recently encountered work on three continents, a certain cross-section of Conceptual art in the contemporary gallery scene, aligning evidence from Taipei to Copenhagen, Los Angeles and San Francisco to London, in which certain works of media reflexivity find a particular flashpoint in an aesthetic of negative reversal, whether in photography or found objects, painting or cinema—including an eerie triangulation of infrared, X-ray, and heat-sensitive imaging in their related deconstructions of the naturalized plane of vision. This essay, almost a *summa* of his earlier (and obviously ongoing) visual interests and methodologies, finds Stewart once again approaching media study at the inner limit of its own (to use his neologism) demediations—often marked by reciprocal negation at one or another transmedial interface.

7 / Negative Imprints in Conceptual Art

ACCIDENTS WILL HAPPEN. *Will,* and in any attempted sampling of tendencies in Conceptual art (given few established subgenres for tracking), almost *must* happen for or any kind of productive forage, let alone coverage, in the mode of pattern recognition. Accidents of venue and schedule, that is, repeatedly aid in bringing previously unstudied practices into unexpected conjunction. If, by happenstance, one thing leads to another like it, the grounds of that likeness may point the viewer elsewhere in turn. And eventually "toward" generalization. In the present case:

Negactivity—Toward a Poetics of Inversion

SUCH MOSTLY FORTUITOUS ROUTES OF DISCOVERY lead here, stateside first, from San Francisco and Los Angeles, cross country to Cambridge and Buffalo, then on via London and Copenhagen to Taipei—and finally back through

Central Europe to Los Angeles (and a final footnote to the latest London retrospective). At which point too many common denominators had been amassed not to benefit, for me at least, from my nominating an organizing trope for their loosely shared ideations in the mode of material negativity. So this essay sets out to chart the sequence of their discovery as a map of coincident (both senses) inferences—eliciting a common if shifting tropology not delineated in terms of regional borders, let alone established art genres. With trip as trope, the transnational ground thus spottily covered, in its exacting artisanal relish and wit, can still seem to mark out collectively, if only implicitly, a global holding action, however beautifully futile it may appear: not just against computerization as the encroaching horizon of all imaging, but, looming larger all the time, against artificial intelligence as the vanishing point of art and human conception alike.

In this commentary's admittedly piecemeal experience of such recent Conceptual art, however finely gauged and distributed the helpings, the charge (both senses again, demand and reward at once) is, as usual, to think about it: to think with it. This amounts to further interlineating the explanatory glosses that so often accompany works of this sort in gallery space or catalog copy, where the image, object, or assemblage has already passed over from (audio) visual episode to discursive event. The appeal of this to a literary sensibility (more specifically, to a scholar with his home base in literary study) is that these works offer undisguised occasions for reading, for thinking about in phrase. Poussin or Rodin, Pissarro or Picasso, can be written about forever, of course, in the implications of their makings, their markings: provocations to an inexhaustible ekphrasis of their separate medial craft in all its inherent visual eloquence. But certain conceptual works, even when painstakingly executed in paint or bronze, are often articulated in the first place mostly in phrased response, their imaged ideas only in this way fully spoken for.

And what one finds to say (if only to oneself) about them, one by one, can found a repertoire of formulations brought to the next deliberate or chance encounter in this line. Including, at least in my case, the combinatory neologisms that the unstable materiality of such practice, in its frequent transmedial conflations, may call up.[1] One way to engage a concept is to recast it in your own words, or word, taking up and on what is often the fine line— the hairsbrea(d)th difference—between blatant and latent, manifestation and production, the obvious and its sometimes obviating inverse. That's what I intend here, and meant by the phrasing above, in "nominating" various disparate practices as operating in the zone—and this particular wording in the first subhead above was no accident, no typo—of a certain negactivity. An italicized mark-up of that loaded term's internal syllabic pivot—nega(c)tivity— was the initial or seed formulation, but it has been leveled out since so as better to catch the coherent transitive force of the effects under scrutiny—including precisely their immanent transactive reversals. And this terminological simplification has an extra minor advantage, I might add, since every time I tried to parenthesize that lexically set off *c* in my neologism, it got spat back by word-processing algorithms, here too, as nega©tivity. So be it: I'll accept copyright on the coinage, at least for as long as the present essay takes to justify it. Suffice it for now to suggest that, within the orbit of such aesthetic reversals share with technical media, the leverage of the negative is not to nullify or neutralize so much as to execute a materialized contravention, a counter*action*, a definitive (and self-defining) transfer at the base of the seen. Negativity, when intercepted in process/progress, doesn't cancel or erase; its force is integral and formative. And is often, as such, the generative locus of a performative irony: a negactivation as ideational as it is visual.

Ideart

I SAY "IRONY" ON THE BEST OF EVIDENCE. In the conceptual practice I'll be sampling, such notionally if not tonally ironic pieces (showing one thing while meaning another, whose involuted logic typically needs piecing out) hold our attention for the thought experiments they instance and in turn generate. For "conceptual," then, some quick dictionary recourse: "theoretic, notional, philosophical," and, farther down the list of synonyms, "general." To extract a concept from a concretized material arrangement amounts to being able to say, odd as it sounds, that "I've seen a version of that concept before." This essay is, as I suggest, a venture in how such accumulated recognition, such generalizable findings, can be brought to bear on new accidental finds. To make it easy on itself, discussion will begin with three makers whose innovative practice this author has previously thought about in writing, though in ways more narrowly focused than here. These include the "deconstruction" of a renowned oil canvas by the simulated results of radiographic probe and photonegative reproduction in the work of San Francisco painter Jordan Kantor (b. 1972); the conversion of negative painting to photogram positives in both the layered and sometimes moving-picture frames of Cambridge- and Berlin-based transmedial artist Matt Saunders (b. 1975); the painterly canvas treatment of abstract photo imprint in the cyanotypes, or as Man-Ray would have called them, "rayograms," of Buffalo photographer John Opera (b. 1975). In all three cases, what we find is a kind of rayographic (or projective) aesthetic: aligned in each artist's feel, sometimes almost haptic, for reverse imagining—or, in a very particular optic variant of the Keatsian aesthetic, for "negative capability."

These works, and others like them, gravitate—for protracted aesthetic response—to the often indeterminate aura of technical inversion and its projective imprints. And it is from the density of such material reversals that the detected negactivity of their related visual practices seeks some such collective designation, and of course a much fuller analysis, in these pages. Allow for now that the some of the most illustrative works in this line (this line of ambivalent demarcation)—images hovering in orientation between painting and photomechanics, for instance—focus our interest on the way they resist the levelling notion of a "post-medium condition" in contemporary image production.[2] Not by offering themselves as traditional "mixed media," they instead take their tacit stand precisely by isolating within a given composite image the transfused media *specificities* from which it issues—and whose convergence becomes a defining issue in the resulting work.[3] Such enacted transmedial conceptions often come forward in this way as works of implied "mediarchaelogy" (another portmanteau term, like "ideart," keyed to an inextricable self-instancing).[4] Designed to equilibrate competing claims on our medial recognition, as for instance between painting and its successor in photography, they may foreground certain traces of the handmade either layered over the indexical imprint or eliciting its antecedent in negative mediation. At which point some preparatory reagent phase of the work—gone but not forgotten, lapsed but still evident in palimpsest—is materially rehearsed in its reconceived visualization. One result is that negactivity can regularly be grasped as catalytic: disappeared from conceptual, as from chemical, process by what it precipitates.

Color Ocularized in Reverse

OVER A DECADE AGO, in *Bookwork: Medium to Object to Concept to Art* (2011), I digressed to the realms of canvas art in order to convey a further sense of the "demediation" I found in the artificial or denatured book objects that I had been cataloging for analysis: strictly conceptual books with no legible surfaces and often no openable pages. I turned to an extravagantly clear parallel of such demediation in painting by Jordan Kantor: an impressionist masterwork reduced first, in the records of curatorial inspection, to the radiographic traces of its underpainting, as repainted in turn in black and white (Untitled [*The Bar*], 2009), then further negated by a full-scale photographic negative.[5] The canvas thus denuded and reversed: *Manet's Bar at the Folies Bergère*, whose waitress has already famously gone into reversed duplication in the angled mirror behind her—and this in the new post-photographic mode of impressionism's tempered retinal blur. This was followed by the third part of this serial deconstruction on Kantor's part: an X-ray of the canvas-mounted photo, x-ing out the image and showing only the material infrastructure (wood frame, staples, hinges) of the radically material support. Coming more recently to my attention, other work by Kantor from the same period involves not just negative imaging in the lab but, if I may put it this way, an *imaging in the negative*: the on-canvas rendition in paint of color-reversed photos. By a further representational irony in the conceptual twist of these *Eclipse* works, his denaturalized color inversions of represented bodies—as if irradiated by some unnatural light—record seated figures against a balcony railing viewing an eclipse of the sun through protective ocular shields. In such a de-activated solarium, the off-frame sun itself would approximate its own negative image in the dead glare of black light.

When writing subsequently on the paint-based photograms of Matt Saunders, for *Cinesthesia*, I wasn't aware of his connection with Kantor, who took his PhD in art history from Saunders' own institutional home, Harvard University, where the latter was then an Associate Professor of art and film. Influence aside, each is an artist of photoconceptualism. Saunders' meticulous craft is designed to widen the space between painting and photochemistry within the same processual image, rather than across a triptych like Kantor's. Widen, or say dilate, protract—introducing a felt temporality into facture across any number of experimental gestures, textures, ocular wagers. His effort, on numerous fronts, and in many layered frontalities, is to convey "outcome embedded in its own process."[6] His is an art of chromatic composition in oil that gets registered in the beamed light of secondary photographic capture—as if occupying the seam between media in the optics of thrown light. Call it:

Permediation

I HAD BEFORE WRITTEN only too briefly about Saunders' serial paintwork in the context of moving-image gallery exhibition. What needs stressing more broadly here is the way his single-image work in paint as well—and its shadow transfers in beamed light—negotiate the *per* of both saturation and transmedial through-ness. And hence the transfusion of another portmanteau coinage: for the permeable as medial. Early in his career, with a more obvious emphasis on the time of viewing as well as the dilated time of making, he would deconstruct film motion in VHS screenings by taking slow-action Polaroid shots of transitional movements in the closeups of Andy Warhol films: going back again and again over the same camera frame, then resequencing the all but infinitesimal transitions in handmade drawings at something approximating, though wall-hung and immobile, the twenty-four-per-second photocells of a single facial gesture on screen. These are experiments in negated action— under reconception as sheer graphic difference—that will return under more conceptual pressure later in his painting. Also early on, Saunders engaged in bolder (at least blunter) cinematic deconstructions as well, ironizing the transparency of the medium by transposing the whole issue from celluloid to mylar and painting a sex scene from a Fassbinder film with one body on the front side of a mylar sheet, the other cast in murky silhouette on its reverse face. With no conjunction possible despite this approach to copulation, here is the material semblance of an embrace where, despite the image's infrathin (because entirely transparent) membrane, never the twain shall meet.

Since then, the doubleness of Saunders' work at the interface of photochemical record and the facture of painting has become more intriguing and oblique, the transmediation at play driven more directly into process itself. In such single-canvas painting, the photogenetic technique of its alter-images resists the stasis of the so-called film "still" (the images typically lifted from cinema frames) by introjecting our cued recognition: not just of the derived image but of precisely the technical challenge involved even before its quasi-photographic relay. In the space between historically rehearsed technical conditions, between painted cloth and light-saturated paper, is sandwiched the time-lag of apprehended concept. Aided in display by explication, it happens like this. First Saunders reverse engineers an imagined photonegative by strenuously thinking through (in yet another double sense, before streaming light through it) the chromatic inversions of the invented image at which he is at work, say blue flesh (in one of his examples) for a woman wearing a light red dress. Whereas I suggested above that we consider Kantor's color reversals as a case of *imaging in the negative*, Saunders must be understood as *imagining* the negative out of thin air—and on fabric almost as diaphanous. He then projects through the canvas weave of these complementary colors, with high-intensity illumination, a reversed positive image of the "merely" transitional painting. The result is a second-degree impression that bears traces of its own original fabric substrate along with the reversed and normalized chromatics of a represented film figure. The self-imposed conceptualist regimen in all this is the direct opposite of the admonition popularized in the old Johnny Mercer lyric: "You've gotta accent-tcu-ate the positive, eli-mi-nate the negative." Encouraged to "Latch on to the affirmative," we were told there, in sum: "don't mess with Mister In-between." For Saunders, however, the in-between—the neither one nor yet the other, neither positive photochemical image nor its negative "provision," but rather the almost palpable emergence of the former from the latter—is the reenacted duration of aesthetic making per se that he seeks to inscribe and communicate. Between the scrim of linen and the permeating trace of light, porosity is elevated from a quality of the former substrate to the very medium of a new layered composite. Three media are in effect overlapped from the original refashioned extraction. The celluloid image of a cinematic face or body, its framing rectangle always losing its functional transparency when reaching the screen, is returned to its founding negative in order to pass through a new painterly support, a secondary screen, on its way back to a projected tracing in pure light.

One phase in the process of Saunders' deliberately "hybrid art" (pitched between photography and video this time) turns to the digital valence of the latter with an interest in the automaticity of black-and-white surveillance footage—including a fleeting CCTV image brushed again onto highly permeable "canvas" and then transferred under the brighter light of medial interrogation, if you will, to a nonmechanical photo imprint. By which point the tiny gaps in the loose weave of the interposed "church linen" have lent a kind of pixelated surface to what resembles all the more closely the fuzzy digital print-out of a surveillant screen capture. In the process (exactly the deep materiality of the process itself), the strictly ocular resistance of this frame grab ends up "reading" as political—seems visibly figured as such—by a low-resolution haze that precludes any usable facial recognition.

Time Stamps

THE STANDARD AUTOMATICITIES of 24/7 motion-triggered camerawork contrast of course with its cloth-sieved transmediations in this derivative case. And contrast all the more so—in Saunders cultivation of such middle spaces—with his handmade painterly negatives. And all the more obviously yet, in turn, when—geometrically increasing the stakes of the painstaking—he multiplies his ensuing photo-positives as if they were celluloid transparencies, projecting them serially as animated film strips. Even this last kinetic effect, like the CCTV treatment, may well weigh in as a resistance to the digital—and to the strictly theoretical way in which new media discourse tends to posit computer imaging as a return to handmade "drawing" (rather than indexical capture) in the work of CGI simulation. Saunders' stopgap measure—so we may come to think of it, to conceptualize it—is in part to halt the historical progress toward algorithmically generated pixel imagery by a sudden reversion (twin senses again, via metahistory and negative switch alike) to the technical paradox of handmade photography. Short of this transmedial arc, what recourse to the time-stamped surveillance image helps to spotlight is the broader emphasis in Saunders' work on capturing—in the very surprise of projected paint—the time-stamp of its own composite making. From easel painting to photographic exposure—and down through the input hours of computer rendering in CGI—medial time is of the essence. Unmistakably so when, made manifest among the essential elements of given imprint, we find the trace of time itself—including its "negative" countertrace—in the details of production. In the reflex action of Saunders' technique, then, this is the conceptual weight of the perceptual: going out of its way to install the negative as facilitating inverse of the pictured form. So time *stamps* indeed: at once a plural noun for results and an underlying predication, phrase and clause alike, instances and their premise at one go. Recovered in contemplation, duration stamps such images by Saunders with its own contributory function.

When this professor of art and film labors over an actual differential series of such photo *oppositives*, derived one by one from his invented canvas negatives, and then runs them together for projection in a moving-image strip, the logic is optically compounded. He thereby animates the definitive intervals previously curtailed, early in his career, by those frame-grab Polaroids from Warhol videos—and their subsequent pencil drafting as miniature, and micro-differentiated, wall portraits. Early and late, Saunders is bent on redrawing—and so drawing out—that "fragment of time in which an image comes into being," on screen as much as on canvas. In further transmedial work with conversant (if not convergent) forms, figure painting and photography, what he calls "resistance painting" operates another foregrounding of the negative, whose "potential energy" is only discovered in the act of impedance. What results is again a "politics of disorientation" in the refusal of facile optics. With works "resistant" in this way both in pigmentation and in recognition, one has first to think what it is that one sees (couched by paratextual discourse), not just think about it. Narrowing the former space between canvas and imprint's photosensitive sheet, oil paint is now applied directly to photographic paper in his figure drawing, then doused in a developing fluid that turns everything black that has not been blocked by the painted heads or torsos. From the continuing bath of such chemistry, the speckled and streaked surfaces of imaged bodies emerge over time in textures beyond the artist's own control. The medium of these works, in his words, is "the liquid material of light." What it seems to be thinking out before our eyes is an aesthetic of pig*mentation* under conceptualist reduction. As everywhere in Saunders' recent painting, his very application of paint, whether in blockage or reversal, may be said to "accent-tcu-ate" the negative as its own form of temporal *negotiation.*

Less Is More: Substrate Subtracted

IT IS THE RARE BEAUTY of Saunders' painterly results—achieved by elision of their initiating medium, as if subsequently haunted by the matter of their own composition—that renders him so exemplary a figure in the conceptual executions of inverted surface. Within an abiding iconography derived from the racing frames of traditional cinema stalled for fixated investigation, the material thinking traced by Saunders' career so far has a marked arc of reversals and inversions that takes us deep into the precincts of a generative negativity. To review its logic is to better grasp its lambent granularity. Celluloid movie images, submitted to painted canvas transfer, are returned to light-seared imprint by a subsequent darkroom projection. The precedent in his formative work is clear. Those early serial drawings, aided in process by self-developing Polaroid photography, slice the screen motion of facial closeups into graphic differentials at once spatial and temporal. From there out Saunders' work can be characterized as devoted to *splitting the difference* within and between media. No sooner does he move from the chemical imprint of his painted cloth negatives, in that tacit palimpsest of difference, than he multiplies his process in quasi-filmic chains of secondary projection on the "screens" of gallery display. In this leap of premise and execution he has traversed a tacit media archaeology of the preceding two centuries, moving from the photogram of cameraless record to the same term used to identify the single frames of the celluloid film strip, its borders disappeared in the pace of projection by the sheer raced trace of difference. And when Saunders has turned more recently to the monotype rather than photoprint, with "drawing" the end in itself rather than the material intercession and "precursor" of an emulsified image, there is still in operation the constitutive inverse inherent to any print process, its mirror-like flip between matrix and impressed image. Here, too, the former, the monotype master, like the painted cloth that articulates by reversal Saunders' darkroom work, is further doubled by a slippage of portrayed faces at the point of impress. The effect turns each print into a kind of gestural "montage" of difference, often seeming to involve a quick shift of position within the drawn rather than moving-image frame. And at the latest pole of Saunders' experimental development, offering the further reverse of its several previous inversions, Saunders has ventured on the abstract overpainting of his paint-abetted photo works, asserting in this way after all—like the return of the repressed—the pigment origin of their subsequent materialization in light.

Among the savvy and evocative commentaries included in Saunders' latest catalog, there is an apt notice taken by fellow artist Matthew Hale of the recurrent fabric surfaces in Saunders' chosen film stills—shirts, bedsheets, etc.— images chosen to be represented by chromatic contrast on the similarly woven material of production.[7] Dwelling on this might well bring further to mind the etymological aura of *textein*, texture, text. Certainly one may be tempted to say of these sumptuous "fabrications" that they are indeed *texts of image-making* rather than straightforward pictures. And texts not least in having their own transformational grammar. Like the folds and tucks of fabric projected through the painted cloth of their representation, the further stage—the effacing of paint on the way to paint-generated photographs—is only another variant in this exploratory material syntax of *double negation*.

In the quintessential form of Saunders' recessional aesthetic, then, what might be described as a *layering* of picture planes (as I have in fact described it) is also a performative *withdrawal* from the sensible (how this reaches us) into the always inexplicable sensuous (how this touches us, in all its spooky—es/ pied—beauty).[8] This very withholding, held up before us, lies at the heart of his darkroom work. Each piece installs its own compendium of performative reversals and subtractions: removals without erasure, gauzy tracings, phantom laminations, sublimations. In what amounts to a multifold retreat from immediacy, a stilled film, yielding a film still, is tracked back in paint to the negative substrate of its own photogrammatic origination. At which point—in a now nontheatrical projection—it is drenched into registration by a different flood of light. What then appears as image includes the folded or frayed edges of the once-negative canvas surface—now unstretched and relaxed in its loosened drape. By a further irony of inversion, however, this image comes to us captured in a high-resolution print that looks more like a gallerist's photo of a stroked painterly rendering, threaded underlay and all, of the "cited" screen image—rather than confessing its actual status: optic residue of that purposive technical negativity where alone pigment has been involved. And through it all, absence makes the art grow fonder. The clothed or cloth-swathed bodies under representation by such means—far under, beneath, and before it—are all the more mesmerizing for the way the staging of absence brings forth their deferred surface in the eerily retained lure of flesh and presence.

UV Light in Photostroke

THE THIRD OF THE NEGATIVE-IMPRINT THINKERS on whose art I have written before, if again only briefly, and who help pave our way forward here, is the Buffalo-based photographer John Opera, whose double-ply conceptual photos, in contrast to those of Saunders, are executed in a reverse hybridized priority characterized above as "rayographic." In Opera's practice, photography precedes painting on the latter's received (as cultural standard) and receiving (as chemically mediated) woven surface: namely, the cloth of former canvas art, but with light-sensitive emulsion and color pigment applied as preconditions for the eradiating effects of projected light—thereby finalizing and a/fixing the photographic composition. One of his works appears, cropped, on the cover of *Attention Spans*, an anthology of my writings; another work bestrides the cover of *Bandwidths*, a critical conversation between me and distinguished colleagues. While thematizing the broad spread of *Attention Spans'* subject matter, the black-on-sunlight gold cyanotype, in its fanned out radials, participates again in the transmedium (rather than "mixed media") mode of photopaint impress. Ultra-violet light poured out across the treated linen substrate of a waiting "canvas" (though literal and harkening back to a painterly tradition) results in a representational effect of seemingly splayed out burnt-black rays. The finished work, in this case and others conjured by similar techniques, issues a subtle and alternating figure/ground dynamic, with arrow-tipped vectors segmenting the painted surface and pulling the viewer inward along the tapering light-seared streaks of the serial exposures. But concept, as usual, exceeds effect. Whereas Saunders "negates" painting by rendering only the negative of the image's eventual recovery as photogram, Opera negates photography by "eliminating the negative" in direct canvas irradiation.

In his extensive separate writing on Opera's technique—and its concept—David LaRocca, editor of *Attention Spans* and *Bandwidths*, postulates the status of such images in medial terms.[9] He conjugates an answer to the more than ordinarily provocative question: what are Opera's images photographs of? In regard to captured subject matter, and not unlike Saunders' isolation of light itself as overriding canvas medium, the answer is that they are "photographs of themselves."[10] By this reflexive logic, Opera's resuscitation of the old-fashioned cyanotype process—recovering in turn, by optic overlay, a much longer prehistory of image making—joins the innovations of Saunders and Kantor in a patiently worked negactivity that can't help but appear, in the dedicated intricacies of their disparate crafts, to resist any eclipse of the artisanal by the digital. That metaphor of cancelled image source ("eclipse")—recalls in part Opera's series of "Black Suns" (2005) as well as the solar collapse he workshops two decades later in the series "When the Sun is Done" (2025), where, via gum bichromate, portraiture and diffraction patterns are applied to canvas, col/lapsed upon one another.[11] In a piece from the series, "Solar Eye"—an overlapping palimpsest of hominid iris and solar/eye/zing star—quantum-level behavior mixes with pigment to shuffle scale and requestion origins. Radiation and diffraction simultaneously convoke disintegration *and* birth: the specter of a black whole. Kantor's painting of color inversions also come aptly to mind in their extraterrestrial dimensions. For instance, Kantor's shielded eclipse-gazers—evoking as they do, without actually picturing it, an intensity of light reversed by solar occlusion to a negating black—recall another California artist working in conceptual photography, though in his case at cosmic scale.

White Holes: Negative Telescopy

AT THE MACRO LEVEL, the negative photographs of Los Angeles artist Mungo Thomson (b. 1969) have a push-pull effect at galactic register, as if converting—inverting—the entire visible span of the universe into its own event horizon: a black hole turned white by negative action. In these photo panoramas, the Milky Way resembles a variegated splatter of spilled ink against the non-color of a whited-out deep space, spangled only here and there by the color flares of exploding stars and the smeared whirl of radiant interstellar dust. When mounted on the ceiling of white-box exhibition chambers and similar museum spaces, these negative skyscapes render astral depth more like the neutral backing of something between pointillist exactitude and Abstract Expressionist drip and smear. And when mounted, alternately, on intensely lit urban billboards and photographed at night, they gash open a bleached breach in the night sky itself, rather than miniaturizing it in replica.

The weird, almost apocalyptic inversions of these chilly astroscapes find a more pointedly ominous equivalent, so I discovered, among the negative experiments of a famed British artist whose career retrospective I happily encountered in the winter of 2022. Negation is an explicit keynote in the work of Cornelia Parker (b. 1958), achieving various manifestations not just in photography but in floor and wall sculpture, where, in the last case, the term is lifted to prominence in her found-object titles. Shown adjacent to these explicitly "Negative" works that we'll return to in a moment, and included among her several displacements of photochemical indexicality, are images—in what she calls the "Avoided Objects" series—where both actual film stock and its chemical processing have been displaced by transmediation.

A/Voidance as Negation

IN A PERVERSE SKYSCAPE that brings Mungo Thomson's work to mind, curatorial paratext explains that Cornelia Parker borrowed from the Imperial War Museum the 35mm camera formerly owned by the commandant at

Auschwitz, Rudolf Höss: an object ordinarily very much to be avoided, but with which, stocked with the wrong film substrate, Parker views the world as if through a brutal past's infernal aperture. (Höss himself, and his camera, return—between voids of graphic depiction—in Jonathan Glazer's negative-reversed Holocaust film *The Zone of Interest* [2023]: the Shoah as *un*experienced from the other side of a walling-off ethical limit and its repressions. To this digitally shot diagnosis of Höss' monstrosity—under coincidental but equally fitting distortions by different optical anomalies—we will return later.) Once Höss' camera is loaded with infrared film by Parker, the resulting "view of the world" exposes, in her appropriated POV, an eerily blackened sky above the War Museum, where the clouds float like accusing ghosts against the optical abyss. Neither a strictly negative image, like Thomsons' *negastronomy*, nor a *negative cinema* in Glazer's bracketing of the film's ostensible but (a) voided subject(s), nonetheless the imagined focal point of such a traditional vista seems to have stained the print with a murderous vision's own unnatural black-on-white darkness.

A different valence of obscene seeing characterizes another work of Parker's that involves a kind of found and detourned object, in this case "avoided" images themselves rather than their ill-omened apparatus. By way of another institutional repurposing, Parker reroutes the efforts of the British government to liquidate the trade in pornographic imports by retrieving from Customs some shredded X-rated VHS tapes intercepted at the border. From the Imperial War Museum to the War on Porn. But Parker then has these discards actually liquefied into a new colored ink for the drawing of Rorschach-like pictograms whose cloven symmetries—in what we might call an un-negatable eroticism— suggest the resurgence of vaginal folds in a whole new recirculation of visual desire. Redaction inverted, cancellation as new incitation: a litmus test of the libido under medial duress.

More abstract and radically conceptual yet, and with Parker's most explicit statement of the negational paradigm, are two works of what we might call constitutive voidance. Above the title "Negatives of Sound," little spun black balls of fragile lacquer filaments—affixed to a white display board—are hung in a vitrine next to their bright metal counterpart, with its answering title "The Negative of Words." The former sonic offshoots are explained as the vinyl shavings left behind by the grooving of recorded sound at Abbey Road Studios; the latter are the slivers sloughed off by the stylus of engravers when monogramming silver. Together, the dark/light contrast of the twin displays establishes its own optical inversion. But more to the point, each work separately excavates the material space where acoustic and linguistic signifiers make their individual mark across the time of inscription—without whose curled residue, in those opaque afterbirths of impress, there would be no recoverable marks (plural), no "legibility" left behind as record. For Parker to have named such material/matricial traces of the signifying track by analogy with the better-recognized mediality of photographic negatives is the true conceptual work of these mounted sculptural recyclings. In the present book's nomenclature—concerned with reading as refraction in a punctuated mediality—what one finds isolated in these tandem works could be *filed* (procedural metonymy intended with this grooved pair) under the heading of *contrafraction*. As so often in this mode of materialized thinking, the negative (not the "re" of refraction but a full obverse with "contra") can be said to *posit* its alternative. Casting this logic up into a verbal antithesis cognate with the reversals thus topically inscribed: what you see or hear isn't what you get, it's how it got there.

Same in a different and, if possible, even more extreme and denaturing version of lexical trace under negation—effacement by total voidance—in an exhibit at the Smithsonian's Hirshhorn museum in 2014, where all that is left of "text" is the unreadable blank surface that words once in their monochrome lacework covered. Where Parker's 1996 "The Negative of Words" gives you, ironically enough, only the linear inches that writing's strokes and curves once covered, spun out in the residue of precious metal, this later and more political work gives you only the square inches of their total ink outlay. If a poetics of inversion is a graphics of integral estrangement that can be traced back to the optical schemata of figure/ground—in its skewing to figured ground—then the black-on-white of imprint culture since Gutenberg would be one rudimentary testing ground for this deactivating practice. Beyond the codex deformations of bookwork, with its conceptual *bibliobjets*, the condition of radical negactivity in textual terms—while operating still at the scale of an entire "volume" rather than a chiseled inscription—finds a probing recent example not in the pulped or burnt book liquefied to new ashen ink for further inscription, still less in the simple white-on-black of a photostatic copy.[12] Rather, matching in its delineated extremity the shaved-away remains of lexical scraping in Parker, this version of irreversible negation comes from Cuban political conceptualist Reynier Leyva Novo (b. 1983) under the title *The Weight of History, Five Nights*. This five-"panel" instance of "negatived" wording comprises five jet-black, inkjet-like wall panels executing the ideological as well as material reduction of world-historical polemics and their dark legacies: a declension from the rhetorical force of their call-to-arms to the raw quantity of ink distribution that originally platformed their messaging.

Nova's fivefold work inverts the whole chromatic ratio of the traditional book format, negating the white space in and around letters, in and between lines, so that only a determinate but illegible surface of illegible ink remains—amounting, in effect, to one unvaried and totalized redaction. The process, let alone the product, is an inversion of codex culture derived, surprisingly enough we learn, from an aspect of computerization that doesn't speak directly to the overthrow of paper by electronic text, as so often happens, but submits the codes of language to a blunter reduction in the black-out of total eclipse. Involved here is a software program (INk.1) with no on-line visibility, designed instead for computing (by font analysis and tabulated word count) the amount of ink used in generating a given text (the sheer "volume" of its potential lettering). The calculation is redeployed in this case to obliterate, literally to de-letter, certain key texts of revolutionary politics in proportion, not to their rhetorical power or resulting human damage, let alone moral darkness, but to the codex ink quotient of their ominous dissemination. See (from the Hirshhorn Museum's web archive) the five solid black rectangles—scaled to the inked surface of manifestos by Lenin, Hitler, Mao, Castro, and Gaddafi—rolled directly onto a gallery wall. Like blood, ink once "spilled," as the saying goes, is literalized in being slathered b(l)ack, regurgitated from the other side of history. In those five emblematically "benighted" shadows of rectangular page (or book) shapes, the canonical Black Square of high modernism (Kazimir Malevich, 1915) has reared its right-angled head again (this time "right"-leaning and anti-revolutionary) in Novo's impenetrable wall work: rectangular stains applied as something like their own drastically censored display texts from the long history of incited violence—as if stenciled all too densely as the self-cancelled text of a former *writing on the wall*.

This broadening compass of the essay's key term from inversion to voidance—condition of possibility to its cancellation—should help delimit its scope while sending us back to the fuller spectrum of Parker's work. Negativity, reversal, erasure, demediation: it's not hard to connect this chain of association, via further optical inversion, to Parker's sculptural countermolds, where the cracks between brick and cement pavement in one work, for instance, set in blackened bronze and transferred to a gallery floor, offer a new figure to a no longer traversable ground.[13] And in this spread of experiments is certainly to be included Parker's homage to founding photographer Henry Fox Talbot and, in turn, to his work with the pre-negative photogram. When John Opera uses the related cyanotype process to record, with the electric UV equivalent of prolonged sunlight, the virtual photogram of his abstract patterns onto linen "canvas," his time-based work of the index can be taken to complement Parker's own return to the Victorian photogram: the "rayograph" sketched independently of a camera lens. This is especially clear in a work whose *registration* divides between imprint and its optical discernment. Traced by light alone in one of her picturings are already-transparent glass objects recognized at first glance—in (and through) their own lack of opaque resistance—as resembling negative images in a spectral confusion of black/white contrast. The results seem alluding in part to Talbot's landmark shelves of crystal vessels under the title "Articles of Glass" in his illustrated manifesto *The Pencil of Nature* (1844): images meant (representatively for the new post-painterly medium at large) to outmode the laborious showy treatment of cut-crystal glint in the still life canvas tradition. As if offering her own take on that breakthrough vaunt—and through the extra conceptualist twist of negation by breakage—Parker's splintered glass articles do more than revert in their traced jagged outlines to the pre-negative photogram and its apparatus-free writing in light. For the title "Being and Non-Being" names its image at two levels. Smashed decanters and their stoppers spill out in fragments across a shimmering plane of negated interiority and containment. At the same time, the time of imprint, the entire image is removed from the ontology of bottling by the ghostly outlining of such glass shards as a mere two-dimensional tracery.[14] Again, if only by titular association: objects voided twice over—more than just emptied out—in the indexical absence of a camera's *objectif*.

Brushed by the Sun: The Found Photogram

A SIMILAR ABSENCE OF APPARATUS characterizes work I encountered later that winter at Copenhagen's National Gallery. Like the cyanotypes by John Opera, though often in tones of a much more faded blue than their method's historical evolution into blueprint technology, these works by Danish artist Maria Lund (b. 1976) are a kind of unaided solar reprography. Looking rather like abstract expressionist "veils" from a distance, they reveal a subtle surface treatment of shades and gradation recorded not on paper, nor on canvas, but on the cloth "support" of ordinary window curtains exposed to uneven bleaching over extended time periods. These recovered curtains are stretched onto canvas by Lund, where they may look on somewhat closer inspection—in the chromatic fades and folds of heir cloth texture—like nothing so much as the *painting* of curtains in some post-impressionist mood piece.

What turns them all of a sudden conceptual in their muted delicacy, rather than merely tantalizingly artifactual, is, as usual, the discourse that attends them: here to begin with, alongside fuller explanation, in the reduced form of the monosyllabic title "Stills." Hard to avoid is its clear invocation of photo imprint—in the received shorthand that distinguishes "still," for instance, from the "movie" whose duration it may be abstracted from. Lund's work, inflected by its naming, returns us to the original transition—rehearsed (and reversed) of course by Matt Saunders as well—from photogram to slow-exposure negative photography. And, by further association, may put us in mind of the later transfer of that very term to the serial "photogram" that makes for filmic motion. The event here, however, the duration, is only the long-term (call it negationary) effort of *screening out*. In some of the cloth photograms in this series, one even detects, stretched on the canvas frame, the faint blueprint, so to say, of the cross-barred window mullions through whose inner framed panes the sun has poured: wide-aperture exposures of (because to) exactly the world's light that these cloth partitions would otherwise have curtained off.[15] Doubly walled in by gallery and canvas p(l)ane, negated functionality becomes art.

And by further association yet, beyond photography and its time-based progeny, there is a distinguished painterly association for Lund's work less abstract than a modernist "veil"—if only because treating the traditional canvas explicitly as just such: a material mantle or curtain, whatever its surface execution as picture. This is to say that Lund's taut surfaces, with their layered hints of windowed depth, have their own negative precedent. Those gridwork shadows outlining the sectoring panes of her light-stained rectangles—as if the cloth were still being sun-drenched on site—call to mind, by inversion, the actual translucency of Sigmar Polke's surface scrim and its material underlay in the German master's outsize canvas from a decade before: not a still life but a narrative scenario of a magician or sorcerer at work, whose supernal labors are intercepted as if in *media* res. But Polke's *Untitled* (2013, SFMOMA) lays claim thereby, with the evacuation of any other name, to a picture of picturation rather than a denominated image. What Jordan Kantor achieved with the X-ray of his own already chromatically negated Manet (also at SFMOMA), exposing to view the wooden infrastructure of the canvas plane, Polke achieves by strategic linen translucency under the thinnest strokes of oil and resin. This is not *Magic*, by title or otherwise, but more like its alchemical deconstruction. In the oil-painted black-and-white simplification of a vague interior space paneled by pastel rectangles, the scene is also more like a cartoon than a double portrait. All realism is foregone. Here's what we see—and see through. A heavily stroked curtain is drawn on a spectral female figure conjured by a wand-wielding mage in medieval garb and sharper delineation, whose ability to summon (with the implicit brush as wand) is implicitly linked to the traditional skull, book, and candle visible next to him on the depicted ground plane. Roughly perpendicular, as usual, to the canvas' own vertical is such a receding floor space, but this time the former's more open-weave fabric is every bit as diaphanous and translucent as the female phantasm that the illusionist's powers are concentrated to summon. The open drape pictured to reveal the scene is in fact painted on a curtain all its own. Through this scrim of manifestation, one result is that the brownish wood stretchers that serve as backing to this painting's filmy, flimsy surface are hazily revealed in tan shadow. One of their verticals happens to intersect and obscure the very face of the female image being conjured. So "sketchy" is all this that the hint of the otherworldly—the ectoplasm of necromancy—hovers as a parable of the everyday "medium" itself rather than any compelling case of its pictured magic. At the same time, there is a further gestalt effect that may serve to negate any stable orientation toward image versus "underlying frame." For the recessional irony of Polke's picture plane, in which substrate shows through demonstration, is on its own specular terms reversed (support turned aperture) when at first glance—or second, depending on the push-pull of one's optical fore/grounding—it may well appear that we are viewing the curious scene (as double portrait) through the wooden criss-crossing of a partitioned window frame on *this* side of the image—upon which an unlikely exterior drapery has been lifted.

Planarity / Depth Deception

By another unexpected conjunction, this time within the same Danish National Gallery, the artisanal wit of Danish/Brazilian artist Andreas

Albrectsen (b. 1986)—in his expert charcoal depictions of screen media, as compared with the appropriationist ingenuity of Maria Lund's "Stills"—helps rethink even those cloth pieces, in their sun/shade stainage, as a mode of interface imaging. Consider Albrechtsen's artful black-and-white drawings of picture-perfect mountain peaks reduced to the simulated photo sublime of backdrop screen-savers behind a blizzard of desktop icons. In one iteration of this "concept" from 2018—identified as *Untitled (Folders)* both for its blank file symbols and for the interface anonymity of the work all told—the desktop shortcuts are marked by skeuomorphic tabs like those of cream-colored manilla folders, yet figured here only by stark white see-throughs to the drawing paper itself. Inverting the figure/ground logic of this black-and-white conception, the effect reminds us, with these merely sharp-edged interruptions in the depicted mountainscape, that a blank substrate is in a sense always the underlying negation of depicted space in plastic art. Breaking back from represented interface to material support, these flagged folders, one level further down, serve also to remind us, by computational analogy, that the evocative landscape itself—as default screensaver—would be only another embedded file in the electronic apparatus.

But returning to the blank paper surface rather than the substrate it infers, and before returning to a different suite of char/screen works by Albrechtsen, we should acknowledge the different negative logic of a more famous charcoal master, photorealist Robert Longo (b. 1953), his giant canvases on display, and grasped together as never before, in a powerful retrospective at the Albertina in Vienna (2024–25). Under the loose rubric of negated expectations, two immediately obvious reversals of the photorealist manner precede his more pointed graphic negations: first the denaturalization of the mode's typical hypermimetic acrylic palette to the micro-controlled black-and-white smudges of charcoal marking; second, the counterimmersive break up of his giant panoramas into discrete panels, triptychs, and beyond. Then, too, there is in one haunting case the regressive rather than negative treatment of photo mimesis in the duplicated black-and-white closeup of a woman's ringed hand holding up before her face, replacing its individuality, the female mourning photo of a notorious Iranian regime victim in slightly foggier registration: *Untitled* (protest for Mahsa Amini; Iranian Embassy, Brussels; September 23, 2022), 2024—where the layered removal from the real (re)cedes back toward death's own absence. Elsewhere, in rendering the sphere of Mideast detection and violence, a more obvious degeneration of the photo grain is built into image definition with the reproduction of a long-distance night-vision photo of prisoners (unidentified as well as untitled) at the Kandahar Airport. Even more challenging conceptual distancings appear on other walls in the Vienna exhibit. There is the fighter pilot whose helmet's visor reflects not the cockpit controls surrounding him but a clear view of the cloud-banked sky through which he is hurled—as if, in some claustrophobic cinema of flight, we were privy to shot and its reverse shot in the same paradoxically kinetic freeze. And then an opposite play with time, labored rather than elided, in which the flaunted spontaneity of a massive multicolored Pollack drip canvas—*Untitled* (After Pollock, Autumn Rhythm: No 30, 1951), 2014—is painstakingly drained of color, in this case its variegated beige-hued background, by the exacting strokes of meticulous charcoal drawing. The painter's very art of chromatic improvisation is negated by the intervening draughtsman's elaborate craft (and figured as such, most strikingly, when the evoked startling strands of Pollock's overlain white paint find their *trompe l'oeil* illusion effected by Longo) like a negative image turned positive—through the sheer stringent (and stringy) absence or erasure of his layered grey scale. The eerie result lays bare what amount to thin runnels of the stark paper base beneath the swirl of charcoal tones. Recalling even more openly Albrechtsen's use of drawing paper's white as the blank screen behind a video mountainscape, though at dozens of times its scale, there is Longo's quartet composite of a shrinking iceberg looking not unlike four framed panels of outsized and lightly wrinkled paper sheets. With the enormous blocks of ice as default white, it is only their occasional jutting shadows and crevices, along with the waterline into which the mass is sinking, that are rendered in light charcoal dusting: art as the faint tracery of the fateful.

A less portentous end is portended in that set of Albrechtsen's images to which, before Longo, I promised a return, where the foundational interface of cinema, rather than computer screening, undergoes a more obvious inversion—or *mirrorotation*. Just that portmanteau term can help partly to recall the inherent double-sidedness of the transparent predigital cinematic photogram—and in a different connection yet in this case, surprising and ironic, with paper surfaces. In a series of works from 2020 to 2021 under the English title *Reversed Endings*, with its alphabetic gestalt of "Reverse Tendings," the onward grammar of film—including the entropic plotting of mainstream screen storylines—undergoes its own kind of negated inversion. In these works of hand-drawn metacinema, we find the flipped alphabetic format "The End" as if seen from behind the screen—thus torqued to variants, in English, Turkish, French, and Chinese, of "dnE ehT"—and superimposed in each case over a given film's last narrative image. It is as if, from the vantage of closure, we are seeing back *into* the story rather than turning the last page *on* its plot. And that passing codex metaphor is by no means forced. Oddly recalled by a further eccentricity of these drawings, one suspects, though it may take a moment for this suspicion to dawn, are the many classic Hollywood narratives that tout their prestige status as fictional storytelling, especially in literary adaptations, by having the credits open to the seeming title page of a book (the hold of "Once upon a time" fervently held in cross-conscious memory). For in Albrechtsen's backwards concept, the inverted alphabetic sign-offs on see-through celluloid are in fact—and remarkably enough—printed as the last (or first) horizontal versos of oversized, wide-format paperback volumes, full of blank unopenable pages. Only their inaccessible inch or so of depth, with no image available, is made visible behind the uppermost drawing (and lastmost screen frame) within the enclosing wooden frame of their gallery display. If we can imagine ourselves seeing through the inverted words of finality to the last image they overtake, the further implication—balked as soon as broached—is that we might page our way back into the world of the diegesis. It's never over till it's over? Or is the point, rather, that the medium itself is now a closed book? The shadow of this latter mediarchaological suggestion seems especially likely in conceptual association with the computer satire of *Untitled (Folders)*. All images, even those once projected through a transparent substrate, are now simply *on file*: awaiting pixel activation.

Historicized T/endings

Andreas Albrechtsen's intriguing rotations of inscribed surface and scenic depth bring to mind, from Ed Ruscha (b. 1937), the famous frameline misalignment of a gothic-lettered *The End* (from 1991) on two simulated out-of-sync frames of weathered celluloid—as if a single film, but also its medium with it, were spluttering to obsolescence, to negactivation, before our eyes. It's hard to suppress the guess that Albrechtsen's transmedial conflations of drawing with narrative imagining in celluloid—and of the latter with the individual cells of the photogram strip that speed the story to conclusion—are meant to come across like Ruscha's drawing, from the early days of digital hegemony, with a decided graphic pang. For in this mood Albrechtsen's "Endings" would only constitute another version of the postfilmic ironies operating elsewhere in his computer-screen mockups. Like them, these subsequent works in the seeing-backward of black-and-white celluloid, each "End" in mirrorotation, would spell more things "over" than in any one plot. Especially with the polyglot array of these inverted last frames, we are looking back on, and only by illusion into, filmic cinema *tout court*—sampled across several national traditions from the vantage of its present global supersession by the computer image. Curtain closed—but not until the still visible *mise-en-scène* of closure has become, in Albrechtsen's negactivation, the *mise-en-abyme* of its own platform and medium alike, stamped *niF*-al.

In this graphically allegorized look back, *Reversed Endings* falls into conceptual alignment with an actual feature length "film" from three years before by Iranian master Abbas Kiarostami, under the counterintuitive title *24 Frames* (2017). Instead of the inherent 24 celluloid frames per second, however, we get two dozen digitally altered 35mm photographs held for four and a half minutes each, while various pixel images—snowflakes, horses, pigeons—invade or overlay them. And in the last of the fixed-frame images, a woman appears asleep on a desk where a computer monitor plays a maddeningly decelerated version of the closing embrace from the postwar Hollywood classic *The Best Years of Our Lives* (1946, dir. William Wyler). The embedded film grinds to a finish here—and then fades out all but interminably on its own "END"-title.

But "end" is not, in this case, as with Albrechtsen's drawings, superscribed on the last image. Instead, putting all images behind it, already used up, the word looms in its own frame-filling three letters—just at the moment when Kiarostami's (en)closing film credits begin to roll alongside that inner screen. "End" of an era, one again can't resist thinking—and this whether Wyler's remediated celluloid is being vanishingly lingered over in dated VHS, DVD, DVR, cable, pay-per view, streaming format, what have you.

So what, in broader terms, have we? I mean what have we seen in what we've been looking at, even when sometimes seeing double in an image's negative valence. A last concerted view(ing) should help answer. Albrechtsen recalling Kiarostami; Lund, Parker and Polke; Parker, Talbot: so it had gone—as I headed off to Taipei National University in the spring of 2023 for three lectures, the last of which on this very topic. And it was there that I found—more accidentally than ever, a whole new ocean away—the true *philosophe* of my building paradigm: a genuine technopolitical theorist of negactivity. This discovery came to me, just in time for my last and most relevant lecture, thanks to a career retrospective on the indefatigable and bracing work in the politics of technical media by Kao Chung-Li (b. 1958). The exposition was mounted at the Taipei Fine Arts Museum under the hyphenated title "Re-Present." The rubric was an etymological inflection, obvious up to a point, whose full weight came through to me only when experiencing, in a last separate gallery, Kao's filmic "remake" (or re-presentation) of Chris Marker's modernist classic, the "photoroman" *La Jetée* (1962), with its own famous "Fin" superimposed on a closing time-loop death scene: a form of reverse tending at the metanarrative level.

Re-Presentation as Techno(ideo)logy

BROUGHT—AND THOUGHT—TOGETHER with the EuroAmerican conceptualist work I had been tracking, Kao Chung-Li's installations were a continuous revelation. The artist exerted his defamiliarizing irony on the whole gamut of representational technology, phonography to film, via a repurposed collection of optical toys and reworked assemblages. These included a "Slide Show Cinema" that, in a dedicated projection apparatus, dismantled the speed of celluloid to one slide-like advance (after another) of entirely discrepant still shots, punctuated by exaggerated black framelines of arbitrary interruption and clocked advance. In another installation, true to the incremental continuum of the cinematic institution and its spools alike, and recalling Matt Saunders' early transfers of Polaroid-caught photogram advance to handmade drawings, Kao surrounds the viewer with a dozen (rather than twenty-four) step-frame images at a time, on separate TV monitors, from Alain Resnais' *Hiroshima, Mon Amour* (1959). These are cross-sectioned slices of motion advancing from one encircling video monitor to the next in the decelerated circuit of counterimmersion. Stressed there, as in all Kao's work, is the etiological link between image technology and the capitalist war machine. While all but negating engineered motion in his parsing of the *Hiroshima* track, in another audiovisual installation Kao inverts the optics of war trauma by showing a gasmask in a kind of Fluxus suitcase, as if found among the remains of the dead, including letters, diaries, and so forth. Staring out at us is a veritable death mask in whose twinned goggle lenses—with a vision of stereoscopic conviction—miniature documentary segments of artillery explosions flare up as if from the retinal mirror of the absent body. Explosions whose broadcast noise fills the whole gallery—offering the ominous sonic outside to this macabre cinematized interiority. And behind curtains next to this tabletop exhibit, at the very innermost sanctum of the exposition: Kao's version of Marker, including its replay of the original film's own motif of Second World War gasmasks.

But another iconicity, more broadly technological than just martial, explains Kao's taking hostage Marker's 1962 film. By interspersing the selectively pastiched images of *La Jetée* with actual photo negatives from his own Asian cultural archive, Kao closes in on the metaphorics of his further political critique. The first black-and-white negative is of a woman in a traditional kimono with an open book of photographs on her lap, looking out at the camera as she has entered upon the process of becoming one of them. Another chiaroscuro negative shows two hands holding a hinged photo diptych composed of two identical images, each tonally reversed, of a double portrait, one man standing next to a seated one. Any negative, it would seem, even two of the same imprint, marks the chain of a further duplicability. Another chromatically inverted black-and-white insert shows, in fact, a newspaper advertisement spread across the page in celebration of just such technology as the photographically pictured (in negative) sound projector. And, hardly least, the last shot in *La Jetée II* is the negative image of a young girl with a camera photographing a boy playmate in soldier's uniform. Distilled without needed comment there is the artist's thesis about the military asymptote—and political symptomatology—of image culture in all of its innovative machinations under "technocapitalism."[16] To this end the photographic negative, reversing the indexical trace of momentary presence en route to its potential as reproducible document, elaborates Kao's deep-going interest—become almost a parable (as we'll read) in the closing metacritique proffered by his intertitles. Stressed hereby is the technically generative latency brought out, or more like transitionally exposed, within the blatancy of all such negative effects.

Doublentendre: Chemistry and Chimera

When Kao Chung-Li's remake—and conceptual rewrite—of *La Jetée* turns at discursive length to the negative images it has inserted, we get his own version of Matt Saunders' emphasis on the temporality of production: "A negative image with the black and white inverted is a delay that happens between the latent image and the photograph." Latency, larval possibility, emergence. Hence the preoccupation, as in Saunders as well, with exactly this technically enhanced and conceptually investigated lag time. The negative, so the well-translated intertitles of *La Jetée II* make clear, "is not the same as the presence of being photographed and the developed object (the photograph)." In light of Kao's useful threefold distinction (explained as one enters the exhibit) among *object* (thing), *object image* (its picture), and *image object* (the site of technological image production), we might instead call the negative an *image-object-in-process*. Neither photographed nor photograph, it is the transition *between*: neither here (as recorded) nor there (as positive display) but rather confessed as the transitional chemistry of manifestation itself: jettisoned, one might well say, on the way to imprint.

In this way the always-repressed backstory of technical inversion in photochemistry figures the functionally unseen in the coils of all mediation. For Kao's politics of perception, the negative is just a technical emblem of perception in general, where the presence of the picture faces outward and away from the unseen but contributory past of its arrival at just that present moment of captured visibility. And thus the photograph is in turn a further touchstone for the weight of historical circumstance pressing in from behind it on the never more than partial authenticity of any technical mediation: history bearing down on the intercepted moment in all its economics of production and its violent exclusions. So that a Janus-faced coin on screen, in another of Kao's breaks with the original Marker montage, is captioned for just this bidirectional simultaneity, rather than reversible sequence, of its "two faces." What one is certainly invited to call negative perception in Kao—or again a neo-Keatsian negative capability—is focused on recovering the process behind the product, as if history's long experiential and often traumatic *durée* could be condensed on site into a recoverable time-lag of technical production.

One delay plays on the other in their shared submersion by the imaged present, each pointing back to causality, historical or technical, and outward to recognition. And here, in the symbolic two-fer (unified by the singular concept) of negactivity, and again from the intertitles of the Marker remake, the logic becomes explicitly textual—as if for such mediation, in the conceptual rigor of the intertitles, pun is the nub: "Like a double entendre, a negative image can instinctively, automatically, point out the technical system and other images; therefore, it is not simply producing objects but is also a reproduction of photography itself." So it is (as noted earlier with the abstract cyanotypes of John Opera) that the negative here is photography taking its own picture, its own reversible and transitional measure. And, for Kao in his "double entendre" trope, finding its own descriptive concision: another case of the deep resonance between Conceptual aesthetics and literary wit— as transacted this time in a sense of the index all but *punning* on its own technical basis through the somersaulted chromatics of its resultant image. In the transformations of Marker's film—via repeated negactivity in image and metaphor—we are reminded that what at origin is black on white, or white on black, is, constitutively, the generative intent (entendre in the other sense) of its own emergent inversion.

Optics as Negative Dialectics

FROM THESE EPISODES OF THE METATEXTUAL, Kao Chung-Li's intertitles lift further, or probe deeper, to the metaphysical. With a probable allusion to Eugène Atget's long-exposure photographs being said to resemble police photos of a crime scene,[17] Kao presses further on his dialectics of the negative in the climactic intertitles of his *La Jetée II*: "A negative image is like as suspect who is unwilling to leave the crime scene, which makes each film negative exude a melancholy on [on the question of] 'who' and 'what'. . . ." In this way the transitive fact of what I have been highlighting (as if in the darkroom of conceptualism) as negactivity stands forth as a function that "tugs at the imagined geography, logistics of perceptions, chronology of consciousness, anthropology of time, and"—the Bazinian inspiration of *La Jetée* coming most explicitly to the surface finally in this series—the "topology of mourning." Regarding these deep cultural litmus tests of luminosity's reversible process, it is the translator's verb "tugs" that catch so perfectly the push-pull effect not just of the actual inverted negative but also of so much medial transposition in art's conversion of life to the lifelike—where the veil of Veronica, the death mask, the chemistry of embalming and mummification are never far from mind's eye.

And media do not just resemble death rites and immortality cults, but, beyond the violence they can implement (Kao's insistent technological subtext), they remain vulnerable, all told, to their own eradication. Hence the meta-hyphen in "Re-Present" as an exhibition umbrella for Kao's parsing of second-order manifestation. At the indexical basis of all technical media down through modernism, as thematized at its height in *La Jetée* as photo-film, and only threatened since by computer imaging, there rests as premise a founding divide—or dualism. The presence of the image doubles for the now-and-here, or the there-and-then, but not for the historical-why-and-wherefore, which lies always behind and beneath it, pressing incessantly upon it—and can be seen to do so, when properly contextualized, in conceptual rendering. It is just this sociopolitical underside of photographic and filmic capture that is figured, in Kao's visual thinking, by optic technology's transitional negative. Such, in sum, is the mediating interface transmuted and consumed in the picture of things it helps manifest—including (and here with CGI certainly on the horizon) the technocapitalism it bets on and abets. And including, in turn, its ultimate destiny in computerization's wired warfare. In the mechanical image's foundation as double entendre, the split trisyllable of "re-present" as exposition rubric can thus be understood to locate in part the intervening work of the negative, which operates—or, again, neg/otiates—between (in Kao's foundational triad) the *object* and the *object image* as the transitional *image object*. It is by this logic that a negative image is a photograph caught in the making. This intuitive sense of integral negactivity depends on a perceptual, and at the same time conceptual, response that lifts such an otherwise invisible function—easily discounted, though in no way negligible—to the plane of the neg*legible*.

In asking above "What have we seen in what we've been looking at?" I was, as fortified since by some further confirming evidence, prepared to say this much. Abstracted to its broadest outlines, negactivity is the foregrounding of a time-sensitive *inter-mediate* process in the emergence of the mediated image. As such, in the recent Conceptual art we have sampled, it comes into play as a transpositional function signalized by, and sometimes instancing, that most radical cultural innovation—before the last century and then some—since the reversed images of Gutenberg's moveable type: namely, the photographic negative. Most radical, that is, before the foundational (and black-boxed) algorithmic negativity of the 1/0 binarity in the reversible on/off mode of computerization. It is from the earlier and visible notion of the negative, of course, that my gathering sense of experimental commonalities takes its name(s)—and very much in the spirit, belatedly discovered, of Kao's stress on the inverted image as a kind of punning double of the positive. By this logic, and in so many arrestingly different ways in recent Conceptual art, does the model of inversion (upending material assumptions) put the mediating action back in the temporal protr*action* of both execution and response—or say, pun-like again, assert the traversing *reach*, as well as the stressed texture of *each* separately, in the confronted aspects of any such transmedial *b/r/each*. The abiding Concept underlying such recurrent encounters doesn't depend on accumulated evidence, however, even within a given artist's output. It is immanent in each work separately, each localized praxis, each materialized idea. Any attempt at synopsis can only be a litany of diversification. Yet each newly enrolled inversion tends to expand and deepen the very parameters of reversability, including of inside-outness, often regarding the rudimentary distinction between figure and ground in optic representation. New kinds of negactivity can thus, from within their own high-definition relief, throw into further relief the scales of luminosity in alternate models.

Ex-Radiant: Light Rays / Unlit Trace

RIGHT ON THE HEELS OF MY ENCOUNTER with the techno-evolutionary negativity of Kao Chung-Li's Taiwanese conceptualism, in a return to the main axis of my transatlantic evidence, another late discovery in the inversion of the canvas image plane struck a further technohistorical chord. The unsettling conceptual practice I came upon in a trip to Central Europe following my Taiwan lectures, alerted by the holdings of the Bratislava City Gallery, was the inordinately gorgeous work of Italian innovator Renato Meneghetti (b. 1947). Inordinately, because pressing as it does beyond the typical ordinations of image making in the realm of painting's "unaided eye." Not, perhaps, since the suspected use of the *camera obscura* in the work of early Renaissance perspective has specular technology been any more directly enlisted by representation. Insisting on the inverted ratios of surface and depth, materiality and image, mass and transparency, Meneghetti's suite of work from 1985 to 2000 engages with a modern optic technology constituting a major step beyond the "pencil of nature" in those photogrammars around which we have circled. Instead of the photo negative, rendering visible the typically unseen transit from optical emission to ocular transmission, Meneghetti paints the ironically illuminating power of invisible X-rays: their tracery imagined from inside out the way Matt Saunders "conceptualizes" the transitional negative in reverse grayscale or complementary colors. Meneghetti's work thus rounds out this survey's purview of reversabilities under the rubric of negaction by arranging, as we will see, that the radiographic tracings of a scientific modernity are pivoted, in their founding invasiveness and inversion, not just upon the anthropology of the human image, its anatomical infrastructure, but, through an extra double twist, upon both the art-history of figural representation and, making distant contact with Kao Chung-Li's concerns as well, upon the political constraints that its technology has separately evolved to facilitate under the functions of the security state.

Set into new perspective by Meneghetti's metatechnical innovation in painterly technique, our most nearly related instances of the inversion aesthetic so far can be recognized to diverge from standard-issue indexicality in complementary directions. Suspending the difference between painting and photo imprint, John Opera negates the representational trace of photography by indexing only the strike of light—rather than stroke of pigment—on an already treated canvas substrate; he orchestrates—by means of hand-fashioned tools and repurposed electronics and photo-generative apparatuses—the pathways of light so they might "land." Opera then uses plain water to wash away the residual elements leaving in their place the permanent "record" of light's impression on these particular pathways. Elsewhere, by a penetration as well as registration, Matt Saunders throws light through the linen mesh of figurative oil imaging on canvas—speculatively negative in its approximated tonality—in order to project a quasi-photographic reversal for emulsification. By a different process of "permediation," Meneghetti projects (either literally or imaginatively) the work of invisible Roentgen rays through the bodily figure—with its own sear-through (rather than just see-through) opacity. The time of either glance or gaze is deflected by the reconstructed operation of the probe, even in its own instantaneous functionality. Meneghetti's painterly application works in this way to generate a newly envisioned depth—and paradoxical documentary flatness—in figure painting. When drawing out and forth the revealed innards of human anatomy, its true "formal" infrastructure, the artist executes his images in the thinning effect of alcohol on pigment-treated canvas. The result is to dilute and lighten either a typical diagnostic grayscale, or his departure into frequent color registers, toward the simulated laboratory transparency of the radiogram's ghostly glow, unnervingly carnal and disembodied at once. Then, from 1999 to 2010, he elaborates on—and further dehumanizes—this practice in a manner closer to the political critique of technological advance in Kao. This happens with Meneghetti's *Invasion of Privacy Invaded* series, based on airport security imagining designed to penetrate the hide not of the animate/animal body but of its human agent's own leather (and otherwise) hiding places in preventatively scanned luggage. Meneghetti's renderings of these monitored disclosures in shimmering aluminum prints alternate, by design, between the look of on-site negatives and evidentiary positives, black background versus white blackground.

Since then, he has turned the cathode ray of his favored operations on masterworks of the art-historical tradition in order, phantasmatically, to block out, as in an airport scanner, the red zone of his selectively heightened interest. These are rectangles of highlighted "detail" that, in effect, flay open the canonical image—as for instance the fingertip meeting of God's hand with Adam's on the ceiling of the Sistine chapel—to reveal, in that case, the shared anthropomorphic skeleton beneath begotten body and Unmade Maker. Then, too, in Meneghetti's adjacent moving-image practice—including its ironies of what we might call the time-based mortal body—there is a transfixing video of Mantegna's *Lamentation Over the Dead Christ*. In its alternating of canvas closeups with Roentgen penetrations, the video cuts between X-rayed highlights of both sacred corpse and hovering mourners in a skeletal eschatology of mortal tragedy and elegiac faith—until the full-scale radiograph of the foreshortened Christ is multiplied heavenward in its chapel setting, lifted like peeled layers of an increasingly gleaming inner radiance into an image of pure transcendent light. But not before an added art-historical irony, one of a proliferating number in the painter's work, has been installed in the founding chiaroscuro contrast of his X-rayed (invisible) medium.

For in all of this Roentgen simulation, long before his treatment of the risen savior, there is an arresting further inversion in his "inward" portraits. Never made explicit, but deeply conceived. What the radiographic technique does in the first place—contrasting cranium or jaw or vertebrae as negative brightness again the flesh-penetrating burn of the X-ray in the latter's manifestation as black background, or *b(l)ackground*—has a sepulchral way of suggesting the stark positive of bleached bones already stripped bare in the other sense (post-mortem) of *exposure*. And that's only half of the extra half of it. Such ironies are compounded and further reversed when what is figured is the idealized *painted* body, dead or alive, rather than a radiographed living specimen. To vary Henry James on "relations," put it that "negations stop nowhere." The conceptual wit involved in directing the cathode apparatus of an imagined X-ray on the Old Masters—on their representations rather than their execution, that is—inverts in its own turn the usual high-tech study of gesso treatment, facture, overpainting, and so forth, including the signature effects of stroke and pigment (think Kantor's version of conservationist's Manet). The frequent inversion of image and support in conceptual representation has in this sense been displaced by Meneghetti into the canvas diegesis as that between human figure and its bone and cartilage substrate. The result is a virtual f/laying bare of the pictured figures themselves rather than their figuration: art-historical forensics turned fantastic, each painting its own raw anatomy lesson. And it is only characteristic of the technological acuity of Meneghetti's exploratory optics that he would have carried his work more recently yet into the backlit aesthetic of LED digital art, inverting his previous surface/depth model with light-emitting diodes rather than X-ray cathodes.

By an almost macabre coincidence, the technological thread of our evidence—from infrared film recording in Cornelia Parker's borrowed Nazi camera through negative laboratory imaging in Kao to Roentgen probes in Meneghetti—returns us now to the same Auschwitz butcher, Rudolf Höss, this time via the use of heat-sensitive military cameras for the fantastic counterpoint footage (spectral alleviation) inserted into the lacerating hygienic exactitude of CCTV in Jonathan Glazer's Academy-Awarded 2023 film *The Zone of Interest*. As if demarcated by its very title, the question of framing on screen—and what it keeps *off*—is the chief formal constraint (simultaneously moral complaint) of this plot.[18] The Auschwitz commandant's household is captured in its servant-heavy routine, often one quick-cut after another, relayed across the neutral surveillance of wall-ensconced digital cameras (no crew on set, all natural lighting in this poisonously unnatural lair). The film's sequencing of an ordered middle-class life adjacent to a human slaughter factory is especially apparent when Höss (seen at one point placidly using his camera to document his family's leisure) battens down for the night by flicking off the light switches in mechanically patrolling from foyer to hall to room upon room, his visible moves shifted from frame to frame with the abruptness of forensic slides, softened by none of Marker's haunting dissolves. Here is regimen met head-on by technique—and suffused with accusation. A hint of this zeroing in (or out) on the ordinariness of moral opprobrium, culprit by culprit, is prosecuted even cinemato/graphically. This happens in a letteral fade (a transmedial collusion between filmic dissolve and concrete poetry) that has the slowly vaporized widescreen title dissipate soonest at its periphery, leaving as its last full-phrase trace the exposed anti-hero as THE **ZONE OF** INTEREST.

With the wife's lavish manicured garden sprawled alongside the camp's stone and barbed-wire wall, that barrier's reworked dramatic effect is less to hold invisible victims *in* than precisely to keep them *out* of view—with only the muffled acousmatic sounds of distant railcars, rumbling trucks, shouting guards, intermittent screams and gunshots, together with the nighttime glare of furnace flarings, permitted to invade, and then only faintly, the fixed-frame treatment of an antiseptically domestic space (invaded only by falling ashes and the putrid smell of burning flesh—so noxious to Hedwig's visiting mother that she leaves without saying a word). So lethal is this genocidal off-screen space—and its register of impinging historical time—that its horror, become brutally screen-cancelling, wholly annihilates the narrative for many long seconds at a time in four metafilmic blottings—"underscored" around the edges by fading or returning diegetic sounds, by a preternaturally deep silence, or at the end by the ominous grind of the atonal score. These narrative elisions include dead black after the dissolving title (for over two whole minutes), white more briefly after an effacing sunlit blur of crematorium smoke, a several-second open wound of red in symbolic bloodbath after zooming in on a deep pink bloom from the garden, then blackout again at the end. Modelled by that opening zoned-out void after the fading title, and marked at points of building rupture, the nominally on-screen is itself offed. And if this stark cancellation of image is to be imagined as its own kind filmic negactivation, not by symmetrical reversal but by total aversion, the color code is narrowly appropriate. Between the play of bleaching white glare and black evacuation falls the drenched red of darkroom processing.

In another and more stunningly disruptive pattern, Höss' reading to his children of the "Hansel and Gretel" story (with its own justified retributive oven, incinerating the Witch) triggers the eerie AI enhanced heat-sensitive sequences of a young girl from the Polish resistance (we find out from subsequent reading) leaving food—under cover of pitch darkness—for the imprisoned workers at a construction site, through whose virtual living graveyard she flits like a ghost. If photo negatives are intruded into Kao's re-edit of Marker's World War II (and III) montage to make the underlying fact of the medium part of its narrative—the intermediary negative serving to figure the historical backstory of any present image—a similar metatech trope seems at work in these spooky interludes, less gruesome of course than what they interrupt. Here images that glow with signs of life (as registered, target-worthy, on the surface of the girl's skin as she moves about) stand for the truth of the human, of human warmth, still moving amid the brutality—and not just against the unlit mounds of construction debris but against the heatless "negative" (direct reverse image after all) of washed laundry collected like midnight-black shrouds amid the whitewashed horror of the camp's adjacent domesticities, ash sullying them before they can be returned to the commandant's quarters.[19]

From Percept to Concept

THAT'S WHERE WE'VE BEEN, then, in our individual sightings. Take Manet taken apart by the new photorealist medium that his competing impressionism once sought to outsmart. In Jordan Kantor's peeling away of image and its technique, serial conjectures to this effect pass through a canvas-scale photographic negative that has reversed the time of painterly production. Kantor thus *unpaints* canvas art in reduction to the invisible frame on which it is typically mounted. Elsewhere, in a complementary reversal, the same artist inverts the chromatic balance of his own more realist figure painting—and this in a scene of occluded solar sighting returned halfway (yet backwards) toward positive image. Every practitioner of such medial deactivation attempts their own unique pivot in this respect. In his own emphatic attachment to the time of production as integral to the aesthetic function, Matt Saunders rehearses a related trajectory of media history. His is an approach to figure painting that disfeatures its mimetic integrity by the imaginative labor of *de-picting* it: once (in respect to filmic duration) via the redrawn track of cellular photograms, later through the inversions of photography. In a similar re-traversal—or retroversal—of media evolution (though calling up by association an earlier sense of "photogram" as optical format), John Opera projects a transmedial energy onto prepared canvas in the form of light-etched, pigment-washed cyanotype (blue)prints of the previously inexistent—free radicals of light as wave *and* particle en route to their settled effects. No technical negatives (other than those of mode and genre) are involved in Opera's laboratory experiments—merely evoked, in some works, by the stark chiaroscuro of light's own abstract rayed traces, part of an all but furtive media circuitry and collusion. At a quite different optic scale, and hard to recognize at first as mere photo negatives, loom Mungo Thomson's inverted, black-on-white night skyscapes—turning, as they do, the time-delayed flares of cosmic radiation, light years in arrival, chromatically inside out.

Synopsis keeps populating itself in review by anomalous modes of inversion and negation. On the European front, in the narrow cross-section provided here, Cornelia Parker's indexical photograms of smashed vitreous transparencies revert in their ghostly black-on-white outlines to the pre-negative phase of "photogenesis." And juxtaposed to her infrared Nazified snapshots of a morally blackened daylight sky are her explicit post-indexical "negatives" (of words and sounds alike: those comparable leavings of visual and phonographic inscription). All are cognate in turn with her sculptural molding of everyday pavement interstices. Repeatedly her work approaches the phenomena of perception and reproduction from the vantage point of a structuring absence traced by one sort of negation or another—if only, in those photograms, of fragile objects by the fixture of their edging shadows. In Maria Lund's work, with its own derivation from pre-photographic record, her pigment-free sunburnt "Stills" also recover the solar magic of early non-negative imaging—while, in the process, negating an initial appearance of a thin painterly facture by the disclosure of sheer sunlight index. Intercepting optic technology in its later commercialized stages, Albrechtsen's inversions of medial determinants take shape in complementary ways. There are those domesticated digital interfaces with their mountainscape desktop panoramas. More recently, there are his charcoal renditions of celluloid's fleeting transparencies in narrative film when transferred in mirror reversal to the uppermost sheet of inaccessible stacked pages. Each conceptual effect—executed with deft artisanal finesse—works to insert the vanishingly handmade into the mass produced, negating both in a kind of suspension of optic belief. And if one were to take together these related bodies of work in Albrechtsen's recent practice as epitomizing gestures in a twofold nostalgia for the *mise-en-scène* of the cinematic shot and the landscape sublime of the painterly tradition, how far would such work fall from a suspected resistance to electronic computation—with its increasingly dominant role in the permutations of image culture—in the resistant negactivity of the other artists we've reviewed? Including of course the decelerated unfolding of a cinematic "END" in Kiarostami's digitized photo animation—or, before him, Ruscha's fixed-frame drawing, *The End*.

With computer imaging repeatedly the unsaid destiny of history's media juggernaut in the re-presencing of the world, certainly Kao Chung-Li undertakes the detourning of an entire media history on the spools and spun platens of its decelerated and interrupted mechanisms, their deconstructed clockwork basis. He then transforms a time-travel allegory from the high modernist canon, *La Jetée*, with the inserted science of its own photochemical basis. Addressing Marker's unmaking of cinema as a chain of frozen photo images, Kao tracks this received parable of an aborted temporal continuum one level down to the optical engineering of the sequential photo image itself. Through his unflinching critique, he exerts this further denaturalization of media art via the surfaced negactivity of all celluloid "development." He does this to lay bare its mostly invisible facilitation of a yet deeper technocapitalist infrastructure—rather than any sensed material substrate—in modernity's thoroughly compromised ways of seeing.

In contrast, we have the works of cleansed and intensified perception on whose complexities we have dwelt—or, better put, whose material intervals we have lingered to inhabit. Such (in Opera, Saunders) are the pivotal developments of the darkroom, for instance, that can knowingly turn the remnants of photonic residue into the investigated positivity of a recognized image *painted in light*. Which is a fair enough definition as well, even though the rays of his light are too short-wave ever to be visible in themselves, for the negated flesh of Renato Meneghetti's luminous anatomies. See by antithesis (as in fact you can't, though in a different sense from any sub-optic x-radiance) those machinations of computer imaging in which the fundament of all sensory apprehension is withdrawn into the bowels of code. Art has scant ingress there. Instead, as eloquently advocated by an artist like Saunders—in the exacting rhetoric of his gallery hangings, projections, and lectures alike—one may otherwise enter upon an aesthetic of perceptibility steeped in the time-based transformations of its own process. Entailed in the coils of such making is a ruminative pro/ tr/action recovered in imagery's temporal palimpsests, the viewer always invited first of all to register conceptually how an image itself has been made to register. That's also what, beyond his military-industrial critique, renders Kao's explicitness so apt for this subset of image practice: turning the negative, seized at the estranging interface between object and process, into a prototype or parable of vision's own elided transactions. With such a material object stalled halfway toward a further materialization, concept emerges directly from transitional percept. Kao's discursive insistence on this splaying of layers in the understood work of manifestation helps us recognize other practitioners in this vein as operating in the same conceptual light: as technicians—and theorists—of the image in action, not the picture on display. This is exactly the way negativity—the text of the *neglegible*—participates in the broader project of Conceptual art. Made especially clear when intervening in automatic functions like photography, it is the disruption of process in the name of its contemplation, its analytic exposure. And it can happen at one medial remove from automatic record, as in the charcoal coalition of grayscaled photorealist surface and paper substrate by which Robert Longo, as we've seen, effecting an ontological flip, negates the drip hierarchies of Pollock's layered, aleatory chromatics to lift the first into the place of the last: paper underlay risen to the look of canvas' final chalk-white oil flourishes.

In Matt Saunders' typifying version of this inverse aesthetic in painterly form, the phases of making are not deceptively cancelled out but, in their intrinsic counterforce, prodigally enacted by conceptual overlap—and this at their own markedly *non*digital interface between painterly facture and mere trace. Negation is in many ways foundational. Regarding recurrent examples here, put it this way in sum: the traditional photo negative is the intrinsic necessity of the image, the backbone of its positing to the eye. And this way as well, for a broader poetics of the negative: at a certain pitch of formal inversion, negativity (activated) becomes a reassertion of defining terms. Its inverting process offers on this score, among countless other ramifications, an often technological touchstone—as maximized under critique, for instance, in the inserts and intertitles that pace Kao's Marxian appropriation of Marker's previous "slide show cinema." Or that submit a Nazi overlord to the entrapping scrutiny of his own police microstate in another version of quick-cut montage in *The Zone of Interest*. Hence the politics, within my subtitled poetics, of inversion. With or without an overt sociocritical "spin," however, yet by a comparable material logic, the reversals, mirrorotations, and transpositives of all such Conceptual art—in the cunning of its material punning, the transmedial palindromes of its production—serve to *accentuate the negative* (to invert again that old song's upbeat advice) with a compelling visual grip. They do so not to deflect, suppress, or "eliminate" any intervening "mess," but rather to bring out the labor, via the texture, and finally the text, of mediation's fertile "in-between." Which never fails to rivet—to affix—the attention of a peripatetic gallery goer in the oblique variety of its latest manifestations. And this even when (below) returned to the mode's definitive first sense, and historical emergence, as the photogram's dark burn of light.

Dateline: press time approaching. On the question of photographic negativity, Kao Chung-Li turns out to have some distinguished Asian company in a succinctly curated show at the Getty Center in the spring and summer of 2024 (no catalog, alas). The chronological oxymoron of its title, "Nineteenth-Century Photography Now," cuts to the quick of the hard-won fixity often at stake in the exhibit. With regard to the "now" of art-historical response rather than the ongoing fate of chemical preservation, Victorian experiments in photo negativity, photograms, and cyanotypes were cannily paired in that exhibit with contemporary responses in both still and time-based media. The early challenge of the "pencil of nature" and its solar jottings—the difficulty of fixing the light-waved trace of image, even at the preliminary stage of the contrapositive index (often stored, unstably, on salted paper surfaces)—is taken up from, and pursued in, diverse and rather opposite directions by the contemporary practice represented here.[20] From famed Japanese photographer Hiroshi Sugimoto (b. 1948) we read how, "With the help of the J. Paul Getty Museum" and its archives, "I toiled away in my darkroom" until able to recover for the first time—to "develop" after decades of latency—a full (and much enlarged) picture from the inverse fragility of original William Henry Fox Talbot negatives. These experiments included for display at the Getty—in a fine balance of art and nature—the bust of Venus de Milo, her marble head, no longer onyx in tone, correctively turned in the right direction, set over against a conversion of the white-on-black tendrils of one of Talbot's famous lacey fronds, as if etched by delicate handicraft, into a b&w positive. Continuing a tour of this exhibit, we come in a moment, a few yards away, to the artifactual response of a Japanese *writer* to photography as writing.

In the meantime, on a nearby wall, in contrast to Sugimoto's achieved teleology of the negative, contemporary artist Phil Chang (b. 1974) explains in another self-authored gallery text that, returning to the mechanical trace before its chemical entrapment, "I produce photographic images that fade and disappear in the light necessary" (not to record—but subsequently) "to view them": a negative evolution of the index. Chang deliberately records images in all photo genres—from portraits to landscapes to mere screenshots—so as to subordinate any thematic topos to the trope of evanescence. All these glimpses are traced on paper shorn of all fixatives, so that the image fades away over a number of indeterminate hours. For display at the Getty, twin cases of such photonic ephemerality are recorded as moving (or removing) optical sequences—and framed in time-lapse video alongside the accelerated carousel of a clock face and its spinning dials, as if to upend the vocabulary of "capture" in the photographic first place. The question of the negative as custodial mold of the preservative—affirmed by permanence—is thus reversed to a case of the cancelled rather than transcribed, a glimpse not saved but effaced, nixed rather than affixed.

Transitional negativity recovered for fixity (Sugimoto); chemical intervention foregone in the name of the fleeting (Chang). After this unspoken curatorial antinomy, a third major conceptual turn (typically research-heavy) comes from the cousin medium of post-Gutenberg imprint. It concerns, by way of historical backcast, French nomenclature's search for the new medium's best name, a term that would—befitting the chemistry of disseminated ink—decidedly stick. Not negating the medium in this way but claiming kin with its own inherent reversability, the writer not the painter Murakami (Hanako rather than Takashi) gives us one unique dialectic "takeaway" from the exhibit: a poster-sized glossy sheet (on offer for all comers) listing in a nearly two-foot-long centered column of elegantly crisp print all the twenty-seven French names (in often Greek derivation) by which the aborning medium was at first known—and came rapidly to know itself. From the ontological equivalence of "expérience," via "point de vue" to "copie de gravure," we move through "plaque" and "planche" to "photologie" and on through obscurities like "iconotauphyse" to "autophuse" before arriving, at last, after "procédé seriagraphique," at the comfortable transatlantic cognate of the namesake "daguerreotype." Thus do we scroll down the cascade of terms in review of the "pictured" lexemes whose function (as imprint) recalls that predecessor form out of which the new medium emerges. Everything remains potently implicit in Murakami's gloss. "The invention of photography is also the invention of its idea." And thus the birth of its nomination among the elder-sister arts and their technologies. Without direct mention of the metal sculpture mounted above the stack of print-outs like a miniature Donald Judd, with its tiers of reversed type, Murakami indicates simply: "The terms are printed with hot metal typesitting" that "evokes the intensity of photography's conception as well as the negative/positive printing process." Enough said, though a Getty gallerist might have noted in addition how the medial link between reverse typesetting and the negative reversal of the photographic plate is a "textual" connection made long ago by Talbot himself in his early backwards image "Imitation of Printing." This was a photographic "page" from his book, *The Pencil of Nature*, consisting entirely of its three-word, three-line eponym legible by reverse in the manner at once of a photo negative and, by analogy, a typesetter's alphabetic array: each manifest together via the mirror of formative inversion.[21] Across the whole arc of this Getty exhibit in its inevitable confrontation with reversability in all its facets (and its type-facings), *photontology* is textualized yet again under the system of the negative, whether back/words, evaporated, or archaeologically recovered as positive. The conceptual turnings of such inversion become their own mode of trope.

Notes

1   [Ed.] For a fresh digest of Garrett Stewart's neologisms (and inventive portmanteaus), see "Terms of Use: Coinages Cashed Out—A Selective Glossary," as featured at the conclusion of *Attention Spans: Garrett Stewart, a Reader*, ed. David LaRocca (New York: Bloomsbury, 2024), 340–47.

2 [Ed.] For more on the "post-medium condition," see Garrett Stewart, *Transmedium: Conceptualism 2.0 and the New Object Art* (Chicago: University of Chicago Press, 2017); and relatedly *Attention Spans*, "Material Transference and Medial Merger," chapter 12, 153–58.

3 In this sense the present essay's negational cluster of conceptual practices serves to extend, though in the narrower scope of their shared visual logistics, the general purview of *Transmedium*. A scope "narrower" here, yes, but at the same time emblematic, since the defining slant of the textualist prism that constitutes the medial inflection point in many of the most complicated works in that more broadly delimited mode is often marked by reciprocal negation—an operational cross-purpose—at some thereby localized (and clarified) transmedial interface.

4 [Ed.] From *Attention Spans*, Stewart on mediarchaeology: "one aptly compacted word for the historical depth of developmental sediment made immanent at certain impacted moments in a single image, whereby, unlike the two-word version of typical film studies, a local node of the medium enacts its own prehistory, as with the digital "aging" of Victorian photographs in Terence Davies' *A Quiet Passion* (2016), 344. See also Garrett Stewart, *Cinemachines: An Essay on Media and Method* (Chicago: University of Chicago Press, 2020) and "Kinetic Textuality," *Attention Spans*, chapter 16, 191–210.

5 See partial illustration in *Bookwork: Medium to Object to Concept to Art* (Chicago: University of Chicago Press, 2011), 117–18, figs. 3.5 and 3.6.

6 The delay by inversion at stake in this phase of Matt Saunders' work, along with the intent and execution of both earlier and later experimental procedures, is carefully laid out by the artist in a video of his 2020 lecture at the University at Buffalo: https://www.youtube.com/watch?v=HcfyId7rZmw.

7 Matthew Hale, "The Light Between Your Shirt and Your Skin (On Matt Saunders' Color Linen-Negative Prints)," in *Poems of Our Climate: Matt Saunders* (Brooklyn: Dancing Foxes Press, 2022), 35.

8 [Ed.] For more on "s/pied beauty," see in this volume, chapter 4.

9 See David LaRocca, "Object Lessons: What Cyanotypes Teach Us About Digital Media," in *Photography's Materialities: Transatlantic Photographic Practices over the Long Nineteenth Century*, ed. Geoff Bender and Rasmus R. Simonsen (Leuven: Leuven University Press, 2021), 207–34; and "A Photograph as Evidence of Itself: Representation, Reflexivity, and Tautology in Light-Based Art," *Social Research*, vol. 89, no. 4 (Winter 2022): 915–45. See also "CHICAGO | The Observers: John Opera; January 6–February 25, 2023" and "LISBON | Blue Dream: John Opera; January 20–May 20, 2023," Document Space, Document Gallery, Chicago, documentspace.com; and "Equivalent Simulation: A Conversation with John Opera, *Afterimage: The Journal of Media Arts and Cultural Criticism*, vol. 42, no. 6 (2015): 16–21.

10 See David LaRocca, *Attention Spans*, 291 n. 1.

11 See John Opera, "Black Sun I" (2005), "Black Sun II" (2005), "Black Sun III" (2006–7), and "Lunar Eclipse" (2009) at johnopera.com. John Opera, "When the Sun is Done," an exhibition at Rivalry Projects, Buffalo, New York (January 17–February 28, 2025). [Ed.] In the obliterated "Pater" (2024–25), a figuration of the father as solar/paternal erasure negactivating a lineage that will culminate when the son is done (*cum sol finitur ergo cum filius finierit*).

12　[Ed.] Another crucial Stewartism, *bibliobjet* is glossed as "the sculptural codex form that has surrendered all bibliographic utility to its material objecthood (as the French elision suggests)–even as it tacitly generates formal 'figures of speech' for its own lost field of reading that become in themselves textually 'legible'" (*Attention Spans*, 340). See especially on this score, *Bookwork*, and in *Attention Spans*, "Reading Foreclosed/Text Reinvented," chapter 9, 130–38.

13　Associations quickly collect around Cornelia Parker's negactivating tactics. With this most laconic of her works, where the mere interstices of minimalist built space (namely, and by title, *Paving Stones*) come to the fore in a new abstract grid, the inverted materiality may well call to mind the white plaster countermolds of her British compeer in Conceptual art, Rachel Whiteread. But literary inversions as well as minimalist sculpture can feel like part of the precedent as well. In the first line of Vladimir Nabokov's first American novel, *Bend Sinister* (1947), the reader encounters a gap in the world's expected surface that seems derived from a quite similar "concept." Negating that surface is an oblong sector of optical illusion brought forward from a depression in the asphalt (rather than paving stones) of the narrator's gloomy prospect after news of his wife's pending death: "An oblong puddle inset in the coarse asphalt: like a fancy footprint filled to the brim with quicksilver; like a spatulate hole through which you can see the nether sky" (New York: Penguin, 1974, 13). To think of this optic reflex as the nether/nor of a momentarily stabilized mirrorotation is to anticipate later versions of this invertability in Nabokov's novel, including, in a passing distraction, the "negative image" of the hero's hands in those of "dark-skinned" elevator operators (42)—and, more poignantly, the reverse image of his own handwriting in that of his now deceased wife, each script "slanting and curving in opposite directions" in a rapport as erotic as orthographic: "Her concavity fitting my convexity exactly" (33). And concavity makes an *outré* return in British conceptual sculpture as well. Helen Chadwick's 1996 sculptural garden of *Piss Flowers* (on display in 2024–25 at the Tate Modern) adds a live-action dimension, of sorts, to Whiteread's negative molds. Where Whiteread (her works previously engaged in *Transmedium*, n. 2 above) often remarks on her poured plaster casts as "mummifying the air in a room," the fluid work of such molding is redoubled (or double-negated) in Chadwick's contemporaneous sculptural send-up by having a liquid stream of the titular piss as itself the "form" being cast in its own freezing mold. In flower-shaped metal containers filled with snow, the urination of the artist and her male partner burns a funnel in the snow that, when its contours are refrozen, can be cast in bronze and then repainted white to simulate either conventional plaster, snow again, or both, but with the upright pistil that results (more phallic than the male stamen of normal flora) fusing the gendered mix of raw material in its inverted, fountain-like thrust.

14　So back for a moment, stateside, from London to Manhattan, for another version of "articles of glass" under an extreme conceptualist duress. Closer to Cornelia Parker's own typical 3D work in negative space, as it happens, is the still life by Charles Ray, exhibited at the Met in a retrospective of the artist's work in 2022, with bottles and so-called glasses (drinking goblets) arrayed on a clear glass table. Their presumed coincidence, or visible redoubling, of surface matter—with transparent bottoms appearing (or disappearing) in indiscernible overlay upon the glass tabletop—is only apparent, or say assumed. On inspection, the assemblage is ironized further by the fact that the circles of contact, in the objects and the table itself, have been cut away to effect the negative contact of pure illusory interface. Instead of redoubled glass, there is only circular gap. In play here is the phenomenological principle of "adumbration" in its double sense, whereby the manifest aspect of an object presumes while excluding its averted face. This is the very thing that facilitated the heyday of the Dutch still life in two dimensions, often approximating *trompe l'oeil*—including the frequent *tour de force* of cut-crystal refraction maximized automatically by William Henry Fox Talbot's lens. But here, in Ray's assemblage, the eye is fooled by what is actually there for it to discern: aligned holes not the abutting surfaces of whole objects. In his deeper (and gradually penetrable) illusionism, this traditional assumption of objecthood from frontal aspect is just what is carved away via the absent glass interface. The result at these elided points of contact is, as in traditional still life, still impalpable—but this time visibly (de)materialized in the conceptualist mode of a sculptural double negative.

15 In a further connection with Cornelia Parker's photo concepts as well, Talbot comes immediately to mind in deciphering and contemplating Maria Lund's work—including what is often cited as his first stable paper imprint made from the instrumental negative reversal of a *camera obscura*'s traced beam. Given Talbot's other self-conscious thematizations of the new medium—as in the reverse-faced typeface "Imitation of Printing"—the pictured subject is in this case a perfect choice for his transmutation of natural optics. Identified as "Latticed Window at Lacock Abbey," the photographer's own residence, it records—before functionally reversing it—the atmospheric fact of light streaming through a cross-barred paned grid of transparency. With cause evoked in its own effect, the seared traces of this reticulated light have been passed in turn, via chiaroscuro inversion, through a negative transfer in order to be printed as light versus occlusion, white versus black, in the positive paper image. Forget the *camera obscura* and insert a fabric layer (if not quite paper-thin) nearer to the window's light source, and such a broad curtained aperture—Lund's work reminds us—might have produced a similar optical index.

16 It is part of this critique of media application that Kao Chung-li's allusion to Thomas Edison's invention of the phonautograph (using a detached human ear to transfer voice to its storage as graphic trace) involves projecting the apparatus forward to the actual retrieval functions of the later phonograph, where, attached to the stylus in Kao's rendition, is the skeleton of an intact human skull—as if only the full cranium could be the sounding board and echo chamber for recorded human speech. Yet, typical of Kao's critique of the technological juggernaut, the skull becomes more monitory when linked to military effect as well as technological cause. This dawns on us when we realize that, though the work is titled for the anodyne lines first read by Edison into his new machine, *Mary Had a Little Lamb*, the printed label on the commercial-style vinyl record—re-tracked here by the needle's prothesis of the human sensorium—pictures two figures in military costumes, army and navy in lockstep. Whatever Mary had, what we have since, in the legacy of such invention, are radio intercepts and military sonar, to say nothing (though the exhibit elsewhere does) about the din of machine warfare.

17 See Walter Benjamin, "The Work of Art in the Age of Mechanical Reproduction," in *Illuminations: Essays and Reflections*, ed. Hannah Arendt (New York: Harcourt

Brace Jovanovich, 1968), where he paraphrases a received view about Eugène Atget's deserted streets: "It has quite just been said of him that he photographed them like scenes of crime" (226).

18   Discussion of *The Zone of Interest* here, in its links back to Cornelia Parker's ironic recommissioning of the Nazi camera, expands on my previous comments when bringing director Jonathan Glazer's technical innovations into evidence in dialogue with Daniel Morgan, on the question of off-screen time and space alike, for our exchange in *Bandwidths: Reading Across Media with Garrett Stewart* (New York: Bloomsbury, 2024),

19   Framed by the right narrative context on screen, as with Glazer's anomalous night-vision technique, the inverted image need not be an actual photographic negative in order to trope such a function as the underlay of the moving-image medium that foregrounds its macabre counterpart. In *Godland* (dir. Hlynur Pálmason, 2022), the conflated title of a divinized earth—openly inviting a mediating and mitigating third term—brings its potential dichotomy to bear on the central protagonist, a Danish priest-photographer outposted to Iceland in the late nineteenth century, who carries his photo equipment on his back, both camera and portable darkroom, and mediates between divine ordination and the forbidding landscape by portraits of living people framed against its stark rocky (and volcanic) backdrop. Shot in a squarish academy ratio (its curved-edge rectangle distinct from today's dominant widescreen format and closer to the shape of the photo images made within its framing view), the film—having shown us the slow development of site-specific portraiture under the tarpaulin of his makeshift darkroom—follows the priest's death with aerial shots alternating between his cloaked corpse and the slain horse whose killing precipitates the retributive violence that has led to his murder. Serial jump cuts pace the horse's sideways-sprawled body, as if in arrested flight, across two years of seasonal decay. Via the optic shifts in this quick-cut snapshot time-lapse—between snow-drift-contrasted flesh and eventual sunlight-shadowed bones—the animal anatomy flashes past in contrastive outline to resemble at times its own fleshless negative image in a denaturalized photogram process (in the temporal and physiological equivalent of Meneghetti's bone-baring X-ray composites). Only in this way can a disembodied overhead shot, in a god's-eye-view of this documented human violence, treat the world the way the photographer-priest, now ripped from it, had sought to do: by putting organic life into relief against a stony, unforgiving land via the fixating force of photochemistry's own living death.

20   With the present manuscript nearing submission in catch-up mode, this was a banner season for conceptual photography, in its political as well as archaeological dimensions, as evident in transit from the Getty to London's Whitechapel Gallery (2024–25) for an exhibition by Peter Kennard (b. 1949), collage satirist and Emeritus Professor of Political Art at the Royal College of Art, the first such professorship in the British academic world. His retrospective show at Whitechapel: "Archive of Dissent." The ferocious two-part pastiche that might well recall the simulated flayed flesh of Meneghetti's work was prominently featured in media advertising for Kennard's exposition. In it, a publicity photo of former Prime Minister Margaret Thatcher, holding up the glossy image of a neonatal incubator—with smiling nurse and featured infant, as if in celebration of National Health—is answered in diptych by the same ringed and braceleted hand

holding an identical image of her face, now as detached photo cut-out, in front of (as if peeled away from) the shouldered symbolic death's head of her own lethal austerity. As with a nearby collage beheading of Queen Victoria, the monarch's serene face replaced by Thatcher's, the force of superposition acts as unmasking. More recent works in the Kennard exhibit follow suit in a 3D version of this implicit surface/depth logic, where a variant of such divisive photo collage, in its mode of twinned or eclipsed portraiture, is in turn redoubled by various mixed (or say conflictive) media formats. The fracture of collage is turned at a right angle into the satirized laminate of discrepancy when corporate logos are projected from glass slides—no prismantic dispersion here—upon indistinct photo portraits (mounted on salvage board in a punning work called *Board Room*): smudged images of the virtually faceless victims upon whose existence corporate practices have been imposed, as figured by the inviting green blossom of the BP logo or the seaside fan of the eponymous Shell (no seaborne oil spill in sight). According to the suggestive gallery text, these amount to the "deconstruction" of Kennard's standard two-dimensional collage practice. Superimposition, made in itself visible across gallery space in such works, becomes a matter, beyond photo process, of sheer dialectical negation (via effaced responsibility). Another related, complex, and in this case time-based work of Kennard's at Whitechapel entails not a severing or direct obfuscatory negation of image, but an intermittent backlit expose. This 2023 assemblage—titled (with a direct photographic pun) "Double Exposure"—intermittently "projects" from behind the financial pages of daily stock quotes, when printed on their verso, the otherwise averted photo evidence, human and environmental, that all this lucrative tabulation tends to put from mind when, as it were, light isn't forcibly thrown on it. Only by sporadic glimpses here, the repressed underside of capitalist accounting returns in flashes when its unpredictably obtruded and glaring *effect* (to economic *causation*) appears in a kind of instantaneous darkroom "development"—the "negative" will out— through irregularly timed LED-light flashes in which exposure shows forth as political precisely because optical, emergent for all to see. Collage, in the flick(er) of the spectatorial eye, is transformed into a kind of shot/reverse shot *montage* within a paradoxically fixed, inflexible, and eclipsing set of frames. The warning about stroboscopic light effects in the mandatory gallery caution, regarding epileptic risk, becomes almost in itself allegorical, given what the insistent political flashpoints of the assemblage may "trigger" when *brought to light*. Far, yet again, from any oblique prismatic refraction in Kennard's projection work, file this assemblage as another variant of the contrafraction (rather than glancing refraction) posited for Cornelia Parker's "Negative" traces.

21   See Stewart, *Transmedium*, 9, where the photo imprint is simulated by the designer's mirror typeface to install a first talisman, formal and historical alike, of techno-hybridity in the unfolding manner of conceptual media works.

III

REVENANT REVISIONS: "GHOST READING"

8 / In this crossover experiment in creative criticism, Stewart's over-close reading propels him just past closure itself to a model of reading-on and -in that generates hypothetical last sentences appended to major novels in performative paraphrase of these fictions' own rhetorical vanishing points—deferred by the investitures of micro analysis. Closure foreclosed, if speculatively. Invested or immersive reading here resurfaces only after extra reflective saturation in the flux of residual impact, spelling out as prose what often lingers as inference in the spilling over of association. Stewart's notional insertions after a novel's final period can be conceived as their own version of "writing beyond the end," t/ending to continue spiritedly despite the implied finality of the terminal punctuation mark.

8 / *Narrative Afterwording: Too Close for Closure*

ONE ALWAYS STARTS SOMEWHERE. In academic criticism, that somewhere is often the classroom, where no established protocols restrict one's effort to ignite engagement—or even to free-associate on the spot. And then there is the peripheral spur to further writing that such teaching may sometimes induce. Of which this essay is a record. The idea for these pages—and I had no idea how many or few of them there might come to be when starting out—was sparked one day in a recent undergraduate course offering. Or say the *instinct* rather than "idea": a dawning itch to try out at greater length, and on prose fiction rather than iambic pentameter, what was at the time only an extemporized heuristic in a classroom exercise. The occasion: an example from Alfred Tennyson used to illustrate, in rare distillation, the peculiar energies of nonfinite grammar in an undergraduate writing seminar focused as well on the complementary habit of "creative reading." It will usefully, I hope, take a while, with examples frontloaded before propositions, to explain this essay's alternate current rubric of spectral attention under the unspoken banner of proverbial close reading. Enough for now to say that the main fictional paragraphs with which discussion ahead will be concerned don't exist in the literary record; they are in themselves fictional, and thus, if only by default, metafictional. Or say instead that their mode of existence is only that of associational persistence: a lingering pressure of content outlasting in stylistic afterthought the actual closure of its text. Call it a ghost of the unwritten still cloistered in embryo by the parent text.

Toward a Grammar of the Nonfinal

MANY TEXTS CAN SEEM FINISHED, both polished and finalized, without being *over* in the reading mind. At the level of linguistic predication rather than plot, there is a name for this form of untruncated action: the infinitive. So here's the classroom moment that inaugurated this current of thought (or instinct) on my part—and launched this essay's exercise in backdoor analysis via invented addendum. I was on familiar ground at the time, and didn't see these further ramifications coming. Whether teaching the dramatic monologue in a literary-history course or the drama of grammar in a course on style, I never tire of charting for students, in the last line of Tennyson's seaborne poem "Ulysses" (1842), an intrepid syntactic voyage all its own, cresting repeatedly on the nonfinite verb form. Propelled thereby, in Tennyson, is a journey in which the variables of syntax seem in their own right mapped in transit—all this dependent, on and from, the deft metonymy of a brave crew annealed in long service like the tempered steel of their time-tested swords. And all this so far, of course, if new to students, nonetheless part of the literary-critical record regarding these famous last lines:

> One equal temper of heroic hearts,
> Made weak by time and fate, but strong in will
> To strive, to seek, to find, and not to yield.

Afloat on this asymptotic voyage, Ulysses' crew is united in a willed momentum clocked by a collective strength—almost, in its pentameter strokes, as if with the propulsive oar-beat of nautical advance. But there is more than mimetic push in this metric exertion. To parse this verbal chain reaction—ongoing, emphatically nonfinite in its impetus—is to mark the build from a verb all but idiomatically requiring an indirect object for specification (to strive *for this or that*) to a form inviting less necessarily a direct object (to seek [*this or that*]), though each semantic range allows for the more generalized notion of "striver" or "seeker" at large. From there the line unfolds to the emphatic transitive form of a more or less mandatory object in a directed destination (to find *whatever*)—followed by a return to a blanket indirect object under negation (never to yield *to anything whatsoever*). Then, too, from the first of this pentameter lockstep, there is the potential dovetailing of the infinitive format, where forward momentum, despite punctuation, becomes in itself unpartitioned, overlapped, cumulative, self-propulsive. Here is a phrasal drumbeat that seems not just insistent but again mimetic, from the pivotal enjambment forward, overriding the commas as if with some implicit muscle memory of slashing sword strokes in a "tempered" unity of purpose. Not just heroic will in general, rather than lassitude, but a "will / to"—as manifest in the continuing phrasal protrusion of *to strive to seek, to seek to find*, and so forth, the grammar going steadily forth again undaunted, phrases agglomerated as if to enact the overarching syntactic continuum of such serially renewed determination. And dovetailed, further yet, by the assonant cross-thread of long vowels in the *ive/eek/ind/ield* pattern that steers the crew's resolve through to the affective double negative of "not to yield."

It was by slowing in class over the grammar of the line's piled-up iambs— and after introducing by association the further dated metonymy of tested "mettle" (a word unfamiliar to newer generations of students) for the crew's affirmed adamant (tempered) purpose—that my further move was for the first time spurred. Suddenly, to encapsulate the point about the stylistic valence of grammar in the open-ended strain of this infinitive cascade, I found myself ad-libbing—for my creative writer/readers—a further predicate vector in an imagined couplet closure ending in a punning rhyme: "To strive, to seek, to find, and not to yield, / Our dream to reach against all meekness steeled." As poetry: a redundancy and a sacrilege. As analysis: a further italics (in the "emphasis-added" mode)—phonetic stress included—on the forward momentum instilled by inbuilt skids of the infinitive in Tennyson's actual closing line. Though negligible as verse, I was inviting my students to imagine this instead as a one-line gloss in metrical tow. The fact of being "made weak by time" once admitted, the real danger must be defended against: so real that it might well haunt even the hero's pep talk with another slippery enjambment in a subliminal commitment "not to yield / Our dream."

Beyond that, part of my nudge to the added past-participial grammar ("steeled") no doubt came, if only half-consciously, from the class' recent discussion of the "absolute construction" in its variable aesthetic valences (hovering between phrase and clause, often with its own ongo-*ing* version of nonfinite [participial] predication). In thinking to highlight, by ramping up further, the rescinded vanishing point of Tennyson's quest narrative, I was thus adding another syntactic exercise to the lesson plan begun with a concentration on infinitive grammar. This second stab at an unfixed closure for a crew undaunted—yet always on guard against a flinching timidity— was again, at least on first pass ("Our dream to reach"), left open-ended in its transitive object(ive)s regarding any set goal. Yet by its latent Necker inversion as "to reach our dream," this elastic rhyming addendum was found, on a moment's further reflection, to insinuate by ellipsis the ambiguity, or better circularity, of *alternate* grammatical absolutes. With "one equal temper" operating as governing subject, the open-ended sense of a receding goal oscillates between "Our dream [being] to reach, against all frailty [are we] braced" and "[We] to reach our dream [being] against all frailty braced." The pure will *to* ______ is once again suspended in defiance of slackening and finitude alike. But by now, as you may well imagine, I was losing many of the recently schooled grammarians among my students in these coils of Empsonian doubleness.[1]

In gently backing off, however, I found I hadn't let go. Something about the alternate current of this ad lib put me at liberty for unexpected reflection later in my office. Was this sudden riff really so new to me, even if spun off for the first time in class? Wasn't this what I was always doing, letting last words survive a text in the reconfigured echo of clarification? Not as an aesthetic, but as a prosthetic, gesture: getting leverage on the said by its generated secondary suggestions, putting tacit phrasings into the mouth of authorship by finding them where they would eventually be found anyway—in my own voice, as commentary. In this newly sprung version of creative reading—in the form of residual writing—I began to wonder if the spontaneity of this little exercise had legs, as it were, in stepping off the implications of longer prose fiction across an extra swatch of shadow text. What would it look or sound like: this stretch (in every sense) of narrative wording not just familiar and implicit in my head— and so affecting the phrasing of my eventual analysis—but now spelled out more actively? I started mental doodling simply by recalling, without having yet to look more accurately back at, famous fictions over whose readily (if roughly) remembered closures I had previously lingered. For this would approximate what I, and surely not I alone, regularly do in finishing a text I've become engrossed by: re-read right away the last paragraph, letting it sink in by steeping attention in it again—and then again. For this new thought experiment—all the more productive at first, with no exact rendition of the sponsoring text in front of me—I tried imagining the texture of such an aftertext as I had imposed on "Ulysses." Imposed, that is, by letting it seem impelled from within by that final laddering-up of infinitives.

This process amounted, I soon found, to making bluntly explicit what interpretive reflection had so often elicited for me from the nuances of a fine stylistic finish (at the *finis*), with its drawing taut of a particular verbal "micropolot"—that last being the keystone term in my approach to "narratography."[2] So I went back to those same books that came first to mind, opened them to their exact last paragraphs, and wrote on. *On*, not over: the effort being certainly not to rewrite, to line-edit, but rather to let implications land more fully (not in any sense more forcefully) with the frequent weight, so it turned out, of a second shoe falling. This essay collects these wide-ranging experiments, sorting them along with the questions they generated. To what extent is drawing out an entwined hint always something like a closet version of drafting a new prose passage in amplification, a kind of countertext? Had commentary as preoccupied as mine with the linguistic contours of a text, as restlessly "stylistic," always been a kind of redrafting after all—somewhere between paraphrase and interpretation, catching a syntactic rhythm, prolonging a figure into explicitness, letting no dead metaphors lie undisturbed? When asking myself this, I supposed so—but only as a methodological exception, in degree rather than kind, to literary fascination's usual rule (over our response). In the hold on us of any gripping narrative prose, the locking in of interest is its own kind of secondary key; what attention fastens on tends to loose a welter of relevant associations. All the more so in closure—where the buzz of inference is met with no immediate further distractions along the route of plot. There's nowhere else to look but quickly back. And then, Ulysses-like, with a vestigial vigor won from reverberation, to forge an extra stroke or two ahead as the tide helps propel you.

Matrimonial in Closure: Some Forgone Conclusions

So LET ME BEGIN with a couple of the fictive examples I myself began with that day in the office—yet before, and in light of which, some still further methodological justification will need to be advanced in order to motivate any such trespass upon the sacred dichotomy of text and explication, paratext and actual added paragraph. The two excerpts to follow first—from the canonical equilibrium of narrative resolution in the bed-curtain-closed prospects of a companionable marriage—invite rumination about what was just last, that is finally, said. What exactly is at stake in just that phrasing, especially regarding the narrative and figurative back-channels it taps, the metaphors it redistributes and transmutes? Mulling such passages in words worked up as if in a continuum with the novel's own prose might—such was the hypothesis I realized I was testing—be evidenced as the *closest possible* reading. Consider it an overbrimming of textual immersion—in response to the proverbial deep dive—in the resulting form of spill-over: a plunge with its own quasi-redundant ripple effects. What gets transcribed in this manner is a brief paper trail in closure's own prose wake. So let the principle behind all this *text t/reading* stand for now in this provisional form: creative reading as one intimate measure of a text's own buoyancy and momentum. There is less tenacity here on criticism's part than acquiescence—letting the text float in attention long enough to register its full inertial force, dwelling with us until it swells with extra surmise. Literary prose is not just the produce of conception but its process. In each famous closing paragraph to follow in this experiment—the nuances of its innuendo spelled out in an extra ratchet of interpretive words following from it—one might expect to hear still at work the latent figurations that have fueled the passage in composition, even when deflected or subsumed by what the author decided on instead. Afterwordings of this sort, accessories after the fact, toggle between the given and the avoided—an impaction of the for(e)gone in both senses of that typography: the felt weight of the previous and the relinquished need (strategically resisted here in my script) for the already sufficiently implicit. In this sense my extra Tenny*sonic* holding action in class was its own kind of quasi-acoustic model. In the prose examples to come, with or without marked phonetic resonance, the backdraft of afterthought is meant not literally to rhyme, but in other ways to chime, with the horizon of finality it overrides, including its closely scanned verbal contours. GHOST READING in this sense haunts the text whose own induced disturbances, or unexhausted tropology, readers in their captivation are slow to exorcise.

Early in the century of the English and American prose that has most concerned me, the nineteenth, there is an ending so famously conventional that its full charge only emerges from the near-miss dimension of its marital plot. This is the conclusion to Jane Austen's *Persuasion* (1817). One can best appreciate this much-debated Austen novel as a kind of remarriage comedy in which a suit once rejected in deference to the wisdom and solicitude of a young girl's beloved elder is, once renewed, warmly (and with new wisdom) embraced. The result is canonized via this metaphor-laden glance into the happier-ever-after of companionable marriage, already solidified in the evolution of British fiction as a privileged format of closure:

> Anne was tenderness itself, and she had the full worth of it in Captain Wentworth's affection. His profession was all that could ever make her friends wish that tenderness less, the dread of a future war all that could dim her sunshine. She gloried in being a sailor's wife, but she must pay the tax of quick alarm for belonging to that profession which is, if possible, more distinguished in its domestic virtues than in its national importance.

When cannot Jane Austen be left to speak for herself? But what is she saying beyond what was eventually sent to the printer? In the act of reading, certainly the passage vibrates under suppression, almost to the edge of parody, with many earlier fiscal tropes in this novel of a calculated marriage market—so much so that it springs retrospectively a pun on the hero's last name. And the result of this admission, by association, may appear in turn to lodge a reminder of the diminishment latent in the phonetic truncation of the heroine's own first name by the family pride—which dismissed her always as "only Anne," no *one* of consequence. With the result that she would emerge confirmed in an extra paragraph like the following: a set of lines superfluous because entirely derivative in respect to suggestion, meant mainly to track the heroine's new status once emancipated, grammatically and otherwise, from the indirect article (only "an Elliott") of her marginalization. And meant to do so here across more than a dozen discounted idioms of social commerce and marital equity. These are laid bare by added italic emphasis—added and thematically toted up (even while here, like all the coming aftertexts, ratcheted down one font point in delivery to mark their inexplicable link to the cited last lines they dwell on, over, and in):

> No longer just "an Elliot," one who barely *counted* with father and older sister in the *ledgers* of their stifling pride, Anne Went*worth* has *redeemed* the full *value* of her husband's surname as well in finally taking it with zeal and affection on its second *offer*. The love that once went away in defeat, that was sent away at the *unnegotiable price* of a higher *debt* of gratitude to Lady Russell and her *costly* persuasion, had returned *compounded* in its *bounty* by the *worthiness* and *wealth* of her husband's devotion. That the latter must be *apportioned* between his wife and his public duty was indeed the one and only *excise* now *levied* on the great good *fortune* of their felicity.

Such a resolution is more, in Austen to begin with, than a maidenly patience having figuratively *paid off*—the one that got away returning worthier yet to be accepted and invested in—but it is no less. Criticism, like fiction, becomes the studied elaboration of dormant bromides and p(re)packaged dead metaphors when tracked through their strategically refreshed manifestations. This isn't new writing so much as the way the printed passage settles out in reflection—like one distended span of italic weight fashioned to bear down on the merely tacit. Ghostwriting is in this sense a textual sounding board reached by rumors of the inferred, rumors and rumblings phonetic, figurative, grammatical, and otherwise.

Same with another such happily-ever-after marital closure, if a far wordier one. A quarter of a century on in the evolution of British fiction, in Charlotte Brontë's *Jane Eyre* (1847), Edward Rochester must be physically humbled—injured and temporarily blinded in his mansion's retributive fire—to warrant his husband's role. It's still all Jane Eyre's story, though: "Reader, I married him." Thus her "tale draws to its close," but not without "one word respecting my experience of married life, and one brief glance at the fortunes of those whose names have most frequently recurred in this narrative." In recounting Rochester's injured dependence on her, she stresses her role in affording a prosthetic vision for the blinded man:

> Literally, I was (what he often called me) the apple of his eye. He saw nature—he saw books through me; and never did I weary of gazing for his behalf, and of putting into words the effect of field, tree, town, river, cloud, sunbeam—of the landscape before us; of the weather round us—and impressing by sound on his ear what light could no longer stamp on his eye.

When, beyond her visualizing for him both the pages of books and the world she translated into similar words, what she adds in the next sentence is at least as metaphoric as literal, blurring those two mediations into a figurative third term: "Never did I tire of reading to him; never did I weary of conducting him where he wished to go." By parallel association, reading emerges in its own right as a conducted progress, in this case a path to recovery:

> One morning at the end of the two years, as I was writing a letter to his dictation, he came and bent over me, and said—"Jane, have you a glittering ornament round your neck?"
>
> I had a gold watch-chain: I answered "Yes."
>
> And have you a pale blue dress on?
>
> I had. He informed me then, that for some time he had fancied the obscurity clouding one eye was becoming less dense; and that now he was sure of it.

The restoration has been economically treated—even before half a dozen more paragraphs follow, summarizing as they do the fate of other characters, mainly St. John Rivers looking forward to that death which is the other face of closure in Victorian fiction. But this structural symmetry, this balancing act between a resituated (thus resuscitated) secular future and a closed story of faith, dulls the end of the novel as we've cared about it to that point. Any reader might forgive Jane for reverting once more, after Rivers' sainted death, to her own domestic story in some such words as these:

> But while we are still making our way in this lower world, Reader, you and I and Edward alike, let me say yet one word more about my troubled road to wedlock, where, as so often, my very name has seemed to whisper a fate. *Ere* now, J*ane Eyre* could *n'er* have been Mr. Rochester's, been Mrs. Rochester, never while his first wife lived. But since then the very *air* we've breathed and shared, our marital weather, has for too long reached his appreciation only through another eye's sight. This is what I meant by my being the "literal" *apple of his eye*: less an object in view than the very globe of his deputized vision. But was this actually for "too long" really? Reader as I became in marrying him, I have translated the world for him in words sounded on his ear like these words here on yours, stamped in turn, as always before, not on your outer eye but only in ink on this last of pages. And just here, Reader, I tremble saying to you what I have never yet, though may one day, say to my husband and friend of friends. For weren't these many months of dependence perhaps a blessing in disguise? Edward being so long deaf to my protestations in refusing to become his mistress, it now seems to me somehow sadly right that he should, "literally" again, have taken some slow time in being able—having finally *come through the fire* restored—to *see me as I really am*: devotedly there before him, not only on his impassioned terms, but on mine, modest ornament included. As I hope I will myself continue to be, an ornament and more, in brightening his new sighted life.

One might conceive of such phantom afterthoughts as located somewhere so exactly between the paraphrastic and the parasitic that their thematic extrapolations (as imagined interpolations) would offer an index to the given rather than an appendix, last-minute inventory more than detached invention.

In Further Consideration

READING ALONG THESE (UNWRITTEN) LINES entails a furtherance of the given—where wording is still dependent as such on the internal kinetics, the inmixed density and tensi(li)ty, of the style that has structured its imprint to begin with. This retention of the novel's own attentive linguistic force field identifies such afterpieces as the work—and the stretch—of *textension*. Yet, not to exaggerate the difference of such procedures, what is even standard-issue close reading but the functional opposite of closed? It pulls in tight enough to pull the plug on all finality in the name of resonance. Such reading is permeated in this way by the text whose rhythmic and semantic energy it has prolonged by absorbing. *Analysis in this mode does more than parse, it participates in, the writing it engages*—and thus labors in the churn and backwash, the spill and undertow, of further(ed) determinations. No less a reverberant stylist of closure than Joseph Conrad pronounced, as a general principle, that "One writes only half the book: the rest is with the reader."[3] The line is frequently misquoted (almost everywhere on the web) as concluding with "the rest is written by readers." But Conrad's alliterative proposal remains subtler. The sense that half of a book's weight and force must rest "with" readers is not ordinarily equivalent to its needing to be *written* by them (except in this essay's anomalous ventures, of course). Yet emphasized by Conrad is more than the obvious symmetry of input/out. The pitch of reception to which he alludes is more than decoding, more than the shadow-play of response from paragraph to paragraph, chapter to chapter. Suggestions must of course be taken up, but on the reader's own re-articulating terms. My investigative attempt at writing along "with" certain enticing finish lines—their phrasing as if calling out for readerly furtherance—is designed to pinpoint Conrad's claim at the point of closure, including a final example of his own below (from *Heart of Darkness*, 1899). Always necessary to reading along the way, the typically passive co-authorship entailed by Conrad's sense of imaginative collaboration is indeed most pointed when the author's at least visible work is done. And thus when and where any further writing, any "performance" (more via Stanley Cavell below; and earlier in chapter 3), would have—perforce is just the word—to be the reader's.

As if in some *peripheral audition* of the inscribed text, what ghost reading provides is not just certain reworded tracks of destination for the drive of plot but a filtering grid of its lingering associations. This is what results, beyond immersive scrutiny, by the triggered engagement of participatory reading: co-author(iz)ed by the evidence at hand, in hand, in script, when submitted to further concerted discernment. In this regard such creative reading is the liberated hermeneutic version of what I have termed "conscripted" reading in the willing rhetorical coercion of Victorian direct address, Jane's vocative endearing of her "Reader" most famously.[4] Call the Conradian prompt, rather, the indirect address to interpretation of all major fiction: pro-vocative not least in the way it invites readers to acquit themselves in closure—to speak up and out. The writer's work done, that half of the book complete, the rest is ours, resting with us, ours to *write through* (not just read through) in uptake.

Ascertaining the heft of things left unsaid, such creative reading underwrites association by delivered subtext. What ghosts closure in this sense is a finality the text has no interest in securing. The pulse of meaning continues beyond the last breath of transcribed text, getting its second wind in interpretive "reflex."[5] Traditional ghostwriting ventriloquizes intent in presentation. Ghost reading, by contrast, takes representation back a step, and sometimes to pieces, in an ear for alternatives. In the closural experiments mounted here, ghost reading stands to close reading as a power of two, squaring the hermeneutic circle in a new paragraph or so of inhabited response. It marks out an occupied (rather than just registered) zone of association. In all but literalizing a contemporary metaphor, it pushes the textual envelope of closure—passing beyond *intensive* reading to something we would have to call *extensive*. It encroaches on the white blank of contemplative aftermath to spell out the already indwelling. Hence the neologism *textension*, whose portmanteau is a compact of adjunct and phrasal agitation. The extra lines are meant to let a text *exfoliate* itself one degree further into reverberation. In terms otherwise lapsing to cliché, and against the sense of any supposedly fixed, literalist, or "surface" reading, such a *ghostext* "keeps the conversation going" in the approximated texture of style's own subsidizing discourse: sometimes as a return of the phrasal repressed. Ghost reading is haunted and diagnostic at once, catching on to intimations in not being ready to let go—a tracking of text as ghost*reading*. The leads it takes *away* from an imposed closure are those of an invested readerly unconscious, dredging hints from sound and syntax alike, guided equally by prods and obstacles. Always on edge, ghost reading entails a séance of undertones.

To shift metaphors, I conceive of these experiments as grafting a tapering last branch of narrative to some remaining flow of nutrients from the rooted parent trunk. In venturing such textensions, of course, I am certainly out on a disciplinary limb of my own devising. But not entirely alone there. I like to think of such freed-up possibilities of analysis in company with Stanley Cavell's brief against the charge of "reading in" in *Pursuits of Happiness* (1981), where he introduces the notion of a "tertiary text" that exceeds both the primary aesthetic document and the correlative secondary text of interpretation.[6] He certainly wants an idea of "reading in" as a thing that may "go too far," but at least "on a real track"—yet that can do so only by aptly questioning any determination of "far enough" as a natural limit.[7] He eventually decides to characterize his own "tertiary" responses to his chosen films as a new "performance" of them, as if of a musical score, always with interpretation—and improvisation[8]—built in: not just a rerun under scrutiny, a textual rescreening, but something more like an invested enactment—as if offering a dialectical third term above and beyond reading a work and commenting on it.[9] So with the yet more obvious "tertiary" status of my closural ghostings in this essay, assuming a manifestly "real track" before inching farther along it: before edging past the narrative's own textual status and limits, that is, toward some newly scored, sometimes expansively orchestrated, cadenza on analysis' own part. In Cavell's terms, this may be an over-reaching "performance," a variant of overreading, but one that goes "too far," again, only as the sole mode of "knowing" just "what the end is."[10] And while Cavell means "end" in the sense of intrinsic limit, exhausting all plausible implications of a primary text, my narrower concentration on actual last lines—along with their alternate sense of an ending—operates in the same spirit. These echo chambers of textension—only when performed as such—locate narrative's last dispensary of inference before dispensing with plot altogether.

Grounding any such claims to the taking-on of a text in performance, and well short of some undue co-optation, is a foundational axiom of the phenomenology of reading. For whether in an avowed (even if fictionalized) first person discourse or in the impersonal depictions of omniscience, "in reading I am the subject of thoughts other than my own."[11] Not just the target, but the *enunciating* "subject." In the clearest case, a narrator's "I" is mine in articulating her words; her thoughts and actions come into my ken by direct cognitive proxy. In close reading, this mental annexation is hardly disbanded. So one more clarification to clear the air: the recycled air in which these forthcoming extra paragraphs aspire to their proverbial second wind (at the close-out of this volume's experimental essaying). The gambit of such writing is simply a reminder that we always think out literary meaning in words (rather than receive it finished, unbidden): to begin with, in the authorial idiom of those words nearest at hand, leached by association from the text in front of— or just behind—us. As a manifesto for critical self-consciousness, the challenge involved is rather the reverse of any gauntlet thrown down to overzealous invention. Try *not* doing something like this in the pondering of major writing: try *not* ruminating on it in language at least loosely borrowed from it while burrowing back to some new but (again) always immanent depth.

To *read reflexively* in this way, as a saturation in the language of story, is certainly to be keyed up for the verbal logistics of the summative, of locutionary closure, in a book's final phrasing. To close in on the convergent vectors of a concluding moment is to press harder—and therefore sometimes push farther, beyond formal specs into engendered speculation. Such extra exertions amount to reconstructions of the latent in the verbal layout: less a surplus than what poststructuralism understands as the *internal* supplement.

In the theater of interpretation as performance, it can seem as if one or more subtexts—given for once their walk-on parts—are taking their own final bows. I stress again that what remains immersive about this approach can only be felt to rest—with the work of language in its working upon you: the channel characteristics of the medium experienced as such. This kind of close reading is never the foreclosure of script in determined sense. It is for this reason that closure itself is no impediment to a text's further repercussions. One lets the best film endings dim slowly on the retina of affect; we live ever after with their afterimages—endings that don't want to end, that we don't want to *let* end. Last paragraphs, too, can have their own penetrating afterimages, spontaneously enacted—Cavell's "performed"—in rereading. To see how in more detail, we turn to further examples: wordings that may seem operating upon us like the slow iris-out on details suddenly foregrounded in their very exit from the field of further view.

Unfinished Business

Taking up with Dickensian closure in the next decade after Brontë's "Reader," we find his most famously rhetorical ending, his most fluent and mellifluous, charting a very different relation of marital intimacy to its social surround than one finds in Austen or Brontë. Arthur Clennam and Amy Dorrit have just signed the marriage register in *Little Dorrit* (1857). They have paused for a deep breath at the last of this penultimate paragraph, precipitating the anaphoric loop of the next with an incremental, marginally advancing emphatics not needing the typographic mark-up (given here) in Dickens' own text:

> They paused for a moment on the steps of the portico, looking at the fresh perspective of the street in the autumn morning sun's bright rays, and *then went down.*
>
> *Went down* into a modest life of usefulness and happiness. *Went down* to give a mother's care, in the fulness of time, to Fanny's neglected children no less than to their own, and to leave that lady going into Society for ever and a day [...].

After another complex sentence fragment, the couple is posited again as plural subject in a final if crowded panorama of descent, adverbially tempered by the inner peace they harbor:

> They *went quietly down* into the roaring streets, inseparable and blessed; and as they passed along in sunshine and shade, the noisy and the eager, and the arrogant and the froward and the vain, fretted and chafed, and made their usual uproar.

Among the many things to note across such cadences of downward progress is the answering "up" buried in the etymology of "uproar." What inevitably rubs against the couple's incarnate modesty and virtue in the friction of social space gets the elaboration it hardly requires in the fervid music of their denouement.

Then, too, this ultimately dissonant music includes, right at the end, another vertical and entirely tacit etymology in the unsaid pressure cooker of "up/rising": exactly what the meliorative function of the new couple's generous domesticity is meant to appease—and against whose French depredations so many of Dickens' conservative closures are poised to stand, even here in what George Bernard Shaw saw as Dickens' most acerbic and Marxian book. The inert axial metaphor of "uproar" might thus have burst its syllabic husk in a final, if only for the reader implicit, seeding of irony. Had the passage gone (gone on) like that below instead, just a little further than that last and perfectly chosen prepositional noun, "uproar," it would only have been moving in an already aimed direction. This is a direction in whose tracks critical rumination is readily led to follow—and in part by continuing to register social friction in the key of phonetic fricatives, where even "forward" as "froward" can be recognized as a typifying pushiness matched elsewhere by phrasing's own phonetic vectors in the rough chafing rasp of society's grating self-interest. If we've picked up the sound play, it may well play on in aftertone:

> Up the roar from all the frenzied desperation, the shove of vast and fevered effort, the avarice and vice, that madden the city's daily race. Up from the clattering carriages in their greedy speed to the Exchange. Up equally from the hawker's street carts and the groaning belly of the pauper's pleading need. Up from the moans of disease and the weepings of grief. Up from fame and vanity and famine alike, of congestion and collision, of humdrum clamor and the bellowing yells of revolt, all lifting thick like choking smoke from the raucous factories of desire and the mills of humiliation. Up it rises: a roar kept from more violent uprising only by the offices of private good. A lifting tumult, into the din and midst of which any committed human industry, our new and devoted couple's now included, must step down, take its bearings, and make its way.

The transparent fact that none of this *needs* saying, in extrapolation from the lexical and phonetic subtext of the said, is in fact exactly the point.

A more complicated sequence of syntax rather than just modification seems covertly in service four years later at the end of Dickens' revised alternate ending (the supposedly "happier" one) to *Great Expectations* (1861). When Pip encounters an obscure, thrice-mentioned "figure" coming along the footpath of "the desolate garden" in the "ruined place" of Mrs. Havisham's former lair, he finally recognizes "it" (after five repetitions of this neutral pronoun) as the very figure of his aspiration, Estella herself in person yet symbol still. At which point he is cajoled by her, against typically thin resistance, to say that they are "friends." But she then adds, with no question mark, "And will continue friends apart." Though cause for erotic optimism is thereby kept quite in check, Pip takes, rather than is given, her hand so as to lead her away (at least a little way) toward the future (across the ambivalent fulcrum I've italicized below). Yet it is a future by no means as palpable in prospect as was the original ending's last and irreversible retrospect, where Estella is recognized, by Pip at least, to have sensed the entirely imperfect tense of "what my heart used to be," a passion over and done with. But even under revision, in his looking out literally in front of him, things ahead have no *positively phrased* expectations:

> I took her hand in mine, and we went out of the ruined place; and, as the morning mists had risen long ago when I first left the forge, so the evening mists were rising now, and *in all the broad expanse of tranquil light they showed to me*, I saw no shadow of another parting from her.

In none of my previous commentary on this notoriously revised passage and the irony of its in/transitive predication—with its expectant wait for a direct object called up short by in-transit reconstitution as a subordinate clause—had it occurred to me, until drafting the essay on Dickensian punctuation included in this volume (chapter 5), and despite the ruined garden locus, to identify Pip's last syntax (ventriloquized by Dickens' elusive irony) as the classic "garden path sentence." Yet we find here a moderate form of self-correcting models like the classically pure instance "the old man the boat," where a nominalized adjectival plural must delink the straightforward modification of "*old* man" assumed first time through. (My opening Tennysonian "Our hope to gain," with its infinitive flip, is another if milder variant. Or, to concoct a further instance, "The electronic micro chips / away at all conception of the humanist macro.")

In the case of Dickens, one can well listen to such an effect as it might have been intoned at the family hearth, no comma in earshot. With Pip's "in all the […] light [,] they showed to me," the sense of "in all this shed light they disclosed the following vision" must retrace its steps to "in all the lighted scene they made visible, I saw […]." The grammatical object is shunted off to an iteration of blinkered subjectivity, optically figured. The comma that can often disambiguate such a garden-path sentence—as in a construction like "Whenever Pip thinks he truly sees [,] the light / may itself blind him"—is already there in his own given sentence, but a split-second too late to secure our own focus at the start. In the essay "Point/Counterpunct" above (chapter 5), partly as a function of just that jarring punctuation, we have seen how easily ChatGPT is thrown when tossed the bone of rewrite (and thereupon chokes). So imagine Pip catching on to the mental grammar that he himself has been caught up in. To do so would be a belated act of critical irony contoured on the underside of a quite natural and transient linguistic conundrum. No technical term is required to see that Pip may still be leading himself down the proverbial dead end of a literalized garden path—as if he himself were trying, not just his author Dickens, to draft a somehow less depleted finish. And yet the result comes across as something like a negative title scene:

> I didn't put that quite correctly, it might seem, in this last page of my poor story. For what indeed can mists—thickening or dissipating, either one—show in their own hazy form? And, anyway, how can we think to see the future foreshadowed in a revealed evening light? But, then again, when have I ever before seen rightly what was there before my eyes? What I really should have written, or maybe in a sense did in the wavering resolve of my own script, is that what the mists always showed to me, whether in themselves or in their dispersion, was nothing in particular, no object beyond what I had it in mind to see or not to see. And in this very moment it was borne in on me, more clearly than before, that I no longer had any expectations whatsoever left, great or otherwise, and that all was a matter of the here and now. And of that now, and there, all I can say is that I wasn't in the mood just then to expect yet another separation from Estella.

What Dickens drafted by way of revision is, to be sure, its own kind of mood piece. Leaving the trashed garden with "no shadow" of parting added to departure isn't necessarily a wish-fulfilment fantasy even for his beleaguered narrator. (No more so was it wholly comforting to see the very "shadow" of that parting-under-erasure in the first printings of Dickens' revision.) But without our imagined coda, what Dickens' actual redrafted passage has tried taking back from privation must still fend off the shadow of delusion cast by its own supple prose.

Afterthoughts: Logging in the Fallout

As SHOULD BE CLEAR BY NOW, ghost reading's manner of writing *on*, not over, is therefore only a mode of reading *back in*, aggravating hints into explicitness, turning idioms to motifs, syntactic slippage to slip-knots of cognition, dead metaphors to final nails in the coffin of a pervasive irony. It is a rounding out by rounding back: a case of perpetuation as interpretation, transcribing the unsaid in the form of the inferred: reading in, on, and beyond. Whatever its interest, ruining the original is not its risk. Its residual wording has no equivalent, even similar, status to that of novelistic writing. In the quite visible excess of its "overstatement," crossing the threshold into some version of inbuilt redundancy, the resulting passages never pretend to match, best, or outwit the given. Far from it. Resulting only from intensive rereading, they are in the dynamic sense its resultant, taking the extra measure of convergent motifs in their vectoral force. By releasing, from stylistic concision, the latent impetus of unnoted semantic and affective energy, ghost reading only attests by these means to the potent dramatic compression under which major writing operates. Such writing's spectral after-trace scarcely labors (under any delusion) to be aesthetically comparable, just thematically compatible, with its prompt text—but that correlation involves, under the narratographic paradigm of microplotting, a certain glancing stylistic affinity as well. Such speculative exercises amount to reverse engineering the thought process—or, better, the thoughts processed in phrasing and figuration—that must be imagined, in the context of all that precedes, to have gone into the author's still entirely definitive half (Conrad again) of the writing. The supererogatory n+1 of the attached paragraphs imagined here—serving almost paradoxically to "open up" narrative closure—are therefore mounted less to amplify a master text than to complement and expand ordinary reading under its more typical conditions of silent interpretive paraphrase. They offer a sometimes ungainly, but not I hope unprofitable, torque of the norm: a norm we are following Conrad in enacting as our *silent partnership*, or say our not-so "secret sharing," in the imaginative labor of textual completion as comple*mentation*.

In receiving the passed baton of hinted sense in the last relay of inference, these narrational paragraphs are by definition too *wordy* to pass for more of the gifted original. Yet since their words "think out" a last passage in some inevitable vestiges of its own style, these cognate operations can seem to weigh in with an integral fitness. Even as mere tagalongs planted to flag a latent thematic pressure point, their role as textual gloss hews closer to interlinear, if you will, than marginal. Thereby encroaching on the nuances they are moved to discriminate, they hover between critical thinking and descriptive writing. We've all been there, more or less often. This is what it sounds like—I discovered at least for myself—if I tried to transcribe the process. The point is hardly to "put the literary back in criticism," but rather to smoke out further dimensions of critique: an extra rhetoric of irony tucked away in literature's most considered turns—and figurative creases—of phrase. The purpose is to appreciate how much of the original novel's closural rhetoric, how dexterously, is maintained at the level of sheer lingering suggestion.

Logging this in, I'm suggesting, is only the natural discourse of afterthought—as one can sense in the further reverb of an actual Epilogue. A decade before our Dickensian examples, in Herman Melville's great work, *Moby-Dick* (1851), the narrator Ishmael also has his own extra say in an official afterpiece—to which any ghost reading must then be subsequently appended in the mode of secondary reframing. The novel ends officially in draping the vortex of the sinking Pequod in a funereal trope binding death to a chiming with time itself ("shroud"/"thousand"): "then all collapsed, and the great shroud of the sea rolled on as it rolled five thousand years ago." With the "as it" a form of immediacy as well as comparison, the sense of an immemorial continuum is there in the continuous echoic past of "rolled" and "rolled"—rather than the more logical, rational, anthropocentrically historical "as it had rolled." Human temporality is reengaged, however, for the rescue of the novel's frame narrator in the Epilogue, where a ship—traced by a stylistic zoom lens—comes "near, nearer" (hear "near 'n' nearer") to rescue Ishmael from the buoy of Queequeg's floating coffin—life adrift after death, like prose after closure And hovering over the last of this Epilogue—"It was the devious-cruising Rachel, that in her retracing search after her missing children, only found another orphan"—might be intuited a potential postscript, tightening again the overall narrative frame by returning to the novel's famous opening line, with its keynote allusion to exile in the wilderness: "Call Me Ishmael." Something like this, then, we might seem unconsciously to read without an extra word written:

> Then it was, after a baptism in reverse from all this lethal sea, that I truly came into the wanderer's name by which I have told you to know me. It was as if I had been christened in fateful rescue by a ship that now plowed on, forward upon the fearsome deep of those wildering waters, its newest foundling nowhere bound.

A "ghostly baptism," in the author's phrase, as we haunt the book at its edges—no horizon in sight.

Last Taunts of the Gothic

THE HAUNTS OF TEXTUAL AFTERMATH can be yet more explicitly postmortem than the examples so far. Two years after the posthumous publication of Austen's last completed novel, *Persuasion*, 1819 saw the blockbuster debut of Mary Shelley's first, with its strategically distancing epistolary frame. In the long denouement of Walton's last letter, dated September 12, the textual transfers of *Frankenstein*'s storyline as documentary lineage close in the crosshairs of a compound irony: the eponymous Victor dead in defeat by the results of his science, Walton the practical explorer and journal-keeper cowed into return from questing by his angry crew. After Walton has already internalized in free indirect discourse his mission to annihilate the creature—"The task of destruction was mine"—Victor's language may be heard to rub it in by an extra smudge of lexical echo: "Yet I canno*t ask* you to renounce your country and friends to fulfil this *task*." Instead, it will be up to the Creature, as we soon discover, to see to his own extermination. But this with a final geographic irony. Victor has expressed surprise and disappointment that Walton has given up his search for the true magnetic lodestone of the North Pole, in deference to the threatened mutiny of his crew, even when this is the very scientific ambition whose egomania Victor had previously counseled against. And now only the Creature himself will achieve this quest, as he explains to Walton in their own subsequent encounter, where he announces that for his funeral pyre "I will seek the most northern extremity of the globe." And with the last seen of him, he is, in more than a triple play of phonetic linkages, "borne a*way* on the *waves* in *darkness* and *distance*." The verbal recession of his phrasing operates like a Shakespearean hendiadys for the distant obscurity—or obscuring distance—of the unportrayed last scene. After so much of "Walton, in Continuation," Shelley might have given us "Walton, Discontinuing":

I hardly know what I write. In distant darkness—or in the dark distance—call it what you will. All perspective now is blackened for me by the same vanishing point. Nor can I drive from this backward view the terrible figure of the Creature in his despair, let alone the disturbing figure of speech in his parting words—as if dictated by Victor's own fear of racial propagation, its threat now to be purged only by conflagration: "Soon these burning miseries will be extinct." Immolation is his only wish, a species purge of one: "I shall die, and what I now feel be no longer felt"—that implied "shall be" almost a prayerful "let it be no longer." But I have tried in my notes, and then when recasting them for you in my letters, to make you feel just how he *did* feel—as if he were a character in a novel, open to reading. That is why I shared with you the way Victor himself, still the demonic artificer even when editing my journal, was bent on "breathing life and spirit" into his "conversations" with his expressive creation and nemesis—as if the poor misshapen being were only an imperfect document of genius, waiting a further animating draft. Be that as it may, my own aggrieved writing is now wholly given up, at last, in being given over to you.

A later gothic tale, in its own greater stylistic concision and restraint, would invite a less wordy and word-conscious aftermath. In a story whose pivotal irony is grammatical—caught in the brilliantly terse double valence of the objective versus intransitive predication in the radical comma splice of "Yes, I had gone to bed Henry Jekyll, I had awakened Edward Hyde"—any such ghostextual p.s. as mine, next, can afford to be decidedly succinct. The novella has closed with the doctor's written narration of his own "strange case." Having reached pharmacology's dead end, Jekyll is afraid that he won't finish his text before his drug-emergent double "will tear it to pieces." On our behalf as readers, internal closure is imperative to secure the manuscript's outer transmission. In testimony's "true hour of death," Jekyll abjures all interest in Hyde's fate as concerning "another than myself." That very word "myself" at once converts the reflexive pronoun to the antecedent of his death sentence in its last distancing demonstrative: "Here then, as I lay down the pen and proceed to seal up my confession, I bring the life of *that* unhappy Henry Jekyll to an end" (emphasis added). But since the reading act is never finalized by set type, we may be induced to imagine exactly the immediate aftermath of which Jekyll has washed his hands—as if in a last surgical scrubbing. How then (a performative interpretation might loiter to ask) might a never to be decontaminated Mr. Hyde take final command of his own christened infamy in a punning usurpation ("myster-y" and "kyll" included) of his capitulated master's textual confession, speaking in the obtruded and foreignized italics of a self-alienated tongue?

"Here, then." But where is that exactly? Hear too, then, for all I know, how the unbridled Hyde is even now worming his own words between the lines that cannot be made final in any barrier between us. *Yes, here I am still, waiting this very moment for your sleep of sleeps, from which it won't be yourself you awake. No longer being Jekyll by springing the new I of my Mr. Hyde from all mystery and suppression at last, you'll kill not me but your own will: dying Edward Hyde, not Jekyll, so that, if only for a while yet, maybe only in this one moment of mastery, all hiding over, I'd alone abide.*

The gothic dark side takes over in Oscar Wilde's *The Picture of Dorian Gray* (1890) as well. But in violating his detested festering portrait, Dorian stabs to the heart of his own ugliness—cutting through the canvas that could otherwise be used to shroud a corpse. In this climactic violence, it is as if passive grammar takes the very agents of recognition by surprise: "There was a cry heard, and a crash. The cry was so horrible in its agony that the frightened servants woke and crept out of their rooms." And soon, in the final paragraph:

> When they entered, they found hanging upon the wall a splendid portrait of their master as they had last seen him, in all the wonder of his exquisite youth and beauty. Lying on the floor was a dead man, in evening dress, with a knife in his heart. He was withered, wrinkled, and loathsome of visage. It was not till they had examined the rings that they recognized who it was.

Final paragraph, yes, but in the residuum of its irony, the last but one. What follows (not there, of course, but only below) is one supplemental transcription of what seems meant by the unsaid in that, for Wilde, uncharacteristically laconic last sentence. Such a rhetorical reflex picks up immediately on the foreboding undertone of that otherwise too routine past tense in the rather flat-footed and anticlimactic "who it was" (as given over below, italicized, to the garden path's sway of "who[m] it once was / [that] they [...]."):

> The inset jewels of those ornate rings, the showy pride of him *whom it once was* they admired and obeyed, glistened sickly against the putrescent flesh. Having served so long his unnatural glamor, the servants saw now all too clearly who he had been by that which lay there, blistered in pustulant corruption before them. What in the pocked and withered visage they recognized finally was the fury of time's deferred truth: the very picture of their master gray, the already ashen waste of his ghoulish lust for beauty, his features as wan and rotted as if torn from the grave he had somehow sold his soul to defer forever.

Gray for the grave. Even Edgar Allan Poe couldn't have topped such a final understatement as Wilde's, after all the story's psychic festering and actual gore, but, as long as half a century before, he would have tried. Remember the byzantine kinks of "Berenice" (1835): to my mind, or ear, the most unstinting distillation of Poe's syllabically embroiled prose aesthetic. In typifying fashion, paronomasia is at one with paranoia, lexical self-reflexivity with other inbred and incestuous enfoldings, pun with rhetorical self-abuse, all luscious tonguing its own palpable indulgence in aural response, every verbal turn a perversification. And thematized as such, here, in the narrator's combined oral fixation and implied castration anxiety. Increasingly obsessed with the glimmering white teeth behind his dying cousin's beautiful frail smile, the narrator cannot bear their loss along with her when she succumbs (make that climaxes) in a fit of epilepsy before their ill-considered marriage can be consummated. Though she is soon laid to rest in other than a marriage bed, the narrator finds his own way of violating her most fetishized orifice. This happens to him in some kind of psychotic stupor that has become the latest but illegible chapter in a lifelong debility caused by an overdeveloped "attentive" faculty (read: monomania). This last incident "was a fearful page in the record of my existence, written all over with dim, and hideous, and unintelligible recollections. I strived to decipher them, but in vain." He is left to read his own body instead when a servant takes up his gouged hand as material evidence—along with a clotted spade nearby—of the master's maniacal grave-robbing. The blocked memory returns decoded in a flash:

> With a shriek I bounded to the table, and grasped the box that lay upon it. But I could not force it open; and in my tremor, it slipped from my hands, and fell heavily, and burst into pieces; and from it, with a rattling sound, there rolled out some instruments of dental surgery, intermingled with thirty-two small, white and ivory-looking substances that were scattered to and fro about the floor.

Enough said, especially in its mix of circumlocution and continued repression in that lethally abstract noun "substances." The once affixed teeth he adored and fixated upon he can no longer recognize—or bear naming. Enough, but in a sufficiency otherwise pressing to be spelled out. What, one might ask in a class on the psychoanalysis of gothic fiction, has gone unsaid in this madness? The unmentioned teeth, while still in place, had been for the narrator more abstract even than these "substances," except as words to turn over in his own mouth. Varying a romantic aphorism, he had believed of Berenice that "*toutes ses dents etaient des idées*" (all her teeth were ideas, hardly doing justice to their coveted materiality). He luxuriates in the sound of this delusion in a phrasing that coasts from sibilant to, yes, dental delectation in "*dent(s) etaient des idées*." After which, as if in one emphatic noun phrase of grasped-at rational probity twice repeated, the narrator emits two more exclaimed and cross-syllabic bursts of "Des idées!"—serving, all too incisively, for the fateful "decidé(e)" of a doom (if not a tomb) sealed. This word-madness might have returned in conclusion, laying bare the whole deranged tale as some prolonged morbid pun on the oral surgery of literacy itself. It's all up for class discussion even if not down on the page. And easy to imagine here in the ratiocinative cadences of our narrator as bookish lunatic:

> All this by dint of my affliction. *Dint*, the very word! Unrelated in the annals of philological science to *dent*, and equally foreign to *dentition*, still the word has hung in hallucination about me, dug into me, and there it was again, in thinly disguised echo, when the servant showed me, so hideously to say, *my hand in that abominable crime*. For there was that soft pale member, so much like my dear cousin's own, newly "indented" by those nails of hers, in lieu of the delicate lustrous tusks she could no longer wield after my quick and savage work. Such had been the ivory treasure that I could not rest without palpating. I craved these fixtures of my *ideé fixe*, so much more eloquent than her withered sheathing lips, so much truer—as the outward sign of her imperishable skeleton—to the doom coming. Now, no man of my wide and obsessive learning could not have known, from lore folk and mythic alike, of the lascivious and macerating *vagina dentata*, though no man alive could have been beset with less fear, I was sure, of the desired woman whose frailty I had so long grieved. In admiration and love only, and yet despite all the normal wellings of desire, it was my obsession with those pearlescent appendages of her upper body that bit so steadily into my imagination, gnawed away at my sanity through the terror of her slow end, spoke to me so keenly without need of adjacent lips. The idea of those divine teeth, even in amorous possession, seemed always a bloodless abstraction, an idea radiant beyond all lust, redolent beyond all desire. But in *extraction*, how terrible! For now their enameled revelations have been wrenched away at last, so the servant tells me—and my own dented hand confirms. Oh, baffling and ghastly horror of horrors, how is it possible that, in her very coffin, Berenice writhed undead whilst I collected my dental mementoes for preservation in this miniature smashed casket—as I now try collecting my tortured thoughts?

If the story can barely be said to mean anything in other than pre-Freudian terms, these (above) would simply be more words—some of them furiously bursting forth from euphemistic cover—for what it isn't saying. Such reading-on (and so back in)—with, in this case, its macabre archetypal read-out—becomes, of course, its own kind of extraction aesthetic. Mining for meaning after the fact.

Finis in Reflex: Following the Worded Lead

MOVING FORWARD FROM ANTE-BELLUM GOTHIC in Edgar Allan Poe toward modernism, we can return to frame narratives operating less for the containment of the marvelous than for the transmission of political irony. A quintessential turn-of-the-century (and of-the-tide) case is the anonymous frame narrative around Marlow's oral field report about Kurtz and the African "cause" in Joseph Conrad's *Heart of Darkness* (1899). The unfinished business of closure in this case is the business-as-usual of colonial ransack and extraction and the moral evacuation it entails. Framed tale returns to frame tale in fading off from Marlow's long narrative across one of the most awkward em dashes in major English writing. It reads like some kind of deep subgrammatical breath taken by the halting voice of the nameless outer narrator, where even the description leading up to this mimics in punctuation the isolating, almost fracturing force of the relayed message: "Marlow ceased, and sat apart, indistinct and silent, in the pose of a meditating Buddha." Yet after setting him apart, prose sets his story into immanent reverberation. It does so as if rephrasing the atmospheric "gloom brooding" over the outset of story and vessel alike. Now, at the end: "The offing was barred by a black bank of clouds"—where "offing" bears the sense of a prospect both literal and figural. And where the phonic blockage at "black bank" invades the next phrase, with its abrupt shift of tone from scene to "seeming." For it is there that, suddenly repredicated after the *ack/ank* dyad, "the tr*an*quil waterway leading to the uttermost ends of the earth flowed sombre under an overcast sky—seemed to lead into the heart of an immense darkness." Sombr*e*, und*er*, ov*er*, with barely any breathing room in the claustrophobic collapse of the latter pairing. Darkness is the very medium of perspective in a grammar loosed to the vague and indecisive—and defensive: honest confrontation buffered by that hint of a merely figurative ("seemed") vanishing point.

Yet the blanks in any such perspective, like that of the Congo outposts on a European map, are all too easy to fill in. Marlow has reframed his own guilt with his last shipboard words about his lie to Kurtz's "Intended" regarding the latter's own last words. It falls to the outer narrator, the unnamed sailor, to reframe our inner narrator's ensuing silence in the global perspective it in every sense adumbrates, both outlines and clouds, maps and morally shadows. Blame not the messenger, unless he seems himself to partake in the collective guilt and occlusion. And so it falls to us, not so much in turn but instead, to imagine what more such a reflective seaman might—as impelling the reflex action of narrative reception—have to brood over in the wake of his last awkwardly tacked-on and hedging "seemed." Especially when such a seaman would be well aware of the river's receding horizon en route to the Congo—out along the estuary of the Thames into the North Sea and down through the Strait of Dover, out across the English Channel and past the Celtic Sea into the yawning Atlantic to just south of the equator at Point-Noire, last outpost before the mouth of the Congo: no implied turning point darker in the unmentioned but readily charted track of Marlow's telling. How would interpretation turn the "seemed" of this placeholding narrator's last words into a fuller imperial cartography? Yes, the Thames in its endlessness "flowed on ...—[and in so doing, after this spacing dash] seemed to lead" into (as *Frankenstein*'s Walton might earlier have had it) "darkness and distance." The abrupt grammatical disjuncture works to induce an imposed geopolitical overlay. For here we are reminded yet again, by this looming case in point, how the author writes only half the book, even in the texture of its last sentences.

So a further methodological generalization that the Conrad passage should readily help solidify. The "hypothesis," rather than premise, I began with—that immersive reading (as one might now rephrase the issue) isn't over till it's over—directs the verbalized "hypotheticals" collected here toward premise after all. Such shadow texts gather to demonstrate, in disciplinary terms, the way formal analysis is always some version of a creative *reading in*. It operates in this way, when directed at the last but decidedly not least among a text's sentences, in sorting out the various threads knotted off—if never quite completely cinched—at the end of any complex fiction. Loose ends send us back to the text's own rhetorical weave. And forward to its thematic castoffs. Hence this one last example from that self-appointed and exemplary half-writer Conrad, where syntax itself feels caught off guard in the rush to choke back political recognition by the language of mere analogy (only "seemed" like the nautical ingress to moral darkness). Can anyone read that famous if anonymized last British narrative sentence—in full appreciation of its wavering figuration ("heart of" as cartographic coordinate and/or geopolitical center of gravity as a corrupt abyss)—without instinctively putting more rotten meat on the bones of its "as if"?

> Seemed to lead—and does. There is no mere semblance in the menace of this truth. Leads on and in. And not just stretches, but leads *us*. In the penumbral gloom of imperial plunder, blunder, and murder, this river of no real return flows pulsing like a reverse bloodstream deep into the darkening heart of ferocity and folly. Past our flanking British life clustered civilized here along the silent widening mouth of the Thames—if that mouth might only speak!—the bloodied flood streams directly on into that nether hemisphere of rapacity and damnation.

To borrow the tacit imperialist ligature from Conrad's "uttermost *ends of the earth*," we may ask where in the end, here and in previous examples, this pressing-past-the-given-end has been tending? What has the extratext (textra?) been meant to excavate? Or ask: in this opposite of foreshadowing, what has the ghostext shown reading to be still haunted by? Summary can't answer, since every case is site specific. But a tendency emerges regarding the inertial momentum of closure. In *Persuasion*, the interpretive ghosting went just so much past Austen's phrasal symmetries as to cash out the hidden metaphor of marital investment and reward still banked for intuition in the actual finale. In *Jane Eyre*, immersive reading "corrected" the denouement, with its eschatological anticlimax focused on St. John Rivers, directing it back to

Jane's own afterthought on a lurking optical metaphor—coloring the reading aloud both of world and books to the blinded Rochester—that has him finally reading *her* aright. In *Little Dorrit*, a lexical reflex—pivoted on the down/up(roar) contrast—unfolded prose's own momentum in an even broader social perspective, where sanctified domesticity is assimilated to the rhythms of a world under further cynical critique. *Great Expectations*, rather than caught sounding the persistent titular note of expectations still clingingly unchecked, manages to equivocate the hero's vision even in its revised ending. Across the Atlantic, and many another ocean, the frame narrator Ishmael, in *Moby-Dick*, is found to float one more trope of unmoored survival in returning, by renewed if still uncited biblical allusion, to the frame's opening sentence of self-naming by direct address.

A fuller network of latent reframings in the gothic tradition began, with *Frankenstein*, in the narrator Walton's residual pity for the very tropes of the Creature's suicidal despair—and pending obliteration. Resisting, instead, the will to finality were two later endings in this tradition. Dr. Jekyll was not let rest in the othering grammar of a distancing demonstrative, nor Dorian Gray in a discovered ugliness assumed separate from his character. But Poe's deranged first-person narrator took us beyond all comparable limits in probing not just the inner linings of literary aurality but its very anatomy in the human mouth, each desecrated by an invasive surgery visited in part upon the author's own habitual wordplay. Returning to the readjusted extra dimension of a neo-gothic nested narrative in the form of a wider political frame, when edged out one more notch past an exhausted main plot, we have the speculative "seemed to lead" of *Heart of Darkness* given starker topographical actualization.

In entertaining just these exceedings of the said, there is no proposed method to be diagnosed mad. There is only the unconscious of first reactions squared, raised to the power of the text's own verbal reserves. Uncensored, let rip, these unraveling intuitions are like *talking back to the text* in the first words that come to mind, always borrowed from the source idioms before any private elaboration. Such back-talk doesn't contest but echoes the plot's outlasted last words. To *Persuasion*'s recovered "worth" we say (in short and at first, to text and ourselves at once): Bingo! Emotional jackpot! To *Jane Eyre*'s uneasy balance between secular and theological destiny: Through a glass darkly, yes, but now he sees. To the marital coupling of *Little Dorrit*: Downs and ups—the name of the game. To the habitually unseeing Pip's "saw no shadow": Enjoy it while it lasts. To the "orphan" metaphor at the end of *Moby-Dick*: Ishmael—of course! To Walton's unsigned last letter: Darkening and distanced indeed, like a tragic tale that is told. To Jekyll's evaporating "first person": You can say that again, and in Hyde's own usurping voice. To Dorian's surviving minions: Seeing is believing—for ugly is as ugly does. To Poe's obsessive narrator: Serves your brutality right—you can't even now name the "substances" you so obscenely craved. To Marlow's auditor/narrator: Seeming is the least of it. Repeatedly, then, the residual inference—even when more fully elaborated—appears to reside by design in the original. Whose leads the instincts of ghost reading do no more than follow.

Such reading in this way laminates a spectral afterimage upon a given node of closure, offering—value added?—a supplemental template of interpretation. But even as I was drafting this essay, a further justification emerged from intermittently breaking news. Exponential developments in NLP (Natural Language Processing) have rapidly reached the point where computation can imitate, however well or not, an extra line of closure for either Tennyson or Conrad, can write an entire stanza or chapter in simulation of a given author's signature effects, from Shakespeare through Henry James and beyond. Or, by the same token (of algorithmically tokenized lexical n-grams), and to the chagrin of humanities educators everywhere, artificial intelligence can, prompted from a given terminal, produce a reasonably expert term paper on the subject of a given writer's literary style. Terminal indeed: the foreseen end of *belles* letters and literary criticism alike, one often heard in foreboding. But ghost reading is its own third term. And less amenable perhaps to being rendered algorithmic. For harder to program is the kind of analysis felt from the inside out, not by the bundling of "optical character recognition" (OCR) but from actually reading (which the computer can't do) the full audiovisual resonance—and reverb—of an author's signature enunciation. And then "performing" it yet again, under fuller interpretation, as if on the same page. This is what I attempted with Dickens' last sentence in *Great Expectations* (in chapter 5), and wanted to try out again (below) on the even more shadowed prospects that bring *Heart of Darkness* up short. As pursued but not inherently privileged by such treatments, closure becomes one among many possible proving grounds. Prolonged beyond the written—trailing behind it in order, as it were, to get to the back of it—may, in this indulged reflex of response, be a way of keeping one step ahead of the software. So far so good, since this is my latest test response from ChatGPT, the best of several tries: "Sure, here's my additional sentence to *Heart of Darkness* in the style of Joseph Conrad: 'And as I stood there, staring into that unfathomable void, I realized that the true horror of humanity lay not in the darkness that surrounds us but in the darkness that resides within us all.'" Amazing enough on its own algorithmic terms, but on Conrad's merely a regurgitation of clichéd buzzwords verging on parody.

We shall have to see how things progress—if that's the word. In the meantime, Conrad's aphorism about collaborative reading doesn't imply that for every novelist's *recto* there is a decipherer's *verso*, but rather that the time-based work of narration is simultaneous with its performance as comprehended text. So I recur again to the grammatical anaphora of Tennyson's last escalated verb forms—together with that spontaneous pedagogic gameplay spurred by the domino effect of my superfluous further wording: a way of tutoring creative readers, on behalf of their writing, in the forward vectors of syntactic effect. Yet the ad hoc tactic has grown for me unpredictably definitive: another case of pedagogic practice as the road to theory. What began as a means of engaging verbal curiosity has become a gauge of reading itself: reading when understood as ingrained by paraphrase, each decipherment a redescription, the energies of the half-said indexed by mental reflection. With the demonstrations here, my curiosity has been directed at moments where there is neither *recto* nor *verso*, no story at all, left. And yet such last moments last. No matter how broad or narrow it looms on a narrative's final page, the white space at the end of a volume, inverting the hiatus at the end of a cliffhanging chapter, concerns not some pending narrative event, all such energy now spent—but the entirely potential event of interpretation. That blank is the white flag of surrendered narrative in appeal to a negotiated (even if never stabilized) truce in the mode, and cued mood, of response. Not a peace that passeth understanding, but that articulates it. Occupied in this manner, across a last page's blank remainder, is a variable swath of unmarked sheet that becomes the very mantle of the ghostext: carrying impact, by implied readerly contract, into a further analytic action pressed just past the threshold of the read. The textensions generated in this way represent blueprints for intuition, case by (unclosed) case, where close reading probes the last membrane of intent.

All the more reason for normalizing this process in review, despite its more colorful gothic figuration (as "spectral" incursion) along the way. Yet graveyard tropes are hard to shake for these last rites (and rights) of response. Again and again in(ter)ventions of this sort, attempting to vent what goes un(re)marked in a given text, do seem burrowing in order to unbury. If a redacted text (from the Latin for "lead back") is one that walks back the details it seeks to suppress, by contrast the *extractive* reading acts performed here (well beyond reference to Poe's gothic oral surgery) are designed to leverage the weight of critical association from the authorial tact of compaction. Appreciatively muscling in on what passive reception might take at "face value" (if that term of presumptive verbal surface can even be let briefly stand without a posited depth), such robust and invested reading—like so-called *immersive* screen viewing, and no less audiovisual in its silent way—becomes, to vary an acoustic brand name, typically "sensurrounded."[12] Repeatedly it is cued by phonics as well as predication and descriptive image in the work of narrative realization. But as a practice rather than a condition, an energy participatory rather than just receptive, creative reading's mode of engagement is less effortlessly engulfed in the text, almost passively, than strategically navigating it. As suggested at the start, this interactivity constitutes an attention, an attendance, scarcely "exorcised" (that was the word) on the spot by the formalism of closure. Which thus renders endings not so much the favored site but just the most readily equipped laboratory for such in-reading, all test space cleared away past the printed last word.

But let it be clear, finally, that the pitch of textual intimacy for which ghostly closeness is one characterization has a kind of inductive derivation from the everyday idioms of narrative involvement—and indeed critical uptake. There is nothing demonstrated or propounded here that should seem more than the work of ordinary literary analysis in allegorical form. Or call it a "conscription" still very much in the rhetorical thrall of imprint—especially when a text's last words are, in the will to interpretation, all one has left to *go on*. Endings are nevertheless comprehended in a manner familiar from any other hermeneutic lure (once baited), any other conjured urge to linger over a passage with a preternatural inquisitiveness (once caught). Gripped by a particular episode of wording, one mulls, dwells, inhabits the prose—its textual haunt—in a preoccupation, a pre-occupancy, hard to dispel. As a tactical amanuensis of sheer implication, you become a mind-reader *manqué*—again, and not only with dead authors, the agent of a narrative *séance*.

So these closural "variants" of mine operate less in the mode of some anomalous fan fiction than as a fantasized archival plagiarism: post script without end—a human drive to counter the abyss of chatbots' tireless resources. These variants comb a conclusion's phantom earlier draft for the phrasing and figuration otherwise laced in by ironic undertone to the finished version, over but not yet done with; they imagine the deleted on behalf of the more tightly complete. Sometimes it is only by encroaching this closely upon unbidden turf that verbal analysis can finally rebound to a synthesizing distance. In any case, one utility of such exercises—their impulse being up to a point involuntary—resides in how directly they can be transliterated from extratext to commentary, from brief clinching sequel to integrated critique. Trust me: it happens all the time. Earlier publications of mine have certainly done this, until now subliminally, in regard to all the passages read (and ghost-read) into evidence here—even as their previously unconscious, and entirely unwritten, post-closural prompts are spelled out now for the first time: addenda helping estimate the writer's achieved tonal agenda.

Satellite writing of this sort, of any sort, can have its own mass, specific gravity, velocity—and determined purview. Its orbit is powered by more than mere reflected glow. Atmospheric diffraction helps with seeing the centering object in variant lights. And then, in terms closer at hand in this volume, there is the further prismatic optic introduced to register traced shape as formal inference, however oblique. A recent study defends "secondary" criticism in general on creative grounds, "because it makes something new."[13] Not just new again, its topic text freshly understood, but a making of new verbal work in and of itself. Understood in this way, criticism is more than a paratext: instead, an original written object sent into the world, subject to its own protocols and rhetorical surprises. To be spurred by wording to an ensuing phase of one's own phrasing is certainly the spirit of ghost-reading as well, though more intimately tied than usual to the language that inspires it: not just making something new *from* literature, but *in* literature, catching the rhythm of a sponsor text, coasting the rim of its exosphere from newly angled tangents under enhanced magnification—and in this way making for its own peculiar version of writing in refraction.

"Ghosting" is one term for the textual deflection induced by such a remove from closure as intractably said and done. If in most cases unconsciously, residual wording generates interpretation as its own mode of apparition. Especially on the point of closure, if you're really *into it*, your attention hovers as a resident if transient *medium* of the very textual intention you can't yet let go of. And for whose still emergent subset of messages your own phrased recognition serves as telepath/telegrapher—routed along lines always partly your own as committed visitant, or mere onward traverser. These, as we know, are paths of stylistic as well as thematic percipience—and empathy—that may well overflow a story's inscribed last words. At this degree of reactive attention, and with all shadings of the preternatural put to one side for the moment, what one understands as ghost reading can be felt indeed to reactivate the very s/pace of composition. In its aspect as criticism, its transferential act approaches (here in both earned senses of the stressed preposition) to reading *in* the author's own voice: a reading that enunciates what it intuits. With a particularly loaded closure, what you *get out of it* may find its best measure in how hard it is to leave behind. Caught up in this way, the critical reader—as all but an involuntary revenant—countersigns writing's own script in phrasing its penumbral doubles. This is why—on exit, but anywhere else as well—ghost reading names a hosting of the meant within the intentionally unsaid.

Notes

1 [Ed.] See William Empson, *Seven Types of Ambiguity* (New York: New Directions, 1947 [1930]), e.g., chapter II on "double grammar"; "double meaning" (x-xi, 70, 81, 138, 228); "double syntax" (2, 49, 55), etc.

2 Previously entertained in the context of my screen readings, this is a close-gauged approach set out first for literary study, and often in my analysis since, in *Novel Violence: A Narratography of Victorian Fiction* (Chicago: University of Chicago Press, 2009). [Ed.] See also Garrett Stewart, "Mapping the Narrative Substrate," in *Attention Spans: Garrett Stewart, a Reader*, ed. David LaRocca (New York: Bloomsbury, 2024), 117–29.

3 Joseph Conrad's ubiquitously cited 1897 letter to Cunninghame Graham.

4 See *Dear Reader: The Conscripted Audience in Nineteenth-Century British Fiction* (Baltimore: The Johns Hopkins University press, 1996). [Ed.] See also "Re: Reading Under Address," in *Attention Spans*, 77–87; a glossary entry there describes *conscription* as "the co-production of textual affect between script and readerly contribution, whether invoked by direct address (interpolated) or acted out (extrapolated from) in an internal reading scene." And to close the circuit, *interpolation* as "the often paired modes of inclusion and induction that divide up the reflexive field in the narrative work of conscription." Ibid., 341, 343.

5 Hence the eponymous trope of my most recent book on literary (and screen) style, *The Metanarrative Hall of Mirrors: Reflex Action in Fiction and Film* (New York: Bloomsbury, 2022), where that level of "actionable" interpretive response can

seem limned in advance by the give-and-take of immediate textual recognitions. This analytic resonance or "reflex" is an inbuilt framing of response by phrase—as carried, in the textual "excess" of the present experiment, out beyond the last words printed into their inertial paraphrase. But in none of this do I imagine myself doing more than exaggerating into the open a process familiar to serious readers when left "with" closure, and to your own devices, in the contemplative space between a writer's last lines and their re-faceting by afterthought in the beveled mirror of response. For it is only then that you follow out (and fill in) given nuances along the slant of a barely delayed and productively skewed *re(fr) action.*

6 Stanley Cavell, *Pursuits of Happiness: The Hollywood Comedy of Remarriage* (Cambridge, MA: Harvard University Press, 1981), 35, 37.

7 Cavell, *Pursuits of Happiness*, 35.

8 [Ed.] For more on improvisation, see *Music with Stanley Cavell in Mind*, ed. David LaRocca (New York: Bloomsbury, 2024), which also includes Garrett Stewart's "'A Voice Deep Inside: Cavell, Streisand, and the Reach of Song's Inner Speech," chapter 4, 97–129. See also in the present volume, chapter 3.

9 Cavell, *Pursuits of Happiness*, 37.

10 Ibid., 35.

11 Georges Poulet, "The Phenomenology of Reading," *New Literary History,* vol. 1 (1969): 58.

12 [Ed.] For more on the thematics (and prismatics) of immersion, see Paul Fry, "Immersion: The Spectator Gets Into it," and Garrett Stewart's response to Fry, "Wading In, Weighing In," both in *Bandwidths: Reading Across Media with Garrett Stewart*, ed. David LaRocca (New York: Bloomsbury, 2025).

13 Jonathan Kramnick, *On Method in Literary Studies* (Chicago: University of Chicago Press, 2022), 12. In a cursory chapter on strategies of "Close Reading," his study narrows attention at one point to modes of citation in which critics either firm up the "grammatical threshold" (41) between cited texts and commentary or try blending the two in an interplay of paraphrase and textual quotation. The distinction is straightforward and familiar. As a quite different and third thing, of course, and fashioning as such an ancillary experiment in hermeneutic procedure, ghost reading serves to spook that threshold by refusing altogether to hold fast in its role as secondary account rather than "mediumistic" participation. Ghost*readers*—roving patiently, biding their time, awaiting.

A DIALOGUE IN DIFFRACTION

DAVID LaRocca: WELCOME BACK. When last we spoke in this format/forum, it was at the conclusion of *Attention Spans: Garrett Stewart, a Reader.* Since then, a still further volume of multidirectional—call it multidimensional—criticism was convened to engage your work in conversation with a baker's dozen of illustrious contributors, a so-called *Bandschrift* operating under the title *Bandwidths: Reading Across Media with Garrett Stewart.* Now a volume of essays in refraction. With this third installment, a first question comes to mind on the heels of a merger of old (but not dated or dusty) and new pieces. After twenty monographs of varying length and scope, what to make of, in a sense, your first "essay collection"? Does a structure without a preordained thematics or thesis give some different picture of your working methods and abiding concerns, I wonder, across a more obvious dispersion of scholarly and artistic points of investigation? A bias line that accentuates a diachronic tally of your abiding scholarly studies and pedagogical preoccupations?

GARRETT STEWART: To me it does, yes, and I hope to readers. Or at least a clearer picture, if not a different one. But with nothing preordained in this miscellany, there is an unplanned symmetry, I now see. Taking a deep breath of retrospect before our resumed dialogue, I looked back at the organization of this book only to realize, really for the first time in this overarching sense, how it's all there in the leap between the first two words of the book's title ("closer reading") and the last four of its concluding chapter's subtitle ("too close for closure"). The bracket is so far from a matter of incidental, let alone calculated, word play that it depends, as witnessed chapter by chapter, on the intrinsic imaginative play of literary wording—or of emblematic image, of course, in visual media. If you're *inclined* to "close reading," your lean-in gets you steadily *Closer* (the premise). Until at the end (the consequence), such attention, having become too close for comfort in truncation, yields a restless residual version of what D. A. Miller long ago called by title *Narrative and Its Discontents* (1981)—in this case a matter of what can't be verbally "contained," as closed-off narrative *content,* even by finished script; Miller's own subtitle: "problems of closure in the traditional novel." What's left, then, is what I have in mind—only in mind, not materialized by words still on the page—as "ghost reading." Getting close enough to the generative energies of narrative you realize—especially in certain masterly and overdetermined fictions, whose rhetorical rhythms have gotten under your readerly skin—how there is nothing "sure" even in "closure" except the wish, re(tro)actively, to speak back to text as if you were penetrating so eagerly its last words as to come out the other side (not *the end* but the "other end") into a suddenly articulated space of prolonged fade-out. It is this split sense of "afterwording," leaving behind what is simultaneously trailed in unscripted phrase, that completes any given reader's move, like this book's, from *closer* to protracted *closure*.

DL: *Closer Reading,* then both book and practice alike, leads one less to closure than to *disclosure.* The "discontents" of narrative refracted here in your essays reveal new *content* and *content.* Reading aslant in this way, even when angling past script altogether, is the ultimate "refraction"—in the sense of our subtitle: ever more pathways to notice, facets to follow after. A *refractive* method is an *essayistic* one. And look how you've just now bracketed a volume that is in fact notably anchored by the first of the new essays, on the "acoustic prism" of Gerard Manley Hopkins' poetry.

GS: To this end (as entrée rather than terminus), the subtitle we hit upon for this volume is meant to forefront the prismatic nature of textuality at large as I've come to understand (and hence read) it—or say traverse it analytically, along one face or another of its interlocked inferences from medium to medium. It is this instinct that keeps me crossing between aesthetic forms, in and beyond their own sometimes inherently mixed status. As I know you agree, the multifaceted dimensions traced by this volume are textuality's own, well before exegesis, mine or anyone else's. My own resulting "essays in refraction" have come about, and are arrayed here, to catch the glint, the hint—and trace the shimmers and shadings—of textuality's own unexpected illuminations.

DL: Just so. Certainly it was no surprise to me that you're disposed to promote the idea of reading as its own kind of prism. Even before the acoustic prismatics of your Hopkins essay (chapter 4), the term reminds me of those actual glass-paged codexes you turned up as conceptualist *bibliobjets* in *Bookwork: Medium to Object to Concept to Art* (2011). Faced with such plied vitreous folios, reading as conventionally understood was both forestalled and refigured as a thing so inscrutably if transparently available—unimpeded by words—that it amounted to "textual" opacity.

GS: And then there were the wood or cement sexahedrons of book form, their own impenetrable prisms cross-sectioned or compacted as *un*written puns on one or another aspect of the presently unwritten *bibliobjet*. Or the battered and defaced books troping on everything from textual vulnerability to deserved radical vandalism. I recall how exciting it was to be led by Bill Brown's essay in *Bandwidths* to works, under his analysis and otherwise, in which Black artists assault an archive of textual oppression in both encyclopedia history and legal practice.[1] Here we find bookworks in which occluded transparency stands as a figure for blocked access, in contrast to those equally illegible see-through forms you are remembering, actual glass constructs of hinged or stacked p(l)anes. Just as normative reading is the gift that keeps on giving, *prism* is the metaphor that keeps on morphing. True, its multisided dimensions recall, by way of formal containment, the sheeted inner layers of the right-angled 3D rectangle (known as a codex) on which this paradigm of interpretation—modeled on deciphered wording rather than cryptic specularity—regularly depends. At the same time, the shifted facets of attention thus conjured as prismatic are indeed always shaving away from one plane of notice to another, at angles acute and obtuse by turns. These deflections in focus, mocking all presumed difference in attention between surface and depth, oscillate until standard distinctions in whatever medium—verbal or plastic or digital—lose hold. Especially the contrast between signifying materialities as either readily transparent or headily translucent is a distinction inclined (and I choose the participle advisedly, in the geometric sense) to vanish facet by facet with each shift of vantage point along the leading edge of the reader's own analytic inclination.

DL: And something else about prismatic or refractive thinking. When titling my Introduction "A Spectrum Analysis," I must have unconsciously wanted, I now realize, a double sense of implicit "wavelengths" entailed: both a shaped tempo ("wave") and a spatial measure ("length"), both waver and gauge at once.

GS: Goes straight to the mystery of light itself, doesn't it? Like nodes of analytic registration in the flux of perception, light is both particle and wave (the way I think of syntax, actually, including screen editing). And for me the deep appeal of the prism trope is its special way of suggesting that each revealing angle from which, in any medium, "reading" strikes an interpretive spark is the mark of an illumination caught in action—or, better, *crystalized* in refraction.

DL: Something like that was the terminological motive going in, to be sure—and that trope of refraction has really paid its dues. But standing back now from the results, there is more at stake than a mere sampling of the various means by which a given critical slant, so to say, can rise to its varied occasions, one after another. We could think of it this way maybe: the effect of retrospect extends well beyond the three reprints we had space for in Part I. Looking back through and beyond their distinctive apertures, I find—and presume readers will too—that many of your career-long predilections seem newly delineated here along the canted zones and angled transitions invited at large by this open-ended prismatic model of text as such.

GS: Again, I would hope so. But with all these slanted planes, oblique angles, hinge-like edgings, tilted slopes of association, and the like, one's attention, verbal included, needs to stay unusually alert. If I may digress for a moment or two in a conversation barely begun, I can give an unexpected example from the everyday walk of life—or, in this case, its routine vehicular transport. I say this just back from London research in time to add new material to a couple of the preceding chapters—London, where some of my most intriguing intramedial encounters have taken place over the years, traversing by Tube between the British Library and the British Film Institute (BFI), as between the two Tate museums, with these dedicated expeditions linked in turn by the rewarding premium placed on Conceptual art at many of the city's public and private galleries. But this time I realized that a recurrent background feature of my more recent visits (make that background tone, if just noise for many others), has, in effect, rendered one minor charm of such shuttling transit almost allegorical (in metalinguistic terms) for my literary methods—even while problematical for some Underground riders, I was surprised to find. I'm bringing this divergence up now, with your permission, because it sums up, for me, many of the issues this conversation is bound to touch on.

So back to my digression. The close surveilling of word borders—model for my sense of prismatic faceting and transmedial linkage in the other arts— has consequences, I discover, for real-world lexical wit and its public-service injunctions. I'm referencing here the considerable debate on the internet over supposed confusions in the Transport Police's motto for suspected irregularities on the Tube. The typically British way with public wordplay in all manner of signage (including phonetic puns in the grand Victorian tradition of *Punch*) is in this instance, though unacknowledged as such, castigated online by numerous disgruntled auditors for the way it can supposedly flummox foreigners as well annoy locals. The audio message under critique, in its variation of the US airport slogan "If you see something, say something," plays deliberately on the indistinguishable shift in enunciation from a phrase of imperative action to one of past-participial achievement. Be assured that all alerts will be sorted out by the authorities, that's the message; your important job is done by reporting: "If you see something that doesn't look right, speak to staff or text British Transport Police 61016. We'll sort it." Brief but dramatic pause on the way to the mimetic leap of faith in the jump-cut, flash-forward finish: "See it. Say it. Sorted." One and done, faster than you can say two words when sounded as one across a broken parallelism. Naturally enough, I always warm to this time-lapse wording—a self-performing case of no sooner *said* than *settled*. It's a case of syntax as wave motion again, I realize: particulate diction swept up into sentence rhythm at the speed of light—or at least of ear's sight. (And I was of course interested to hear since from a British colleague that "sort it" is mostly a middle-to-lower-class idiom whose strategic effect in this case may be to soften the authoritarian imperative of the message, to cozy it up as something of a home truth.) For some voluble members of the interpellated public in their

Web venting, however, this verbal transposition is too clever by half(tone). "Is it sort it or sorted?" asks a chorus of Google disquiet, more than one respondent objecting to either possibility as misleading. Where is the agency in all this? So it goes. To generalize by audible example, many a clever verbal turn—in full phonetic leverage—may not charm all ears. Over those London loudspeakers, the homophonic trajectory is for many a flop. One person's catchy internal rhyme (*sort it/sorted*) is another's nagging snag. Why resort to that sort of thing? Poetics and civics, it would appear, aren't always a perfect mix.

DL: Your exegesis has a fine way of suggesting that you yourself might have written that slogan, rather than just speaking now (tacitly out loud) about it, indulging its wide imaginative ramifications for the complexity of everyday language use.

GS: I'd surely have been prepared, if so assigned by municipal administrators, for the consternation it courted, even if disappointed that verbal wit couldn't win the day. But I have been featuring this wordplay as all but "allegorical" for me, not just pleasing. Where the civilian vigilance enjoined by this transit catchword, a literalized surveillance *watch*word, falters for many at the level of verbal persuasion, for me such a "turn" of words (especially in its ubiquitous poster form) elicits, on reflection, its own kind of model for a mode of phonotextual—and eventually narratographic—reading: *seeing* what is written, precisely by *saying* it (as you suggest, virtually out loud), and thus tracking (*sorting* through) its twists of inference in the mind's ear. As an itinerary of the word even when such wording is not flashed past in subterranean transit, this phonic attunement is what Hopkins insists on, as discussed in chapter 4, as the *reading out loud of the page* in both senses, as if "paper," in his odd personification, were enunciating its own slippery inscriptions. Seen, sounded, sorted: the art of reading. Or in the alternate registers of visual art to which London has so often offered me medial access: noticed, annotated, read.

DL: So let's call this so-called digression an excursus on verbal as well as research excursions—one that, we may also say, *un*packs quite a wallop, to say nothing of a punch line. In terms of chapter 7 above, "sort it" develops the *negative imprint* into a proof-positive—"sorted"—under your instinct to see what is said in the sounding out (for us, with us). Courting aural attention to counsel sensory impression. At which point, long after we've disembarked from such urban transit lines (heading for sentences instead), your complementary motto "noticed, annotated, read" would include a spur to (long *e*) *read* on.

GS: I'm with you there, in part because literature is full of such ludic double plays. It's a matter, in this case, of inverted delineation: an operational either/or. Flop or not in that Underground messaging, the fillip is a cognitive flip. You can't keep both "sort it" and "sorted" together in the same plane of determination.

DL: Nor keep even other contingencies warded off, I suspect, once that plane of loosened association becomes the proverbial slippery slope. Given that London is one of the most polyglot places on the planet, one feels special empathy for the unsuspecting linguistic immigrants who may think they hear (perhaps via their audio-translation apps or AI transcription aids) neither "sort it" nor "sorted," but "sordid." A kind of false-positive pun?

GS: That's the way the dice roll, tossed into such contrapuntal "sorting," whenever, as in the intended Underground case, the ear dices one word into two, or splices vice versa. If, at a different scale of syllabic slicing (sort/ed; sor/did), that softer *d* hardens the phrase to the critique of an unsavory security state, more Orwell than Empson, there's no "policing" the ear against this kind of linguistic license. But no guarantee either—students stand warned!—that a given pun may "work" in literary analysis. As with the prose poem of that Tube mantra, you're at least *expected* to have signed on for the echoic ride. Context sets certain parameters, if not in stone. One plane of determination, albeit slippery, is not hospitable to all possibilities at once, which reminds me to say somewhere—and here is as good a place as any—that the Necker cube may be the purest of prisms in this book's audiovisual sense, its gestalt alternation drawing us into the abyss of reversibility along edges and angles that can't finally be stabilized.

DL: And its equilateral prism might have offered a fallback cover design—with its own push/pullback wavering—for this very anthology, whose chapters have a way of revealing, not just in "Negative Imprints in Conceptual Art," the often inverted relation of source to an output in which the former causality is still found latent or oscillating. (Readers can look to page 131 of *Attention Spans* for a graphic variation on the Necker-effect by your own Escheresque hand, and also consult direct references there to the cube on pages 70, 259, and 290.)

GS: Drawing the denatured codex into the conversation, your mention of "anthology" form routes us round (again) to your earlier question about what feels different for me in offering up this kind of essay collection. A case for the kind of fluctuant textuality across media we've begun discussing is best made, I like to think, as spaciously as it has been here, with a spread of evidence not indulgent, essay by essay, let alone unfocused, but simply freed up. And on this score—all thanks to you—the genealogy of this collection is not just fortuitous but instructive in regard to its final shape and potential use. *Closer Reading* ramifies in detail, one essay at a time, a sustained (and I want to say sustaining) interpretive tendency even in the present departure from my normal habits. In the past, as you know, I always tried to make "books" (a highly loaded term when under press duress to hone the topic closer to the bone)—tried to or was told to—not cullings of disparate essays for collection. This often meant dropping the most peripheral interpretations among the test cases for a given monograph's thesis—for reasons of volume length or topical overreach, the latter whether historical or thematic. A kind of "tough love," those excisions. One such cut-away chapter was an earlier version of the second essay reprinted here, "The Foreign Offices of British Fiction," as originally rerouted from *Novel Violence: A Narratography of Victorian Fiction* (2009), where it illustrated (one referee found) the method of the subtitle, alright, but not directly the eponymous theme or the bracketed period. (Out it went, being concerned with E. M. Forster as well as Charles Dickens, and less with violence than with its figural equivocations around the tropes of death and immortality). These perennial university press limitations on breadth or spread, or call it these guardrails against mission creep, have had their own rewards in the tightening of overall claims, but there was always a price to be paid, cumulative over time, a curtailing of curiosity in the name of expedited argument.

DL: As you imply, though, this honing and hewing certainly has had its advantages. But then there seem no paucity of "occasional essays" either, in your formidable catalog, recalling on this front "Timelines: A Topographical Bibliography" assembled for reader-researcher convenience in *Attention Spans* (348–54), and handily so with your writing subsumed beneath orienting thematic subheads.

GS: I wasn't exactly hamstrung, that's true. But my point here is that your editorial instinct to retrieve that Dickens/Forster essay, together with those reprints on either side of it, and to put them into a foreshortened perspective with new writing of mine has staked out a quite different kind of analytic volume—a Necker cube of volumetric effects, shifting prismatically when read individually and together, in sequence and out. To be sure, monograph-making is its own unique textual discipline, and I kept in training, book by book, for the next "big enough" idea. The closest I ever came before this volume to simply following my omnivore instincts—unleashed from a thesis, tethered only to curiosity in regard to textual (and metatextual) questions still waiting be addressed—was in my catch-all rubric, its subtitle especially, for *The Ways of the Word: Episodes in Verbal Attention* (2022).

DL: One sensed the liberation there, and yet felt a center of gravity still—an irresistible pull.

GS: Sure, the "verbal" itself. Usually, though, I had tried for the linear, narrowly monolithic argument, even if my readers may have wished for more breadcrumbs marking the path—always preferring as I did the methodical to the sporadic. And I was back at it again quickly enough, moving from "episodes in … attention" to a fairly continuous cross-medial argument in *The Metanarrative Hall of Mirrors: Reflex Action in Fiction and Film* (2022). And that's, indeed, where you came (back) in.

DL: In deliberation and deed alike. With a decade of collaboration behind us—and four installments of your work featured in as many of my edited volumes[2]—something about the round number twenty in a tally of your books, a total struck with *Streisand: The Mirror of Difference* (2023)—encouraged me, with no new project of yours on the horizon to look *forward* to any time soon (I found when inquiring), to think instead about looking *back*. Luckily, you had the time and eventually the inclination for an innovative "reader." But it is only now that I see how the subtitle to number nineteen (which you just mentioned) anticipates our own main title here—where the "reflex action" you distinguish from postmodern reflexivity or metanarrativity is a tacit factor in your unique way of intercepting textuality's *prismatic* faceting.

GS: Hadn't occurred to me either in just those terms. But "reflex," you're right, is as much a term from optics as from muscular anatomy. Certainly this terminological link wasn't in play when you first broached the notion of a collection of excerpts and commentary on my cross-disciplinary career, since this was before my work on acoustic refraction and diffusion in Hopkins had rendered prismatics so tempting a template. Back then, in the preparation of *Attention Spans*, we just had that title's noun/verb play on scope and focus in mind. Once my new prose in the framing and critical revisitation of earlier work—squirming with its if-onlys and corrective second thoughts—was turned over to you for editing, time opened up at my end. I seized the opportunity for following out a few new leads "on the side"—while also bringing to completion preliminary drafts of separate essays until then on rather slow burn, or let's say no more than intermittent percolation. But there was something else as instigation as well, rather than just a temporal window while your editorial sleeves were so tightly rolled up. After answering your call for a "Stewart reader," I was now doubly self-conscious about the *way* I read, rather than just its divergent span of topics and provocations.

DL: Uncannily such a double self-consciousness proves a unique power of *Attention Spans*, if I may say so on your behalf. The volume brings that kind of reflexive consciousness to its readers as well as to its author.

GS: What I mostly recognized in *Attention Spans* was that the very act of stock-taking in retrospect had a way of breaking open unforeseen paths of investigation in several—and distinctly separate—directions at once, ranging from art practice to poetics. "Episodes" in the "ways" not just "of words," then, but of texts more broadly understood: that's what these new (s)trains of thought amounted to. I was liberated, more than ever before, to say something at length about what I saw. Then further opportunity knocked for following through as soon as possible on such "incidental" writing (freed to a full engagement with the potent aesthetic *incidents*—the broadly defined reading *events*—

that inspired it). It was your knock again, with the door opened being just as unexpected and intriguing as that of the previously suggested "reader" whose threshold we had crossed months back.

DL: I had hoped you'd see it that way. Plans for a companion volume under the title *Bandwidths*—featuring freshly rendered critical commentary from readers of Stewart set in syncopation with Stewart's own newly composed responses—might both confirm and extend the range of your influential methods.

GS: That was the new pitch alright, whose appeal seemed at first to risk putting on further hold the essays I had returned to almost simultaneously. But not for long, this fear of back-burnering. There was plenty of time left for me while you strategized and negotiated. The idea now asimmer was in effect a sequel to the "reader" on other readers' reactions over the years to my lines of inquiry—resulting, as per the working title, to shared *Bandwidths* of investigation. But which readers, ideally, and would they be interested? Have the time to engage? David LaRocca certainly had his self-imposed task ahead in the patient labors of solicitation and acquisition and in due course editorial shepherding, line by line. Given two new books in the works with you and Bloomsbury, then, but with you doing the heavy lifting at this point, first with editorial work on the compendium of excerpts (*Attention Spans*), then scouting volunteers for the subsequent print "colloquium" (*Bandwidths*), the book-writer in me could default again to the leeway of the essayist—and bring some of those new things to completion.

DL: In the bright heat of that happy season, I hardly knew you were moonlighting (how could you be?), given the considerable burden of our shared labors. And all while teaching too, as you were.

GS: Teaching was part of it, part of a particular disciplinary issue quite apart from time management. In any case, you eventually caught on, as I leaked mention of what I was currently thinking and writing about. Somewhere along the way, in the throes of those tandem anthologies you and I were engaged in planning or already wrestling into shape, first rehearsing my publication, then in the early stages of garnering responses to it (and finally my own to those), you learned that I had been otherwise writing away with no thought of book format, nor any imagined niche audience in various journals for this cluster (barely that) of latest essays. Your suggested holding-action was perfectly timed. "What about saving them, storing them up, in light of *Bandwidths'* keynote subtitle, with a twist: '*Writing* Across Media'—which is just what it sounds like you're doing in them—and then we can use them to ballast the solicited essays I'm inviting for the sequel volume, especially if they are a sparer crop than hoped for?" Words to this effect landed at just the right moment.

DL: Then we both know what happened to "derail" that provisional notion, happily enough, along current lines.

GS: Yes, as *Bandwidths* widened its titular scope, turns out that the approached potential respondents said not just "yes" but had their wonderfully full say, one essay after another. And in my thus energized responses I had, almost before I knew it, written another small hundred-page embedded monograph (on what? Let's say: reading style/styles of reading) braided through the collection. Here were thirteen new little essays of mine making for something like (counting our intervening work on *Attention Spans*) my twenty-second book—but in the process (good trouble, though disconcerting at the time) edging out any chance of collecting those (these) incidental essays alongside it.

DL: So here they are instead, #twenty-three: essays not finally made space for in the previous anthology but making space now, in a collection of their own, for some predecessor articles never before reprinted and profoundly suited to orienting the later work. Fortuitous turn for sure, since those recovered studies have of course been included as glimpses into the backstory of an evolving method so fully demonstrated in your most recent dispatches, book-length and otherwise.

GS: And not just evolving, but synchronic, one thing latching laterally (as well as leading forward) to the other. That's what strikes me now, though with an effect entirely unplanned, after reviewing the work in our marathon edit of these gathered new essays on such disparate topics.

DL: Do tell, since you've already caught the gist of my enthusiasms in the introduction, where I tried to capture (as a lure and a promise to readers) how one excitement in reading the whole array of these diachronically composed essays is discovering the way they can—and do—feel very, very much of a piece. A book indeed—a promise kept in the deed of reading.

GS: But I want to confess that such patterns and undercurrents in the latest work have been partly drawn to my attention by you, a tireless reader in *deed*. When I started tracking the editorial endnotes you were inserting, I felt the broadest scope of my procedures was being annotated, even anointed, in a subtending coherence of method or emphasis never consciously designed from one piece of writing to the next. And soon enough, more analytic issues started sorting themselves out by those interlinks of yours. It's one thing to alert readers that Joseph Conrad keeps coming up (chapters 1, 6, and 8) in postcolonial contexts related to the imperialist ironies of chapter 2 as well. Those flagged connections offer a kind of localized indexing for a book that we weren't at all sure, at that point, would end (up) with one. But your continuing (key)notes helped even the author to see conceptual "tetherings" (your figurative *and* accurate image) among the separately conceived and supposedly freestanding essays. And, at the scale of whole books—interconnections and alignments between *Closer Reading*, in all its prismatic ambitions, and predecessors *Attention Spans* and *Bandwidths*.

DL: Pattern recognition of a certain (editorial) sort, I guess. (It helps that you write without patter or padding.) Noticing the presence of common elements across time and terrain provides its own intellectual satisfactions, but the further step is mapping what such rechartings, revisitations, and in-text reflexivity might portend—even if not intend. In any case, as intervener to your inventor, I'm pleased such annotations don't feel distracting but instead heuristic.

GS: Not in the least distracting. And more suggestive than you could have realized. For in looking back over the newest of the essays in Part II, I'm led, via the spirit of your notes about tacit ligatures among the chapters, to imagine (recognize?) for the first time how two of the most narrow or arcane aspects of these investigations actually traverse all the writing. Not in a way, I should quickly add, that would have made for their gathering, under further elaboration, for some sweeping and emphatically "necessary" monograph—like *The Poetics of Punctuation in an Expanded Field*, let alone *Adversification: The Power of Negation in Media Forms*. But right there—in those fantasy/parody titles—are what I now see, thanks to your instinct for comparison, as the highest common denominators of this anthology (and its kin).

DL: I'm eager to hear what you make of such cross-referential linkages, *un*common denominators, and catalyzing precipitates. While you mull, I might simply note how—in this and related collaborations over and within your work—there is ever the question what is best said (or made explicit) by me (say, in framing remarks or endnotes) and what by you (in essay form and post-scriptural commentary such as this dialogue)—realizing all the while how much similar work is accomplished unseen and "off-site" in our email correspondence and in traded, marked-up Word files with their running lists of "threaded" marginalia.

GS: I like to assume that such labor, even though unseen by readers, is tacitly felt, and that, if so, these readers may finally have been joining me—with shared gratitude for connections first sparked by your notes—in lifting away from compartmentalized medial details in the recent essays to shared analytic entailments, squinting past separate textual challenges to an emergent unscheduled pattern. Dare I put it this way? It's as if one only gets the big picture when looking through the prism. In chapter 6, the most recently written of the pieces, I followed the lead of the *Cambridge History of Literary Punctuation* in seeking to broaden the definition of the *punct* beyond the typographic mark, only realizing long since that I had been doing this kind of expansion in the rest of the essays as well. Syncopated phonetic effects jostling the alphabetic tread of poetry were as much a matter of such "punctuation" in Hopkins as were the notorious markings of his sprung rhythm (chapter 4); beyond the explicit *punctum* of maternal photographs in two of the John le Carré novels discussed in chapter 6, decisive narrative *points* were repeatedly made by his deft shifts in "cinematographic" point of view, breaking the frame with a new field of vision; optical reversals in Conceptual art (chapter 7) punctuate the given by the made; discursive afterthoughts in prose fiction (chapter 8) are like "explanation" marks burst upon the texture of narration's own pre-coded response.

DL: Your rich and refractive response in this very rehearsal confirms the (continuing and expanding) virtues of this forum, as in *Attention Spans* and *Bandwidths*, as a space in which some of these implicit associations can be made readily manifest. Citation and allusion in your work make contact here with varieties of metamethod in the literary-critical arts—ruminations upon what we cite, what we gesture toward, and how we manage to conjure certain effects in readers (those who are company to the texts we care about). Stoking the engines in this deliberate way—and guiding the rudder for readers—has been part of the editor's keen satisfaction in piloting this triple-decker Stewart ship, a multi-modal vessel afloat all these years in its own peerless stewardship of a critical tradition the author keeps alive by reinventing and now delivering to the open seas of circulation (in conveniently curated volumes) a patrimony of wares for our judicious uptake and profitable exploration. For instance, punctuation in the fifth chapter's cited sense of "pause and effect" is certainly worth *making a point of* in all your work. As you say of Dickens, I could say of Stewart (in playful hyperbole), in style as well as topic: Stewart is all punctuation, all italics.

GS: I'll try holding my font to roman in spelling out a second through-line I found myself tracing in retrospect, back to front in Part II. Pivot point here: my turning an extra page on closure in those thought experiments of ghostly phrasal traces (chapter 8). This is an experiment that strikes me now as its own version of negactivity (in prose action), inverting printed closure to the skeletal underside of its structure as a residual impress on the reading mind. Such an effect thus aligns for me, if only when looking back, with screen narration's closed book in the mirror-flips of graphic artist Andreas Albrechtsen's "The End" series discussed in the preceding chapter 7: those simulated photogram transparencies of redrawn last film frames seen as if from the other side of the screen and the uppermost leaf of a book—and from just beyond the movie's expended plot. So, too, with ghosted closure in John le Carré (chapter 6), as signaled by the quasi-cinematic curtailing of the "finishing line" in his narrative prose. And so on, as I look back in reverse over the sequence, this time with negatory rather than punctuational emphasis—or the two together. For isn't there also a negactivity of medial function to be felt in the work of inverting expectations (precisely in order to clarify them) in the flashpoints of Dickens' comma-triggered double or otherwise troubled grammar? I'm thinking (thinking back to chapter 5) of the "birth scene" of the hero at "beginning to cry, was Pip" or the comma-pointed "close/cloze upon" death scene of Carker in *Dombey and Son* or, in *Great Expectations*, the obfuscating virtual white-out of "in all the … light they showed to me, I saw the shadow of no." Such tautly nerved prose can take back what it gives at the negating pressure point of a single punctual mark, whether melodramatic or quietly equivocal.

DL: How right it seems—yet exactly how is it?—that punctuation should be sometimes understood in light of marked negations in the speed of prose assimilation. From your penultimate chapter, for instance, one could take your treatment of Taiwanese conceptual master Kao Chung-Li's insert of image-inverting negatives into the already cinema-cancelling still frames of Chris Marker's *La Jetée* as one of your purest models for the *action* of negative punctuation.

GS: Exactly. Where the medial underlay (of the still-latent image) negates in advance what it is in the process of propagating by reverse transfer.

DL: So I'd want to ask again, not dubious, just curious, "how is it" that you are now seeing so many of your cited textual events as some such *punctum* of the medium made manifest from beneath its verbal or visual results?

GS: Textual density is certainly the beginning of any answer there, where so-called inflexion points can be far from obvious in the thick of things, with no exclamation marks as signposts. Working all the way back across the chapter sequence, I would now claim that the principle of negactivation can apply even to those enjambments in Hopkins (chapter 4) where the rove-over, in either grammar or rhyme, cancels one node of linear closure to refigure a momentary new continuity. One verse line can require, I might also say, the perverse ghost reading of the last, with syllabic or alphabetic susp/endings as revenant eventuations. Then, too, a figure/ground gestalt like that, where verse seriality reverses or revises grammatical expectation, can be construed as its own kind of double punctuation, emphatically and/or. But getting too thickly in the weeds like this may spoil the overhead vantage I'm finally trying for.

DL: Yet, from what you've been charting just now in your examples, these on-the-ground micro-accounts are very much in the service of aerial surveillance.

GS: Well, certainly the kind of roundtrip chapter-by-chapter flyover I've just attempted, coming and going, shows off, however late in the game, one benefit of such an anthology of essays: it helps "collect" at least the writer's own thoughts.

DL: Collection and recollection in tandem. And the teacher's thoughts too, I would imagine.

GS: Sure, but in a very special understanding of e-duced interest, it should be admitted. More pointedly than in teaching any particular swath of the expanded canon, there is a bit of "mission," rather than mentoring, in my broader medial work. That penultimate chapter on Conceptual art is the outlier here, certainly, as always in my recent writing: concerning zones of aesthetic thought otherwise mostly overlooked by critical analysis in the literary (or even inter-media) academy. My impetus amounts to a kind of fandom without the fanfare, just instead a mode of amplified "sharing." As tracked anecdotally in *Attention Spans*, my *proselytizing* instinct goes way beyond the sense in my first book that nineteenth prose should be treated with the same care for phrasal detail as Romantic and Victorian verse: reaching for a narrative *poetics* in that intensive sense.[3] The next phase of the proselytizing campaign: to read film that way; then Conceptual art, whether in its openly verbal "lexigraphs" or in the unlettered materialist puns of sculpted (including defaced) bookworks.

DL: Proselytizing, in the case of your work on fiction, as prose/*italicizing*—yet as also seen to pleasing effect, when transferred to song lyrics, in Ross Posnock's treatment of your Streisand studies.[4] So, truly gratifying to have you spell out what I can't be alone among your readers in having noticed: a line of development—an art of "closer reading"—that is not disabled in any way by the nonverbal or even the nonnarrative object. Rather, we find your approach complemented by one of the eye-opening pleasures of *Bandwidths*, as you alluded to above: to encounter a critic such as Bill Brown, exemplary thing-theorist that he is, taking up your terms for textually-expunged book objects, and in other commentators pursuing your ear for the inner wordplay of pop melody (Posnock just mentioned, but also Herbert F. Tucker, Susan J. Wolfson, and James Chandler[5]). And a fine thing that all of this capable handling of (art) objects and material artifacts—in song as well as in substantial if unalphabetical forms—has a way of returning one to the world of letters with a replenished energy undimmed in your promotional encouragement to look and listen ever closer.

GS: Yes, the promise of that return journey is part of the hoped-for propaganda. Currently rereading Dickens for an upcoming graduate seminar, I realized I had forgotten, in *Dombey and Son*, his description of an overworn (figuratively careworn) dictionary as having been thrown open so many fruitless times that its present limp splay of pages amounts to personification. Though the phrase "yawning open" is of course a dead metaphor for gaping wide, it recovers the full force of figuration when, under wearying requisition from the pedagogically beset pupil Blitherstone, "his Lexicon has got so dropsical from constant reference, that it won't shut, and yawns as if it really could not bear to be so bothered." Tedium transposed from effect to cause across the special pleading of that "really" free indirect discourse. Suffice it to say—my basic point here—that it's a only a step or two from that zany trope (Bill Brown's uptake in mind, yes) to all of the frozen-open, cement-embedded, seared, shredded, stitched, taped, painted, modeled, excavated, and otherwise defiantly inoperable anti-texts of Conceptual book art, including their materialized politics: their call (often answered by discursive gallery text in fine print) *to be read in their very illegibility*. And from there, another emblemizing step or two, to a wider range of inverted or vacated norms (of pigment, celluloid transparency, vinyl grooving, X-ray pastiche, on and on) in the "negative imprints" toward which I've hoped, most recently in our chapter 8, to bend some readily rewarded attention among "cross-over" readers.

DL: Which brings me, beyond your inviting sense of "mission," to the intended pedagogical leverage of these new and newly collected essays. In our dialogue for *Attention Spans*, and in your autobiographical remarks there, it was clear that graduate courses and monographs were alternate and self-propelling stages in your career, decade by decade, research everywhere feeding back into teaching pursuits. Do you have that same feeling with these "incidental" essays, I'm curious to know: a sense that any one of them would on its own, or especially in some similar combination, fuel or fund a seminar?

GS: As for doctoral seminars spawned by these latest pieces: "No" is the short answer. Too specialized, I fear, even if methodologically representative. In sitting down to them, well before you had the idea of taking them up together, I had fantasized certain readers from the roster of former graduate students I knew to have shared one or other of these "ancillary" interests, or distant colleagues aware of, and perhaps still curious about, where these preoccupations were carrying me in my continued writing. In a given run of paragraphs, an imagined reader might be pointedly interested, perhaps, in some transmedial corner of the Conceptual art scene or in the metamedial scenography of digital cinema, while elsewhere someone might be keen on the minutiae of punctuation's implicit narrative drama or the auditory nuance of Victorian poetry. One of the essays was drafted with thoughts of the several (other) rabid John le Carré fans I'd met over the years, through conversational accident, in the upper echelons of the literary academy. Talk about (though they mostly don't) secrets well kept. Certainly all of these essays begun in the 2020s felt in composition (Covid-19 no doubt factoring-in) more private or at best "interpersonal" than programmatical. But that doesn't make them— if not easy to foresee teaching a course around, like the conventional one on Dickens I mentioned preparing for—any the less typical of the kinds of attentions on my part that have previously cast their net at book length, as of course your footnoted stress on interconnections has helped me just now to review.

DL: Certainly not atypical. Which is why they are so usefully convened here—and I might add: at the ready for classroom adoption and distribution. So I wonder about the slackening of pedagogical traction you suspect. Wonder, by which I mean doubt it. Where do you see the problem, the tapering off? Is it just that there are more urgent things to cover in graduate programs?

GS: That's part of it, absolutely. Following out, just for instance, one level of methodological investment in this volume, let's say there might be a tantalizing fringe course devoted to "reading the unwritten" (whether the inferential textual messaging of nonverbal media or the white space at the end of a classic novel, viz., chapters 7 and 8)—intellectually profitable, but not cost-effective in a reduced resource economy besetting every corner of the academy, and decidedly not in the current drought ecology of graduate studies at my home institution.

DL: And too rich for undergraduate blood. But when last we pressed the "record" button on a dialogue like this, you were actively throwing yourself into your department's rapidly escalating undergraduate creative writing major, trying to do your part in the face of faculty shortage, shifting emphasis from a prose style course you had occasionally offered to an actual creative writing seminar.

GS: I gave it the old college try—and, after three whole-hearted iterations of the experiment, I didn't think it was sustainable. It was a course in "Reading Movies for Prose Writers," designed to inspire a literary kinetics that would match some of the editing techniques that make for exciting screen style, from jump-cuts to flashbacks, tracking shots to reverse zooms, on and on. And I had examples from a wide range of exciting contemporary fiction (by Nicholson Baker, Richard Powers, Colson Whitehead, among others). But these were not the kind of authors (or novels) students were reading, or wanting to write about (fantasy and memoir being the modes *du jour*), and the discrepancy between illustration and expectation seemed widening all the time. Traces of my classroom experiments can be found in the current essays, but I was energizing myself more than the students. Without being able to stir up the majority of them even in the concept, let alone the execution, of a cinematographic prose, I turned (in private deliberations and drafting) to an author I had rarely taught, John le Carré, in an effort (again above now) to appreciate what I find more cinematic in his novels—as *prose* fictions—than in m/*any* of the films based on them.

DL: Despite enthusiasms, there is a definite trend toward the elegiac in your reports from the front. Even so, and trying to carry on in the face of headwinds, we find in your le Carré essay (chapter 6) critical notes on the interaction between prose and cinema, between literary description and narrative plotting as, outside of classroom writing, they find their way (or fail to) from page to screen. Indeed, the extracurricular seems the order of the age. When you were still caught up in the activity of that creative writing instruction, we talked in our *Attention Spans* dialogue about the multiple threats posed by artificial intelligence, ChatGPT in particular, its challenge not just to authenticity but to creativity, a matter of sapped inspiration as much as of at-the-ready plagiarism. We were told that (already) the majority of "knowledge workers" use generative AI to "assist" their daily writing errands—and more: to become agents for AI, facilitating the sly takeover until it is too late for take backs. Was that latent crisis of "originality" an extra factor, I wonder, in your backing away from such teaching?

GS: Not as much as we might have predicted. The plagiarism issue is real, and graduate students teaching introductory literature courses for non-majors are being predictably worn down by the office hours devoted to detected but unacknowledged bot submissions. The only good model, besides the drastic fallback of strictly in-class writing—as if this were a nineteenth-century grammar school—is designing ways to work with and against the Machine: feed it a prompt and then openly critique the limitations of its "literary sensibility" with students. Or have them do it on their own as part of their assignment.

DL: That strategy sounds encouraging, if also fraught. Some universities have already capitulated by simply hiring faculty who specialize in "AI writing applications." Ready converts across academic ranks attest to AI's largesse as a "research assistant" and "collaborator" (for themselves as well as their students)—however much it requires further fact checking (that may never happen) or silently adapts the findings, style, and intellectual property of others. Subcontracting for retrieval becomes soon enough subcontracting for invention; the long-term temptation to rely upon such a frictionless relationship may be too much to resist. Use AI enough—feel emboldened by its confident offerings gifted without cost or mental labor—and the role of competent collaborator slips effortlessly into the key of intimate companion; no longer belaboring one's own mortal agenda, distracted by efficiency and effectiveness, AI accountability and rights permission, incrementally unguarded, increasingly lie beyond "user control" (a phrase ominously paradoxical, evoking at once power and its negation—the user nominally in control being in fact usurped, under unmanned management by the hired hand). From authentic to synthetic in a keystroke. The rapid "improvement" in such simulations is touted, then, as serviceable—and increasingly so. But by what metrics, what standard of judgment, and to what end? Even as we hold out for the transgenerational pleasures of close reading, there appears pressure to lay wagers on one's level of tech optimism. Will AI do for us or do us in? Another spectrum to (slip)slide upon.

GS: Right, encouraging only up to a point. But deep down, or maybe the right phrase is shallow bottom-up, it's the literary sensibility of creative writing majors that worries me, schooled as they are by so few courses in literary *history* and analytic *reading*, so addicted to free writing and workshop protocols (and the still-prevailing ethos that encourages attention to identity formation and its motivated expression). Artificial Intelligence is less to blame than an untrained literary intelligence. Whatever its value in the moment, my course died on the vine less as a result of LLMs (Large Language Models) than because of SLM: my acronym for how *slim* the student's own language models tend to be, how hard it was to have great moments of writing, isolated as such, get under their skin—or its phrasal variety into their data storage—for eventual deployment in stories of their own.

DL: A case of too little ambition, I'm suspecting you mean, at the level of the sentence. Putting their eggs primarily into the hatching of plot?

GS: Exactly. I couldn't blame them, but neither could I inflame an alternate interest. Still, I felt good about trying, which was of course never entirely futile. I realize now that what I'll miss about the teaching of writing per se, alongside the teaching of reading, is the chance to demolish just that distinction. I enjoyed helping students, or trying to, find in their own writing certain possibilities left dormant even on second or third drafts: to show them the *difference* between living their language, as if from the inside out, and just writing in language. Or let me revise that vitalist metaphor. I liked encouraging them, where feasible, to let their words loose to a life of their own. I wanted the students, the most adventurous of them at least, to feel the power of prodding an oddity of expression into a more engaging play on words, mining an etymological twist that wouldn't need to be tortured to be made less sheerly latent, building nuance with apposition, nudging a run of syntax one notch further into a miming rhythm. With the novels and prose excerpts we read and discussed, the point was to train the eyes of "creative reading" on their own prose.

DL: What more could one want from workshopping? But then, like dedication to learning Latin, I realize it's just too much work for many undergraduates to undertake.

GS: Yes, and increasingly for graduate students as well, this kind of "creative reading." The practice (requiring a good deal thereof) is known, if at all, to those who do (or don't) "do it," as a vestigial form of the "close reading" you mention (now more often than not in scare quotes, since it too has become suspect, a holdover on life support), especially in the case of master's students who were themselves (just) recently undergraduates, which means increasingly in some cases having mostly creative writing rather than literature courses on their application transcripts. Known, that is, the very idea of intensive "reading," more by rumor than habit: a reflex of attention for which they were never really trained, thus never acquiring what one might call the muscle memory for its regimen. To say nothing of its being frequently swept aside as "apolitical," exactly what the "Foreign Offices" essay above is meant to debunk. So, at graduate and undergraduate levels alike, I've found myself writing less with an eye to the next course than simply to setting down and getting straight the record of my own responses. The work was becoming, I suppose, more private, maybe even introverted—as attested, no doubt, by how much of it was accumulating unpublished, unsubmitted, even before you suggested my banking it for our previous volume—and now for this one.

DL: First sent to the vaults, then vaulted into action. Given how we have, in this book and the two previous volumes (*Attention Spans* and *Bandwidths*) dwelled upon the overlap of your career and a catalog of critical "turns," it wouldn't surprise the savvy that audiences for your work would be unpredictable, fluctuating, seasonal. Yet hidden in the question of a critic's fashion is the critic's capacity to fashion—and your career in its many phases finds unity in this fact. Your practice of reading is a practice of writing, where exegesis s/ melts semantics, in which ekphrasis extracts sense. *Writing* is so obviously what it is *doing*, not just "commentary." One of your avowed narratological heroes, Roland Barthes, famously distinguished in literary history between the classical "readerly" novel and a postmodern "writerly" fiction, but I always think of your close "readings" as inherently writerly in themselves. Acknowledging you as among the most intricate and accomplished living stylists in the critical academy—and certainly as unflagging as any in the urge to *phrase your way* to insights, rather than just deposit them—I wonder if this isn't, after all, the open secret of your transmedial offerings, including your productivity? You write as a prose stylist about the style of prose, but you discourse in a comparable manner (as if you were actually "translating" image into words) in your extensive and vividly written work on painting, sculpture, assemblage and installation art, and of course film. Is this writerliness, verging so often on a texture of imitative form, some kind of baseline common denominator?

GS: How can I agree, let alone thank you for noticing, without congratulating myself on some anomalous artistic bent? But I guess such tendencies of mine were after all why I thought, overconfidently, that I could teach creative writing, as if it were continuous with film criticism under the rubric of the "cinematographic sentence." Why should screen analysis be limited to the straightforward terms (vocabulary and determining limits) of journalistic movie reviews? Reactions are one thing, analytic enactions another. Why shouldn't an interpretive paragraph be as carefully shaped and edited as the montage sequence it seeks to evoke as well as report on? Or the solution to a narratographic puzzle be as tightly grooved and interlinked as the increments it has troubled to decode and reassemble? So yes, the urge to think through a formal pleasure or conundrum, on screen or wall or page, is always for me an intuitive (aesthetic) wish to find not just words for it, but the keenly right (just) ones, as multifaceted in syntax as the work's own structure. There is no dream of interpretive poetry here, but the means are not "merely" prose. I once wasn't so alone—and certainly had inspiring precedents in this line (including, beyond my own literary discipline, philosopher Stanley Cavell, of course, and art historian T. J. Clark, to name but two)—yet it seems to me a vanishing wish in criticism. When I can instill its thrills in a student here and there, now if mostly then, I know I'm still teaching.

DL: Because you've been in classrooms for more than fifty years, is it worth a moment to diagnose what you think is going on in the drop off of lift off on such matters—why students, for the most part, seem cycling through without upshifting?

GS: The usual culprits, I suppose. Distraction by many names, whether in the hunt for paying work (rather than intellectual payloads) or by the devices that call out to them: devices electronic rather than formal. At the undergraduate level: after too few books assigned in high school, aligned with little grammar before that, too many apps to leave room for literary application. But as for the graduate ranks, in screen as well as literary studies, the lure of conference work both socially relevant, on the face of it, and thus potentially public-facing—pivoting around whatever "turn" (or return) of politicized commentary has lately taken hold in their coursework (post-theory, post-historical, post-colonial, post-secular, post-human, post-gender)—can easily leave students feeling, in an increasingly identitarian institutional environment, that one-on-one *textual* "intimacy" is too laboriously private for well-advised (or even well-adjusted) professional investment. Or leave that occasional student fascinated at this level by screen or page inscription with no topic mandatorily non-textual under whose sponsorship to display any such scale of notice, thus steadily widening the methodological gap between academic claims and their demonstration. Tendentious writing overruns read attention. "I'm writing about x in y," goes the often thin "prospectus," rather than finding in the reading or viewing of y where x actually marks the spot in a genuine interpretive network. In sum, then, in the terms of our building trilogy, compromised attention spans under constraint by cramped bandwidths.

DL: That's why those books are joined by this new one in striving, even if just a bit, to right the balance.

GS: But let's face it. In my "home discipline" (yet it applies more widely as well), the real problem—and copped to in a way hardly self-promotional for a volume like this: most current literary scholars-in-training have scant acquaintance with, and little passion for, literary scholarship. Inspiration, emulation, rhetorical aspiration: these are things more completely bygone, in regard to critical writing, than it is easy to explain to someone outside "the system"—which is no longer that of apprenticeship. Sharing with students any number of essays devastatingly smart and intellectually elating can leave them seemingly unmoved (maybe secretly deflated)—and, in any case, seldom motivated to further engagement. It's not a genre that counts. As undergraduates, they have read anything but—even while, if busy creatively writing, they have read little else. Then, as doctoral students, funding pressures give them no time to "read around" in their (both senses) nominal discipline. There are exceptions, of course, here and there, and they make it still "worth it," to the dispenser of a legacy at least. But the norm persists. Aside from teacher-training, graduate life in literature programs, with all its radical precarity as a career track, is mostly sought out as a transitional place apart: temporary shelter, to various extents communal, for the harboring and sometime airing of non-institutional viewpoints, not for inculcation into a vanishing profession. The shame of this is scarcely to be blamed on the enrolled participants, whether on entrance to a doctoral program or once entrained by its cost efficiencies. A logic strictly institutional has them in its grips after all. We turn out instructors, and temporarily employ them, rather than nurture interpretive erudition; the premium is on lecturers rather than lectors.

DL: The lament verging on pain inherent in your layered account—sensible to sensitive readers—gives us pause, and occasions a kind of mourning: the passing of an age. Still, as a kind of host to your reflections, I reach for cold water: not to numb us further but, Thoreau-like, to wake us up to these regretful realities. Given the cool (because untutored) reception of your generous offerings, you'd be forgiven for feeling put off or put upon—an inward turn being a reasonable form of self-protection. And yet, classroom experience aside, the communicative force of these essays is undiminished, each of them uniquely vivid in turn, maybe more pointed than ever. And certainly ready for an eager public reception—wherever readers are at the ready.

GS: I would be glad to think so, now that these pages are going public. Yet there's still a target-audience dimension to each piece that makes the sequence inevitably choppy. I can, though, imagine that fans of punctuational nuance might be happier with the included account of Dickens than with my previous two books on the Victorian novelist (*Dickens and the Trails of Imagination*, 1974; and *The One, Other, and Only Dickens*, 2018). Lovers of Victorian poet Gerard Manley Hopkins may well be happier to see him explored in isolation, rather than folded in with a dozen other phonetic technicians to make for a "teachable" book chapter in *Reading Voices: Literature and the Phonotext* (1990).

DL: No doubt there are separable rewards in *Closer Reading* for certain niche audiences. But I'm confident of more. I hear you, as it were, on how hard it is to catch the undergraduate's ear in hearing the beauties of nuance—and the further challenge of aiding those same minds in conjuring their own distinctive, resonant prose. Those twined difficulties call me back to how we both embarked on this volume with the sense of a *pedagogic utility* in such specialized essays once constellated together around the question of textuality across media—*and* with light thus shed on the prismatic quality of the reading experience. In effect, such a diffused spectrum of diverse offerings becomes focused in its cumulative force. Like Stanley Cavell's *Must We Mean What We Say?* subtitled "a book of essays," in *Closer Reading* you too have offered up a resolute *book* of (the) essays therein.

GS: I had forgotten that Cavell subtitle, and the way it blithely transcended oxymoron. I don't hesitate to accept the precedent. What's more, I do think we were right, at some level, however we describe it: that these essays are, as the saying goes, "better together." And that's why we put them, in turn, together with some earlier work that would help delimit the transferably wide scope almost paradoxically inherent in their closeness of focus.

DL: To this end, titles are again entitling, not just we hope enticing. Subtitles too. With the latter for *Attention Spans*, shuffling the traditional syntax of "A Garrett Stewart Reader" brings out the ultimate intent of our volume in exploring what it means to lay stress on the singularity of *Garrett Stewart, a Reader*. In the modesty of this switch, as you were eager for it, lies the deference to broader methodological issues. Here, too, *Essays in Refraction* refers not to the essays themselves as facets of a varied career but to their collective if diversified address to a textual prismatics at stake in the reading act, in and beyond literary formats. In just that, from my perspective, lies their availability as texts to be taught, including the urgency of their address to contemporary classrooms.

GS: You make a good case, despite countermanding evidence, especially by reminding me of what we hoped for in sketching out the volume.

DL: I'm keen to bring the keynote of pedagogy back once again, renewing my initial question at broader scope (by now so engrossingly answered at one level in your back-and-forth scan of the essays' micro-agendas above, regarding both overt punctuation and negactivating medial puncture points). It remains a question about what you yourself, in herding and lassoing together these disparate essays, may have learned, at the most general level, about their deeply shared and interactive characteristics—and that students might in turn learn from them, from you, in their (that almost anachronistic term) "professionalization." (For who can be become a professional when there is no longer a profession to join, to serve, to honor?) Furthermore, I'm curious whether the very heterogeneity of these new offerings, on topics previously spaced out a book at a time, gives you any fresh sense of what has always drawn you, now and again, away from literary study to cinema and, even more unexpectedly, to Conceptual art, which is represented here most saliently in that globe-trotting, multimedial essay, "Negative Imprints in Conceptual Art" (chapter 7), exploring as you do an eye-opening panoply of optical inversions and material negations in current art practice "across media." And, in fitting *fort da* fashion, what has pulled you back (again) to books not just sculpted but printed, as it were, for us to read. And, in turn, what might attract students to precisely this cross-medial scope of fascinations.

GS: Okay, whether or not a solo history of hermeneutic evolution shows students a potential way of their own, it is perhaps useful to outline a methodological lineage as varied as mine. Not long after *Bookwork* (2011), yes, with its illegible codex sculptures, came the literary-philosophical emphasis of *The Deed of Reading* (2015)—with a film publication in between: *Closed Circuits* (2015). Withdrawal symptoms, partly, one medium after another. But I was always yearning to write about something else while seeing one thing or the other into print—with narrative, or its overt erasure, one common denominator. Moving from Dickens to Chaplin, let alone from celluloid to digital cinema, or from Conrad to Coppola, seemed natural enough to me from almost the beginning: on the twin fronts of narrative structure and stylistic detail, equally weighted in my "reading" of both media. I just had to saddle up my hobby-horses differently for whatever split-level terrain of this sort I counted on them to traverse and survey. Art criticism came later, where neither narrative exactly, nor style in the sense of technique (brush or scalpel), caught and held my attention as tightly as formal inference: not visible in stroke or cut but legible only as text. As I moved from the painting of mostly illegible read pages in the canvas scene of textual absorption, biblical or fictional, to the material ironies of Conceptual practice, I was enthralled by objects and assemblages that increasingly needed accompaniment by "gallery text." I was fascinated by works for which interpretation needed to be all but inbuilt. Reading about (in the tacit reading *of*) was mandatory in helping museum goers to discern the layered intricacies or mute formal ironies of the works I kept coming upon—including literal twists like those tiny spools of black vinyl or jeweler's silver in the "negatives" of recorded sound and stylus script in Cornelia Parker's diptych ("Negative Imprints in Conceptual Art"). The more involved I became in such "viewing"—and its own material involutions—the more I was either adding my own text or further glossing the wall-displayed collaboration between maker and curator: that discursive supplement to immediate observation that inevitably roots such art practice in a secondary art of medial translation. And translation is there, or course, to facilitate further reading.

DL: I take your point about translation as trope for these *outré* viewing experiences—but it's almost literalized, across many a foreign-language sector, by the remarkable travel that has gone into your encounters with international gallery work. Like your other textual obsessions, to be sure, wide-ranging, eclectic, always on the move, but in this case not just topical but topographical—mappable.

GS: Well, funding has certainly helped, but it's less necessary all the time. Unlike the case with my book on the scene of reading on canvas (*The Look of Reading: Book, Painting, Text*, 2006), researched in eleven countries before the widespread use of internet files for museum holdings, these new finds were just that, not tracked down by dedicated research trips, but encountered by happenstance when I was away—abroad or not—on other scholarly business. That's part of the thrill of being eager to find "text" wherever one encounters the intentional artifact: the lucky break that affords some kind of interpretive breakthrough. Decades before, in fact, that was indeed part of my motive in writing the article on *Apocalypse Now* included here (chapter 1), when I happened to be living in Westwood, California—while commuting to my teaching post at the University of California, Santa Barbara—and had the chance of snagging a preview ticket to a test screening of Coppola's film. I was thus one of the few to know how his rough cut was originally intended to end the film (as discussed in the essay), with the chiaroscuro ambiguity of Captain Willard's (Martin Sheen's) face bisected by shadow, perhaps symbolizing his own accepted deification by Kurtz's Cambodian followers—rather than plowing a path through and beyond that cult of power, as the release print ends, in an attempted if narratively truncated return. There was a readable moment in the good old-fashioned form, if you will, of genetic textual history.

DL: Your good luck is contagious here, especially when multiplied in the stirring exactions of that "negactivity" essay (chapter 7), since we're all alerted to works in your treatment, from Taipei to Bratislava, that we wouldn't have ordinarily stumbled upon, or even known to "look up." The work of another mentor of mine, Giuliana Bruno, has me thinking anew—in the context of your artful wanderings worldwide—just how much perambulation matters for the "taking in" of art.[6] There are analogies to be noted between following lines of prose, strips of film, and lanes that usher one in and through museum spaces. Linearity of a certain sort is inbuilt as is the invitation to pay attention to one's surroundings, including the art works thus enclosed, and by that conditioning availed. A mentality for environmentality, even when the lines add up and lead to a roving attention.

GS: And that attention—singular or spread out—is best repaid when understood as being poised in advance to "read." Levels of legibility tend to take the viewer by surprise. Maybe that's the particular mental thrill, at least for some of us, of gallery-going in the realm of experimental practice—when an instinct for interpretation is rewarded by forms far less discursive than screen narrative and its cinematographic codes, let alone than already verbalized fiction. Reading's leap is greater at such moments—so that its spontaneous exercise can sometimes feel more immediate and exhilarating under track lights than in the reflected glow of screen sequences, let alone under a reading lamp. And thus lend new dimension to the term "reading," a new facet of prismatic textuality. Just the sort of thing, I might add, that the embedded video cam of a mobile AI robot wouldn't (yet) be good at turning from object into concept in the process of generated commentary. Or, putting it otherwise, one suspects that informed gallerists have less to fear so far, in the job security of their wall text preparation, than many other "information workers."

DL: Your invocations of artificial intelligence—first of LLMs and now of optical "recognition" in an algorithmic key, however limited its resulting "cognition" of the Conceptual—call to mind concerns aired between us in our *Attention Spans* dialogue. And what you surmised just now reminds me of why this rebooted conversation inevitably takes us back, and quite directly, to doubts raised there about the future of creativity (across the human-AI threshold). AI can render a stunning landscape, or in NFT art (nonfungible tokens for unduplicable images) produce a unique mode of beauty. But what it can't do, or not yet, is materialize from scratch a compelling audiovisual *idea*, a concept, in other than digital code, pixel or audial, or maybe not very gripping even then (since it is at every byte abetted by its necessary recycling of the extant). The digital sublime beckons from around the corner. Aided by 3D printing, AI might follow instructions in the fabrication of an ironic book sculpture, one of the *bibliobjets* you've so often studied and theorized, but it couldn't *conceive* Conceptual art on its own. Or would it be art if it could?

GS: Nor, as I was suspecting just now, can it persuasively meet such art face on with enhancing commentary, even lens to screen regarding one of its own NFT kaleidoscopic designs.

DL: Then, too, when tasked with literary analysis, one senses—implicit in AI's frequent shortfalls and lapses—the limits not just of its interpretive acumen but of its literary chops.

GS: So I've found. We keep hearing that progress in such algorithmic intelligence is asymptotic, outstripping expectations (and explanation) by leaps and bounds. No doubt true, but not in its automated mastery of literary studies, so far as I can see from checking back in occasionally.

DL: When we talked first about this, in a similar format for *Attention Spans*, it was during the early deluge of ChatGPT and the first wave of widespread AInxiety. The End of the English Major and serial signals of linguistic—and semiotic—degradation by AI . . . even as its capacious computational maw unselfconsciously hoovers up the sum total of humanity's efforts at literary expression, reducing it to source material and study guides for mimetic affrontery. The span of that particular cultural worry has only widened since (not proved a moment of false-positive panic), with everything from the vulnerability of writing and teaching jobs, as you mentioned, to actors' and writers' strikes against robotic replacement in Hollywood studios. Even if the chatbots end up merely quoting themselves, the specter of nonhuman creation—and interpretation—appears to have put a rent in the confidence we have in, or want from, *literate* analysis of prose. And so, back then, we tested some of AI's likely literary-critical limits—as you recalled doing again, with students, in my subsequent interview with you for the journal *Philosophical Investigations*, where you reported on the difficulty ChatGPT had, on repeated tries, in unpacking Macbeth's two senses of the past participle in "If it 'twere done when 'twere done" speech.[7] It's therefore particularly arresting for me to see, now, your return to chatbots in not one but two of the new essays here, first, in "Charles Dickens and the Plotting of Punctuation" (chapter 5), when computerization is used to call forth a rewrite, and in the process a normalizing re*punct*uation, of a kind of hiccup syntax in Dickens; then once again, in the formidable closer, "Narrative Afterwording" (chapter 8), to summon what amounts to a pallid imitation of Joseph Conrad. Since our previous conversations, have you come to some new sense of ChatGPT's procedures, especially after such further forays into the matricial Artifice?

GS: Only enough to wonder, in the algorithmic mix, what would make computerized phrasal disambiguation have such a hard time with outright syntactic punning; or to pose it from the other side of the coin, what that very difficulty might say about the power, in Wittgenstein's terms, of the language game when played with the stakes of human wit rather than machinic computation.

DL: And played at a scale more narrowly gauged than implied by Large Language Models, I assume.

GS: Yes. But that brings up something more specific that I've learned, come to think of it, since our exchange in *Attention Spans*—about what is (for me intriguingly), called "subword tokenization."[8] Whereas the dominant former nodule of linguistic computation was the word, since around 1990 instead, and under the protocols of "decompression," the < w o r d > has been broken open to more arbitrary junctures and subsidiary latchings that now operate, even subsyllabically, as the pertinent units of transmitted data bits that fall under "interpretation" as coded integers or "tokens," not functional (or fungible in the NFT sense above) symbolic units. I in fact learned of this from an article by a former student of mine who suspected, in sending it to me, the crossover interest (even if by loose analogy) I was likely to take in this algorithmic rather than literary form of such "concatenative textuality."[9] He guessed right—and not just in relation, say, to the phonic enchainments of Hopkins' gradient phonemic linkages but, in addition, for the parallel of "decompression" in the cybernetic sense to the term "decontraction" in a famous essay, "The Voice of the Shuttle," by my own former teacher, Geoffrey Hartman, with one of his best examples being Hopkins' "Brim, in a flash, full!"—the phrase overflowing from within, leveraging a seemingly nonexistent space for superfluity.[10]

DL: The literary implications seem palpable, even with hermeneutics' very different notion of text and interpretation than what AI is programmed to manipulate, scarcely prismatic in its fracturings. Far from entertaining idle comparisons, your interest in this—What else to call it?—*de-construction* of words to the letteral scope of the alphabetic unit itself seems an attempt at the very rough (but revealing) adequation of different scalar perspectives across radically divergent media systems, including poetry and numeric code. A, B, C. 0, 1, 0, 1. (Alas, your academic appointment takes on new signification in so far as you are a [rare] Professor of Letters. But then you've also staked many a claim on the syntactic microstructures of the cinematic apparatus as well.)

GS: Cinema's celluloid *gramma*, yes, continue to fascinate me, and in defining contrast to the bitmap arrays of digital imaging, well above the imperceptible algorithmic level. But "concatenation" has its own unique verbal nexus. The analogy between digital decompression and telescoped syllabification, for instance, is of course a loose one, but that only helps me realize how, from 1990 on in my own work (starting with *Reading Voices*), quite independent of the down-shifting protocols of the coders to narrower and narrower units of "data," I've been interested (without having the terms) in the "bigram" or "trigram" pried from its host word, or spanned across the space between words. This fascination has returned me to Hopkins in this collection with new ears for the auditory forms of his own sublexical tokens—as, under pressure, they can seem to betoken some extra slant of enunciated inference, can even at times skew back into the symbolic as the facet of a new sounded lexeme.

DL: What you're suggesting is that if AI hasn't yet learned to read well, and may never, its modes of text processing have something to teach about reading after all.

GS: Odd as it sounds, I guess so. Or at least about the word-formation necessary to any and all lexical decoding.

DL: A case, here and there, of the subword upped again by happy accident to a newly unfolded (decompressed) word in itself, is that it?

GS: Yes, as never more apparent than when one confronts a closely textured literary experiment with the normalizing bias of AI. Or even a piece of public wordplay. For just now, long since digressing about its transgression of lexical expectations, it occurred to me to run the London Underground triad of my early conversational detour in this dialogue past a gratis chatbot to see first what AI thought it meant—and then, after a predictably flat response, what made it verbally effective. Alliteration was stressed by the bot, and then, under "Flow and Rhythm," in its bullet-point breakdown, this "result": "The structure of the phrase flows smoothly, creating a sense of progression from observation to resolution. This flow helps reinforce the idea that each step naturally leads to the next." Okay, I pursued, so why does it confuse and annoy some passengers? Here: nothing but the obscurity of institutional process, not the scudding play on words: "The term 'sorted' might be seen as too vague. Some people may not be clear on what exactly happens after they report an issue." True enough, but that's what the phrasal automaticity is meant not just to finesse but to figure: a behind the scenes inevitability. So what began as a travel-journal sidebar about incidental word play as oblique model is now—if you will, my patient editor—a lynchpin instance in the matter of the syllabic rather than the numerical bigram as it leaps from a lexical "it" to a past-tense "ed" suffix.

DL: I *surely* will. Before the recirculation of your thought through this telling case in point, bringing your research commutes together with the textuality of computation, I was wondering if you had tried gaming the chatbot system in a hands-on way with Hopkins' continuous lexical challenges. Such results typically clear the head—and divert anxieties from literary obsolescence and aesthetic alienation to more immediate social and political dangers.

GS: Very much so in this case. You guessed it. Prompted, without my citing the titular first line, to do a phonetic analysis of Hopkins' "As Kingfishers Catch Fire," ChatGPT gets alliteration (again) quite mechanically right, is dumbly intrepid in spotting repeated word-opening consonants, but flubs assonance disastrously, identifying the tacit common *e* in "each" and "tells," for instance, and other such pairs, without hearing the difference. And then it identifies "stones ring" as "onomatopoeia"—perhaps from a sense that this is what critical discourse about the poem (which it has swallowed without absorbing) says that such stones do in the metaphysical thematic of the poem, ringing out their names, even though the words themselves are sounding out, as the stones s/ tumble into ubiquitous wells, neither a mimetic stoniness nor some essentialized reverberant splash. To "hear" onomatopoeia in the two words themselves is one of AI's notorious "hallucinations," or call it an acoustic mirage.

DL: A new category of the undigested, as when it kept telling you (in another variant of the imagined) that your punning line from *Macbeth* was from *Hamlet* instead.[11]

GS: Yes, but that was almost unaccountable; this other problem is more symptomatic. The misnamed "chat," which neither talks nor listens, is also quickly caught out, even beyond its unreliable parsing of formulaic rhetorical patterns, as completely incapable—on multiple tries—of imitating any specific Hopkins effect, no matter how studiously prompted ("add syllabic echo," "make wording more obscure, " "complicate the syntax," etc.), but instead turns out doggerel on any of his favored themes. It isn't lazily complacent on my part to say that so far—for of course we have far yet to go—that AI in its standard laptop use, among other deficiencies and terminological gaffes, is entirely aluminum-eared in its phonetic audition. Despite coded voice-recognition elsewhere, its search engines might seem to have been scanning through Large Language Literature for too long in indexed silence. And that's to say nothing about how little an artificed intelligence would be likely to engage, in imitation or explication, with some of my other artifactual preoccupations in the museum world.

DL: Misnomers abound, like "chat," often churlish instead. But the misnaming of these "tools" by tech bros should not surprise, since they are "branding" their wares for mobilization in markets (cattle prods and branding irons of another sort), for IPOs, and other moments of capital ventured. Whereas chat remains as interlocutor fairly coarse (even when not veering too far off course), "artificial intelligence" is neither entirely artificial nor fully intelligent. Still, as you suggest above, whatever time-savers the "generative" functions of AI are now mark(et)ed to implement, certainly this dubious Intelligencer couldn't wander on robotic wheels into the Danish National Gallery, with autofocus lens affixed, and come up, by the luck of the draw, with two such fascinating artifacts of negative optic energy as you do in chapter 7.

GS: Nor, even if planted in front of them, know what to say about what its surveillant lens has transmitted to its data files.

DL: Back to literature for a moment, where chat/tering can be more like static electricity than like an analytic probity. Exhibit 101 of late, a late-breaking (and potentially soul-crushing) development in the e-reader business—not "e" for expert, rather, all but e-rasing the work of reading entirely. The lifeless proteus rises up to underwrite your poignant sense, above, of criticism as a non-genre even for many (contemporary) graduate students (studying literature), the literary essay more or less passé as model of disciplinary expression. The new "affordance" that brings that brooded-upon obsolescence to mind is called "Rebind," compacting together as it does the electronic file of one notable modern novel or another with, in supplement (as if to pad the shock of encounter), a companion essay about the text commissioned from "literary experts" ranging—scholars need not apply!—from bestselling mid-range novelists to TV writers, from *New York Times* op-ed columnists to Deepak

Chopra; I'm not making this up. Masterclass 2.0: Dilettant/ext. Such "essays" are not just included but embedded in the computer sense, whose lucidly "accessible" commentary is meant to gloss and plumb the particular novel's wonders and mysteries. "Accessible," that is, by touchscreen in an instantaneous AI search of its own. Chat with whomever whenever you're stumped or lose track of a motif.

GS: Seems like this grotesquerie might boast of being the opposite—but really it's the shadow double—of the Spritz speed-reading affordance that is laced through my *Book, Text, Medium* as a countermotif.[12] That handy tool sweeps the words of electronic text past you, one word at a time, with the screen optically focused on each lexeme's central and most identifiable alphabetic rather than phonemic feature, making sure you don't "spend too much time on any one word." In short, fast and stylistically unfastened: Book turned to e-Text with no Medium left. So that Spritz wouldn't even let you appreciate the swift punning name for another speed-reading affordance, its competitor Sprint. Begone with all that, we're supposed to think, thanks to this latest "slow reading" gimmick? Let's "rebind" our energies to interpretation: decelerate enough to find out what someone else thinks they have read in this passage as a way of "making up" our own minds about it.

DL: So what, finally, are we to think about the emergence of Rebind as a symptom of present-day/AI circumstances? The sales pitch: "experience a whole new way to read."[13]—What's wrong with the "old" way of reading (you know, reading)? Why does the commodification of the humanities so often appear unhandsome, crass, and worst of all wrongheaded, missing the point— edutainment for those who don't like to read? We want the study of literature— dare to say the *culture* of literary analysis—to survive, but at what cost? Non-nihilistically adapting to the uncancellable business school curriculum?[14] Or turning the other way: founding a school for close reading—as an *art* that can't be outsourced to AI—after the fashion of the guild-based American College of the Building Arts (ACBA)?[15] The Rebind promise on offer (for a fee): "Ask countless questions and get personalized answers drawn from original commentary, distributed by AI." Answers? Distributed? Call it the "offshoring" of humanistic labor—the art of close(r) reading—to LLMs. ©lose® reading.

GS: This "innovation" is so impoverished it's hard to see how it will ever be lucrative: the e-vehicle of bookish "investment." So much for the best that has been thought and said, however mangled by the usual search engines. An almost comic case of Small Language Models, but even there—I do certainly get your symptomatic point in linking this back to our earlier discussion— anything would be better, more efficient, than consulting the full embedded lit crit essay, although that laborious option (I see from the Rebind website) is made generously available as well by further upload, for those who might wish to bother—an essay, however, no doubt written with the aid of AI in the first place, just to "prompt" and prop-up the confidence of non-professionals in their touted authority over a classic text. But, then again, what's worse: this off-shoring of searchable if ersatz lit crit or the preference for none needed, all interpretation counter-indicated—as in the scientific field report you recently alerted me to in its neutral account of experimental respondents preferring the lucid simplicity of unidentified AI poetry, guessed as the work of human talent, to the murky complexity and often assumed "hallucinations"—including no doubt unwelcome types of Empsonian ambiguity—in the frustrating side effects of supposed machine writing? You can't win (back) by losing.[16]

DL: Not so suddenly literary theory needs therapy. Spinning the compass a bit, let's touch base for a moment on another angle of approach, quite unprecedented: begun here, one might have sensed in your encounters with the textual prism in verbal form—make that Hopkins and the *acoustic* prism (chapter 4). Unprecedented, even as it may seem to epitomize, in a bold experiment, the work of reading *on* by reading further *inward* (to the point where, to borrow your terms, depicted natural "instress" is at one with textual "inpress"). Boasting perhaps, including that last coinage, more of your proprietary neologisms than ever before in a similar range of pages, chapter 4 presses to typically unexpected limits—and beyond—the scope of writing's own energy in the work of analysis, spilling over into … what to call it? in light of the end-cap essay (chapter 8) … the unwritten in its own evocation.

GS: Ah, "ghost reading," yes. Hopkins, too, certainly invites it. But I thought I was half crazy when I started uh, *writing* it in that final piece on prose, and then sensed instead that the guiding notion was rather too predictable once I had tried arguing it into inevitability. As I found the unwritten useful to spell out (the ghostly powers of the magical *spell* felt with the act of inscription in mind), this was one of the essays that was triggered by classroom experience. Since then, a retired colleague, interested in the ad-libbed Ulyssean prototype that begins the essay, wondered if I was deliberate, not just in reading on in Alfred Tennyson's poem, but in allegorizing the seafarer's refusal of closure as model for my extra novelistic sentences. How could I not have been, even if in fact I wasn't knowingly? (An irresistible sentence has now been added to this effect.)

DL: Someday you'll no doubt be asked if you didn't intend, by closing with that essay—last but not least—to install a parable of your own future endeavors (against whatever tides of critical fashion) in the many more essays to come. (As we look beyond our mortal limits, I'd posited in the dialogue for *Attention Spans* something like the continuation of your work by computational means— by way of the bespoke large language model GS-p.s.—the Garrett Stewart Prose Simulator.)[17] And since then (not long ago), Google NotebookLM refracted your prose into a pretty savvy podcast episode; it was terribly sufficient at getting the measure of your work (if with uptalking and vocal fry to round out the reality credentials of the simulation). All this musing, of course, in the spirit of an afterlife for what happens after (your) words are no longer possible. AI offers without solicitation, requiring merely a quick upload, its rendition of afterwording.

GS: Where are the ideal emojis when one needs them? I'd rather consider that final essay—a curtain call for this book—as operating on a different kind of parabolic model, if not operating system. I think of it as staging *in extremis* the extent to which (in exaggerated extension) interpretive reading is already a kind of rewriting, not by simple elucidating paraphrase but by inferential extrapolation—a fact only italicized when closure withdraws any further words to contemplate but one's own in reverberation.

DL: Same with the dimming (or cutting) away into a suspension of all further shots at the end of a film, as you evoke in a passing analogy, left as we are only with a verbalized afterimage in our own heads. It is in the spirit of such cross-medial alignment that I note with pleasure the way this volume begins and ends with *Heart of Darkness*, filmed and otherwise, where Conrad's own haunted closural prose (as well as Coppola's cinematic adaptation) has its comparable way of fading out on the invasive superimposition of past upon present (even as GS-p.s., along with your own experiments in writing the unwritten, betoken the impress of the present upon the future). Here is a bracketing of a special sort that comes through quite strongly upon reading the chapters consecutively—not only along the internal paths of argument as written but across the sequence of their presentation here.

GS: And there's another curve to this path, as well, one occurring to me only in proofreading that last chapter for this volume. Quite belatedly, I must admit, I realized not just the connection to Ulyssean late-life industry but, quite separately, to the way the essay's logic, as applied to the unsaid ramifications of *Jane Eyre* (1847) and other Victorian novels, was very much what that particular book's author, Charlotte Brontë, had in mind with her later satire of marital closure in *Villette* (1853). That was a novel about which I had written extensively almost four decades before in *Dear Reader: The Conscripted Audience in Nineteenth Century Fiction* (1996), a study identifying by subtitle the kind of addressed or embedded reader whose responses are written *in* by inference. As were mine in turn as critical commentator. *Villette*'s plot is one of a kind, notably postmodern in this one respect a century ahead of its time. After a devastating storm at sea, in which the narrating heroine's fiancé is imperiled and presumptively lost (since we hear no more about him), she calls a sudden halt to narration ("Here pause; pause at once. There is enough said"— where the "here" swiveling to "there" marks the present moment of arrested discourse in its vantage point on the retrospective momentum that has led up to it). It is at this point that Brontë's narrator turns over the reins of closure to "sunny imaginations" among her readers—even as her imperative to "leave sunny imaginations hope" can easily be heard (repunctuated, re-"pointed") as its own auto-vocative leave-taking from "imagination's" entirely imagined hope. The happily-ever-after formula, with the reader filling in the post-marital blanks, has been evacuated with no subtraction of readerly engagement, which is suddenly made necessary to project any future whatsoever for the couple, to script it ex nihilo rather merely to occupy in imagination its amorous lacunae. Precisely by our being invited to draft our own happy ending, the possibility seems doubly forestalled. In all this, and recurring to our earlier exchange, *Villette* is an eminently teachable novel (as international Victorian syllabi attest) in a way that I'm not at all sure "ghost reading" would come through with any pedagogical grip—beyond nods of understanding about participatory reading.

DL: Maybe not there, with that one hypertrophic version of the unfinished, but as part of a broader seminar methodology, I'm not as dubious as you are. In any case, it doesn't surprise me that literary history is never far from your own metaliterary experiments—one Brontë novel shadowing your treatment of another, even if only "unconsciously." Yet just this intertextual association for the way you've overstepped closural thresholds with many other novels in that final essay, not just in plot formula but in printed formulation, offers an apt last faceting of the readerly prism, a refraction angled just off the print *page*.

GS: There are, I would agree, some novels that can be put into lively conversation with students on the score of closural reverb. And, though untested as yet, one by Richard Powers comes immediately to mind—and to hand, because brand-new and just finished. Borrowing the title of his last novel, *Bewilderment* (2021), the pedagogical imperative is always to turn bewilderment to wonderment, and *Playground* (2024) offers just such a playing field for imagination with its complex hermeneutic grid. You and I have talked a good deal about AI as the evident (or exaggerated) dead end of literary art, let alone its literate commentary, and discussed in passing, in our previous dialogue, Powers' prescient 1995 novel *Galatea 2.2*, in part about teaching a computer to do literary criticism. Published just last month, as we're about to send this manuscript to press, *Playground* contemplates this same endgame, but precisely as an asymptote of play per se. I'd have been half tempted to write a separate chapter on it, if we weren't already at our contracted length and up against a submission deadline, but I'm more than tempted—if you think we can make room for one more rumination in this vein—to include a brief look at (and just past!) its enigmatic ending. For to my ear it openly invites a ghost reading of its last ambiguously sourced italics in connection with a slowly self-ghosted protagonist, a tech billionaire named Todd Keane (shadowed by the

German *Tod* as "death keen"?) suffering from an extreme and rapidly brain-erasing form of dementia.

DL: Let's by all means train our attention at another un-ending: a newly tested phantasmal aftermath. Not long ago, you spoke of "ghost reading" as a "curtain call" for your narratographic close-ups, but that hardly precludes an encore, a specter that outlives the book's final chapter: a revenant analysis, a ghost reading of "ghost reading."

GS: And in this case, cinematically speaking, a fade-out after another of Powers' quick-cut montage novels.

DL: It does seem very much in the textualist nature of that kind of ghostly afterglow, and therefore all the more illustrative, that it wouldn't stop with the nineteenth-century nimbus of a stylist like Conrad.

GS: Right. But unlike the case of *Heart of Darkness*, what goes unsaid in *Playground*'s last sentence is not a swollen, spreading, incremental version of the title itself ("the heart of an immense darkness"), but its title's unsaid second syllable. The play-loving billionaire architect of the website Playground, which steered technology into the realm of generative AI with his recourse to DeepDive learning, has, after his auto-piloted mega-yacht has brought what's left of his consciousness to his desired Pacific peace, been buried at sea in a ceremonial canoe after willing his billions to a Pacific Islander (for whom a passive passion, back in college, once broke through the ambitious shell of his celibacy). She devotes her legacy, we hear in flash forward, to saving her people from the campaign of "seasteading" he himself had bankrolled, diverting her wealth to oceanic restoration instead.

DL: From immersion in the digital web to the deep seas, a topic (in its nineteenth-century sociocultural and literary dimensions) broached and deliberated by you and Paul Fry in *Bandwidths*,[18] now experienced anew in Powers with his customary poetic exchanges between the realms of computation and ecology.

GS: Good to be reminded of that conversation with Fry, since Powers does I think, like Conrad with his call to "immerse" oneself in the "destructive element," find ways of engulfing attention in the sea changes of phrasing's own tidal force—including in *Playground* its micro-organic pulsations. So back to unfolding narrative time. Stunned by the leaps and dive-bombing frolic of the manta rays in the waters closing over the burial, onlookers realize, beyond a host of possible biological reasons for this exercise, let alone supernatural, that the mantas are simply having fun, playing without stakes. This perception is glossed in the italics previously reserved for the intermittent and directly addressed autobiographical text of the dead tech guru. One of the italic passages has recently reminded us of the stories "I have told you," though these narrative episodes are ultimately aimed, we realize only at this late point, not at print culture's "dear reader" but at his symbiotic brainchild, an AI system manifested in the astronomically funded bot Profunda. By the last italicized and post-mortem sentence of the book, however, we don't know who is speaking. Or to whom/what. There is no subject position left: "*What are all creatures—even me—doing at all times but playing in the world, playing before their tinkering Lord?*" Whatever the source of this formulation, seldom could a rhetorical question have seemed to earn anymore decisive a claim to closure. But the living mind of the forgotten reader as partly addressed "you," if I may speak for myself, whirrs on, steeped in what is alluded to earlier as the game of games, Wittgenstein's *Sprachspiel*—or ruled-bound "language game" mentioned above.

DL: As with Wittgenstein, so with Powers, the games are serious, the playing consequential.

GS: And with Powers' language, this is a game whose moves we keep retracing after the fact in *Playground*. A chapter before we've learned that in his loss of conscious identity the demented web inventor has been listening to stories told by (once to) the computer, including perhaps the one we've just read, an algorithmically reconstructed narrative, a tale so convincing that "I mistake your characters," those borrowed by Profunda's narrative, "for the people they once were." After all: "You've read a million novels, many of them *plagiarized*," whose first syllable is also stolen to cap the paragraph in its next chiastic turnabout (as fair play): "You've watched us play, and now you're playing us." But that capitulation is itself couched in the idiom of chiastic *human* wit, with all its typical twists in Powers.

DL: Am I right to recognize in what you value about *Playground* a verbal ingenuity familiar from those earlier novels of his you devote three chapters to in *The Metanarrative Hall of Mirrors*?

GS: Though tempered somewhat, Powers' latest stylistic gaming in *Playground* is very much in the same vein—including especially the passages in which the narrator analyzes the writing of prose itself in its supple mimetic dimensions. What a plagiarist AI could never filch into genius is the way one of the book's main characters, the oceanographic diver and later bestselling author Evie Beaulieu—there at the end, overseeing the manta rays—has struggled in print to immerse "the ears of her readers" in the undersea dazzlements she's seen. As of course Powers works to reinvent them for us, in the ear-evoked sights of his own synesthesia. The result is a prose that AI could no more read right than write. When clinging bioluminescence follows Evie, in her own hard-won prose, out from the water across radiant stretches of beach sand, there is this in phrasal resonance about her own wordscape: "The words that she used to capture those glowing tracks sparked in her wake as she propelled herself forward." And not just in the unearthly glimmer described, but in the tracking grammar *inscribed* and enacted. We might have expected, via past-participial subordination and expansion, something like "The words, so scrupulously used to capture those glowing tracks, sparked in her wake *a trail all aglimmer in its own right*." As with Dickensian counterpunct in chapter 5, however, the enunciated lack of a decisive comma marking, as much as its aural override in the last sentence of *Great Expectations*, becomes commanding. Instead of the expected grammatical route in Powers' case, the words in sequence (organized around the finite past tense "sparked" in its intransitive sense of "sparkled") are doing the tracking, the retracing, in and for themselves (with no resultant grammatical, only a rhetorical, object)—and with no loss of phosphorescence by osmosis. And no sooner, two sentences later, have we read this (with added italics only cumulatively intuited): "Three *q*uarters of ocean species, from zooplankton to *g*iant s*q*uid, were si*g*nalin*g* in a lan*g*ua*g*e of living li*gh*t"—and wondered about its uncanny play of visible even when silent letter variants in the orthographic flutter (q/g/q/g/guage/g/gh), which AI might again misidentify as alliteration—than we know, a sentence later yet, that we have been meant to indulge such wonder: "And now," as for instance right here and now in this sustained flickering interlinkage, "her syllables blinked in imitation," those plosives like tiny lightbulbs popping on and off. If, once prompted, either ChatGPT—or the novel's Profunda—were to audit this wrinkling of prose, as the former did by mistake with the phonics of Hopkins, as an "onomatopoeia" of twinkling syllables, one could hardly resist such a nod to the metatext.

DL: So the prose is playing us as well, luring us to partake phonetically in its performed mimesis: the "signal" as well as signature Powers gambit.

GS: Exactly. And in the end, not bluffing with its foreclosing rhetorical question, but tempting us to up the stakes, I'm betting, in the imaginative bonds of response. I'm particularly glad to see again how inclined I was, with this new fictional closure, to track along its inclined plane of suggestion, because it allows me to reflect further on this refractive "method," this mode of "reflex." To "gloss" derives from the Greek for tongue, and by association the clarification of foreign or obscure terms. As an interpretive reflex in this mode of glossing as ventriloquism, ghost reading is simply the latent twin of explication in a process by which, when all else is said and done, and rather than a marginal paraphrase of the implied, it gives liminal tongue to the unsaid. So we come (again) to the last sentence, not in Evie's book, but in Powers' novel. I had read these words again and again before triggered to write *on* about their, yes, ghostly phrasal aura, resisting the Divine Artificer of this "tinkering" deity as a mere robotic bricoleur in the DeepDive of algorithmic currents, resisting it by dredging a little extra insistence "sparked" by its own traces. Again, then, the reverb: "*What are all creatures—even me—doing at all times but playing in the world, playing before their tinkering Lord?*" With the novel's playful disyllabic title in mind, its own "blinking" *figure*/ground oscillation, I incline, forward one extra notch, to put it, push it ahead, this way: *For isn't ocean, beyond material paradox, in evolutionary as well as ludic terms, and in the unfathomable profound of its teeming depths, ultimately the blue-black but phosphorescent* ground *of all such animate play, including that of the tinkering writer?*

DL: If your fallout phrasing is on target, it sure sounds like Powers is trying again, as in *The Overstory* (2018), for some last word of his own on the vanishing divide between cybernetics and human craft against the broadest possible environmental backdrop. Or rather, given the issues at *play*, back*ground*. And with the "reflexes" of style as both terrain and map at once: should we say narratography as (newly refashioned) stylistic oceanography?

GS: Certainly in reading *Playground* I often thought that the prose was operating almost like an undersea refraction—and in very much the sense we wanted to stress (after the colon) in subtitling this collection. Each distinct essay of *Closer Reading* is an interpretation in tune, or better in close illuminative alignment, with the contours of any text—in one medium or another (including the rippling mimesis of watery ones)—that the act of reading is engaged in holding up to the analytic light, however bent. We both agreed from the start, as you alluded to earlier, that this refractive reading was positioned to identify my response to the essentially three-dimensional and prismatic contours of any complex text once penetrated—shot through—by the spotlight of interpretation. A foundational trope, in short, that mocks the very notion of surface reading (excuse this vestigial polemic), given that any face of the prism is only one angled factor in the epiphenomenal multiplanar envelope of its light-penetrated depth—and chromatic expression. Reading rises to just this polyhedral call, each constituent shift of position and dimension changing under attentive rotation, with depth inherent in the variant surfaces across which any and all radiating refractions alone can be tracked.

DL: As one among the readers of this volume, and your other books, I'm pleased to have your peroration situated here in our conversation—along with the essays themselves that bear out such stated effects, your thoughts on *Playground* certainly included.

GS: Well, I wasn't thinking to convert you further, of course, my longtime collaborator. But I wonder if you've begun converting me. I liked getting that last organizing logic off my chest. In fact, the more I explain away any likely classroom cachet for this cross-medial *topic*—or to put it anagrammatically, this prismatic *optic*—the more it gains hold as a possibility. Are your questions nudging this, or am I talking myself into it? No need to decide. What are "interchanges" for, after all? I'm just remembering how much my usual graduate offerings in theory and method depend on breadth of representation, a survey of methodological divergences (in critics other than myself) in search of what might sink in—and find new outlets in the students' own work. Why not share with them the energy I've found in transgressing disciplinary borders, and not just with new material but in the departure itself as a methodological challenge? Why not a course on "Multi-Media Reading"?

DL: Sign me up. A program—or say a clinical trial—devoted to learning how to let the multi-modal polysemy sink in, another kind of depth psychology. That's truly the point. Prismatics and parallax, variation and triangulation, overground tracking and oceanographic tacking, the close-up crafting of humane letters set against the tokenization of artificers divine and digital. The interplay of this volume's representative pieces has its own luminous angles of incidence, which is why I called my introduction a "spectrum analysis" roving across the various "wavelengths" upon which ride and rise these surprising inflections of approach. Rather than distracting from each other, the coordinated amplitudes of these chapters *gain* from each other across unusually wide gaps in topic, all the while measured—and not incidentally, because issuing from your hand—at something of the same scale of intensity and brightness. The potential "lesson plan" that spans them is all there in this volume we're looking back on (the Table of Contents yet another syllabus in the offing and offering). Just let it breathe the air of fresh acquaintance around a seminar table and it will have done its destined work. If my questions have inched you toward this auspicious prospect, then I've had more than my intended say in this dialogue as a summarizing back-and-forth.

GS: The seed is certainly planted. Forth-and-back-again so far—and soon perhaps forth again into the curriculum. Why, you're helping me ask myself, why, just for instance, harbor largely unaired a passion for, let's call it, museum "readings"? Why limit it to the occasional in-class allusion—without the many slides I have on hand for public lectures—rather than try sharing it with more than my own pages and a few known fans in my circle of former students and friends? Since it has been so much a part of my sensory and imaginative engagement with aesthetics—and with critical possibilities—for the second half of my career, and since any facility I've developed in such gallery encounters has been fueled directly by my experience with literary and then film study— why not inject some of this enthusiasm into the pipeline for student scholars? The rhetorical question answers itself, even in the face of tactical obstacles that may keep it a schedule-of-courses pipe dream.

DL: That's the tune to sing. And "just right" with respect to your dedicated critical forays in Conceptual art-making farthest afield from your credentials and appointment. To put it by way of literary allusion, everything that (a)rises here in these far-flung essays must be noted to converge. Thinking back to those original journal submissions so eye-openingly reapportioned in Part I (the first three chapters), you wouldn't need now a clientele, as you did then, separately interested in screen adaptation or postcolonial readings of Victorian and Edwardian fiction or the irony by which skeptical criticism blinds its advocates to the critique of skepticism in Stanley Cavell. Now, in cross-weaving the pieces, you would only need readers—and I'm confident, if I may borrow from your moving take on Cavell's phrasing, that *they're there* waiting, interested in how chiaroscuro lighting or syllepsis or phonetic pattern ("They, there, are free") can operate at the same granular level of interpretation—and thus potentially explicate each other.

GS: The more minuscule, it does sometimes seem, the more medial. In short, I'm listening. Even while remembering how tactical, rather than openly and freely quizzical, students tend, even need, to be about their graduate coursework in these straitened and constraining days.

DL: Precarity is the watchword for more than just vocational prospects. And yet still. . . . The excitement is all there in the way you phrased it just above: sharing not just the wherewithal in method but the dialed-in desire that motivates it wherever occasions present themselves and attention spans permit. All this potentiality is what comes to the fore in our previous volume, that is, in all your varied conversations with such different and diversely trained critics, across all the frequency modulations of the *Bandwidths* project. In whatever medium you take up, you seem also taken up at the same levels of intensity. And once spreading that across several of these media(l) instigations in this one volume, if I may add an Emily Dickinson allusion to the fate of convergence in Carson McCullers, what we get is a collective manifestation of "internal difference, / Where the Meanings, are—."[19]

GS: Meanings through such differential means, exactly. Getting their message (even before trying to get it out via commentary) is the thing—in whatever key, by whatever mode of transposition. It's rooted in that galvanizing moment known, I assume, to any practiced critic of whatever analytic stamp: knowing in a flash what can or might be done with the come-upon. The "here I go again" moment—when your trusted antennae pick up a signal (a wavelength!) you can see or hear your way to decoding. In my case, the triggered instinct sets in when some friction in the seamlessness of a verbal or visual or audial performance renders imperative the need to bear down and bore in, testing for how much analysis of a certain kind the text can bear up under.

DL: *Under*, indeed—at its solicited depth.

GS: Right, no surface complacency in the eager severity—or otherwise intimacy—of my notice. In the verbatim words of my long-standing film and art editor at the University of Chicago Press, the gifted Susan Bielstein—spoken with some trepidation regarding the lengths (in word count at least) to which it might lead: "There you go again, down one of your black holes." Guess so: primed for the "event horizon" of interpretation.

DL: Because the vortex you enter at such moments has as its main thrill—in whatever quantum recognitions—that you are taking us with you, buckled up, as we are, for the ride. Not ultimately headed for devouring black holes, but instead—beginning with a sometimes minimal glimmer—approaching g/ listening wholes.

GS: Your own sympathetic sound play there—with its all but audial sense of "sympathetic vibration" along the shaved-off graphism of that prismatic phrase—reminds me why an essay featuring the synesthesia of an "acoustic prism" in its title was the inevitable choice to lead off this run of new work.

DL: Yes, where attention is always directed at a kind of "internal difference, / Where the Meanings, are—" and this in the refractive mode of "telling it slant," in refractive commentary as well as in the poetics of phrase.

GS: Now that you've got me going on the pedagogic energy this could potentially unleash across divergent media as well as diverse literary forms, want to indulge me with a recent and complex case of prose poetics tried out in the graduate classroom? Where the "catchiness" is more like a roughening "catch in the throat"?

DL: All ears for this extra sounding.

GS: Just a week before we launched this iteration of our dialogue, I had co-hosted a visiting lecture on James Baldwin by Stephen Best of the University of California, Berkeley, a celebrated scholar of Black American writing known as well for his much-cited resistance to ideological critique under the reparative banner of "surface reading"—a polemic from which, as he wrote me in opting for another podium topic, he had lately distanced himself. In a subsequent exchange, he thanked me for "stylistic" suggestions I had made, after seeing an early draft of his paper, "Baldwin's Inarticulacy," about its longest quotation from the author—and did so, it amused me to note, regarding my "deep dive" into its cited prose.

DL: Aha, one of those dead metaphors you delight in finding juiced back to nuance under a certain contextual force—and, in this case, with a poignant semiotic irony.

GS: Especially in this case, yes, because, despite the lecturer's admittedly doomed effort to recover the affect of Baldwin's originary and faltering human voice behind all the code-switching of his public rhetoric on page or at mic alike, there was, in that unpacked block citation I had briefly glossed, a strand of evidence for this autobiographical baseline in textuality's own *voicing*: a layered effect of "surface script" and (double sense, as with yours a moment ago) its *sounding*. The fraught paragraph on deposit came from "Down at the Cross: Letter from a Region in My Mind," the second essay in *The Fire Next Time* (1963). On the way to bringing it, glossed, into the graduate classroom, for further discussion with students who had attended the lecture, I myself heard, on rereading, an extra dimension yet in the writing's own obsession with an excess of having "heard." Representing for Best the pervasive "chafe" of Baldwin's subject position from an early age, the passage unfolds in such a way, I had suggested, that the speaker's abraded consciousness could actually be felt obliquely manifested by the fricative variants of the "fear" instilled in his boyhood mind, the very word hammered out ten times in fewer than three times as many lines—and released to begin with from a broader *f*-alliteration whenever, which was then always, anxious Black parents work to make racial "difference . . . felt and feared." Fraying away the confidence of every "Negro" child, such is the primal "fear heard in his mother's or his father's voice," the past participle then stretched in the next sentence to the semi-stutter of "fear he hears." Fretting such offspring with distress on every side, the suffusing fear is that the child wouldn't be afraid *enough* of crossing color lines, leading to the double beat of "another fear, a fear" that this freedom from justified paranoia would lead to "destruction," with that immediate stutter of repetition ("fear, a fear") seemingly caught on the cusp, because in the tensed throat, of the associated participle "afeared." All this rasping *friction*, wearing away at any aspiration, isn't the kind of letter-counting graphic alliteration that ChatGPT can be counted on to tally if asked about pattern. It is, instead, an insidious overriding counterforce audible precisely in the monitory tremors of the *overheard*.

DL: I hear you, or make that hear Baldwin's prose in action—aspiration and consternation cohabiting in diction—while appreciating how the theorist of *Reading Voices*, decades after its 1990 publication, remains convinced that you—that is, anyone—can't read *for* voice, in pursuit of it somatically or metaphysically, but only *voice* what you read: not as speech but as linguistic medium.

GS: Exactly. Baldwin claims his "Letter" is a missive "from a region in my mind," himself therefore its first relay point on the way to a readership. At the receiving end, I pronounce—rather than intone—his words in a cognitive zone or region of mine (own mind), to which the suppressed musculature of enunciation (mine, not his), operating by silent proxy, sends its signals. And most directly via the shared parental voice of that passage, at its phonic matrix, in the "fear heard"—and heard by and within us, in reflex audition—

by, of all things, a Hopkins-like instress of transegmental compression (and with all graphonic play on "ear" quite to one side). For it there in that word-b(l)ending, where autobiographical writing turns narratographical, that a chafing second-hand fright (theirs, now his), after pummeling repetition, is both heard and *audibly internalized*—as the "fearrrd" per se. If I may ride the *sub-surface* transport model from my London forays one last time: such a phrasal irony *seen* as prose, then *said* as silent speech, is already to that extent potently *sorted*. Or, to borrow another audio ubiquity from the London Underground—focused here on the likes of "fear heard" as cross-word pressure point, yet applicable at once to verse wording and to the most "pedestrian" of prose spacing ("sort it" versus "sorted"), as well as to the readable interstices of screen editing—one must more than ordinarily "mind the gap" in overstepping mere disjunction as recognized transitional ingenuity.

DL: May I in turn warm to such a transport precaution, turned to encouragement, since the phrasing distills a motive for our two previous volumes in the way it "minds" (pays a rewarded mind to) medial Spans as signifying Widths of attention—closes certain gaps, harmonizes varied concerns from one volume to another, make that three, and beyond them, of course, to your interlineated library of twenty interpretive excursions—tracked and dove into, sighted and sonically picked up?

GS: On the model of gapped lettering in homophonic chains ("sort it"/"sorted")—concerning the infrastructure of aesthetic media more than that of urban transit—a time-lapse call for investigated structural crevices could strike the "saying" ear this way: *mind/mined.*

DL: And the directly *listening* ear, since among the gaps min(d)ed in your recent work (their "bandwidths" addressed by four of the contributors in our previous volume by that name[20]) are—very much in the vein of Roland Barthes' "grain of the voice"—the microtone negotiations of vocal performance within a single legato syllable, as "mined" in Barbra Streisand's case (some would say not just miked but milked) for the note's own latent lyric wordplay.

GS: There too for sure, and abundantly so: the play of and within the note, the phrasing in that sense, not just the wording. Which is why that convergence of several *Bandwidths* contributors upon the Streisand experiment, beyond any "last but not least" gesture, felt so right, true rather than skewed, as method-defining.[21] My audit of Streisand's recording booth as well as live concert miking stresses not so much the lyrics of her music as the music of the lyric sound in phonic-become-phonetic execution—and sometimes its extra semantic reverb. Much is summed by that shift in level. There and elsewhere, *what closer reading reads is the medium itself* in its immanent field of performance.[22]

DL: Yes, perhaps never a clearer case of your working hypothesis across each new "decoding" challenge.

GS: And so, too, in that recently invoked example on the authentic Black voice. Have it that the "inarticulacy" confronted by Best's paper on Baldwin—racial constraints traumatically withdrawn into the never directly sayable—is at the same time enacted by Baldwin's own iterative prose through such slips of the written tongue as "fear heard" heard as "feared." Remembering the algorithmic model flirted with earlier, we might identify this as a subword—but also as a cross-word—tokenization in the mode of sliding bigrams and trigrams, long versus short e sounds here in their consonant bracketing (*ee erd*). None of this analysis gets us closer than before to the corporeal materiality of the biographical Baldwin's embodied speech rhythms (or for that matter, their moral claims), but it does help sort his prose's own insistent *voicing* of the constrictions—of vocal enunciation as well as social scope—that might have come close to silencing his creative energy early on.

DL: Leaning on one of your coinages, I would say that the *vortext* there, in your re-miking of Baldwin's prose, delivers us an event horizon from which light does escape, sounds made newly audible in the process. Maybe we can agree to call the "min(d)ed gaps" of your so-called black holes a 3-D mapping of data mines—resource rich terrains for the renewable energy of textual articulation and hermeneutic critique. As exhibited by your persuasive new evidence from Baldwin, I recognize your long-standing way of motivating phonemic drift as a rehearsed (reheard, re/verbed) slippage. As usual, you pursue such effects within a thematic "infrastructure" (your trope for it just now, identifiably recalling the London Underground from which you periodically emerge) that is anything but "superficial." In the Baldwin example, it is a lexical slippage from cause to resultant d/effect, to borrow, this time, one of your own transegmental latches operating in this case literally, that is letterally, as a phonetic transcen/ dental.

GS: Your treatment relieves my concern over having gone on too long about this brief Baldwin passage, even as a down-to-the-wire instance of my ingrained approach, in all its granularity, "chafing" or otherwise. You're definitely right in spotting there the recurrent "causeffect" merger, inspired yet again by the work of my first graduate school instructor, Geoffrey Hartman, especially in his classic essay I mentioned earlier, "The Voice of the Shuttle." Across a remarkable variety of figural and phonetic evidence, one was shown in that justly celebrated article how lexical and syllabic displacements alike tend at their most compelling to bridge the gap, or in other words mind and map it, between a triggering force and instigated result, however minimal the differential field in question. In older-fashioned terms, form is saturated by content; motifs unfold their own motive. I always like thinking in this respect of Wallace Stevens' title "The Motive for Metaphor" as instancing obliquely, prismatically, its own likening impetus (motehfor/metehfor).

DL: "Form saturated by content"—so fully at times, in any of the media that concern you, that form is coterminous with meaning.

GS: At times like those latest examples from Baldwin and Powers, certainly. The insistent rhythm of that Baldwin passage, its rasping voices of fear threatening to intimidate into silence the subject's own voice, does further recall for me—once condensed to that stranglehold wordplay of "fear heard" conflated or condensed to "feared"—Hartman's interest in the phrasal condensations by which "excluded middles," narrative and phonetic alike, are elided by overdetermined "ends." So with thanks to Stephen Best's visit for this eleventh-hour provocation in going, as Hartman wanted it, "beyond formalism"—but only by building on it—maybe we can let stand this provisional response to Baldwin's prose s/pacing as the last, because latest, of these new refractions in the prismatics of reading.

DL: And doing so in ways linked, even before chapter 6 on John le Carré here, to your previous investigation of a "cinematographic" prose, evident not just in the syllabic (indeed fricative) "Fframe advance" of the Baldwin passage but with the more playful stylistics under auto-commentary in *Playground*.[23]

GS: Your allusion to the medial frame rates of lexical formation (and deformation) actually leads me, beyond the cinematographic analogy, to a further clarifying (I hope) comparison between the Baldwin passage and that other eleventh-hour interpolation when taking up (in the resistance to putting down) Powers' novel under the aspect of ghost reading. In sum, each approach is so "close" (even when post-closural) that it re-sorts (to) pregnant "gaps," whether between or just past wording. On the same tacit analytic spectrum, then, falls the logistics of *deferred inference* and—in a case like Baldwin's, or for that matter in the metatext on Evie's performative prose in *Playground*—a narratographic reading inward and *differential*.

DL: I add only how palpably this moment seems emblematic of one of those interpretive flashpoints you must be most energized to take into class for discussion. As I've recognized so often from your published film work and even art criticism, Hartman's is the kind of dynamic model you bring not just to wordplay but to transmediations in Conceptual art as well as to figurative jump cuts in cinema, even thematized pixel breakups in the reflexivity of metadigital sci-fi. So it's not just in a Brontë or a Baldwin that prismatic textuality induces this kind of hermeneutic moment(um), but just as much in a Stanley Kubrick or an Anselm Kiefer. I don't mean to harp (though the sounds may entrance), but in that recognized transposition of analytic fields lies a renewable pedagogic agenda itself, no? Where students could learn from you the kind of lifelong lessons you learned from Hartman.

GS: Not any final "no," I will grant—however iffy the institutional "yes" might be. File the fantasy, if not under feasible course planning, at least under "courage of one's convictions."

DL: My sense is that you've always let that interpretive fortitude lead you, taking unstinted dictation from such a prodding and productive impulse in your writing. And then there's the companionable (even while admittedly challenging) way, so unmissable in your engagement with the Baldwin passage, the Powers too, that your analysis often walks us through, students each, the stages by which illumination (including audition) is a power that only slowly dawns—until, like light through a prism—it suddenly breaks (brilliantly, chromatically). We don't see it until we see it. Or, as the case may be, hear it.

GS: I do want to show, yes, in publication as well as in class, the way even recognition, let alone interpretation, is likely to be processual, in any medium.

DL: Let me land right there: "as well as in class." That's not so much the adjunct—as the equivalent analytic engagement—I keep pressing for as a reader inclined to imagine yet new work of yours generated through such a familiar circuit (from page back to pedagogic lab and then on to the page again). So looking afresh at the new essays: built up from poetry to prose to cinema to Conceptual art and back to prose again, if only now in conjured rather than cited form (for a conceptual experiment of its own in, as you allowed earlier, *reading the unwritten*). Hopkins, Dickens, le Carré, gallery transmediations, photographic negations, filmic adaptations, fictional closure and its subliminal resistances: an ever-expanding "spectrum" (to use your word above for the shared axis of Powers and Baldwin). You wouldn't need dedicated thesis-bound students of enjambed rhyme and mimetic etymology in some imaginary doctoral cohort; nor philologically-trained young scholars cued to the contrapuntal play of commas and semi-colons in the fugal figurations of prose. Nor—continuing this not very covert editorial summary—students of free indirect discourse as displaced into quasi-cinematic shot exchange in the spy novel; nor of experimental art practice, including its recurrent tendency toward the inside-out and surface-depth inversions of Conceptual art; nor of the narratology of closure in the form of the over-and-done-with (when immediately done more with in the form of Stewart's signature narratography). You wouldn't need *any* such advance constituency to congregate apprentice "readers" curious about the analytic common denominators that crisscross all such strikingly different torquings of concept (idea, theme, trope) by the vectoral pressures of form.

GS: It's not as if I have to excuse myself now in rushing straight off to draft the syllabus under this burst of inspiration, throwing all curricular prudence to the wind. But it does seem like this dialogue has reached, dare I say it, an almost empowering plateau, a point less of rest than of recharge—and thus the very opposite of pointless. Who knew that our attempt at wrapping up would do this extra work of opening up? I had never, as is clear from my demurrals above, thought of this "sampler" as another of my pedagogical instalments: books returned to the classroom commitments that had engendered them. Yet I've been seeing slowly, as we talk, that even this book, to which our conversation is an appendix, has itself mapped the most practicable way of conceiving it as just such an experiment in tutelage and mentorship: that is to say, in the venerable mode of "comparison and contrast" (that tried and true instructional blueprint), where in this case similar scales of mircrostylistic attention would reflect and overlap each other in the analytic field of view. If I should ever see a curricular path open to such a course (of analytic action at the graduate level), then textual *prismatics* would have found a set of ultimate classroom "refractions" after all. No bad aftermath, that, for this book of new and renewed exemplifications, which, ending with our conversation, would thus have begun a number of new ones.

DL: The venerable made available to the vulnerable—those tender hearts in search of textual illumination, whatever the medium and the case may be. Syllepsis and all the other interpretative traits (and treats) await the earnest if encumbered mind of the present moment. *To be cont.* That's a fine note, as with your last essay in resistance to closure, to refuse to end on. Too bleak, otherwise, to think that the truest glories of a discipline had outlived the reach of the teachable. But your editor and interlocutor can't resist pressing further, on this very point of continuance. If this question strikes you as too disheartening, it won't of course find its way into print. But I *am* curious—and have been since we started collaborating on these three volumes. Stanley Cavell, who mentored me, and who was widely lionized toward the end of his career, and then in memoriam, had early spells of feeling substantively ignored, wondering about the fate of his carefully wrought prose. You've written more, though have been less feted and revisited—that is, until these volume of ours, which were for me (not for you in your modesty, I well realize) part of their compensatory intent. But at this late stage, how do you feel about reputation and enduring citation? Or, more broadly, and in a word: futurity, however impersonal. I'm wondering about admiration, continuation, and thus emulation of the *kind* of work you do—methodology and cast of mind—more than praise and uptake of individual monographs, neologisms, and favored texts. I'm thinking in part of Cavell's remarks on this matter in the concluding pages of *Contending with Stanley Cavell*, his admitted worry addressing the unknown(able) and uncontrollable destiny of one's work, in that anthology from which your "Avoidance" essay is carried back into new circulation here (chapter 3). To pose, if you permit me, such a huge and admittedly imponderable question is an urge I must have had in naming "diffraction" as the leitmotif—as much as the method—of this closing conversation. As in optics, the size of an aperture affects the diffusion of the visible wavelengths that pass through it—and so the resulting patterning upon the screen. In a similar act of dilation, I'm opening now to the broadest gauge of y/our concerns, with an exposure time that allows for—invites—speculation about tomorrow and the day after tomorrow.

GS: Actually, Cavell moved me very much, in a personal note after that essay came out, saying how moved he himself was by my appreciation of the literary quotient in his writing that, with the bitter irony I had diagnosed in the chapter here re-presented, tended to keep it from serious engagement among none other than leading literary scholars in two of his main fields of philosophical interception: the respective "Renaissances" (already a dated because too ahistorical term) of Shakespeare and Emerson. I treasured that note. But I had almost forgotten the printed "response" of his you mention in the *Contending* volume, where, in my essay for that collection, the problem I had wanted to explain was the paucity of sufficient engagement one way or the other, whether con- or even at-tending: a situation Cavell saw "summarized in the sadly lovely phrase [of mine] 'avatars of disregard.'"[24] This wasn't, he wrote there, new to him—his remarks surprising more readers than me, I'm sure, with the sense that he had, for a couple of earlier decades at least, felt a paradoxical isolation even under the barrage of half-baked regard, as if he were speaking into the void, or at least into an echo chamber stripped of its sounding board. These are my metaphors. In other terms, he himself was sardonically amusing on this point, recalling the occasional piece of writing sent his way earmarked as "prompted" by his work, but in ways the vaguely grateful author could find no words in the actual publication to make any more than implicit—as if, as Cavell wrote, the two of them were involved in "some illicit trade." An under-the-table exchange finding its place in neither Table of Contents nor even index. Admiration, yes, but inert.

DL: And all but invisible. I too sighed mordantly at that passage—in part because the process of negotiation, to say nothing of nega(c)tivity and negation, reveals so much about the state of affairs in variously related, if as often estranged, academic fields.[25] Hearing, even now, his wry consternation, though, it has always sounded laced with genuine pain (an emotion I had earlier invoked in thinking of your own rough trades in the [d]evolving fate of the humanities). As the Cavell centennial approaches, as with America's quarter-millennium marker, I did the math, whereupon I learned that Cavell was alive for nearly forty percent of America's history (thirty-eight to be precise). But are such durations—personal and national—however long, long enough to off-set counter trends and temperaments? And when we zoom in on those moments of reader and "response," as illustrated by the scene of Cavell and his removed admirers, what should we do with such pain, neglect, confusion, and deferred intelligibility?

GS: My variant of such a limited acknowledgment of my work by others—less annoying, certainly less painful, but like you rightly say, *revealing*—has happened two or three times lately in almost the same words, quoted here verbatim from a renowned cultural theorist on our first personal encounter after their visiting lecture: "Glad to meet finally. I've always gotten a lot out of your work." With no way of putting it into theirs, it seems. Fine. To each his own. And generating some take-away has always been, at one level, the whole point, part of the pleasure principle, I guess. One thing may lead directly to another in one's own work, but the flow can thin to less than a trickle in the matter of influence. I certainly feel neither starved for local publication compliments nor thirsting for a collective toast. But, increasingly, the dearth of real print conversation on terrain I've so carefully mined, including the emaciated gestures of actual footnotes when rearing their infrequent heads, makes one wonder about a sense of "contribution," certainly of "continuance." Yet any personal sensitivity in this regard vanishes these days into conditions more epidemic, even epistemic. At that scale, certainly, and with apologies to Cavell for using the term in its loosest sense, one must be philosophical about it.

DL: Too true, but true, too: be resigned to these historical currents, yes, yet without needing to tender any wholesale resignation to the forces of forgetting—not while readers are still out there interested in such thin*GS*. If the avoidance of Cavell remains an open issue, the attractions of Stewart should be a refractive effect of *Closer Reading* and its sibling volumes. As the epigraph addressed readers directly, this concluding word might complete the bracket: What luck, as ready readers, to have in Garrett Stewart a writer yet to be discovered by widespread audiences; of course, if his work is familiar to many, all the better that these notes toward the rediscovery of his durable goods (chapters 1–3) may be matched by delight in his fresh testings (chapters 4–8)—gathered precipitates of a life's labors achieved, once again, at peak performance, at a pitch of intensity and perspicacity all his own.

GS: I can't deny that if serious literary criticism survives either artificial intelligence or institutional rejiggering (synonyms of a sort?), or if screen analysis, for that matter, survives social media and the videogame, it would certainly be good to think that some of my pages, occasionally read by design rather than "randomly accessed" by the search function, would be part of that legacy—as Cavell's on literature and film, though variously marginalized in his time, have been for my hermeneutic enthusiasms. As well as for yours. Hard to think so, sometimes. But I suppose that's what the teaching of such enthusiasms, in or out of class, has all along, even while solving immediate analytic problems, all but unconsciously sought to promulgate. Or say to advance. Now there's a word, visionary or not, we should be content to end, or at least come to rest, on.

Notes

1   See Bill Brown, "Infratextuality and the Art of Samuel Levy Jones," in *Bandwidths: Reading Across Media with Garrett Stewart*, ed. David LaRocca (New York: Bloomsbury, 2025), 211–21; and in the same volume, Garrett Stewart, "From Textual Refuse to Conceptual Reuse," 222–32.

2   See Garrett Stewart, "War Pictures: Digital Surveillance from Foreign Theater to Homeland Security Front," in *The Philosophy of War Films*, ed. David LaRocca (Lexington: University Press of Kentucky, 2014), 107–32; "'Assertions in Technique': Tracking the Medial 'Thread' in Cavell's Filmic Ontology," in *The Thought of Stanley Cavell and Cinema: Turning Anew to the Ontology of Film a Half-Century after* The World Viewed, ed. David LaRocca (New York: Bloomsbury, 2020), 23–40; "A Metacinematic Spectrum: Technique Through Text to Context," in *Metacinema: The Form and Content of Filmic Reference and Reflexivity*, ed. David LaRocca (Oxford: Oxford University Press, 2021), 63–84; and Garrett Stewart, "'A Voice Deep Inside': Cavell, Streisand, and the Reach of Song's Inner Speech," in *Music with Stanley Cavell in Mind*, ed. David LaRocca (New York: Bloomsbury, 2024), 97–129.

3   The "proselytizing" in—or pedagogical motive of—Stewart's work is embodied across his corpus and distilled to a heady elixir in *Attention Spans: Garrett Stewart, a Reader*, ed. David LaRocca (New York: Bloomsbury, 2024), see the introduction (2, 14, 22–24) plus 27, 29–35, 39–44, 91–92, 255, 294, 303–08, 337, and elsewhere in op. cit.

4   See *Bandwidths*, chapter 10.

5   See *Bandwidths*, chapters 1, 2, and 5.

6   See, for instance, Giuliana Bruno, *Atlas of Emotion: Journeys in Art, Architecture, and Film* (New York: Verso, 2002) and *Atmospheres of Projection: Environmentality in Art and Screen Media* (Chicago: University of Chicago Press, 2022).

7   See David LaRocca, "'It's All There in the Language'—A Conversation with Garrett Stewart," special issue, "Literature and Philosophy," ed. K. L. Evans and David Rozema, *Philosophical Investigations*, vol. 47, no. 3 (2024): 278–97.

8   Tyler Shoemaker, "Concatenative Textuality," University of California Digital Library (October 1, 2023), escholarship.org/uc/item/20k8q4xc.

9   Ibid.

10   [Ed.] Geoffrey H. Hartman, "The Voice of the Shuttle: Language from the Point of View of Literature," where Stewart notes the general principle of "overdetermined ends" and "elided middles" might account more broadly for the inlinked consonant brackets and the pulsing vowel sounds (*The Review of Metaphysics*, vol. 23, no. 2 [1969]: 240–58). See also Geoffrey H. Hartman, *The Unmediated Vision: An Interpretation of Wordsworth, Hopkins, Rilke, and Valéry* (New York: Harcourt, Brace & World, Inc., 1966 [1954]).

11   See again David LaRocca, "It's All There in the Language," *Philosophical Investigations*.

12   [Ed.] See Garrett Stewart, *Book, Text, Medium: Cross-Sectional Reading for a Digital Age* (Cambridge: Cambridge University Press, 2020), 61, 110, 178–79, 193; and "Bookhood in Evolution," in *Attention Spans*, 171–89.

13   See www.rebind.ai.

14 Phil Christman, "Does Teaching Literature and Writing Have a Future," *Plough*, December 3, 2024.

15 Alex Sosler, "School for Philosopher-Carpenters," *Plough*, December 3, 2024.

16 Brian Porter and Edouard Machery, "AI-generated poetry is indistinguishable from human-written poetry and is rated more favorably," *Scientific Reports*, vol. 14, article no. 26133 (2024).

17 See *Attention Spans*, 315.

18 See *Bandwidths*, chapter 9.

19 Emily Dickinson, "There's a certain Slant of light" (1861).

20 See *Bandwidths*, chapters 1, 5, 6, and 10.

21 See again *Bandwidths*, chapters 1, 5, 6, and 10.

22 [Ed.] Stewart's sentiment here on sound (as form and medium) offers a mellifluous reverb to his take on the letters that constitute inscribed musings, written to be read (closely); see again "'It's All There in the Language'—A Conversation with Garrett Stewart," special issue, "Literature and Philosophy," *Philosophical Investigations*, vol. 47, no. 3 (2024): 278–97.

23 Richard Powers, *Playground* (New York: W. W. Norton, 2024). [Ed.] For similar attention to the frame-shift kinetics of prose, see *Attention Spans*, 223–25, 236–38.

24 Stanley Cavell, "Responses," in *Contending with Stanley Cavell*, ed. Russell B. Goodman (Oxford: Oxford University Press, 2005), 174.

25 See David LaRocca, "The Education of Grown-ups: An Aesthetics of Reading Cavell," *The Journal of Aesthetic Education*, vol. 47. no. 2 (Summer 2013): 109–31, in which Stewart's reading of Cavell's scholarly treatment by others exemplifies a path for further productive criticism. See also, "Acknowledging Stanley Cavell," ed. David LaRocca, a special issue of *Conversations: The Journal of Cavellian Studies*, vol. 7 (2019): 1–276, and *Inheriting Stanley Cavell: Memories, Dreams, Reflections*, ed. David LaRocca (New York: Bloomsbury, 2020).

CONTRIBUTORS

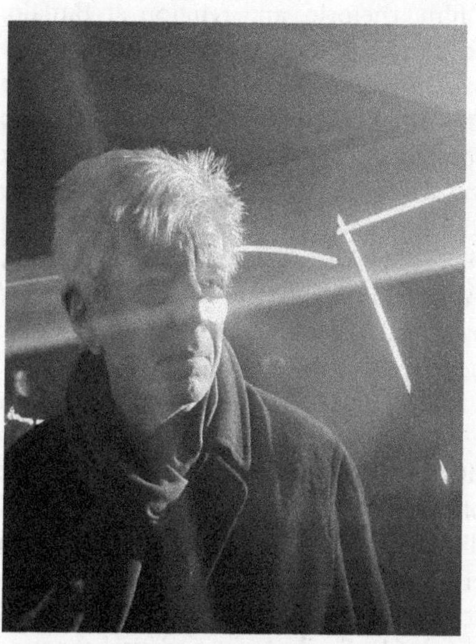

Garrett Stewart has taught fiction, film, and textual theory at the University of Iowa since 1993, where he is the James O. Freedman Professor of Letters. Besides his previous long-term positions at Boston University and the University of California at Santa Barbara, he has had visiting appointment at Stanford, Princeton, the University of Fribourg (Switzerland), the University of London (Queen Mary), and the University of Konstanz. Pursuing always a methodology of close-grained verbal or visual analysis—in books on language in Dickens (1974), the death scene in British fiction (1984), the phonetic undertow of literary writing from Shakespeare to Woolf (1990), and the "Dear Reader" address of Victorian novels (1996)—Stewart was led by that last topic to a subsequent study of the scene of reading in painting, from saints with books in illuminated manuscripts through Rembrandt to Picasso and Francis Bacon. In approaches to the moving rather than the still image, his 1999 investigation into the "photogrammar" of traditional cinema was brought up to date in 2007 by a sequel volume on the new digital conditions of screen narrative, *Framed Time: Toward a Postfilmic Cinema*. In 2009, *Novel Violence: A Narratography of Victorian Fiction*, awarded the Perkins Prize from the International Society for the Study of Narrative, named in its subtitle the method of this and the previous film book, searching out the "microplots" of narrative development in the inflections of technique, audiovisual or linguistic. Since then, concentrating on the conceptual violence done *to* rather than *in* books, *Bookwork: Medium to Object to Concept to Art* (2011) follows up on the 2D image of reading with a close look at the ironies of illegibility in conceptual book sculpture, whether in found, altered, or fabricated volumes, engaging again with the digital epoch on another front: its rapid transformation of the reading experience. Stewart's work on cinema continued in regular reviewing for *Film Quarterly*, and he was elected in 2010 to the American Academy of Arts and Sciences. His dozen monographs since then, including an interactive e-book on moving-image art in museum display, have continued to probe the medial infrastructure of film and literature, ranging from an account of "surveillancinema" to his latest crossover study, *The Metanarrative Hall of Mirrors: Reflex Action in Fiction and Film* (2022).

David LaRocca studied philosophy, film, rhetoric, and religion at Buffalo, Berkeley, Vanderbilt, and Harvard. He is the author or contributing editor of twenty books, including *Attention Spans: Garrett Stewart, a Reader*; *Bandwidths: Reading Across Media with Garrett Stewart*; *Emerson's English Traits and the Natural History of Metaphor*; *The Philosophy of Charlie Kaufman*; *Movies with Stanley Cavell in Mind*; *Metacinema*; and *Werner Herzog / Rogue Filmmaker*. He is also the author of over a hundred articles, chapters, and reviews published in, among other places, *Afterimage, Cinema, Epoché, Estetica, Film and Philosophy, Liminalities, Religions, Transactions, Post Script, The Senses and Society, Social Research, The Midwest Quarterly, Journalism, Media and Cultural Studies, The Journal of Aesthetic Education*, and *The Journal of Aesthetics and Art Criticism*. Currently Associate Editor at the journal *Philosophical Investigations* and on the Advisory Board at *Conversations: The Journal of Cavellian Studies*, he has held visiting research or teaching positions at Binghamton, Cornell, Cortland, Harvard, Ithaca College, the School of Visual Arts, and Vanderbilt. He served as research assistant to Stanley Cavell and Giuliana Bruno, apprenticed with painter Philip Burke and photographer Alessandro Subrizi, made documentary films with William Jersey and Robert Elfstrom, participated in the School of Criticism and Theory as part of a seminar led by Emily Apter, and workshopped with Abbas Kiarostami, Edward Tufte, and Werner Herzog. As a documentary filmmaker, he produced and edited six features in *The Intellectual Portrait Series*, directed *Brunello Cucinelli: A New Philosophy of Clothes*, and codirected the award-winning *New York Photographer: Jill Freedman in the City*. A recipient of the Ralph Waldo Emerson Society Distinguished Achievement Award (an honor previously conferred on Stanley Cavell), he received a teaching commendation from Harvard Extension School and a teaching innovation grant from the State University of New York at Cortland. Formerly a Writer-in-Residence at the New York Public Library, he contributed to a National Endowment for the Humanities Institute and conducted research as Harvard's Sinclair Kennedy Traveling Fellow in the United Kingdom. DavidLaRocca@Post.Harvard.Edu, www.DavidLaRocca.org

<h1 style="text-align:center">INDEX</h1>